THE CLEVER

Coyote

Frontispiece painting

Courtesy of

Frederic C. Walcott Memorial Fund

of the

North American Wildlife Foundation

WALTER A. WEBER.

Plate 1. Mountain Coyote (Canis latrans lestes) meditating, not too hungry.

THE CLEVER

Coyote

PART I
Its History, Life Habits, Economic Status, and Control
By STANLEY P. YOUNG

PART II
Classification of the Races of the Coyote
By HARTLEY H. T. JACKSON

A Wildlife Management Institute Publication

UNIVERSITY OF NEBRASKA PRESS
LINCOLN AND LONDON

Publishers on the Plains

UNP

Copyright 1951 by the
WILDLIFE MANAGEMENT INSTITUTE
WASHINGTON, D.C.

First Bison Book printing: 1978

Most recent printing indicated by first digit below:
2   3   4   5   6   7   8   9   10

Library of Congress Cataloging in Publication Data

Young, Stanley Paul, 1889–1969.
  The clever coyote.

  "A Wildlife Management Institute publication."
  Bibliography: p. 343
  CONTENTS: Young, S. P. Its history, life habits, economic status, and control.—
Jackson, H. H. T. Classification of the races of the coyote.
  1. Coyotes.   I.   Jackson, Hartley Harrad Thompson, 1881–   II.   Title.
[QL737.C22Y67   1978]   599'.7442   77–14026
ISBN 0–8032–0976–2
ISBN 0–8032–5893–3 pbk.

Bison Book edition published by arrangement with The Wildlife Management
Institute.

Manufactured in the United States of America

FOREWORD

The night song of the coyote is as much a part of the West—and of America itself—as the Grand Canyon or the Great Plains.

No other carnivore has been more intimately associated with the romantic history of the western plains and none has been more heavily persecuted by man than the little wild dog of the sagebrush and buffalo grass. And certainly no other American mammal has shown greater adaptability and stamina in the face of ruthless oppression than he. In spite of guns, dogs, poisons, and traps, pursued by hired hunters and carrying a price on his head, he has managed not only to survive but to extend his range into new territory.

This volume, written by two of the most distinguished and experienced American biologists, brings together in orderly sequence a wealth of carefully sifted facts from a vast scattered literature on the coyote throughout its range from early settlement to modern times. This research has behind it field studies of nearly a century, when the combined experience of the two authors as biologists of the U. S. Fish and Wildlife Service are totaled.

The authors neither defend nor condemn the coyote for his forays against livestock or his raids on desirable wildlife. They present the facts as they see them. But they make it clear in their writings that the clever, resourceful coyote is a fascinating part of our fauna. When not in serious conflict with man's economic pursuits or his efforts in game management, it deserves a permanent place in the American scene.

Ira N. Gabrielson

President, Wildlife Management Institute

ACKNOWLEDGMENTS

Our sincere thanks are extended to the large number of individuals who so kindly cooperated with us in the preparation of this monograph. Most helpful were: Dr. I. McT. Cowan, Professor of Zoology, University of British Columbia, Vancouver; Dr. Wm. Rowan, University of Alberta; E. C. Cross, Royal Ontario Museum, Toronto; F. R. Butler and J. G. Cunningham, British Columbia Fish and Game Department; Dr. A. L. Rand, Chicago Natural History Museum, formerly of National Museum of Canada, Ottawa; J. Dewey Soper, Dominion Wildlife Officer for the Prairie Provinces, Winnipeg; Hal Denton, Managing Editor of the Northwest Sportsman, Vancouver, British Columbia; Dr. Clifford Carl of Provincial Museum of British Columbia, Victoria; Everett E. Horn, F. E. Garlough, W. E. Riter, Nelson Elliott, Everett Mercer, E. R. Kalmbach, Paul Quick, E. C. Cates, Lawrence Cheney, Hugh Worcester, John Gatlin, Leo L. Laythe, C. R. Landon, Noble Buell, William H. and Lucille Stickel, and Dr. Walter P. Taylor, of the Fish and Wildlife Service, U. S. Department of the Interior; George Montgomery, Associate Editor, Capper's Farmer; Dr. Remington Kellogg, Director, and Dr. David H. Johnson, U. S. National Museum; and Blanche W. Mahlman, Emma M. Charters, and Katheryne C. Tabb, of the Fish and Wildlife Service. Edward A. Preble, one of America's foremost naturalists edited the manuscript.

In addition to material in the U. S. National Museum, the specimens examined included 611 from other American museums and private collections. Many of these were of critical importance in determining the status of the species in particular regions, and a few of them were type specimens. For the loan of specimens and the privileges of doing research at museums, as well as for other courtesies our gratitude is due to Dr. H. E. Anthony, American Museum of Natural History; Dr. Rudolph M. Anderson and W. Earl Godfrey, National Museum of Canada; Dr. W. J. Breckenridge, Minnesota Museum of Natural History; Dr. William H. Burt, Museum of Zoology, University of Michigan; Dr. William B. Davis, Texas A. & M. College; the late Donald R. Dickey, Pasadena, California; J. Kenneth Doutt and Miss Caroline Heppenstall, Carnegie Museum; the late Dr. Joseph Grinnell and Dr. Seth Benson, Museum of Vertebrate Zoology, University of California; Dr. E. Raymond Hall, Kansas University Museum; Dr. Donald F. Hoffmeister, Museum of Natural History, University of Illinois; Laurence M. Huey, Museum of Natural History, San Diego, California; the late Dr. Wilfred H. Osgood, Chicago Natural History Museum; and Randolph L. Peterson and Stuart C. Downing, Royal Ontario Museum of Zoology, Toronto, Ontario.

CONTENTS
PART I

PART II

ILLUSTRATIONS

Plates

Figures

TABLES

THE CLEVER

Coyote

PART I
Its History, Life Habits, Economic Status, and Control
By STANLEY P. YOUNG

Chapter One

Introduction

THE COYOTE, which sometimes is commonly called brush wolf, and also the American jackal, because of its close resemblance to that South European and African mammal, and such other names as prairie wolf, heul wolf, and steppen wolf, is a small wolf weighing usually between 18 to 30 pounds, or about a third as much as the average sized gray wolf. Many coyotes closely resemble the modern collie dog in appearance, or the so-called "toy shepherd." However, it has slenderer proportions, including a long, narrow, pointed nose; small rounded nose pads; large pointed ears; slender legs; small feet; and a bushy tail, which gives it somewhat the appearance of an animal midway between a fox and a wolf. With its fox-like contours goes an acute fox-like mentality that serves it well in its struggle for existence.

Because of its general distribution, abundance, and exceeding fertility, sometimes having as many as 19 young in a litter, the coyote is in the aggregate the most destructive of all our North American carnivores. It kills not only domestic fowl but every kind of small livestock, and the young of all the larger kinds.

At times it can be exceedingly destructive to big game as will be noted later. As with certain gray wolves, individual coyotes sometimes become well known locally as exceedingly cunning destroyers of livestock and poultry. It has long been a foe of the barnyard hen, much to the ire of the farmer's spouse. Possibly the coyote's tidbit in the way of chicken is responsible for the legend related by Juan Ignacio de Armas (1888: 44) who relates: "Among other peculiarities ('singular, dade') of this animal, Sahagun related that a traveler liberated one from a snake that was coiled around its neck, and that the thankful animal brought to his house that day a chicken ('gallo'), and other birds on the following days."

To many outdoor enthusiasts, the coyote is clever and interesting, and hence a fascinating animal. To others it seems a shame that its picturesque presence and voice should ever be extirpated from our plains. It is the subject of many old Indian legends, and the inspiration of many a lyric, such as Lew Sarett's (1941: 166) *Colloquy with a Coyote*:

3

"Ki-yoo-oo-oo-oo-oo-oo!
Speak now. O coyote, rumped upon the knoll!
Into the bowl of desert night—
Clinking and cool with stars—oh, roll
The melancholy of your soul.
When sentimental with the moon, you cry
Your longing to the lady in the sky,
Know that you do not grieve for her alone,
That your deep yearning, sprung from blight
Of solitude, is doubled by my own.
Speak then, O coyote, speak for me;
With your seductive melody cajole
The lovely one to be more intimate, invite
Her to linger for a moment of delight
The virgin, you and I, we three
On such a night should be more neighborly.

"In the homeland whence I came, a solitude
Dark with its regiments of lancing pine
That march from peak to water-line,
I know another spokesman for my mood—
Oh, he was suave, ingratiating, shrewd!
When balsams muffled their voices in the cowl
Of sable dusk, and tranquil, cool,
The beaver pond was but a chip
Of silver, soundless, save for flip
Of a beaver's tail, the flapping of an owl—
On such a night as this,
When the silver-lady put a kiss
Upon the bosom of the pool,
The gibbering loon, disconsolate, forlorn,
Flinging upon the sky a rain
Of silver tones, the tremole of pain—
Would always gain her ear and mourn
For me, befriend me; oh, the loon
And I!—we had an understanding with the moon.

"Speak then, O desert coyote, speak for me now.
Be to me kinsman in this valley of the dead,
This waste so unfamiliar, so dispirited.
Among the bleaching bones upon the brow
Of yonder butte, fling back your head.
And stabbing moonward with your wail, impart
Our sorrow till it breaks the vestal's heart;
Tell the indifferent one that she is beautiful;
As lovely and as cool
As a peeled willow bough;
Request the lady to leave off her gown
Of clouds, and ask her to come down . . .
    Ki-yoo-oo-oo-oo-oo-oo!"

In song, concerned with the out-of-doors, and especially in the life of the cowboy, it is the symbol of the picturesque interest of the wilderness. So the coyote holds a place in the American mind that cannot be otherwise filled.

No such sentimental feelings as the foregoing, however, are to be found in the hearts of the stockmen. Summed up in toto, this feeling on the part of the majority of the livestock interests is: "To you, Mr. Coyote, unending vengeance, and warfare to extermination!"

"You coyote!" is the worst insult that one Mexican can offer another.

"The animal's ways are devious, his wiles many. With a persistency that has defied all efforts to permanently control him, he perpetuates his atrocities and perpetuates his kind. A parasite on civilization, he lives a life of baseness, snooping about in search of plunder, or skulking away from his victims with his ofttime mangy tail between his thin legs. When at last Nemesis overtakes him, he snarls at his captor with an evil leer which arouses a loathing disgust in place of pity.

"The coyote has cast his lot with civilization. His fortress is a barbed wire fence; he can sleep undiscovered in a bed chamber walled by corn, wheat or grass; orchards and gardens are among his pantries. The localities in which many of his plunders occur prove that much of his food is the fruit of man's labor.

"The animal is the most successful in contending against civilization. It has kept pace with settlement of the country, and with astonishing versatility has adapted itself to new conditions, spreading from the plains into mountainous country, and constantly increasing the variety of its depredations." This is the coyote as the rangeman sees him.

Its distribution and extension of the coyote's range forms probably the most romantic story of any American mammal.

Although Lewis and Clark during the course of their expedition gave the first good description of the coyote, Thomas Say, who might be called the "father of American zoology," was the first to give the specific name to this interesting prairie mammal, with which he became acquainted during Long's Expedition to the Rocky Mountains in 1823. Two years later, in 1825, Missouri legislated a bounty act on the animal, which permitted counties to pay bounties, and was one of the first western States to do so. It has had, therefore, almost a continuous price on its head since the very earliest beginning of U. S. western settlement (R. S. Mo., 1825, 797).

The type locality from which Say named and further described the coyote was near the present town of Blair, Washington County, Nebraska. Since that time to the present nineteen subspecies of the coyote have been described ranging in size from the diminutive form of the southwestern deserts to those of greater size found in the higher mountains. Say named this unique and distinctly North American mammal *Canis latrans,* meaning the "barking dog," and with this sobriquet the coyote has, through the centuries, lived up to its name. The name "coyote" comes to us from the Spanish—a picturesque modification of the Aztec word "coyotl."

Throughout the western United States many natural features—mountains, creeks, and arroyos—have been named after this creature, attesting to its wide distribution and local interest. As an example, in Arizona one finds Coyote Creek in Apache County, Coyote Mountains in Pima County, Coyote Peak and Coyote Wells in Yuma County, and Coyote Spring in Navajo County.

In California, during 1850, the mushroom town of Coyoteville came into existence. Its name was derived from the coyote, because of the tunnel method of mining then in effect that resembled coyote dens.

COYOTE HOUSE

The well known trait of the early Mormon settlers in the Great Salt Valley, Utah to bring wherever possible a mountain stream down into the valley, was thus the beginning of a settlement. With available water, the first thing the pioneer did then was to build himself a "coyote house" which was built in a day. It was a small cellar dug in the ground with a few boards placed up over the hole as a roof. It was occupied until the settler was enabled to build a more permanent adobe brick home. "Coyote House" took its name from a similar but smaller hole (minus the boards) dug by the coyote when establishing a den for its young (Pine, 1870: 307).

Within the Apache Indian nation, during the heyday of this tribe, was a group of Apaches called the Coyoteros. These were geographically divided, one known as the Pinal Coyoteros, the other White Mountain Coyoteros, applied by the Spaniards to these respective groups the name meaning "wolf men." It was known as Mista-chagonis (big belly) by the Cree and Saulteaux Indians; Mica or Micaksica by the Dakotas; Mikasi of the Omahas; Scheke by the Mandans; Motsa by the Hidatsa; and Stshirits pukatsh by the Arikarus. The Klamath Indians of Oregon called it Ko-ha-a; the Piute, Eja-ah. The Chinooks called it Italipas, the Yakima Indians Telipa, and in the Chinook jargon, or trade language of the Pacific Northwest Indians it was known as Talapus, God of the Plains.

Among the Flathead Indians, to whom it was known as Sinchlep, the coyote was "regarded the most powerful, and favorable to mankind. . . . Sinchlep's howling foretells the arrival by the next day of somebody either friend or foe, provided he only howls three times." (Father Mengarini, 1872, Flathead Indians. American Naturalist 6: 180-183.)

Throughout most of its recorded history, the coyote has been killed at every opportunity, and in no instance has been offered any asylum except on the part of some early aboriginal Indian tribes, one of which is the Navajo by whom it was in earlier years treated as a Diety. Between the years 1860-1885 the animal was subjected to one of the most intensive killing campaigns fomented and carried on by the "wolf poisoner," seeking the monetary returns from its pelt along with those of the large gray wolf. This involved an immense expanse of coyote habitat on the Great Plains from middle Saskatchewan and Manitoba in Canada, and extending southward through present-day Montana, the Dakotas, Kansas, eastern Colorado and New Mexico, Nebraska, Oklahoma, and the Staked Plains of Texas. During this quarter of a century, figures are lacking on the kill, but judging by some of the returns such as that contained in the diary of Robert Morris Peck wherein it is recorded more than 3,000 wolves and coyotes were poisoned and pelted during the winter of 1861-62, it is safe to assume that the entire take of coyotes would run into the hundreds of thousands. (Grinnell, G. B., 1914: 286.) (See Fig. 1.)

More adaptable to a modified habitat than its relative the wolf, which practically disappeared from the former western ranges for this reason, the coyote will long remain a part of the western faunal make-up. Whether it will ever be lessened in numbers as with the present-day wolf can only be conjectured. So far it has been able to persist in appreciable numbers. Its present-day habitat, however, is being subjected to more and more intense modification; more modern instruments are being brought into use against it, such as hunting from airplanes and other improved methods. Judging from present experiments, these are apt finally to put the coyote behind the so-called "eight ball." That it has little place in a habitat shared by man engaged in livestock production has long been recognized, and to this end its local control is constantly sought. Other places, where its habitat is found and where it is in no direct conflict with man, are being intensely worked most of the time for the monetary returns that are derived from the creature's pelt. Prior to the recent depression, the pelt brought a handsome price, but in later years a $5-a-pelt average has been considered a good price. But with our unemployment problem as it has been recently, many men have turned to the out-of-doors for work in coyote trapping.

Figure 1. The approximate area poisoned during the heyday of the professional poisoners, 1860 to 1885. Within this area strychnine was widely applied in carcasses of buffalo, antelope, deer, elk and birds as bait. Hundreds of thousands of coyotes together with wolves and the smaller mammals, such as kit fox and prairie skunk, were killed in this region.

Possibly the great strides now being made toward national recovery and the opening up of new jobs may take some of the pressure off the animal, thereby giving it a chance to build up its numbers throughout its range to the extent it did following the poison onslaught of the 1860's and onward for the following quarter of a century. If so, more intense control may be required as a consequence in the livestock areas of the West, where it never has been nor ever will be willingly tolerated. Further impetus might likewise be given toward more intensive coyote control in livestock-producing areas than at present on the part of the Federal Government as a national recovery measure, for people must be fed. The Nation's meat supply for its population in such cases looks better hanging in the storehouse than meat lost on the ranges as a partial toll to the coyote's food habits. No one shouts this louder than the producer of beef and mutton, and poultry.

Thus through the years this western prairie animal has contended with ups and downs. Elliott Coues, the distinguished naturalist, wrote ". . . theoretically he [the coyote] compels a certain degree of admiration, viewing his irrepressible positivity of character and his versatile nature. If his genius has nothing essentially noble or lofty about it, it is undeniable that few animals possess so many and so various attributes, or act them out with such dogged perseverance. . . . The main object of his life seems to be the satisfying of a hunger which is always craving; and to this aim all his cunning, impudence, and audacity are mainly directed." This was our North American coyote as Coues knew it from his association with it by 1873, midway in the poison era. Through the succeeding years it has changed but little; if anything, it has become tougher, though not to the extent that we cannot deeply admire it and hope that in its proper place it will continue to form a part of our western fauna. Judged by everything involving the animal in the past, the coyote, of all the mammals in North America, appears to be the acme of permanence and will always be with us.

A prominent dentist with years of practice in his profession, once remarked to me: "I'm never surprised at what happens to individual teeth in the human mouth!" To that attribute one might well apply to the habits or traits of the coyote. Hence to some who peruse this monograph, it may be judged with a feeling by some readers, particularly those whose experiences with the animal qualify them as critics, that the author overlooked this or that trait, and thus this treatise lacks in its completeness. With any of these critics, the author has no argument, for there is no American predator that approaches the coyote in its ability to veer at times from the expected, and do just the opposite. This versatility is many of the answers to the animal's ability to persist, exist, depredate, and increase in the face of what seems unsurmountable odds and obstacles to its existence and extension of its range, where it may be either an asset or a very detrimental creature.

Chapter Two

Distribution

GENERAL

M Y OBSERVATIONS of the distribution of coyotes convince me that originally it was strictly an animal of the open plains, but that in the United States and in a lesser degree to the northward in comparatively recent years it has followed livestock and game into forested areas of the mountains. In doing this it has followed sheep herds to the pastures above timberline in the mountains of the western United States, and mountain sheep to the bare mountain tops of the Rockies and of Alaska. In Mexico and Central America it is still an animal of the open plains, being absent in the tropical forested country on the eastern slopes from Veracruz southward and present on the treeless tablelands of Mexico and similar open highlands of interior Chiapas and Guatemala, and in open areas at intervals along the west coast where desert or semi-desert conditions provide suitable territory from Baja California and Sonora south to Sinaloa, then again in Colima, and in Salvador and on the Peninsula of Nicoya and adjacent western Costa Rica, its southernmost point of distribution. Within the last 35 years it has extended its range to the eastward in the northern United States and Canada, and north to the mouth of the Mackenzie and not far from the coast of Bering Sea.

It is my feeling that the great and constant pressure exerted upon the coyote by man has been a real factor in its spread through the centuries. Even among the human races may be found cases where persecution has encouraged the constant seeking of newer and greener pastures in the attempt at survival. The sum-total of the causes behind this urge to spread on the part of the coyote is a field yet to be thoroughly explored for final answers. It is one of the few animals that has been able to extend its range within historic times.

From all accounts, the coyote apparently began to extend its range southward into the Central American Republics beginning with the introduction of livestock by the Spaniards in the 16th

11

century. That it existed in large numbers northward in what is now Mexico prior to the Spanish invasions of Central America and the subjugation of the native Indian tribes, and that its migration southward was caused by trailing livestock is most possible. As will be noted later a similar migration moving northward from

Figure 2. Present distribution of the American coyote.

Canada into the Yukon, and finally Alaska some three centuries later, in some respects parallels the animal's southern movements into the Central American Republics.

The north-south range of the coyote now extends from near Point Barrow, Alaska, to tropical Costa Rica, approximately 7,500 miles (See Fig. 2).

Plate 2. Sheep grazing on Northrup area—logged off land, Clatsop County, Oregon. Here the coyote has put in its appearance where it never occurred at the turn of the century. (Photo courtesy of Herb Howell.)

The coyote in extending its range might be properly called an "edge animal." The amount and type of "edge" is one of the determining factors in extension of the animal's range. The "edge" is produced by such phenomena of nature as where glacier moraines have been laid down; or forest fires that produce clearings, or man-made "edges" such as those forest park areas resulting from logged off lands (See Plates 2 and 3), such as the Douglas fir areas of northwestern Oregon, and also the eastern portion of the Olympic Peninsula in Washington. Into this former terrain the coyote has of recent years extended its range, bringing it to the northwestern coastal area of Oregon, such as the Nehalem Valley area of Clatsop County, and surroundings. This section, the boyhood rendezvous of the author, did not harbor the coyote until well into the present century. These "edges" to the coyote's liking, while often vast open clearings within forest areas and often park-like, may also be open glades containing new tree and low shrub growth. Use of such areas by livestock such as sheep and goats is also an important factor in coyote migration because this often affords a dependable food supply. Such an example is the Nehalem Valley in Clatsop County above mentioned.

UNITED STATES

The coyote occurs throughout or the greater part of all states west of the Mississippi River with the exception of Arkansas other than the extreme northwest section and all of Louisiana.

East of the Mississippi it is found more or less regularly in Wisconsin, Michigan, Illinois and Indiana. Other eastern states where it has been taken or recorded within the past two decades are: Maine, New Hampshire, New York, Pennsylvania, New Jersey, West Virginia, Ohio (probably an invader from Indiana), Virginia, Maryland, Tennessee, North and South Carolina, Georgia, Mississippi, Alabama, Florida, and Vermont, where one showing some dog characters was taken in a fox trap near Irasburg in November of 1946.

Some of the recordings of coyote occurrence in our eastern states show that one was taken November 9, 1938, in Gaston County, North Carolina. It had been observed in this section for several months previous because of its depredations on poultry, killing 100 chickens on one farm. Another was taken in North Georgia in September 1929, estimated to be approximately 18 months old. It was presented to the Grant Park Zoo. Likewise, former Regional Forester Joseph C. Kercher reported on Decem-

Plate 3. U. S. Government Hunter trap-setting on Northrup experimental area to control coyotes there. (Photo courtesy of Herb Howell.)

ber 26, 1930, that 5 coyotes had been killed in Habersham County, evidently offspring from coyotes that had some years previously been released by persons unknown. Previous to this, one was killed 3 miles from Waycross near Satilla River swamp.

In 1925, 4 coyotes were liberated in Palm Beach County, Florida, while 10 were reported liberated near Arcadia the same year, followed by the liberation of 16 in 1930-31. Other Florida coyotes have been reported killed in Collier County, and on Key Largo, Monroe County, and 7 miles east of Sparr, Marion County.

A single coyote was taken in Maryland in 1922 near Poolesville, but how it got there is not known.

On November 24, 1944, a skull, presumably that of a male coyote, was so identified (Goldman and Young) that was shot on October 24, 1944, near Holderness, Grafton County, New Hampshire. Hilbert R. Siegler, Biologist, of the Fish and Game Department of New Hampshire, reported that it weighed 35 pounds, 4 ounces. Total length, 52 inches; tail, 12.

The following article, along with a picture of O. R. Gilbert holding the coyote, appeared in the March 1943 issue of the *Ohio Conservation Bulletin.*

"Above is pictured O. R. Gilbert with a coyote he shot in Greenfield Township, Huron County, January 22. This is said to have been the first coyote ever known to have been killed in Huron County since pioneer days, says Game Protector Joe Walker. It was a fine specimen weighing 35 pounds and was shot at long range while at high speed by rifle shot. The female accompanying the ill-fated prowler escaped for the time being.

"An exceptional number of coyotes have been reported killed and sighted in various western and northern counties, and they have done a lot of damage to farm poultry, sheep and wildlife. They are doomed to eventual extinction, but in the meantime are giving farm folks the jitters in sections where they are in evidence, not from peril to humanity but on account of the damage they do."

In Tennessee, coyotes were reported depredating in Hickman and Maury Counties on lambs and ewes in the early 1930's, which resulted in a cooperative project between the Biological Survey and the farmers of these areas to remove them.

Kellogg reports (1939: 267): "Coyotes are reported to have been introduced in Tennessee in recent years, though no information is at present available as to the source where they were obtained. A female killed in Maury County was acquired by the Tennessee State Museum in 1930." This "it is believed that it is from a stock of coyotes that were liberated in west Tennessee at Grand Junction [Hardman County] for the purpose of training hounds."

Many of the coyotes that have been captured or reported in the eastern United States, have come as prospective pets in the autos of returning tourists, only to escape later from their owners. Others have been planted inadvertently by fox hunters who, unknowingly, had coyote pups shipped to them for planting instead of young foxes. The differences between the young of the fox and the coyote are hard to distinguish at times by the average layman. This fact was apparent in the case of one of the southern states (Alabama) during the introduction of supposed fox puppies as an aid to replenish the diminishing supply of foxes for hunting. The release of these took place in 1924 in Barbour County. Five years later, in 1929, these animals began to make themselves known by the livestock depredations they were committing on the ranches or farms in the locality of their original liberation.

Some have been deliberately turned loose. In reporting upon the coyote's recent appearance in one eastern state, the state's game department stated: "This is not an unusual case, as several coyotes have been introduced into the state by persons purchasing them from the West for pets, eventually getting tired of them and then turning them into the wild." Those coyotes that were reported in northwest Florida are believed to have been the result of a liberation by a gentleman from Idaho who, on abandoning his farm in Gadsden County, liberated 11 coyote pups that he had kept on the farm as pets.

The occurrence of the animal in New Jersey was proven by the taking of a female in 1938 near Ringoes. Several reported crosses between the coyote and dog were also captured. Because of the depredation that had occurred on livestock in this state, legislation was enacted making anyone liberating a coyote liable to a fine of $100 for each offense, as well as making it illegal to possess the animal except under certain regulations. Violation of this law likewise called for a similar fine for each coyote illegally possessed in New Jersey.

Whether the plantings of the coyote, accidentally or otherwise, in the eastern United States, where in all of our history it has never been known or reported as occurring naturally will result in its final establishment, only the future can tell. Much of the far eastern and southern states contains suitable habitat for it. If its present eastern extension of its range and that northward into Alaska in the past 40 years are any criteria, it may well

establish itself in the East and the South if given enough en-
couragement. Wherever the animal has shown itself in the eastern
states, it has in some instances created nearly as much local excite-
ment as did the armistice of World War I, or VE Day of World
War II, judging by the efforts that have been made by the local
inhabitants, or in some cases by personnel of state game departments, to get rid of it—and generally with success.

MEXICO AND CENTRAL AMERICA

In the early 1880's, Alston (1879-1882) speaks of the coyote
occurring in abundance in the northern "provinces" of Mexico,
as well as its wide distribution throughout all of that Republic.
Generally speaking such is the case today.

Farther south, he mentions its occurrence in Guatemala where
it was observed first-hand near the confines of the hacienda of
San Geronimo in Vera Paz. Here it proved a decided nuisance
to a flock of sheep.

With regard to its medicinal value in Guatemala and at the
same time showing the occurrences of the animal in this Republic,
Juan Ignacio de Armas (1888: 44) stated that one "Fuentas Guzman affirmed that the ladies of Guatemala did not hesitate
('notenian repaio') to carry against the skin of their stomach the
testicles of the coyote as a preventative against pregnancy troubles
(or mother diseases, 'mal de maire')."

With respect to the coyote's distribution in Guatemala, I am
indebted to Charles O. Handley, Jr., who reported to me the
results of his findings, based on field work recently conducted in
this Republic, as follows:

"Apparently the coyote is recorded in literature only from
Hacienda Chancol on the southern escarpment of the Sierra de los
Cuchumatanes a few miles from the town of Huehuetenango. However, a biological survey of the Republic made in the spring of
1947 leads to the belief that the animal has a much more extensive
range than was previously supposed.

"People in all parts of the country told me that when I visited
the higher reaches of the Cuchumatanes I would find coyotes,
ravens, and sheep. I found all three. The Cuchumatanes are a huge
mountain mass situated south of the Chiapas border in the department of Huehuetenango. In the south and west they rise sharply
from the surrounding 6000 foot plateau country, but to the north
and east they dribble off gradually to the humid cloud forest mountains of Chiapas and Quiche. For many miles the crest of the
mountains is above 11,000 feet and at some points rises an un-

determined distance above 13,000 feet. The mountains are in the form of a big plateau with many gentle sloped valleys and irregular ridges. It is a region of old limestone with many crumbled out-crop ridges, and many sinks and caves. The valleys that I saw seemed to be blind. The floors of all the little valleys are devoid of trees and grasses, while the ridges are pine covered. At the south end of the plateau is a great saucer shaped plain perhaps 20 miles long and 10 miles wide, lying at an altitude of 10,400 feet and completely treeless. Because of the savannahs and altitude, this is the most important sheep grazing section in the country, but it is inhabited only during the dry season, from December to May, when the lower pastures are parched and almost devoid of grass. Because of the inhospitable climate it is deserted by all human inhabitants during the rainy season. It is never hot and is often quite cold, with snow being of frequent occurrence. On the morning of May 2, 1947 the temperature was 25° F. and there was a heavy frost.

"This area is not unlike many parts of the Rockies in the western United States, so it is no surprise to find coyotes in num-bers. On the night of May 1 they were heard howling on the ridges above camp, but as there was a full moon, it was useless to try to hunt them. Dr. Saunders believed they sounded different from Rocky Mountain coyotes, but I've never heard one so I don't know. Probably with the exodus of the sheep herds in late May, the coyotes too desert the region for lower country.

"They are also reported farther south in the big valley north and west of the town of Quetzaltenango. This is between 6,000 and 7,000 feet, but the open country extends on up to 10,000 or 11,000 feet on Cerro Calel. Much of this region is given over to the growing of wheat, but there are also many sheep. Edwardo Caret, Manager of the Pan American Hotel in Guatemala City, has seen three coyotes cross the Pan American Highway just west of Quetzaltenango in broad daylight.

"My assistant, Ricardo Camacho, who was for some time in charge of the National Zoo at Aurora Park, Guatemala City, and who had a small farm near Fiscal, assured me that coyotes were common to within 8 miles of Guatemala City on the northeast. He said that they were most abundant to the south of the road which runs from the City to Progreso, and that they were a menace to poultry. He had frequently heard them howling at night and had seen ones that other farmers had killed. This is a region dis-sected by many deep barrancas. The flat country on the divides between the ravines is open and given mostly to cattle grazing and poultry. The soil is too shallow for crops. The ridges and the steep sides of the barrancas are covered with second growth deciduous scrub which never passes the scrub stage because the Indians are continuously cutting it back for fire wood which they carry into Guatemala City. This habitat is quite different from the Huehuetenango country, but is characteristic of much of the central highlands.

"The only other place where I heard of coyotes was in the arid Rio Motagua Valley between El Rancho and Gualan where the landscape is quite like Arizona. Cactus, thorn bushes, dry grass and sand dominate the scene, while there is dry scrub oak on the ridges. The whole valley is given to cattle raising. All the natives talked to here reported coyotes in abundance but there was no other evidence. This is the only place within the Tropical Zone where the coyote was reported, all the others being in the Temperate Zone. Similar arid country prevails farther south toward the borders of Honduras and El Salvador, and in the valleys of the Rio Salama and Rio Negro to the northwest.

"It is quite possible that the range of the coyote in Guatemala includes all of the central highlands north and east of the Continental Divide, except for the islands of cloud forest which occur on the high mountains at Mataguescuintla, Tecpan, and Totonicipan, and in northern Quiche. It is undoubtedly absent from all of the Caribbean lowland and Peten, except in the arid portion of the Rio Motagua Valley, from the Pacific volcanoes and from the Pacific lowlands, for in all these regions the forest is continuous and only broken by occasional openings. However, it is possible that it occurs in the Pacific lowland near the Salvador border, where a savannah type association is reported to occur. I was unable to visit this region so I would be unable to say.

"Theoretically the coyote of the western part of the highlands at least should be *Canis latrans goldmani* (Merriam). As the range appears to extend all the way across the central part of the Republic, probably to the Honduran border, it is quite possible that it may be coextensive with the range of *Canis hondurensis* (Goldman) of Tegucigalpa, Honduras. This is an interesting possibility, but one which cannot be proven with the facts now at hand. I am not one hundred percent positive that the coyote occurs anywhere in Guatemala except in the Northwest." (See Plate 4, Fig. 3.)

Based on other information, Alston says of the animal farther southward in Costa Rica that it was at the time confined to the northwestern provinces of Guanacaste and Nicoya, where it does great damage to the haciendas by carrying off young calves.

Plate 4.

Near the close of the 19th century Alfaro (1897: 18-19) stated that:

"The coyote, which formerly was found as far as Turrucares, near the city of Alajuela (approximately central Costa Rica), today is found only in the province of Guanacaste. I observed it and heard its howling in Tamarindo and Junquillal, near the Bay of Salinas during 1890. Later, Underwood, taxidermist of the museum, brought a fine specimen from Miravalles, and a neighbor from Nicoya presented me with a skin of considerable size; both specimens are now in the Museo Nacional."

An intriguing account of coyote occurrence in Costa Rica 80 years ago, and describing its cooperative method of hunting, is given (Anon. 1868, Temple Bar 23: 66-75) under the title The Hounds of the Jungle:

"As a Protestant I utterly scorn and detest the instinct which drives a man from among his fellows into a solitary or Essenian life; but as a rough-and-ready student in natural science, I recognize the force of that same instinct throughout the animal world. . . .

". . . . Before it grew quite dark, I was stretched upon the hilltop with my feet close to the hot fire, a saddle beneath my head, and rifle under my right shoulder. And in an hour after I was dreaming of the hermit coon.

"Between three and four in the morning the hunter always wakes: if a novice, roused by the sudden chill of that coldest hour; if an old hand, from habit. That night I awoke with a consciousness of being out later than usual, and sprang suddenly to my feet. Our fire was very low; the black and awful darkness seemed to be visibly shrouded and smothering it as with a mantle. Not a star shone overhead, but dim, steamy sheets of vapor floated

---

Plate 4. Scenes showing coyote habitat in the Republic of Guatemala, Central America.
Top to Bottom:
(a) Cabanas, Zacapa, Guatemala, May 8, 1947. Arid valley of the Rio Motagua, 700 ft. elevation. Sedge, thorn, and cactus. Reported habitat of coyotes.—C. O. Handley, Jr.
(b) Zacapa, Zacapa, Guatemala, May 7, 1947. Arid valley of the Rio Motagua, 700 ft. elevation, reported habitat of coyotes.—C. O. Handley, Jr.
(c) Chemal, Huehuetenango, Guatemala, May 2, 1947. The "great plain" at the south end of the Cuchumatanes above Chiantla, 10,400 ft.—C. O. Handley, Jr.
(d) Chemal, Huehuetenango, Guatemala, May 1, 1947. Grassy valley at 11,000 ft., typical of the Sierra de los Cuchumatanes. Coyotes were heard howling from these ridges.—C. O. Handley, Jr.
(e) Chemal, Huehuetenango, Guatemala, May 2, 1947. Close-up of the "great plain" showing scarcity of vegetation due to overgrazing by sheep.—C. O. Handley, Jr.

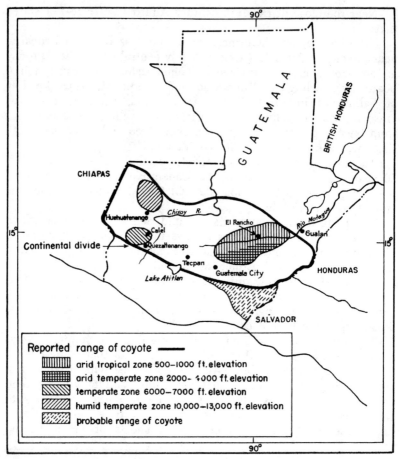

Figure 3. Coyote distribution, Republic of Guatemala.

above the surface of the ground. We had camped in the midst of a long ridge, and the last faint radiance of the fire lost itself in air, not lighting up even the short mountain grass. As I stood within a few inches of the embers, their glow failed to reach me, and I shivered with the cold. But long habit teaches the traveller not too hastily to stir his camp-fire, at least in quarters which he does not know. Some wild beasts are scared by light, but wild men are always drawn thereto, like vultures to the prey. So, for a moment, I stood still, listening to the voices of the night, striving to catch, through the long deep boom of the bull-frogs and the hylas, those keener, shriller sounds which tell of a man's approach

—the rattle and clank of harness or weapon, the thud of horses hoofs. But no such warnings were audible. The frogs thundered on without a break; the night-birds screamed and twittered. All other things were dumb at that hour, gone to their rest, lying in wait, or not yet risen. With a shudder, half of cold, half of unreasoning superstition, I turned from that black void, which floated round me like a sea of mist and darkness. Feeling the way carefully with my feet, I passed round the fire, stepping over the big logs which stretched like the arms of a cross, far out into the grass. Cautiously through the blackness I advanced, until reaching the spot where a heap of fuel had been piled up overnight. And there I found myself in the arms of a man, upright and on the watch!

"His strong limbs closed round me like cables, restraining my movements. "Tsh!" he whispered, in that warning note which, through all lands and times, has commanded another's attention."

"What is it?" I asked in the same guarded tone, recognizing my faithful peon.

"Coyotes, senor!"

His manner, and the fact of his standing thus carefully on guard, showed me that the Indian was alarmed, but who had ever dreamed of danger from a coyote, or from a pack of such brutes? Yet Manuele was brave I know.

"Are you afraid of wild dogs, Indian?" I asked, feeling inclined to laugh.

"Si! Tengo miedo!" he answered, simply, but in a tone which seemed to rebuke either my rashness or my ignorant wood-craft. I said nothing, but stood in thought. Just then, from the farther end of the ridge as I judged, a low whimper broke upon the night, audible, as are all musical notes, above the deep chorus of the frogs. After a moment of silence another call answered it from the opposite quarter. Then, low and soft and most grateful to the ear, reviving happy recollections of old days from all points of the compass rose the gentle murmuring of the pack. I made a movement. "Steady, for your life!" breathed the Indian in my ear. I could not comprehend what peril there was for us, two well-armed men, from such cowardly assailants as are the wild dogs of tropical America. I had met them before, and never yet had used, nor seen others use, against them, any weapon more severe than a stone or a stick. But perhaps it might be well, before proceeding farther, to describe the creature which thus alarmed my trusty peon.

"The coyote has a very extensive range over the central part of North America. He is found from the Colorado to the *Oronoko*, and perhaps still farther to the southward. His appearance varies considerably according to habitat, but in general he is clothed in a warm, thick coat of white or fawn colour. His nose is very sharp, eyes large and protruding, ears broad and long and pointed. In general they hang over like a bloodhound's; but a coyote, unlike the dog, has a power of erecting them, which gives him a very curious aspect. He is said to be descended from the hounds brought from Spain by the Conquistadores, but this opinion is rather founded on the tradition of the Indians than upon scientific deduction. Very probably it is correct, although coyote is a pure Aztec word, with the final "l" softened into "e" as in many other instances; but certainly there are points of great difference between any modern race of bloodhounds and the North American coyote. The latter cannot bark, which perhaps proves nothing; his jaws are sharp almost as a greyhound's; his tail is bushy—very much more so, at least, than that of any smooth-haired dog. In habits the coyote wanders yet farther from his supposed type. He cannot be tamed to any useful purpose; he has not the faintest idea of gratitude or affection; cunning and cowardice are the main features of his character. Of his manner of life something will be learned in the continuation of my story.

"I had perfect faith in Manuele's courage, and he had given too many proofs of clever woodcraft to leave any doubt on that score, but why we should be alarmed at the approach of a thousand of such animals I could not conceive. Nevertheless I stole quietly back to my bed for the arms left there, little consoled in my mysterious perturbation by the Indian's gloomy whisper: "You can go, senor; but a rifle won't be much use if they attack us!" So I fetched the guns and machete and resumed my place beside him. Scarcely had I done so, when the silence that had followed that low chorus of whimpers was suddenly broken by a clear bell-like challenge, softened indeed, but unmistakable. Perhaps it was fancy, but in that moment I thought I could hear the rush of many broad paws over rocks and dewy grass. For a moment all was still again, but Manuele's heart beat loud. Then a second and a third challenge rang out less clearly. Then, after a pause of four or five minutes, the whimpering was resumed. The Indian drew a long breath. "We are safe for this time senor!" he said.

"What are they doing?" I asked, astonished at the silence. "I have always heard coyotes cry on the scent like a pack of hounds."

"You'll hear them loud enough presently," he said. "They are turning the river now. What do I mean? Why, sending on some of their best dogs to drive the game back if he should take to

water, as he's pretty sure to do when they put him up. Coyotes
hate water, like monkeys, though they swim so beautifully. In
half an hour you'll hear them give cry; and perhaps see them
bring their game in if you wait long enough. It's all right now!"
he added, throwing an armful of wood upon the fire.

"Following the Indian's example, I threw myself down again,
after stirring the ash-smothered embers. In the morning would be
time enough to ask an explanation of the night's alarm. Once more
I fell fast asleep, and no dread of these mysterious dogs disturbed
my dreams. It was still dark as a mine when I awoke, startled
afoot by the sudden outburst of twenty clamorous throats. The
coyotes were on the trail! Their musical cry, reckless and un-
guarded now, resounded from hill to hill, and echoed in the deep
forest. All at once it burst upon the ear, as if some messenger
from the front had just arrived. Past the lower ridge, down the
forest to our left, swept the pack, each hound seeming to rival
another in noisy glee. Across the wind they galloped, and the
rising gusts bore to us that cheery music long after they had
passed far away through the long glades and green savannahs. I
looked around. No star nor moon was visible, nor any break in
the heavens; but far above the horizon to the southward a line
of great cones, rosy and purple, hung like lamps in the black sky.
The earth was unseen; the sky spread out as a cloak of velvet;
no light above or below save those magical cones which, like
vast crystals set in ebony, hung suspended in glowing radiance
above our heads. It was a lovely sight, but strangely awesome to
those who understood it not. I knew the vision well. Many a time
had I watched the dawn thus strike the volcanic peaks of Costa
Rica, a hundred miles to the southward. I recognized the great
shafts of the Merivalles, and the fiery crown of Torialba, which
the misty atmosphere of day hid from our view. In each con-
tinent have I seen that fairy vision, which never loses its beauty
nor sublimity, but rather seems to gain with each occasion.

"Within ten minutes light began to spread over the eastern
horizon, and the Costa Rican volcanoes faded slowly from sight
among the clouds, to be beheld no more until the following dawn.
Then my peon arose, blue and helpless as are all Indians at that
chilly hour. Our kettle was already singing and steaming among
the embers; we took a pull of coffee each from the tin pannikin
I carried, changed the caps of our guns, and strode off towards
the misty forest. But on the verge I remembered a remark of
Manuele's the previous night.

"Do you think the coyotes will come back to this spot?" I
asked, pausing.

"Of course," he answered, "and bring their game with them. At this time of year all animals must drive the prey toward their dens. How could the pups and heavy bitches catch a deer, or even a pig? They would be winded in five minutes. And those who went on to the low land last night, are they to get no share for their hard work?"

"How long will they be, do you think?

"It depends on the game afoot. If it be a fine deer, they may not return for three or four hours yet; if a drove of pigs, they will not be so long."

"And they will drive it to this very spot?"

"As near as they can."

"Then take this shot-gun, Indian, and bag the 'pisote solo,' if you can find him. I shall stay on the ridge, and wait the coyotes' return. He laughed, and entered the dusky forest. I went back to camp, and waited the results, sitting on a log by the fire.

"It was now broad daylight, and each dewdrop on the rocky hill was sparkling in the sun. . . .

"East and west and north and south over the watery plain towered those great volcanoes which are the emblems of the land, known by sonorous Indian names, full of threats and mystery—Mombacho, Madera, Momotombo, and a thousand more. . . .

"For an hour I sat and gazed upon this scene, drinking in all its radiant glory. The monkeys passed beneath us toward the water, clashing and chattering among the boughs. The congos sat all melancholy and listless upon the outer limbs of the forest, howling lazily. Crickets and tree-frogs sang among the leaves. Parrots croaked overhead as they fluttered from glade to glade. Scarlet macaws flashed like fire about the tallest trees screaming and croaking. At the bottom of the ridge a half-grown boar showed himself, but bounded grunting away before I could use my rifle.

"At length I fancied the breeze brought a faint clamour, as of dogs upon the scent. Five minutes more, and a tall buck his coat all staring and wet, his tongue hanging low, bounded across a rocky stream, choked with big-leaved plants, which intersected one of the glades, within my sight. The distant cry of the pack came each instant louder to the ear; at top-speed they swept along the trail, heads up high, and bushy tails waving. They followed over the stream without a check, and disappeared under the arches of the wood. Presently I heard the crashing of undergrowth, and threw myself flat upon the ground. Labouring terribly, the buck broke cover at the foot of the ridge, and ran along the forest on my left. The coyotes' triumphant cry rang louder and louder, and then they too appeared, running as fresh as at the beginning of the chase. They dashed along in a compact mass, eight or ten couple of grown dogs, and tailing after were three or four heavy bitches, and a dozen sturdy pups of all ages; these had plainly joined the chase only a few moments before, for they were playing and biting one another. I rose to my feet, and watched with the greatest interest, for it seemed certain that the buck must have overrun the coyotes' trail and his own scent. My guess was correct. On the edge of the forest, a big old dog which led the pack raised his muzzle and howled. Each hound stood still, and I then could mark that some of the finest animals were much more blown than the others, thus showing that the game had been turned by a forced gallop. The leader sniffed about for a moment, then uttered a sharp whine, on which the pack opened like a fan, while the whelps shrank far into the rear. Scarcely had the last dog vanished in the undergrowth, nose and tail to earth, when a short challenge rang out. There was a moment's pause, while the old dogs verified the fact, I suppose. A bolder cry proclaimed that all was well, and the pups, which had been standing still as statues in their place, dashed off into the wood. Then the music of the pack broke out again; they swept away under mysterious trees, and I saw them no more. But the buck had not a quarter of a mile of "run" in him when he passed my hiding place. . . .

"And now tell me, Indio," I said to Manuele, an hour after, as we trotted back to the "rancho," "Why were you frightened last night?"

"I heard the coyotes moving," he answered; "and I knew there was danger. You see, they are not like other beasts, afraid of fire; wild and untamable as the creatures now are, they have not quite forgotten the instincts of their forefathers. Coyotes know well enough that there's food of some sort to be found in camp, and so they cluster round it at night; and the larger your fire, the more coyotes. Ay! there's cause for fear when one is alone and the pack is out. They're worse than tigers or cowardly pumas, though there are few who believe it. They come sneaking up through the black glades, noiseless and silent and they squat round on their haunches and their eyes shine like stars. They wait and watch, and will not be driven off. You shoot one, but others come. They sit like ghosts, like pale devils, round your fire, never stirring, never taking their shining eyes from off your face. Ah!

I tell you, senor, it is terrible to be beset by coyotes! Hour by hour they sit there, just out of reach, in a circle about you. It is a nightmare! From very weariness you doze off, and, waking with a horrid start, you shout to see how near the devils have crept. As you spring up, they slink back again, and take the former ring, licking their foxy jaws, but making no sound. And you—you rush at them and they glide away, and vanish on the instant in the black undergrowth. But as you return, they come forth again, they sit down again, and stare with never a wink in their green eyes. It is very terrible, senor!" said Manuele, whose gaze was fixed in front, as if detailing a horrid memory."

Some authorities opine the coyote in early times was not native to Central America, but came as an invader coincident with the introduction of livestock by the Europeans in the first decade of the 16th century, and also that the spread of the animal was subsequent to the Spanish conquest. (Fig. 4).

The most illuminating account concerned with the coyote's spread southward into Central America, and which supports my contention, is that concerned with Frantzius (Barrentas, 96-97) who contributes the following, in regard to *Lisciscus latrans* Say, a subgenus of *Canis* L., and refers the reader to the following publications: Say, Long's Exped. Rocky Mountain I, 1823, p. 168; Richardson, Fauna Boreali-Americana, 1829, I, 73, Tb. 4; Prince zu Wied, Reisen in das innere Nordamerikas, II, 96; and *Chrysocyon latrans* Gray, Proc. Zool. Soc. London, 1868, p. 506:

"The *lobo de pradera* [wolf of the plains] of Costa Rica lives only in the province of Guanacaste, including Nicoya, on the natural savannas given over to the breeding of cattle, which extend to the southeast from the volcanic region. It causes much damage on the cattle ranges, attacking and killing the calves. Formerly it was found in the Rio Grande Valley and on the plains of Turrucares, and sometimes in the vicinity of Alajuela, but since these have been turned into agricultural land in place of cattle breeding and some small towns have been formed, it has retired to the province of Guanacaste, above mentioned.

"Its numbers have greatly increased there in recent times because the population of that province [Guanacaste] instead of increasing has diminished each year. In order to destroy them the breeders of cattle use quantities of strychnine because the inhabitants of the warm climates are so partial to repose that they do not take the trouble to hunt the wolves with firearms. In spite of much labor to obtain complete skulls and skins I have never been able to obtain even a complete skin.

"Mexico has been considered up to the present time as the

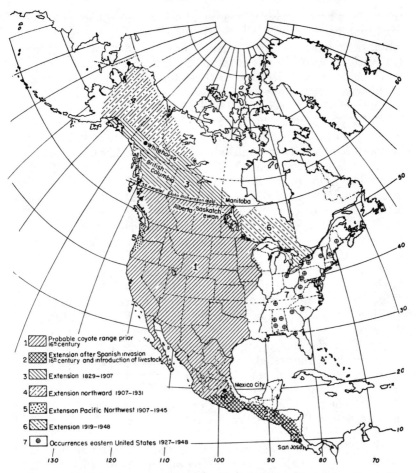

Figure 4. Progressive extension of certain parts of the coyote's present distribution since 1685 to date, as determined from the literature and field observations.

southern limit of the plains wolf, whose true homeland is Missouri and California; but today one encounters it in all of Central America to Costa Rica. In my opinion it is not entirely improbable that the plains wolf, after the discovery of America, that is to say, after the introduction of cattle, has spread from Mexico over all of Central America to Costa Rica, where today it is known by the Mexican name of "coyote." In all of the part of southeast Central America from the Bay of Fonseca to the Gulf of Nicoya, precisely where today extend great plains inhabited only by a small number of people, the Spaniards encountered a dense population of Indians, partly of Mexican origin, and partly of Chorotegans origin, whose semicivilization is full of surprises. It is certainly difficult to understand in these times how the plains wolves could have existed, epecially in bands, in the center of a population so compact,[1] but it is well understood that after the extermination of the aborigines by the Spanish conquistadores, with extraordinary and incredible cruelty, the wolves also followed the trails of those immigrants through whose efforts the herds of cattle increased.[2] It is known that the European cattle were introduced in Central America in the first decades of the 16th century, and that already in 1576, according to a Royal [Crown] report, they speak of the first herds of cattle in the province of San Salvador; in the year 1685, according to Lionel Wafer, the coyotes molested the filibusters when they were encamped in El Salvador close to Choluteca."

In the latest publication on the mammalia of Costa Rica that has come to my attention, Goodwin (1946: 438-439) states that "Most records of the [Costa Rican] coyote are from Guanacaste and the Nicoya Peninsula in northwest Costa Rica, indicating that it is closely allied to, if not identical with, the Salvadoran coyote.

"In Central America coyotes are more or less restricted to open savanna or semi-forested, arid country, mainly along the Pacific coast region. They do not regularly occur in the unbroken forests that cover so much of the general region."

It is probably the large areas of unbroken forests that hinders its spread into Panama where as yet there are no known records of its occurrence.

Belt (1928: 40) found the animal in the late 1860's on the plains between San Ubaldo, located on the northern part of Lake Nicaragua, and Acoyapa, stating that "On top of one of the hills we just got a glimpse of a small pack of wolves, or coyotes as they are called. . . . They are smaller than the European wolf, and are cunning, like a fox, but hunt in packs. They looked down at us from the ridge of the hill for a few moments, then trotted

---

[1] Only in case of necessity and when it is not possible to hunt deer do they [wolves] resort to eating wild plums [jocotes] and other fruits. See Long's Exped., p. 174.

[2] In the same manner the jaguar and other predatory animals have increased notably in the plains and pampas of South America after the introduction from Europe of cattle, horses, and mules. See Von Humboldt, Ansichten der Natur, 1860, Bd. I, S. 234.

off down the other side. Their howlings may often be heard in the early morning."

Re Honduras, Moe (1904: 19) stated at the turn of the present century ". . . . the coyote (is) not uncommon."

The type specimen *Canis latrans hondurensis* described by Goldman (1936, 26: 32-34) comes from Cerro Quinote, northeast of Archaga, on the Talanga road located north of Tegucigalpa, and was collected by the late C. F. Underwood, August 18, 1934.

Goodwin (1942, 79: 183) records a coyote taken at La Cueva Archaga.

One of the earliest if not the first recording of the coyote for El Salvador is the mentioning of "wolves" by Wafer (1934) while journeying to the mainland from his base camp maintained on Tigre or Manguera Island in the Gulf of Fonseca in 1685. Frantzius (1892) places this observation as "close to Choluteca," and it was here while in search of beef produced on a farm hereabouts that Wafer says he was confronted with: "a multitude of Wolves, which are the boldest that I ever met with; for they would come so near, as to be almost ready to pull the Flesh out of our Hands." This boldness as mentioned by Wafer is occasionally observed today with respect to the small coyote of our southwestern deserts (*C. l. mearnsi*). The calling of these coyotes "Wolves" is of course an error as the large gray wolves have never occurred in Central America.

CANADA

Near the close of the last decade of the 19th century, J. B. Tyrrell (1888) gave the coyote's distribution as "Plains and partly wooded country throughout Manitoba and the North-West Territories, though much more plentiful on the Upper Saskatchewan than elsewhere; also on the plains in the southern portion of British Columbia."

A quarter of a century later, Edward A. Preble, the noted American naturalist, in Seton, E. T., 1911: 352, stated:

"The coyote has recently extended its range northward from the prairie country well into the woods. Ten years ago we were told that there were none of the species near Fort McKay. Five or six years ago they first appeared, and now are abundant along the Athabaska nearly down to Athabaska Lake, and extend in less numbers for some distance farther north. E. Nagle [fur-trader] got one coyote from Fort Simpson last year, and one from Fort Liard. Inspector A. M. Jarvis of the R.N.W.M. Police, got one at Grand Detour, Great Slave River, and saw another on Salt

River ten miles west of Smith Landing. It is usually called the 'brush wolf.' During our northward trip we collected a number of skulls from trappers' cabins along the Athabaska, and while returning up the river we saw its tracks almost daily, and frequently caught sight of the animals themselves. Signs observed along this part of the Athabaska showed that the animals had been feeding on the berries of *Arctostaphylos uva-ursi*, Rosa [acicularis], sarsaparilla, and water insects."

At present, the coyote occurs over a vast area of Canada. With exception of a recent occurrence near Ottawa, the animal is unknown anywhere in the province of Quebec. With respect to this Quebec occurrence Rand (1945: 122) records:

"The National Museum has secured a specimen from near Luskville, Gatineau County, Quebec, taken Oct. 29, 1944, apparently the first record for Quebec. [This area is northwest of Ottawa.]

"In the summer and fall of 1944 many sheep were reported killed by 'wolves' in the area just west of the City of Ottawa. About 100 sheep were said to have been killed from the flock belonging to the Dominion Experimental Farm and pastured about the Connaught Rifle Range. Organized hunts resulted in the killing of one coyote and one dog, which probably properly allocates the blame."

Thus the coyote is found in more or less abundance from the Ottawa River westward throughout the other provinces and territories.

Ontario

According to verbal statement of the late E. C. Cross of the Royal Ontario Museum to the author made August 14, 1946, if the extent to which the coyote has spread in its distribution in this province the past decade is any criterion it will be only the matter of a short time until it will have extended its range throughout all of Ontario. Population trends for the period 1935-1939 show the coyote to be moving steadily to all parts in Ontario, its advancement northward being the slowest and all of this in spite of a liberal provincial bounty on the animal. Its heaviest distribution in Ontario at this writing (1947) is south-southeast from approximately the 47th parallel to its southern border and eastward to the border of Quebec, along the Ottawa River to its junction with the St. Lawrence (See Fig. 5).

What is believed to be the first record for the coyote in Ontario was identified by the late E. W. Nelson. It was taken north of Thedford, Lambton County, on January 10, 1919. The body measurements were length 58½ inches (1480 mm.), and tail 11¾ inches (300 mm.). The skull and skin were purchased by the National Museum of Canada at Ottawa, where that specimen is now deposited.

Figure 5. Coyote distribution in Province of Ontario, Canada.

Manitoba

In Manitoba, the coyote is well known. Its most northerly concentration is from the flood plain and delta of the Saskatchewan River west and east of The Pas. While in this province during the winter of 1947, I found that one occurrence of the coyote was recorded from near Churchill on Hudson Bay. Canadian naturalists held the opinion that this was probably a straggler. Another interesting occurrence is near Split Lake, southwest of Churchill.

Saskatchewan

In Saskatchewan the coyote occurs in all of the districts south of a more or less straight line connecting the center of Lake Athabaska and the northern end of Reindeer Lake.

Buchanan (1920: 217) on May 10, 1914, observed a single coyote at Big River—and heard many howling at night. None were seen or heard at Ile a la Crosse Lake. On June 10 while on Sandy Lake, Churchill River, he observed that not one coyote had been seen or heard since he reached Ile a la Crosse Post. Also "Solomon Cook, halfbreed servant, tells me there are none in neighborhood of south end of Reindeer Lake." Buchanan investigated the country lying between the Saskatchewan River and the Barren Grounds, leaving Prince Albert on May 6, 1914, and descending the Beaver River to Lake Ile a la Crosse and Churchill River, thence continuing upstream on Reindeer River and Reindeer Lake, entering Cochran River on July 18, and Lac Du Brochet on August 1. This was his base camp where he proposed to winter, but on receipt of news of the World War I in late October he decided to return, and reached Regina on January 15, 1915. His trip thus covered 2,000 miles of travel by canoe and dog sleigh. Part of his collection is in the Provincial Museum at Regina, Saskatchewan.

Alberta

Coyotes occur practically throughout most of the province of Alberta. They are a real economic problem in the area bordered on the north by the Red River; on the west by No. 1 Highway; on the south by the international boundary, and on the east by the Saskatchewan border. More coyotes are taken in this area than anywhere else in the province. Here were taken one-half of the total number bountied in Alberta from April 1 to October 31, 1946. This part of the province contains all of the sheep producing ranches of any importance; and some cattle are also produced. The total bountied during 1946 was 4,934. A typical Canadian bounty act may be appropriately quoted at this point.

GOVERNMENT OF THE PROVINCE OF ALBERTA

REGULATIONS GOVERNING THE PAYMENT OF BOUNTY TO BE PAID ON PRAIRIE WOLVES AND TIMBER WOLVES

(O.C. 886-46)

1. During the fiscal year ending the 31st day of March, 1947, there shall be paid out of the sum appropriated by vote of the Legislative Assembly for the payment of bounties for destruction of pests to persons who are residents of the Province, and who are the captors of Timber Wolves and Prairie Wolves, by way of bounty the following sums:

For every Timber Wolf taken (including Timber
Wolf Pups) $25.00
For every Prairie Wolf taken (including Prairie
Wolf Pups) 3.00

2. Bounty payments will only be made on Timber Wolves and Prairie Wolves killed or taken during the period April 1st, 1946 to October 15th, 1946 (both dates inclusive).

3. Bounty payments will only be made on Timber Wolves and Prairie Wolves taken within the boundaries of the Province of Alberta, exclusive of the National Parks.

4. Applications for the bounty must be made in writing not later than the 31st day of October, 1946, in a form prescribed by the Minister, containing such particulars as the Minister may require, and the form must be delivered, together with the pelt of the animal in respect of which the bounty is claimed, to a Constable of the Royal Canadian Mounted Police, a Justice of the Peace, a Commissioner for Oaths, a Salaried Game Officer or Forestry Officer, and when making the application for bounty the applicant shall furnish the official before whom the application is made such evidence as he may require as to the time and place of taking the pelt in respect of which the bounty is claimed.

5. The Royal Canadian Mounted Police Constable, Justice of the Peace, Commissioner for Oaths, Game Officer or Forestry Officer receiving any application for bounty shall forward the application, together with his own report, to the Fish and Game Commissioner, Department of Lands and Mines, Edmonton, and upon the application for bounty being approved by the said Fish and Game Commissioner, the proper bounty shall be paid.

6. Both ears shall be intact on all Timber Wolf and Prairie Wolf pelts on which bounty is claimed, and the official before whom the application for bounty is made and to whom the pelt is delivered, shall split both ears, from tip to base, of each such pelt, and return the pelt to the applicant to be disposed of as he may desire.

7. No person who is the holder of a valid and subsisting license to buy, sell, trade, barter or traffic in the skins or pelts of fur-bearing animals shall be eligible to make application for bounty in respect of any Timber Wolf or Prairie Wolf, or any Timber Wolf or Prairie Wolf Pup.

Form No. 73, 4M-5-45

PROVINCE OF ALBERTA
DEPARTMENT OF LANDS & MINES
GAME BRANCH

BOUNTY WARRANT

Affidavit

CANADA
Province of Alberta
To wit:
} In the matter of Destruction of Timber Wolves, Cougar and Coyotes.

I, ... of ....

make oath and say as follows:

The pelt of the .... now displayed
was taken by me in Township .... Range ....
West .... Meridian, ...
killed by me on the .... day of ....
194..., in the Province of Alberta, and not having previously received
bounty for the .... pelt, I am, therefore, entitled
to such bounty.

SWORN before me at ....]
.........................in the[............................
Province of Alberta, this day of[Signature of Party making Affidavit
.... 194..]

....
Royal Canadian Mounted Police Con-
stable, Salaried Game Guardian,
J.P. or Commissioner for Oaths.

Recommendation for Bounty payment:
I hereby certify that .... of ....
is entitled to the payment of bounty on the animals mentioned above,
and that I have today slit the ears of these pelts.

....
Royal Canadian Mounted Police Constable,
Salaried Game Guardian, J.P. or
Commissioner for Oaths.

During the course of two extensive field trips through Canada during 1946-47, I found the majority of the Canadian conservationists and many public officials opposed to the bounty plan as a measure for predator control.

The distinguished Canadian naturalist, J. Dewey Soper, has long made a study of the Canadian coyote. His work has taken him into most of the Canadian National Parks, and he studied particularly Wood Buffalo Park, located partly in northern Alberta and southern Northwest Territories. Herein coyotes, like many other mammals, appear to be cyclic in population. As of 1945, coyotes were less numerous than 10 to 12 years previously. Soper (1945) reported "In last 10 year period, the peak catch was made in the winter of 1934-35, and lowest in 1940-41. Since 1935, the average annual take of coyotes has only been about 18% of those captured in season of 1934-35." Early in 1947, Soper sent me the following which adds to the record:

"Regarding this race, *Canis latrans incolatus* Hall, in Wood Buffalo Park, I write as follows:

"The coyote ranges in suitable districts throughout the whole of the park. According to Indian report, a few stray north of this and may reach Great Slave Lake. It is certain that the species has increased considerably during the past 40 years. When Preble visited the Athabaska-Mackenzie region, 1901-1904, only an occasional animal ranged so far north. Numerous coyotes and their trails were personally seen in the southern two-thirds of the park. The species appears well distributed in the Peace-Athabaska lowlands, and west all along Peace River to the west boundary. The largest numbers, however, are found in the central part of the park north of Peace River, and particularly in the eastern half. Substantial numbers frequent woods and salt plains west of Slave River, and locally in the more rugged uplands to the west, from Peace River northward about Crane, Pierre, Lane, and Pine Lakes to the Northwest Territories. It seemed especially common in the salt plains section west of Fort Smith in September, 1933. In January, 1934, a few trails were seen on the Lobstick Creek Plain and north along Little Buffalo River. Indians reported scattered individuals in the highlands westward, and north to Nyarling River; a few also in the lowlands of these latitudes between Slave and Little Buffalo Rivers.

"On November 25, a coyote, two-thirds grown, was seen in an Indian trap 8 miles northeast of Pine Lake; it was pale-coloured with areas on face, shoulders, flanks, and tail of a light tawny shade. Judging from its small size it was doubtless an immature of the year. An adult female (N.M.C. 12319) was secured for the collection on February 27, 1934—taken in a set made for wolves near Murdock Creek. This specimen measured 1310, 360, 220 mm. and by skull characters is definitely referable to *Canis latrans incolatus* Hall (1934: 369-370). A skin without skull taken by John Bloomfield at Fort Smith, in winter of 1924, shows a trace of *C. l. latrans* or *nebracensis* character in a faint streak of blackish hairs on fore legs.

"In a memorandum of April 26, 1941, Dr. R. M. Anderson remarks: 'This subspecies was described in Mammals collected by T. T. and E. B. McCabe in the Bowron Lake region of British Columbia' by E. Raymond Hall (1934b: 369).

"*Wood Buffalo Park, Alta. and N.W.T., March 17-April 14/45:*
Evidently not very common at this time, as sign of the species
was very rarely observed. Trappers assert that relatively few
inhabit the country, being scarcer than a few years ago. While
poisoning timber wolves, Patrolman Philip Bourque accidently secured two coyotes in the vicinity of the 30th Baseline and Patrolman Bill Braiden secured one in a similar manner west of the
Bay Camp.

"A few signs of these animals were noted in muddy reaches of
the military road between Little Buffalo River and a point near
Nyarling River, on June 5, 6, and 7, 1945. The species is apparently
nowhere common in Wood Buffalo Park at the present time."

Finally, before leaving the distribution of the coyote in the
Canadian Prairie Provinces, Manitoba, Saskatchewan and Alberta,
Soper's further observations hither and yon are given, for they
convey to the reader the immense area of these respective provinces
over which our wild barking dog is distributed:

"The following notes were written as a result of observations
made along the International Boundary in 1927:

"It is doubtless this race, *Canis latrans nebracensis* Merriam,
somewhat smaller than *latrans*, with lighter dentition and paler
colours, which inhabits the entire region of the semi-arid plains.
Here it was found of such universal distribution that it will not
be necessary to enter into details regarding its occurrence in the
various collecting localities. It may be said briefly, to be common
practically everywhere. In a few places its comparative abundance
was more noticeable than elsewhere, these localities being Lodge
Creek, Alta., and Val Marie Rock Creek, and Big Muddy Lake,
Sask. The species was very common in the two latter localities.
Daylight wandering was observed with frequency, while their
weird howling was a nightly occurrence.

"Coyotes were found scarce on the prairies from Estevan east
where the country is less wild and more thickly settled, though
a few individuals were noted. At Max Lake, Turtle Mt., they were
quite numerous. Possibly these are typical *latrans*, which are known
to range into eastern Manitoba and there called 'brush wolf'. The
distribution of the subspecies in the prairie provinces is not very
well known.

"On June 19, 1936, an adult and at least three immatures were
seen at a den on a shrubby ridge close to the east end of Johnston
Lake. One youngster was caught by hand and photographed, then
liberated. Another animal at this time was observed running over
the dry southeast bottom of Chaplin Lake.

"Hugh Green (Oct. 1932, C.F-N) states that this race occurs in the southern part of Riding Mt. Nat. Park where the country is more open with small detached prairies and thinner woods.

"*Frenchman Riv., Sask., at International Boundary, June 15-18/41:* A few plains coyotes inhabit this valley and surrounding plains. None observed, but heard howling on several occasions.

"*Middle Creek, Sask., June 19-22/41:* Occurs sparingly throughout this district south of the Cypress Hills. Two individuals were observed.

"*Nemiskam Nat. Park, Alta., June 23-27/41:* Several were observed in the park during the period of general faunal investigations, both in the rugged badland coulees and on the high plains.

"Northern coyote, *Canis latrans latrans* Say was personally observed at numerous places in the aspen grove or parklands section of the three Prairie Provinces and in some places farther north. Animals were several times seen during the fall and early winter of 1913 in the Fish Lakes-Hay River sector of western Alberta near Jasper Park. Also signs and the howling of the animals were noted at Rocky Pass (S.E. Mountain Park) in September, 1922.

"Green (1932) says of the species in Riding Mountain National Park: 'An average number of these predators exist throughout the main Wapiti range. In the spring of the year they are responsible for the destruction of many wapiti calves. From the size, colour and actions of numerous specimens observed they could easily be mistaken by a casual observer for timber wolves (*Canis nubilus*).'

"*Quill Lakes, Sask., July 1936:* A few reported for the country surrounding the lake.

"*Sandilands Forest Reserve, May 19/37:* Reported as occurring sparingly at least throughout reserve.

"*Douglas Lake, Man.:* Tolerably common.

"*Ekapo Lake, Sask., June 1937:* Reported by D. Bettschen as still relatively common in this district.

"*Cedar Lake, Man., Oct. 23-24, 1937:* Several heard howling at night while camped in this locality.

"Recorded by Hall (1938) from the Touchwood Hills of Saskatchewan.

"*Sunwapta Pass, Jasper Park, Aug. 10, 1938:* A fine, large individual was observed during the early evening as the sun was setting over the mountain to the west. The animal was obviously hunting and travelled slowly along the margin of a meadow and the "last spruces" near timberline. The altitude here is approximately 7000 feet above sea-level.

"Anderson (MS. 1938) says the species is uncommon in

Waterton Park; numbers were seen in Banff Park and considered to be somewhat more numerous here than in Waterton Park; considered to be comparatively few in numbers in Jasper National Park.

"Occurs in some numbers in Prince Albert National Park. Several trails were noted in the vicinity of my Spruce River Camp, Tp. 55, R. 1, July 5-10/40. On several occasions coyotes were heard howling, once during the middle of the forenoon.

"A few are known to occur in Elk Island National Park, Alberta. 'Dust trails' were noted on several occasions on roads, in buffalo wallows, etc. They are occasionally heard howling in the wilder sections of the park.

"These animals are fairly common in Riding Mt. Nat. Park. Many are reported by the wardens in various sections of the plateau both in prairie-parklands areas and in heavy timber. While camped northwest of Lake Audy coyotes were heard howling on numerous occasions from Sept. 18-22/40 and on the 23rd an individual was seen near the west end of Clear Lake.

"*Edwards Lake, Riding Mt. Nat. Park, Oct. 27/40:* Several were heard howling in this locality last night and again today. Probably they are fairly common. *Oct. 28-Nov. 1:* Coyotes were heard on many occasions during the days indicated; most of them were howling along the east side of Edwards Lake.

"*Oak Lake, Man., May 15-18/41:* A few individuals still persist in this district; the species is not nearly so common as formerly.

"*Riding Mt. Nat. Park, 1941:* In late May coyotes were heard howling on several occasions in the Vermilion River and Kennice Creek district. In early October one was also heard howling some little distance west of Kennice Creek. The coyotes occurring here and south in Manitoba may be referable to *nebracensis*, but for lack of specimens the subspecific identity is unknown.

"*Windy Pt., Sask. River, Bighorn Mts., Alta., Aug. 21-24/41:* On the night of Aug. 22nd one was heard howling in this locality; tracks of the animals were also seen in various parts of the district.

"*Overflowing Riv., L. Winnipegosis, Man., Oct. 17-23/41:* Heard howling on several occasions during the above period.

"*Carlyle Lake, Moose Mt. Sask., May 21/42:* Coyotes, presumed to be this race, are fairly common on the mountain. Many are taken here by the Indians each trapping season.

"*The Pas Dist., Man., Sept. 17-28/42:* Scattered individuals are reported in this region by provincial game wardens and other local residents.

"*Breadon Lake, Turtle Mt., Man., Sept. 19-22/43:* Coyotes were occasionally heard howling in this locality during the above period. From all accounts they are fairly well represented and generally distributed.

"*Lake William, Turtle Mt., Man., Sept. 23-26/43:* One heard howling on the evening of Sept. 24th. Said by local residents to be fairly common in the wilderness on top of the plateau and around its edges.

"*Uak Lake, Man., Sept. 28/43:* One was sighted in the woods today at a distance of about 25 feet. Tracks were noted at several points along the lake shore and on dusty trails.

"*Oct. 26-30/43:* Well distributed in the wilder sections of country east of Red River. Commonly heard howling in the vicinity of camp on the night of the 27th southwest of Sundown. Said to be common in the country from the latter point to and in Sandilands Forest Reserve. Many were also heard howling about camp from Oct. 27 to 30th, 4 miles east-southeast of Marchand. One was observed near Steinbach.

"*Baptiste Lake, Alta., May 27/44:* Numbers occur in the district; to be referred to as moderately common.

"*May 30/44:* A fine example was observed close to the road today about 7 miles east of Slave Lake. Reported as fairly common in this part of the region.

"*Sturgeon Lake, Alta., June 13/44:* Ranges widely in this territory. Reported common and increasing in numbers during the past few years.

"*Bear Lake, Alta., June 21-25/44:* Not personally observed, but reported as fairly numerous in the territory as a whole. They range completely across the Grande Prairie parklands area from expansive wilderness areas which completely surround it.

"*Ray, Updike and Sinclair Lakes, Alta., July 7-10/44:* Said by local residents to be more or less plentiful in the district as a whole. The animals were personally heard howling at Ray and Sinclair Lakes.

"*Region south of Wapiti River, Alta., July/44:* Common and widely distributed. Tracks were common along the trail all the way from Pipestone Creek, south of Wembley to Torrens River, Rocky Mts. The animals were heard howling on several occasions. The species has been especially plentiful during the past several seasons. Large numbers were taken by trappers during the past season.

"*Henderson Creek, Tp. 78, R. 10, west of Spirit River, Alta., July 30-31/44:* According to report, fairly common in this area

and undoubtedly similarly so over most of the region at large.
Many fresh trails were seen on various dusty trails and animals
were heard howling during both nights while camped at this
creek. An old hunter's skin of a coyote obtained here (No. 4884—
no data) is being shipped to the National Museum of Canada,
Ottawa. The dorsal area on this pelt is very dark.

"In the whole region north of Peace River this species has
been unusually plentiful for several seasons and particularly during the trapping period of 1943-44. The same conditions prevailed
south of the Peace to Magloire Lake. Tracks of animals were seen
on several occasions and animals heard howling nightly while
conducting investigations at the latter lake during mid-August,
1944. Also common in the Kimawan Lake district.

"*Winnipeg River, Whiteshell Forest Reserve, Man., Sept. 25-
28/44:* Reported as occurring in fair numbers throughout this
district. Several heard howling during the above period.

"*Blue Lakes, Duck Mt., Man., Oct. 7-11/44:* These animals are
apparently rather common in this locality, as several spoors were
observed and various individuals were heard howling both in the
vicinity of the lakes and to the north and east.

"*Singoosh Lake, Duck Mt., Man., Oct. 12-14/44:* Generally distributed throughout this locality. Individuals were heard howling
on several occasions.

"*Turtle Mountain, Man., Oct. 16-17/44:* Comparatively common
in this territory, according to reports of forest rangers. Individuals
were heard howling on numerous occasions at Breadon Lake, where
two nights were spent in camp.

"*Duck Mt., 4 miles west of Watjask Lake, Sept. 20/45:* One
example was observed early in the evening mousing in a grassy
depression in the forest among the hills. It paid scant attention to
the car when it stopped at a distance of about 40 yards. It was
only after I got out of the car that it became alarmed and ran
off into the bush.

"*Riding Mt. Nat. Park, Oct. 3-5/45:* Reported by the wardens as
relatively common. Two were personally observed while travelling
by motor car in various localities on the mountain.

"*Lake Manitoba, west of Moosehorn, Man., Oct. 20/45:* Reported as moderately common in this district. One was said to
have killed a sheep a few days ago a short distance south of
Steeprock.

"*Winnipeg, Man., Jan. 17/47:* Through the courtesy of Mr. G.
Malaher, Director of Game and Fisheries, many additional records were secured with respect to the distribution of the coyote

in northern Manitoba. The game branch has records of the animals having been taken in the following localities: Port Churchill (rare occurrence; first and only record); Cross Lake; Pikwitonei; Nelson House; Kississing; Thicket Portage; Granville Lake; Berens River; Little Grand Rapids; Norway House; Split Lake; and Wabowden."

British Columbia

With the exception of the fiord-like region of extreme western British Columbia, the coyote occurs throughout the entire province. A few occur in the lower Fraser River Valley, as is the case to within almost the city limits of Vancouver where during the winter of 1947, they were reported to be eating garbage. In this province, the coyote has consistently invaded new terrain. Prior to 1892 it was unknown in the Mt. Baker region of extreme northern Washington, but according to Allan Brooks (1930: 66) from that date coyotes began to "invade the region from the dry interior." By 1930, they were common.

For the past several years a late spring and summer bounty has been paid on the coyote by the province, but latest advice is to the effect that the bounty plan is being discarded in favor of trying the so-called paid hunter system as a coyote control measure.

As in Alberta, the main antipathy toward the coyote comes from the sheep producing areas of the interior, and to a slightly lesser extent from sportsmen.

There are no coyotes on Vancouver Island, although the large wolf occurs thereon.

Mackenzie Delta

Concerning the coyote's northward migratory movement, that recorded by Porsild (1945) is of more than passing interest. It is known as Amarognag by the Eskimo. Porsild states:

"At least for some years preceding 1927, coyotes had been invading the Mackenzie delta, apparently from the west, and a number of pelts were traded each year at McPherson and at Aklavik, as well as at trading posts up the river. During the winter of 1927-28 coyotes were very common between Arctic Red river and Norman and did considerable damage to fur caught in traps. Above Sans Sault rapid the writer saw the pelts of 12 coyotes taken by one trapper.

"In December 1927 on the Arctic coast just east of the delta, the writer saw a coyote which had been taken in a trap. The coyote was then unknown to the Eskimo of the region, who thought this particular animal a 'cross between a dog and a red fox'. The skin and skull are in the National Museum of Canada.

"As far as the writer was able to learn no coyotes were taken in the delta during the years 1931-35.

"Mr. Lang informs me that in late years coyotes have been rather infrequent visitors to the Mackenzie delta."

Yukon

Of its first appearance in Yukon Territory, that to be noted with reference to the coyote's invasion of Alaska, puts the date as 1907 near Whitehorse.

According to Rand's findings (1945: 36) the coyote appeared in the Yukon Pelly Valley country about 1912, and since then has become common, then "scarce," probably because of a fluctuation in food supply.

In a manuscript by C. H. D. Clarke (1943) it is stated:

"Coyote tracks were occasionally seen in southwestern Yukon and I collected an old skull at Tepee Lake. Two years ago (1941) coyotes are reported to have died out, and abundance altered to scarcity. Mr. Jimmy Joe, of Kluane Lake told me that he knew of sick specimens found recently."

Plate 5. Alaska coyote.

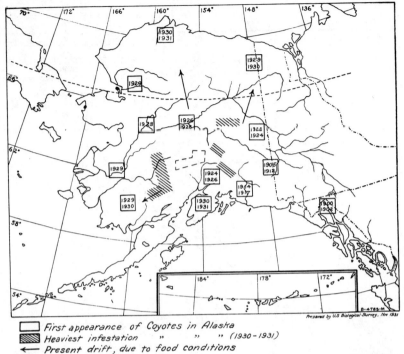

First appearance of Coyotes in Alaska
Heaviest infestation " " " (1930-1931)
⟵ Present drift, due to food conditions

Prepared by U.S Biological Survey, Nov 1931

Figure 6. The extension of range of the coyote according to literature and field studies.

ALASKA

Dufresne, long a resident of Alaska, and for nearly a decade Executive Officer of the Alaska Game Commission, states in his annual report to the Secretary of the Interior, for the fiscal year ending June 30, 1940, that: "The coyote reached Alaska less than a quarter of a century ago from Yukon Territory, but in this short space of time it has penetrated to almost every far corner. It has been taken from the Stikine River in southeastern Alaska to and near Point Barrow on the Arctic Ocean. Its numbers have steadily increased, although it has failed to establish itself in the swampy coastal areas. The center of abundance at the present time is from the upper Tanana watershed southward and westward to and including the Kenai Peninsula. The territorial bounty of $20 per animal is paid on the wolves as well as the coyotes but does not appear to be producing comparable results. That the number presented for bounty each year is constantly increasing is borne out by reports of shipments of pelts from Alaska. During the past year 1,507 coyote pelts were exported, nearly 3 times the 15-

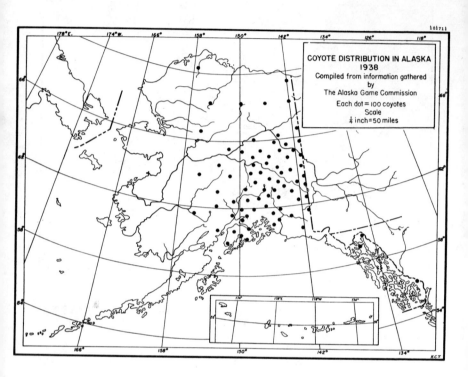

Figure 7. Coyote distribution in Alaska.

year annual average of 568, and 25 times the 61 skins shipped in 1925." (Dufresne, F., 1940: 11.) (Fig. 6), (Plate 5).

The spread of the coyote toward the polar region unfolds an intriguing story. Richardson for instance by 1829 put its most northerly distribution limits at about the 55th parallel or roughly the northern boundaries of Alberta and Saskatechewan (Richardson, John, 1829: 73). Approximately three-quarters of a century later (Allen, J. A., 1908: 584-586) records the animal taken in February 1907 near Whitehorse on the Alsek River, Yukon, and at that time was "by far the most northern record for any form of coyote." From that time nearly a quarter of a century elapsed when it made its appearance (1930-31) just south of Point Barrow on the Arctic coast, its most northerly habitat. (See Fig. 4.) The first coyote to be taken at Circle, Alaska, was during the year 1923.

For the years 1942-1946, a total of 2,496 coyotes were presented for bounty payment in Alaska. (Fig. 7.)

Chapter Three

Habits and Characteristics

THE COYOTE is by far the most successful of all the larger North American predators in contending with advancing civilization. Contrasted to the North American wolf, which has been eliminated from much of its former habitat, is being gradually restricted to the wilder mountain recesses, the coyote seems to be holding its own, adapting itself to constantly changing environments, and slowly but surely spreading from the plains section to the high mountains. All this in spite of the continual warfare against it. In this respect it is a most astounding mammal. According to present indications it will always be a part of America's fauna, regardless of the fact that it will never be tolerated, with but few exceptions, throughout its vast range by a majority of the general public. The nature of the beast together with its physical make-up are assets that appear unbeatable by the hand of man. Personally, the author, though in full sympathy with whatever measures are necessary in the local control of its depredations, nevertheless feels like Ernest Thompson Seton: "If ever the day should come when one may camp in the West, and hear not a note of the coyote's joyous stirring evening song, I hope that I shall long before have passed away, gone over the Great Divide. . . ."

However, the foregoing plea is not "to advocate [this animal's] protection in areas occupied by the homes of civilized man and his domestic animals." To do so is only to "invite being discredited as practical conservationists and to risk through prejudice the defeat of measures which may be vital to the future welfare of the country" (Goldman 1925, 6 (1): 28-33) not to overlook the future existence of the coyote as well. This seems to fit in to Graham's recent program, Summarization of the Thirteenth North American Wildlife Conference, March 8 to 10, 1948, when he stated ". . . . that on most land wildlife must remain a byproduct. But there is no alternative. The goal is the survival of man."

Never have I seen any sympathy directed toward any of our North American predators wherever they were a menace to livestock or poultry production, or the public health.

SIZE AND WEIGHT

Often one may be easily misled about the weight of coyotes. (See Plate 6.) A matured adult of either sex taken when the fur is prime appears, when first looked upon, to be comparable in weight to the smallest of the gray wolf forms, the Sierra Madre or Mexican wolf, which occurs in Arizona and New Mexico. These wolves generally weigh between 60 and 90 pounds. Generally speaking, the coyote weighs somewhere between 18 and 30 pounds. Exceptionally heavy individuals occur. Noted are the following:

A male coyote killed in February, 1944, on the Merle Forbes farm north of Bancroft in Kingsbury County, South Dakota, weighed 42 pounds.

A male coyote taken near Jackson, Mich., weighed 53½ pounds.

The heaviest coyote among the records obtained by the Fish and Wildlife Service is that of a male weighing 74¾ pounds killed near Afton, Wyoming, on November 19, 1937. This animal was very fat, had been killing sheep, and measured 63 inches from tip to tip.

Other weights are:

446 male coyotes from New Mexico averaged 24.4 pounds.

383 female coyotes from the same state averaged 22.2 pounds.

Hidalgo County, New Mexico, produced the largest male coyote, weighing 41 pounds; the largest female, taken in Eddy County, New Mexico, weighed 33 pounds.

7 male coyotes (Crabb, E. D., 1925) taken during 1917 on the then Wichita National Forest, southwestern Oklahoma, averaged 30.50 pounds.

93 coyotes taken in northwestern Oklahoma during 1947 averaged 25 pounds each, while 96 coyotes taken in the northeastern part of this state during the same year averaged 27 pounds each.

38 females taken from the King Ranch in Texas weighed from 17 to 32 pounds, or an average of 23.14 pounds.

46 male coyotes from the same area weighed 18 to 42, or an average of 27.69 pounds. Fourteen in this group weighed 30 pounds each.

The author is indebted to I. McT. Cowan, Professor of Zoology at the University of British Columbia, Vancouver, for the following data on coyotes taken in the Rocky Mountain region of western Canada.

Plate 6. Average size coyote.

TABLE 1.—Coyote Measurements and Weights

Locality	Sex	Total length Mm.	Tail length Mm.	Hind foot Mm.	Ear from notch Mm.	Weight (lbs.)
Jasper, Alberta	Male (juv.)	1130	355	204	114	20
Banff, Alberta	Male (yearling)	1150	370	195	117	26½
Jasper, Alberta	Male (ad.)	1215	342	207	117	..
Jasper, Alberta (Brazeau)	Female (ad.)	1010	342	180	105	23
Jasper, Alberta	Male (ad.)	1070	295	192	100	27
Banff, Alberta	Male (ad.)	1155	320	190	120	30
Banff, Alberta	Female (ad.)	1130	375	190	102	25
Banff, Alberta	Male (ad.)	....	...	...	...	30
Red Deer River, Banff Park, Alberta	Male (ad.)	1265	...	...	...	33
Banff, Alberta	Male (ad.)	1260	360	215	125	32

Coyote Pups in July

Kootenay Park, British Columbia		Banff Park, Alberta	
Sex	Weight (lbs.)	Sex	Weight (lbs.)
Female	6¾ (healthy)	Male	6½ (mangy)
Male	7¾ (healthy)	Male	6 (mangy)
Male	8¾ (healthy)	Male	8 (mangy)

Yukon Territory Coyote Body Measurements

The following coyote specimens from Yukon Territory are in the Zoological Collection of Royal Ontario Museum, Toronto, Canada:

Male, No. 31.2.16.10, White River, February 1930; total length, 48 inches; tail, 18 inches.

Old male, No. 32.10.16.14, White River, December 31, 1931; total length, 49 inches; tail, 13½ inches; hind foot, 2¾ inches.

Female, No. 32.10.16.15, White River, February 10, 1931; total length, 48 inches; tail, 17 inches; hind foot, 2¾ inches.

Male, No. 32.10.16.16, White River, January 24, 1932; total length, 48 inches; tail, 14 inches; hind foot, 2½ inches.

Male, No. 32.10.16.17, White River, December 31, 1931; total length, 56 inches; tail, 14½ inches; hind foot, 3 inches.

Male, No. 32.10.16.18, White River, March 1, 1932; total length, 50 inches; tail, 14½ inches; hind foot, 2¾ inches.

Young female, No. 32.10.16.20, White River, November 14, 1931; total length, 46 inches; tail, 14 inches; hind foot, 2½ inches.

Male, No. 33.9.20.9, Yukon River, 1932; total length, 50 inches; tail, 14 inches.

Male, No. 33.9.20.10, Yukon River, December 1932; total length, 48 inches; tail, 14½ inches.

Female, No. 33.9.20.11, Yukon River, January 1933; total length, 46 inches; tail, 13½ inches.

Female, No. 33.9.20.12, Yukon River, January 1933; total length, 48 inches; tail, 14 inches.

Female, No. 33.9.20.13, Yukon River, January 1933; total length, 47 inches; tail, 13¼ inches.

Female, No. 33.9.20.14, Yukon River, February 1933; total length, 48½ inches; tail, 13 inches.

COLORATION

The color pattern of the coyote varies less than in the large wolves, which are notoriously subject to melanism and somewhat to climatic variation. The predominant hair color is a light gray and red or fulvous interspersed over parts of the body with black and white which holds generally for the species, with certain modification in some of the races. Altitude of habitat is a factor in coyote coloration, those found at the higher elevations tend toward gray and black, while those on desert areas are more fulvous, or often a whitish gray, a color that is generally protective from its blending with so much of the desert growth. The author has always felt that in general Merriam's description

(1897: 23) of the coyote's color can be little improved upon when he wrote: "muzzle dull and rather pale fulvous, finely sprinkled with gray hairs (chiefly above) and with black hairs (chiefly on cheeks); top of head from front of eyes to ears grizzled gray, the pale fulvous zone of underfur showing through, but the gray predominating; ears deep rich fulvous, sparingly sprinkled with black hairs; upper parts from ears to tail coarsely mixed buffy gray and black; under parts and upper lip whitish; long hairs of throat sparingly tipped with blackish, giving the broad collar a grizzled appearance; fore-legs and feet dirty whitish; becoming dull clay color on outer side of leg; hind legs and feet dull fulvous on outer sides, white on inner side and on dorsal surface of feet, the change from fulvous to white rather abrupt; tail narrowly tipped with black, its under side whitish basally, becoming pale fulvous on distal half and tipped and edged with black."

It is not common to find albinism among coyotes. When this occurs, there is generally only one in the litter. However, where more than one to a litter has occurred as that observation made by Barnes (1936: 137) where in a litter of coyote pups taken in western Nebraska by Charles Grepes of Boone, Nebraska, 4 were albinos. Instead of the eyes being pink, however, they were a

Plate 7. Albino male pup coyote (right) taken 7 miles north of Killdeer, North Dakota, Nov. 10, 1945, compared with ordinary coyote specimen.

Plate 8. Normal color, left; albino, right.

milky blue in color. Only one case to the other extreme, a black animal, is known to the author, and pertains to a single individual trapped in Colorado during the early 1920's. The eyes in this instance also were a milky blue color.

It is interesting to note that of a total of 750,000 coyotes killed by Federal and cooperative hunters between March 22, 1938, and

June 30, 1945, only two albinos were captured in the main United States range of the animal.

While albinism among coyotes appears to be rare, albino coyotes have been captured in most of the Western States. Very often as stated there is but one in a litter as was the case of one killed by an automobile 5 miles east of King City, California, on October 18, 1931. Approximately 9 months old, it had for sometime previous been the target for numerous riflemen. Another was trapped during February 1939, near the White Sands National Monument in New Mexico, described as being "snow-white." Its skin was reported sold to a railway employee for $30.

Another albino coyote killed November 10, 1945, 7 miles north of Killdeer, N. Dak., was apparently one of a litter of seven, the remainder of which were normal in color. (See Plates 7 and 8.)

Among 1,672,604 coyotes taken by hunters of the Fish and Wildlife Service for the period July 1, 1915, to June 30, 1945, only 6 were albinos, which according to D. D. Green (1947, 28 (1): 63) "were taken in California, Idaho, New Mexico, Oregon and Wyoming. This record is one per 278,767 coyotes captured."

What was at first believed to be a form of light bluish black color phase among 6 adult coyotes trapped in the early winter on the west side of Tennessee Pass in Colorado, close scrutiny revealed to be nothing more than large quantities of almost microscopic cinder dust. This had worked into the pelts as the animals had used the main line of the Denver & Rio Grande Railroad for runways in hunting the garbage thrown from the passing railroad diners. Several miles of the railway road bed in this locality had been ballasted at that time with furnace slag and then crowned with cinders. A thorough shaking of each pelt resulted in a fine cinder dust cloud that finally settled to the ground.

LONGEVITY

Coyotes appear to have about the same life span as do the larger wolves, i.e., 10 to 18 years. One kept in captivity in the London Zoological Garden lived 12 years, 2 months, and 10 days, while a female and male kept in the National Zoological Park, Washington, D. C., lived 14 years, 1 month, 14 days, and 14 years, 5 months, 2 days respectively (Flower, S. S., 1931 (pt. 1): 172-173).

Other longevity records of coyotes kept in captivity are given in Table 2:

TABLE 2.—Longevity Records of 16 Coyotes Kept in Captivity at National Zoological Park, Washington, D. C.

| Born | Acquired | Died | Period of confinement | |
			Years	Months
. . . .	Jan. 28, 1891	Prior to June 30, 1909	18	6
. . . .	May 12, 1888	Mar. 3, 1904	15	10
. . . .	Apr. 26, 1906	Sept. 28, 1920	14	5
. . . .	Apr. 26, 1906	June 10, 1920	14	2
. . . .	June 11, 1928	Aug. 12, 1940	12	10
Apr. 17, 1911	Apr. 17, 1911	Aug. 1, 1922	11	3
. . . .	Apr. 22, 1901	Jan. 8, 1912	10	9
Apr. 17, 1911	Apr. 17, 1911	Jan. 7, 1922	10	9
. . . .	Sept. 5, 1893	Mar. 3, 1904	10	6
Spring of 1921	July 8, 1921	June 30, 1930	9	. .
. . . .	Jan. 12, 1932	Feb. 25, 1940	8	1
. . . .	Dec. 29, 1897	Exchanged Dec. 7, 1905	7	11
Apr. 23, 1925	Apr. 23, 1925	Jan. 12, 1933	7	9
. . . .	Oct. 29, 1904	May 14, 1912	7	6
. . . .	Apr. 7, 1925	May 30, 1932	7	2
. . . .	Oct. 23, 1937	Jan. 11, 1944	6	3

Chris Twisselman, a livestock operator in San Luis Obispo and Kern Counties, California, took a male coyote pup from a den which on approaching maturity became quite tame. It had the freedom of the ranch home and around the holdings of Twisselman's San Luis Obispo County Ranch. Here it lived for seventeen years, dying but a short distance from the ranch house.

STRENGTH, SPEED, AND ENDURANCE

The old saying "In union there is strength" is no better illustrated than that displayed in teamwork among coyotes when obtaining prey. There is a plethora of information based on hundreds of observations concerning this trait of the animal. While "Forest Service studies of the Rocky Mountain mule deer in Modoc County [California] showed that a lone coyote can kill a 200 pound buck if a wire fence is present to deflect the deer, and that two or more coyotes can kill a healthy buck in open country" (Horn, 1941) it is generally in pairs that coyotes proceed to chase and kill their prey. If a pair of coyotes pursue a deer upon crusted snow surfaces sufficient to sustain their weight, but not that of the heavier deer they usually make a kill. Even a single coyote under like conditions, is often successful, as the prey flounders around in attempts to obtain firm footing. The uncanny and almost human-like craft employed by coyotes when hunting in pairs is no better illustrated than that observed in the fall of 1929 on the Charles Sheldon Antelope Refuge in northwestern Nevada. On a small flat containing a dozen adult antelope, 2 coyotes were observed approaching from the windward side. As they neared the edge of the sagebrush surrounding the alkali flat which kept them concealed, one coyote separated from its companion, circled through the sagebrush and around as well as above the antelopes. When it reached a point below the herd, the other coyote which had intently watched the movements of its companion, immediately sprang into the open, and started the herd which swirled and started on a fast run headed for the other coyote hidden below. As the herd passed, it immediately gave pursuit, and was close enough to grab onto the flank of a passing doe. The two rolled over and over like a large snowball, giving sufficient time for the other coyote to come to the aid of its partner. Between the two of them, it was but a short time until this female antelope was so severely maimed that it became helpless, and was greedily fed upon. From the point this was observed it was strongly evident that the antelope gave signs of life for a considerable time after this pair of coyotes started to feed upon it.

Many of the larger prey such as deer and male antelope while

Plate 9. Jack rabbit in full leap.

attacked often succeed in making a get-a-way as evidenced at the scene of an attack which show signs of a terrific struggle, but no victim.

In a running chase, it is doubtful if a single coyote can catch a jack rabbit in a fair race on open ground. When the coyote does overtake a jack rabbit it generally is in terrain which is covered with bunches of greasewood or other shrubs that enables the coyote to approach close to the rabbit and probably to catch it before it gets fairly started. The leap of a jack rabbit from 18 to 21 feet as first measured by Captain Meriwether Lewis while leading the memorable journey across western America in 1804-1806 was probably made by a jack rabbit in full leap. (See Plate 9.) The coyote in full jump makes approximately only two-thirds of this distance.

It is the author's opinion that most jack rabbits are caught by the coyote when working in unison with another coyote, as in the antelope case mentioned. If the jack rabbit during the chase doesn't slip into some hole, he eventually becomes fagged and is overtaken, as its endurance cannot outlast a pair of coyotes teamed up for its capture.

R. Scott Zimmerman records a party of 4 men driving a light car across a Utah desert lake floor giving chase to a coyote about 2 years old. For 47 minutes the race kept up, at times showing a speed of 43 miles per hour. In the course of the chase this animal turned, doubled and dodged to elude the pursuing car before finally becoming exhausted and killed (1943: 400).

Cottam (1945) records a coyote after a 2-mile chase by auto going the last 0.6 mile at the rate of 35 miles per hour at the Malheur National Wildlife Refuge, Oregon.

Harper records the statement by William Brown of Fort Smith, Mackenzie, who was noted for his prowess in running down on snowshoes such animals as the moose, and both species of the caribou, as well as the wolf, but could never overtake the coyote which invariably outdistanced him (1932: 26).

An interesting episode transpired 4 miles east of Findlater, Saskatchewan, Canada, during January 1935. Here a young farmer experienced in hunting and trapping rode down a coyote with a saddle pony at the end of a 7-mile ride. He then attempted to make his pony step upon the animal in hopes of killing it. However, this only resulted in the pony's legs becoming badly mutilated from coyote bites. So the rider finally had to dismount and kill the coyote with a pair of fence pliers.

Reporting upon an observation made in Yellowstone National

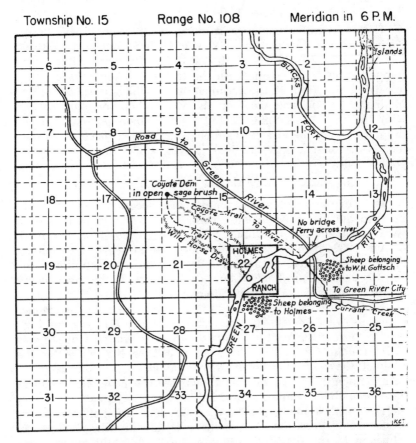

Township No. 15   Range No. 108   Meridian in 6 P.M.

Figure 8. Map showing remarkable hunting routes which were used regularly by a female coyote from den to lambing areas. Both runways necessitated swimming the Green River (Wyoming). Depredations on lambs were considerable and victims were either carried across the river or eaten and disgorged later to pups for food.

Park, Long (1941: 23) says that a coyote carried a still warm but dead coyote, which had been killed by a buck deer a few moments previously, up a 30° slope for a distance of 28 yards at a "dead run."

STAMINA

That a coyote sometimes survives what seem to be unsurmountable odds against it is shown by one recently captured (Anon. 1947: 28) in New Mexico, near Canjilon. After being trapped it made its escape with the trap on its foot. For 17 days it carried this trap at the termination of which it succeeded in pulling out of it, and went on its way. While traveling around with the trap on its paw it fed upon a blue jay, and in the droppings were found a bird's toenail and toe, a piece of its own foot pad, some acorns and oak leaves, some sheep wool, and gopher hair.

SWIMMING ABILITY

The coyote is not at all timid when necessity requires it to get into the water. Many observations show this animal to be a good swimmer, often exhibiting this trait when obtaining food. Couch (1932) mentions an outstanding record of coyotes swimming the Columbia River to raid poultry roosts, and returning "the way they came" in Ferry County, Washington, the river being nearly a half-mile wide at this point.

Another observation showing the coyote to be a good swimmer is the case of a female that had denned under a canopy of high sagebrush near the lambing grounds used by Messrs. Gottsch and Holmes along Green River in Wyoming (See Fig. 8). After the birth of the pups this coyote began to make periodic raids on both lambing herds. To do this, the coyote was compelled to swim the Green River coming and going. In some instances she swam the river with a young lamb in her mouth to bring it to the den, or she would gorge on a lamb that she killed, swim the river in returning to the den and disgorge the food to the pups. Here Green River although wide and generally shallow was nearly 6 feet deep in the narrow main channel.

Bryant (1920) records an observation of a coyote swimming a channel 30 feet wide and 8 feet deep in the Salton Sea area of southern California, and concluded in this instance that "narrow channels of water formed no barrier during the food-getting expeditions of this particular coyote" which in this instance was preying on waterfowl.

Similar cases where the coyote was seeking waterfowl and

their nests for food that necessitated swimming narrow channels and wading in marshes have been noted in the San Luis Valley of southern Colorado, particularly along Spring Creek.

TRACKS

The coyote track (See Fig. 9 and Plate 10) is elongated and not nearly so rounded as a dog track. The animal's side-toe impres-

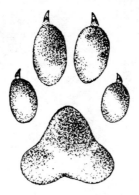

Figure 9. Diagram of front foot track of the coyote (average size).

sion is longer than that of a dog of the same size. The tracks of young coyotes and barren females, and those that have recently lost their pups can be distinguished from a denning pair of coyotes, for the latter usually travel by a direct route, the tracks of the female generally smaller and are more pointed than those of the male.

USE OF RUNWAYS

Generally, coyotes follow a runway or circuit, often referred to as a hunting route. It may be a combination of trails of game, cattle, sheep, old wood roads, dry washes, swamps, marshes, or ditch banks. Sometimes but one of these may be a predominating run such as an old wood road or ditch bank, from which the animal will deviate from side to side in search of food. These runways do not approximate in length those used by the large wolves, which at times may be more than 100 miles in extent. The coyote runway may cover no more than 10 miles, and be used throughout its life span, providing sufficient food is always available. What causes the animal to forsake old established and localized runways is usually the food factor, or continued persecution. It tends to have established runways where plenty

Plate 10. Coyote and its tracks in snow.

Plate 11. Wanderlust from the Plains.

of food is available, such as hanging about a band of migrating domestic sheep or goats leaving winter ranges for the higher summer ranges. However, the coming of winter storms will cause it to return to lower elevations and generally to terrain with which it is familiar. This return may be to the former runway it abandoned in the late spring or early summer. Most of my experience in connection with these migratory movements from old established runs have been in connection with field studies that indicated that the migration was influenced by the movement of livestock, mainly sheep and goats.

Banding studies now being carried forward should throw more understandable light upon this intriguing problem. Details, partially determined to date are discussed under migratory movements.

VOICE

The main voice of the coyote is a high quavering staccato "yip-yap" that often ends in a series of high, shrill-toned, ear-piercing howls. Contrasted with the deep bass, chesty howls of the wolf, it is several notes higher on the scale, and at times it is as prolonged. One western man has aptly described the coyote's cry as a "prolonged howl which the animal let out and then ran after and bit into small pieces." It might be rightly termed the "chatterer" of the American predators. (See Plate 11.)

The natural howling of the coyote when heard by one for the first time leaves a never-to-be-forgotten impression. The animal is usually silent during the day, but is generally heard at any time between sunset and sunrise. The twilight and the breaking of dawn seems to be the favorite "yip-yap" period. Several coyotes may give vent to voice at one time, producing a mournful medley hardly describable. Two coyotes thus yapping in unison emit a chorus that sounds like a dozen or more of these creatures were howling at once.

Mills (1922: 96) says of the coyote's voice that it is used "for other things than pleasure. He has a dialect with which he signals his fellows; he warns them of danger and tells of opportunities; he asks for information and calls for assistance. He is constantly saving himself from danger or securing his needed food by cooperating with his fellows. These united efforts are largely possible through his ability to express the situation with voice and tongue."

With respect to the foregoing Alcorn (1946) lists three distinct coyote calls: the squeak, the howl call, and the distress call. The imitation of either of these or a combination of them has brought coyotes within rifle range in several of Nevada's counties. Likewise, gadgets have been made from the cow horn that when blown imitates the distress squeal of the jack rabbit when first overtaken by a predator, and when used on the open range will call coyotes from out of hidden cover.

The animal is capable of emitting a well-defined bark similar to that of a collie dog. I have generally heard it break forth from a trapped animal when approached. Occasionally it will be heard also mixed in with the higher toned yipping emitted on the open range.

High promontories overlooking large or small valleys, canyons, or dry washes seem to be favorite yip-yapping points for the animal, and once I overheard one give vent to a prolonged "yipping" from the top of a pile of hay that was stacked for curing in a farmer's meadow.

Some naturalists aver that different races emit distinct howls. As an example they distinguish a voice difference between the coyote of the mountains and the race that has its main habitat in the valleys, but I have never been able to recognize any difference.

COYOTE BITE

The bite of a coyote is comparable to that of its larger brother, the gray wolf, but as would be expected, it is only in proportion to the superior bulk of the wolf's skull, which is about 1½ size larger. As with other members of the canine family, the bite of the coyote produces a shearing effect, and is obtained by the action of the carnassial teeth (or the last premolar, and first molar on each side). The tearing effect is done mostly by the canines. The snap of a coyote's jaws resembles that noise made by clapping two shingles together often made when a trapped coyote is approached. The average length of the canine tooth is about 1½ inches.

Thus the bite of this animal can be very severe, as attested to by the mutilated condition of young lambs or adult sheep attacked (See Plate 12). Furthermore, the author, while removing a supposed dead coyote from a trap in the Canelo Hills of southern Arizona, had the sad experience of having the animal come suddenly to consciousness, and at a time when I was in a very awkward posture. This aided the animal to take a good bite into the calf of my right leg. In doing so, the animal drove both canine teeth through my heavy blue denim trousers, a heavy suit of underwear, and well into the flesh. When it finally released its jaws, flesh and clothing came out. Result, a very sore right leg for several weeks, which necessitated vigilant treatment to prevent infection.

As in wolves, coyotes in old age show teeth much worn, and incisors broken (See Plate 13, d).

SCENT GLANDS

As with all members of the dog family, the coyote has a scent gland. It is located on the upper side near the base of the tail, and though smaller than in the large gray wolf, it is of the same bluish black color. It functions when coyotes meet, and the usual smelling prevalent among dogs takes place. As with the large gray wolves each coyote possesses a definite individual scent. (See Plate 14.) Coyote scent glands form the basic ingredient as a lure for most hunters' trapping lines.

Coyote urine is very strong, and the animal generally relieves itself on some definite spot as does the dog on the telephone or fence post, which is followed by the usual scratching with the hind feet, and occasionally all four feet may be used in motion in the attempt to cover the deposit.

CANNIBALISM

The coyote possesses no qualms when it comes to eating or feeding on the carcass of its own kind. Coyote fat has been used successfully as a trapping lure or as a poisoned bait. During the period of the rut, coyotes will often eat organs of females that have previously succumbed in a trap or been poisoned.

Walter P. Sharp of the Fish and Wildlife Service, stationed in Arizona, recently observed:

"On November 16, 1946, a poison station was placed at a point 6 miles below the old Miller ranch on Date Creek, westerly and a little north of Congress, Arizona. When the station was checked one week later on the 23rd of November, all poison baits had been taken and it was found that a coyote had died about 50 yards south of the station.

"All sign and tracks here showed that the dead coyote had been eaten entirely by one or more other coyotes. The carcass had been dragged some 50 yards in the time that it had taken to devour the dead coyote. About 50 yards west of the station, a coyote tail was found buried in a small sand wash with 4 inches of the tip of the tail sticking above the sand. All tracks here, and the sand that was dragged up over the tail was done by coyotes.

"At the same time, a male coyote was killed by poison baits about 10 miles north and east of the Date Creek station, on Lawler Creek between Date Creek station and Hillside, Arizona.

"The next time this station was checked, a female coyote was found close by. The female had visited the station and eaten 3

Plate 12. A sheep with throat nearly severed by bite of coyote.

poison baits, then had eaten all the flesh and fur off one side of the back of the dead male. The flesh and fur were in the female's stomach—something of a gallon of it.

"Two weeks later the station was checked again and coyotes had dragged the female away. The trail of the dragging could be followed for about 200 yards and was then lost in rocky ground.

"There is no doubt about these carcasses being eaten by other coyotes, as the tracks proved this and there was no sign of eagles or ravens around the stations anywhere."

DOMESTICATION AND SEMIDOMESTICATION OF COYOTE

From early available records, one is led to conclude that the coyote had been domesticated by various Indian tribes prior to the voyages of Columbus. By the middle of the 19th century, much of the outdoor literature contains comments on the Indian

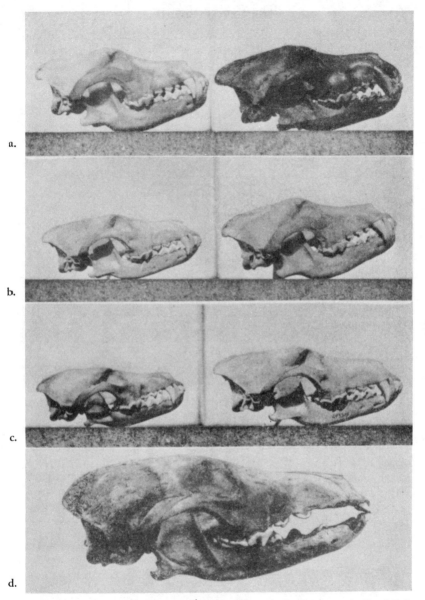

Plate 13. (a) Skull of interior Alaskan wolf *(Canis lupus pambasileus)* left, compared to skull of dire wolf right, the wolf of the Pleistocene Period, from Rancho La Brea tar-pits, California. (b) Skull of Mississippi Valley red wolf *(Canis niger gregoryi)* left, compared to skull of interior Alaskan wolf *(Canis lupus pambasileus)* right, (c) Skull of coyote *(Canis latrans)* left, compared to skull of Mississippi Valley red wolf *(Canis niger gregoryi)* right. (d) Old coyote with teeth much worn or lost.

Plate 14. Coyote scenting. (Top photo courtesy of Tappan Gregory.)

domesticated coyote or coyote hybrid. Coyner (1847: 38) in commenting upon the Indian villages on the Great Plains, states the "Indian dogs seem to be wolves of the smaller kind [coyote]." They were used as draught animals in the absence of horses, as was the case in the large gray wolf-dog hybrid.

The coyote is easily tamed when taken as a young pup, and readily adapts itself to the surroundings in or around one's field camp, farm or city home. On full maturity, however, the tendency is for it to become quite destructive to anything it can get its teeth into, be it the fringe of an expensive parlor rug, or milady's poultry in the family's hen yard. (See Plate 15.)

Apropos of the latter comment is a recent reversion to wild instincts of a pet coyote in Arizona owned by Government Hunter Teg Riggs. It is recorded that this pet coyote enjoyed a short but happy movie career. It appears that

"Although Riggs became richer by the sum of $100, he is minus his pet coyote, 'Butch', which he acquired in the summer of 1945. Last fall when the movie set moved into southern Utah to produce the picture 'Smokie', the coyote 'Butch' was rented for a part of the film. He played his part so well that his services were again contracted for in June of this year for the production of 'Ramrod', which was filmed in the vicinity of Zion National Park.

Plate 15. Coyote as a pet, Ft. Davis, Texas.

"Prop men decided that the means of securing the animal by a dog collar detracted from the natural appearance of a supposedly wild coyote so conceived the idea of fastening a fine wire to his foot as a means of detaining him. 'Butch' gained his freedom from this encumbrance the first evening and made haste to the closest ranch where he proceeded to raid a turkey flock. The lady ranch-owner appeared on the scene and promptly dispatched the marauding predator by plugging him with her trusty 'thutty.' As Butch was insured by the movies for the sum of $100, Mrs. Riggs is compensated for her prize pullets that he outwitted during the past year and to us this little incident lends further support to the suspicion we have entertained that 'once a coyote, always a coyote.'"

E. M. Mercer of the Fish and Wildlife Service at Phoenix, Arizona, commented further with respect to the foregoing, saying:

"One of the interesting things about this particular coyote was that he never misjudged distance. Hunter Riggs kept him tied at the end of a 20 ft. chain. He would lay back in an old barrel that was his regular home and if a chicken ever made the mistake of getting within the radius reached by that chain its number was up. That coyote never misjudged the distance that the chain would permit him to travel after a chicken."

E. T. Morgan, of Houston, Texas, during April of 1948 owned a pet coyote, but because of its inroads on the family's valuable poultry flock, decided to give the animal away. At his request the Houston Post ran a story to this effect. By actual count 219 phone calls were received between 12 noon and 6 p.m. It was estimated that more than 500 calls for the coyote were received. Different reasons were given for wanting the animal: Seamen and Boy Scouts wanted it for a mascot, some wanted to breed it with dogs hoping to produce better hunters. So in spite of the general antipathy to the coyote, such instances show that it still has many friends.

Concerning its early domestic history in Mexico, Packard (1885: 900) found "In a . . . visit to Mexico, not only along the railroads, but in the course of a stage ride of about five hundred miles through provincial Mexico, from Saltillo to San Miguel, we were struck by the resemblance of the dogs to the coyote," and he concluded, "there can be little doubt but, that they are descendants of a race which sprang from the partly tamed coyote of the ancient Mexican Indians."

As will be noted later, coyotes and dogs readily hybridize, the offspring remaining fertile, and some coyote hybrids seem to make good animals.

While on a journey to the Upper Missouri Elliott Coues (1873: 385) observed hybrids between the coyote and domestic dog.

Packard (1885: 900) also was "struck by the coyote appearing Indian dog among the Crow Indians near Ft. Claggett on the Upper Missouri in 1877," and compared with those he had previously seen among the Mexican Indians. "The color was a whitish tawny, like that of the Eskimo dog."

Again adding to the record Packard (ibid.) quoting a field note from J. L. Wortman in the report of the Geological Survey of Indiana for 1884 says: "During extended travel in western United States, my experience has been the same as that recorded by Dr. Coues. It is by no means uncommon to find mongrel dogs among many of the western Indian tribes, notably among Umatillas, Bannocks, Shoshones, Arapahoes, Crows, Sioux, which to one familiar with the color, physiognomy and habits of the coyote, having every appearance of blood relationship if not, in many cases, this animal itself in a state of semi-domestication."

Joe La Flame of Canada (Young & Goldman, 1944: 188) used a full blooded coyote together with a gray wolf as part of a draught team hitched to a sled for hauling supplies to an aeroplane.

During the summer of 1947, the National Park Service reported that "Two coyotes in Yellowstone National Park have been giving the bears keen competition for the tourists' attention—and food. During the past few weeks they have been begging for food along the main park highway between Midway Geyser Basin and Nez Perce creek, some 10 miles from Old Faithful geyser.

"The coyotes have caused traffic jams seldom excelled by the so-called 'bear jams.' The two coyotes have been photographed extensively.

"Yellowstone visitors in the past were lucky to even see a glimpse of gray coyote stalking his prey off the sagebrush plains or darting among the timber. However, the coyotes give the tourists a fine vocal show nearly every night with their loud yipping and barking.

"For coyotes to beg for food and pose for pictures along the road has been until now unheard of in Yellowstone's colorful history.

"This diamond anniversary year of the founding of Yellowstone Park finds two 'little wolves' putting on a very unusual show, much to the delight of visitors."

MIGRATORY MOVEMENTS OF THE COYOTE

Migration studies of the coyote by ear-tagging of both young and old animals are bringing to light some interesting information. First initiated by the former Bureau of Biological Survey, for more than two decades periodic tagging and marking of coyotes has been carried on.

There has always been considerable speculation as to the distance that individual coyotes travel from their place of birth and as to the factors that influence their movements. The Biological Survey desired to have detailed and definite information to aid in determining the best locations to concentrate coyote control operations to give required protection to domestic stock, wild game, and the public health during rabies outbreaks.

The early procedure was to concentrate in areas where coyotes were thought to be denning in numbers. Such areas were searched for dens to obtain sufficient numbers of pups in order to furnish enough records to guarantee reliable conclusions. Special tags were made resembling those used in cattle marking but smaller in size. Instructions for the hunter were on the tag. Only pups old enough to shift for themselves usually 6 to 8 weeks old were selected for tagging.

For about ten years data have been gathered as time and funds permitted in New Mexico, Colorado, Montana and Wyoming. In the tables following a summary of the records of releases and recoveries for New Mexico and Wyoming is given.

TABLE 3.—Tagged Coyotes Released and Recovered in New Mexico

No. In Den	Tag No.	Male Pups	Female Pups	Distance Miles	Length Time	Stock Influence	Natural Food Influence	Climatic Influence
7	1	x		100	1 yr. 16 days		x	
	2	x		5	9 yr. 3 days		x	
	3	x		18	2 yr. 31 days		x	
1	6	Trapped Adult		5	4 yr. 5 mos.		x	
	7	x		1	1 day	x		
1	8	Trapped Adult		7	1 yr. 34 days	x		
9	6			Av. 22.6	2 yrs. 5 mos.			

TABLE 4.—Tagged Coyotes Released and Recovered in Wyoming

No. In Den	Tag No.	Male Pups	Female Pups	Distance Miles	Length Time	Stock Influence	Natural Food Influence	Climatic Influence
1	74	x		90	8 mos.	x	x	x
3	75		x	0	5 mos.		x	
	151		x	15	4 mos.		x	
	158		x	3	2 yr. 6 mos.		x	
1	96	x		20	2 mos.		x	
4	117	x		5	2 yr. 2 mos.		x	
	118	x		7	2 yr. 7 mos.		x	
	119		x	2	6 mos.		x	
	175		x	6	1 yr. 3 mos.		x	
6	154		x	12	11 mos.	x	x	x
	155	x		30	1 yr. 0 mos.	x	x	x
	156		x	50	1 yr.	x	x	x
	157		x	80	9 mos.	x	x	x
4	160	x		12	1 yr. 8 mos.	x	x	x
	162		x	0	4 mos.	x	x	x
2	172	x		30	2 yr.	x		
	173	x		18	3 mos.	x		
6	185	x		15	2 yr.	x	x	
3	201		x	25	6 mos.	x	x	
	202		x	30	6 mos.	x	x	
	203		x	50	6 mos.	x	x	
4	204		x	40	7 mos.	x	x	
	206		x	60	3 mos.	x	x	
	207		x	9	5 mos.	x	x	
3	226		x	1	6 mos.	x	x	
	227	x		6	6 mos.	x	x	
	228		x	1	1 yr. 6 mos.	x	x	
5	231	x		6	8 mos.	x	x	
6	234		x	18	5 mos.	x	x	
	235	x		15	1 yr. 8 mos.	x	x	
	236		x	45	5 mos.	x	x	
	237	x		1	5 mos.	x	x	
	238		x	37	10 mos.	x	x	
	239		x	20	1 yr. 8 mos.	x	x	
8	240	x		25	5 mos.	x	x	
	241	x		100	1 yr. 3 mos.	x	x	
	242	x		12	5 mos.	x	x	
	243	x		12	1 yr. 7 mos.	x	x	
	244	x		50	1 yr. 6 mos.	x	x	
	246	x		40	5 mos.	x	x	
	247		x	36	5 mos.	x	x	
4	248	x		8	6 mos.	x	x	
	249	x		6	8 mos.	x	x	
	251	x		85	1 yr.	x	x	x
5	253	x		50	11 mos.	x	x	x
8	257	x		45	5 mos.	x	x	x
7	269	x		2	9 mos.	x	x	
5	273	x		48	5 mos.	x	x	
	276	x		25	1 yr. 4 mos.	x	x	
6	283	x		30	8 mos.		x	
	287		x	25	4 mos.		x	
1	289		x	60	6 mos.		x	
	290		x	1	5 mos.		x	

Summary of Tagging Results
NEW MEXICO

In New Mexico nine male coyotes were tagged on the Jornada Range Reserve. Two were adults when tagged and seven were less than one year old. All were trapped to tag. There has been a 66⅔ percent recovery in an average length of time of 2 years and 5 months, ranging from 1 day to 9 years and 3 days.

The average distance that these coyotes were caught from the point of release was 22.6 miles. All but one were taken on or nearby the Jornada Range Reserve near Las Cruces, New Mexico. There was plenty of natural feed for them in this locality, so there was no need to wander off any distance. One, however, did roam 100 miles away following North along the San Andres Range of mountains to some stock ranches bordering the salt marshes, where it was caught.

The coyote taken after 9 years was about 10 years old for it was about 1 year old when tagged. It was recaught only a few miles from the point of release.

WYOMING

The records in this State are of considerable interest and value. Sixty-two male and 48 female pups were tagged and released at the dens, a total of 110. Of these 28 males and 25 females have been recovered by trappers, making a total of 53. This is a recovery to date of 48.1 percent.

For males the average distance taken from the place of release is 28.32 miles, ranging from 1 to 100 miles in an average length of time of 1 year, ranging from 5 months to 2 years 7 months. For the females it is 25.04 miles, ranging from 1 to 80 miles in an average of 8½ months, ranging from 2 months to 1 year 8 months. The males thus were taken slightly farther away after about the same time.

By referring to the map (Fig. 10) the lines of drift can be readily seen. At the den site is a fraction shown in black ink. The numerator of the fraction is the number of the den and the denominator is the number of pups tagged and released there.

In the Jackson Hole area the pups from the dens along the Gros Ventre River Valley and the Hoback Basin are no doubt influenced by the movement of domestic stock, amount of available natural food and the deep winter snows. They show a definite tendency to drift to lower altitudes in the fall and early winter to the winter sheep range, traveling as far as 85 miles in an airline. Three of the four recovered from den No. 20 traveled down and were caught on the winter sheep ranges. Three of the four released at den No. 19 in Hoback Basin were drifting into lower country when caught. Six out of ten recovered from these two areas, or 60 percent, drifted to lower country. The dens are apparently fairly abundant in the Gros Ventre area as three were located fairly close together.

The fact that a barrage of effective control poison stations, placed around the border line of the Wyoming National Forest from about Thayne on the Western Slope, around the southern point to Hoback on the Eastern Slope and in good strategic locations to the south in Lincoln County, almost completely removed the coyote population from the Lincoln County sheep areas where previously they had been abundant, indicates that the source of supply of coyote to that area is located in the Wyoming National Forest and the Jackson Hole area. This reduction of coyotes was felt down on the Uinta County sheep ranges as far as Evanston, Wyoming.

At dens No. 17 and No. 18 near the Colorado-Wyoming line we have a different situation. This area is full of rough breaks and draws. It is of little value for grazing but is good for coyote dens. This area is about the same altitude as the Continental Divide Basin of which it is really a part. Note how almost all the coyotes retaken have drifted good distances out of this rough country to the winter range lands in both Wyoming and Colorado on the Divide Basin. Within an average of 9 to 10 months the coyote went an average distance of 22.5 miles from den No. 17 and 40.7 miles from den No. 18. Almost none of them stayed about the home area, as was shown in the New Mexico area.

Den No. 14 is on the northern border of the Continental Divide Basin. Note that the three recovered coyotes out of the four tagged drifted down into the Basin.

Dens Nos. 23, 26 and 27 are in the Basin and there is no one definite direction the coyotes drifted.

Den No. 21 was well up in the Shoshone National Forest area. These pups were not released at the den where taken but brought from a location lower in altitude. The only one recovered was caught in much lower country. There were not many hunters trapping in the Cody area so there was not much chance of getting a report on these.

Other migration records of coyotes by means of ear-tagging from Washington are as follows:

A male coyote ear-tagged August 20, 1932, 2 miles west of

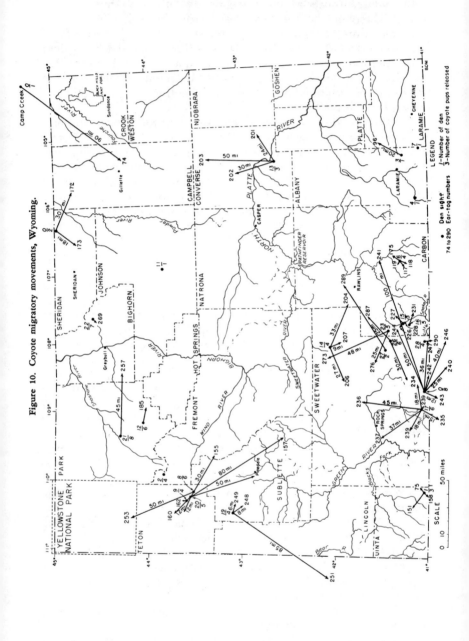

Figure 10. Coyote migratory movements, Wyoming.

Cold Creek Store, was recovered on January 13, 1933, 8 miles west of this point, and 6 miles west of the point released.

A male coyote tagged on September 7, 1932, 19 miles east of Tonasket, was recovered in March, 1933, 1½ miles from the point of liberation.

A male coyote tagged and released on September 16, 1932, southwest of Blue Creek, William Taylor Flats, was shot on September 22, 1935, 5 miles west of Wellpinit, 50 miles airline distance from where it was released 3 years previously.

During the year 1918, 7 adult coyotes were marked near Phoenix, Arizona, and released on a southern desert mesquite winter range used for sheep during early February. One of these coyotes was trapped in September of that year a short distance from the south rim of the Grand Canyon. The animal had traveled more than 250 miles after being released about 8 months previously. The movement of this coyote was influenced by the shifting of livestock, in this case, sheep. The release of these coyotes was made on the sheep driveway that began south of Phoenix and continued in those days to the summer ranges of the former Tusayan National Forest in Coconino and Yavapai Counties, Arizona.

The apparent long distances individual coyotes will sometimes travel is confirmed in the case of the coyote specimen collected near Southwick in Clearwater County, Idaho, on January 30, 1934. This coyote, when shot, was found to be wearing a sheep bell around its neck. Carved on the bell strap was "H. H. Burns, Oregon." Burns, Oregon, is more than 400 miles by airline from Southwick, Idaho. Between Burns, Oregon, and northern Idaho, lies the winding Snake River, so it is evident that this coyote was forced to travel many additional tortuous miles to make the trip. At what date the bell strap was tied around the animal's neck before it was released it was impossible to ascertain.

While the foregoing data are of interest, they by no means give the complete picture that leads to a much needed and fuller understanding of coyote migration which has a far-reaching economic effect. At this writing an intensive cooperative coyote ear-tagging project is underway between the National Park Service, the Absaroka Conservatory Committee, Montana, and the Wildlife Research Laboratory of the Fish and Wildlife Service. It is being conducted in the Yellowstone National Park and contiguous areas. Improvment over those practiced in the earlier experiments in ear-tagging techniques have been perfected, and it is anticipated that much more comprehensive knowledge of coyote migratory movements will be gained than is available at the present time.

SEX RATIO

For more than a quarter of a century the sex ratio of predators has been a particular hobby of the author. However, up to the present time, when summaries of collected data were made, it was found that all predators, such as the wolf, puma, bobcat, and the coyote, throughout their ranges hold reasonably close to the proportion of 50:50.

Other co-workers have studied this particular problem. In segregating all of the accumulated data, that pertaining to E. M. Mercer's findings in Arizona present an illuminating picture concerning sex ratio of coyotes killed between July 1, 1919 and June 30, 1946, involving a grand total of 56,595 animals. For the record these findings are quoted as Mercer submitted them to me following a conference with him at Phoenix, Arizona, during February 1947:

"There is attached hereto a table of sex ratios of coyotes as recorded by the cooperative hunting force of the Fish and Wildlife Service in Arizona, from July 1, 1919, to June 30, 1946, inclusive, or a period of twenty-seven years.

"You will note that the number of female coyotes exceed the number of male coyotes taken during the years 1920, 1935, 1936, 1939 and 1945. During other years of this period the number of male coyotes taken have exceeded females.

"It came to my attention a number of years ago when checking Forms 3-133, on which the sexes of predators taken by the hunting force are recorded, that there were generally a few more male coyotes taken than females. This led to the checking of itinerary reports of individual hunters and it was soon discovered that on occasions a hunter would take a great many more of one sex than the other during some months but by the time the years work was completed the sex ratios of the coyotes that he had taken would compare very favorably with ratios of all coyotes taken by the hunting force that year. It occurred to me that perhaps there was some particular time of the year when a greater number of one sex might be taken than the other. Tables were then compiled of the catch made by the hunting force each month for a period of years. This yielded nothing of value. The catch of one hunter might be predominately females while in some other part of the State a hunter would take principally males. Later the thing would even itself up when the same hunters would take greater numbers of the other sex.

"I gave some thought to the matter that hunters might get

careless in recording the sex of animals when taken in the field and that in recording them later at their camps they might get into the habit of saying "male and female" and in this manner set down too many males. I checked some of the hunters very carefully on this score and found that there was no difference in the records of those that set down the sex of the animal when it was taken, or those that set it down when they arrived at camp.

"The thought then occurred to me that perhaps male coyotes were attracted to lures and scents used by hunters in trapping the animals more often than the female of the species. While males are apparently more often caught in a single trap when a pair of coyotes are traveling together, the females are readily taken in traps when alone, or when two traps are set near each other.

"It was then that I checked the sexes of coyotes killed with poison by members of the hunting force at widely scattered points of the State. The ratios were practically the same as for coyotes taken in traps during the same year.

"I have no idea as to why more female coyotes are occasionally taken during a year than males. The percentage in 1920 was 48.38 males, to 51.62 females. In 1945 the percentage was 49.61 males, to 50.39 females. These figures are based on 1,207 coyotes taken in 1920 and 4,479 taken in 1945. It is believed that in 1920 most of the coyotes recorded may have been taken by poison. You perhaps know something about this. I do know that poison was used extensively in control work until about 1930. From 1930 until 1944 most of the coyotes taken in Arizona were taken by traps. Since that time more than half of the annual catch has been made by poison and coyote getters. Regardless of how the animals are taken, and how many methods may be employed in their control during the year it appears that ever so often more females are taken than males. On the average males exceed females to a considerable extent in numbers and in 1932 the percentage was 57.43 males to 42.57 females.

"During the fiscal year 1946 the hunting force in Arizona recorded a total of 2,407 coyotes as taken with lethal bait. Of this number 1,205 were males and 1,202 were females. During the year a total of 5,556 coyotes were taken by all methods and of this number 2,842 were males and 2,714 were females. The percentage on these figures is 51.15 males to 48.85 females. During the present fiscal year we have taken 939 male coyotes and 947 female coyotes with poison. Since females of the species were taken in excess of males during the fiscal year 1945 it is apparent that we are probably in a cycle favorable to the female of the coyote at present.

"I have checked the sexes of 4,926 coyotes taken by poison in Arizona during recent years. Of this number 2,479 were males and 2,447 were females."

TABLE 5.—Sex Ratios of Coyotes as Recorded by the Cooperative Hunting Force of the Fish and Wildlife Service in Arizona, From July 1, 1919, to June 30, 1946

Fiscal Year	Male Coyotes	Percent of Total	Female Coyotes	Percent of Total	Total Coyotes Recorded
1920	584	48.38	623	51.62	1,207
1921	588	51.44	555	48.56	1,143
1922	687	50.96	661	49.04	1,348
1923	611	53.22	537	46.78	1,148
1924	515	55.94	379	44.06	894
1925	447	56.00	352	44.00	799
1926	621	56.76	473	43.24	1,094
1927	528	50.05	527	49.95	1,055
1928	616	55.39	496	44.61	1,112
1929	684	56.25	532	43.75	1,216
1930	655	54.11	555	45.89	1,210
1931	738	55.36	595	44.64	1,333
1932	749	57.43	555	42.57	1,304
1933	938	56.10	734	43.90	1,672
1934	475	50.69	462	49.31	937
1935	709	49.48	724	50.52	1,433
1936	1,450	49.37	1,487	50.63	2,937
1937	1,171	50.62	1,142	49.38	2,313
1938	1,003	52.95	893	47.05	1,896
1939	1,379	49.91	1,384	50.09	2,763
1940	1,580	50.74	1,534	49.26	3,114
1941	1,895	54.77	1,656	45.23	3,551
1942	1,761	54.15	1,491	45.85	3,252
1943	1,754	53.01	1,555	46.99	3,309
1944	2,416	53.44	2,105	46.56	4,521
1945	2,222	49.61	2,257	50.39	4,479
1946	2,842	51.15	2,714	48.85	5,556
Totals	29,618	52.33	26,978	47.67	56,595

These statistics show a tendency for a slight excess of males over females, as was the case for the puma in this State (Young & Goldman, 1946: 110).

Sex ratios for a 5-year period 1943-1947 for Oklahoma as embodied in Table 6 shows a slight excess of females taken than males during the period.

TABLE 6.—Coyote Sex Ratio Data, Oklahoma, 1943-1947

Sex	July	Aug.	Sept.	Oct.	Nov.	Dec.	Jan.	Feb.	Mar.	Apr.	May	June	Total
Fiscal Year 1947:													
Male	38	42	48	84	67	84	67	101	48	91	147	29	846
Female	44	52	54	97	62	94	85	88	60	88	138	35	897
Fiscal Year 1946:													
Male	28	31	25	42	41	36	44	50	22	91	111	73	594
Female	24	31	27	42	32	42	46	54	44	105	99	65	611
Fiscal Year 1945:													
Male	11	10	7	16	19	13	8	24	8	37	89	54	296
Female	15	15	23	15	15	10	14	17	9	54	90	38	315
Fiscal Year 1944:													
Male	52	28	47	72	80	45	49	93	46	102	130	41	785
Female	62	31	38	75	81	39	36	57	60	132	138	43	792
Fiscal Year 1943:													
Male	30	18	19	45	52	52	65	81	47	76	138	85	708
Female	34	26	17	43	45	47	51	51	54	77	135	70	650

Total male coyotes taken during 5-year period   3,229

Total female coyotes taken during 5-year period   3,265

6,494

REPRODUCTION

As a rule coyotes do not mate for life. Some pairs may remain together for a number of years, however. There is evidence that females breed when 1 year old. In the mating season coyotes may be heard yelping much more than usual, and packs of three to a dozen animals may be seen. Later the breeding animals pair off.

The whelping season in the United States varies with latitude. In general, according to studies of a large number of embryos by Hamlett (1938), the season in the northern tier of States seems somewhat earlier than farther south. In Montana, for example, breeding begins about February 1 and lasts throughout the month, the height of the season being about February 15. In Texas, breeding apparently begins somewhat later, although data are inadequate for definite conclusions. In some States, as in Oregon and Arizona, Hamlett found a variation of at least 2 months in the time of breeding, probably because of great diversity in altitude and other environmental factors.

Coyote pups are born 60 to 63 days after mating. The parents in breeding couple much as do domestic dogs. (See Plate 34.) The eyes of the young, the pupils which are circular as those in the wolves and domestic dogs, while the red and gray foxes are elliptical, open when they are 9 to 14 days old. The average number of young in a litter is 5 to 7.

In working up records of government hunters in New Mexico of the number of embryos taken during the years of 1928, 1929, 1930, and 1931, totaling 120 cases, Aldous found that litters of five occurred most frequently. The average number of unborn young per female was 5.54, and that 77 percent of all the females carried from four to seven young. (1933, C. M. Aldous report dated March 11, in files of Fish and Wildlife Service.)

In Arizona, out of a total of 396 litters of unborn coyotes recorded for the fiscal years 1942 to 1945, the average litter for 5 years was found to be 5.05. Some naturalists feel that sizes of coyote litters may depend upon the available food supply: the less the food, the smaller the litter, and vice versa. However, in Arizona, a coyote heaven, all around year conditions are ideal. Plenty of food is always available such as acorns, prickly pear,

a.

b.

Plate 16. Litters of coyote pups are found at times to number 9 to 12. (a) Newly born. (b) Approximately 6 weeks old.

Plate 17. A single litter of coyote pups totaling 19. Utah.

apples, mesquite beans, grasshoppers and other insects, besides both wild and domestic fruits. The foregoing, coupled with food from the different species of non-hibernating rodents, and domestic livestock and wild game animals Arizona coyotes fare well at all times of the year. Attesting to this is the rendering of 4 pounds 13 ounces of fat from a coyote taken in Yuma County, one of the hottest sections in the United States.

Although there may be smaller litters when food is scarce, at other times it is not uncommon to find litters of 9 to 12 (See Plate 16), and some females have been known to have as many as 17 and 19 respectively (See Plate 17). On March 29, 1947, a female with a litter of 14 was taken near Alturas, Modoc County, California, which is believed to be a record for this State.

In the coyote den later described, the pups lie in the dry dust on the floor.

Dens often contain two litters, one of young with eyes not yet open, and the other of pups about a month old. One litter may be large and the other small, the latter probably belonging to a young female that apparently at a loss for a place to den, had taken up quarters with her mother. (See Plate 18.) Young females usually whelp about 10 days to 2 weeks later than the older ones. Occasionally a den may harbor three litters. At a den where two litters are found there is usually only one male which would suggest that polygamy occasionally occurs.

Plate 18. A coyote den sometimes contains two litters of pups of different size.

Under normal conditions a pair of coyotes is found with every den unless one parent has been killed. If the female is killed and the pups are young they die. If they are old enough to eat meat, the male parent cares for them, as he does his part in providing food.

Occasionally deformity will be found among coyote pups in the same litter. In midspring of 1947 a coyote den containing pups 2 days old near Vale, Oregon, in Malheur County, contained one pup with a foreleg undersized, and the foot turned right back up toward the body with only three toes on the foot. Another pup had a large skinned place on its backbone near the hips, the hind legs were crossed and reminded one of the rear flippers on a hair seal. The feet were normal but useless.

Some wildlife students believe that possibly vitamins may be controlling factors both as to the size of the litter and the sex ratio.

This is a field left for some further research student whereby experimental feeding under as natural conditions as possible might give the answer.

DENNING AND REARING

As with the large wolves, coyotes generally use a den (See Plate 19) when bringing forth and rearing their young, though there are exceptions to this general rule, such as the choosing of cover beneath sagebrush and giving birth to the litter above ground.

Coyotes do not select denning sites according to any recognizable rule, but many of them return to the same general locality year after year, even though the dens are regularly dug out and the pups killed by den hunters. If the female is killed, the male may bring his new mate to the same den the next season. A dug-out den that has not been badly damaged in removing coyotes may remain unoccupied for two or three seasons and then be used again.

Dens may be found in a canyon, wash-out, or coulee, on a bank or Hillside (See Plate 20), in a rock bluff, or even on level ground, as in a wheatfield, stubblefield, or plowed field. (See Plate 21.) They have been discovered under deserted homestead shacks in the desert, under grain bins, in a drainage pipe, in a dry culvert under railroad tracks, in a hollow log, in a thicket, and under a clump of thistles that had blown into a canyon. An unusual denning location sometimes is found as noted from the following:

While Junior District Agent Oliver S. Robinson was den hunting with Leonard Holst, predatory animal hunter, on the Belle Fourche River in Crook County, Wyoming, Holst located a den of pups in an old hollow cottonwood tree. The tree was on a slant and the mouth of the den was 5 feet from the ground. The pups had been out on the ground and were walking back and forth on a big limb that made a passageway from the den to the ground. The tree was hollow for about 15 feet and Holst and Robinson had to chop holes in it to get the pups out.

As a rule, instead of digging entirely new dens, coyotes will enlarge abandoned badger or rabbit holes or use deserted porcupine dens in rocky promontories or canyon walls. Usually they start cleaning out the holes several weeks prior to whelping. They generally claw out the dirt in one direction from the mouth of the den, where it piles up into a mound (See Plate 22), although some dens have no such mound.

The female continues digging and cleaning out den holes, sometimes a dozen or more, until the young are born. Then, if one den is disturbed the family moves to another. Sometimes the

Plate 19. Terrain admirably suited for coyote denning, north central Oregon.

a.

b.

Plate 20. (a) Coyote den in the bank of a dry wash. (b) Typical coyote denning ground in the Midwest. Arrow points to den site. (Photo courtesy of Missouri Conservation Department.)

animals move only a few hundred yards, apparently just to have a cleaner home, leaving many fleas behind. Occasionally a female that has lost her whelps will clean out several holes before becoming reconciled to her loss. Barren females sometimes prepare dens, but they are not found traveling with a mate. Male coyotes also work at many holes in spring but generally to dig out dead rabbits. The tracks of the male will usually be seen at these freshly dug holes, which have a different appearance from those cleaned out for dens, and dried-up rabbit carcasses will generally be found nearby.

When entering the den, the coyotes almost always go around, not over, the mound, if one is present. Dens may have one or several entrances in use, and several passages may branch from the main one. After the pups are born, small balls of rolled fur and hair from the mother's belly may be found in the dry dirt in the mouth of the den.

Parent coyotes have no set time for being at home and may be found near the den at any hour. Although they do most of their killing for food early in the morning, they sometimes visit the den only at night. They are clean about their dens; so there is little refuse or odor.

The coyote den is usually in rougher surroundings than are dens of small burrowing rodents and is normally within reach of water. Contrary to general supposition, however, coyotes do not always make their dens near water. In hilly areas they usually do, but on the large deserts of eastern Oregon dens are often found as far as 6 miles from water. Coyotes do not go to water regularly unless the weather is warm, and pups do not need water until they are several months old. If one listens at the mouth of the den he can usually hear any whelps inside, especially when they are very young, as they are then seldom quiet. If a nursing whelp loses hold of a teat, it is rather noisy until it regains its hold.

The whelps emerge when about 3 weeks old, and then their

Plate 21. Coyote den on prominent sand dune, well screened with greasewood and sagebrush. (San Luis Valley, Colo.)

Plate 22. Coyote den in rough coulee. Such situations, if reasonably near water, are excellent for denning. The arrow points to the mouth of the den. (Lance Creek, Wyo.)

tracks and other sign are easily noted. At this age they do not whine, but can be heard moving about when in the den, where, if crowded, they sometimes growl. Curiosity to see what is going on outside will bring some to the entrance. When the burrow is steep they are unable to clamber out at as early an age as when it is nearly level. Little scratches made in their attempts to crawl out will often be noted on the side walls and floor of the den.

When the pups are about 8 to 10 weeks old the dens are abandoned, and the entire family roves about, remaining together until early fall. (See Plate 23.)

As far as stock losses from coyotes are concerned, the most severe often occur at the time young are in the den in late spring, though a later denning period such as the middle of summer seems not to mitigate against similar losses.

Occasionally the mother coyote will take her pups to an area a short distance from the den which is used as a sunning place, when weather permits, after which they return to the den.

As already mentioned coyotes are particularly destructive during the denning season because of the greater need for food for both parents and young. It is then that lambing bands of sheep on open ranges suffer the heaviest losses, for invariably in the West the whelping of coyotes and the lambing of sheep as well as nesting game birds occur at approximately the same time in the spring. The availability of an ever ready food supply will sometimes cause coyotes to den close by. (See Fig. 11.)

Unfortunately, at the time Sperry (1941) was well under way with his food analysis of coyote stomachs, nearly a thousand stomachs stored in small barrels that were taken throughout a

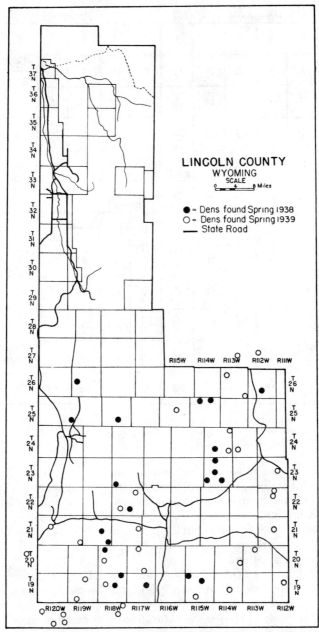

Figure 11. A study of coyote denning concentrations within a portion of Lincoln County, Wyo., and points adjacent thereto, important sheep ranges. (Courtesy of Noble Buell, Fish and Wildlife Service.)

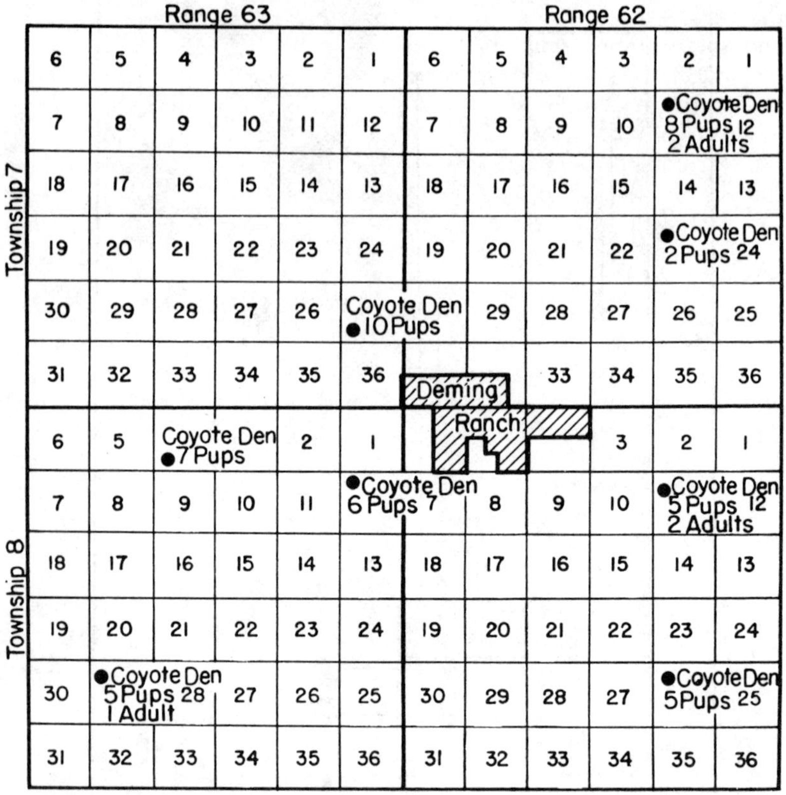

Township	Range 63						Range 62					
	6	5	4	3	2	1	6	5	4	3	2	1
Township 7	6	5	4	3	2	1	6	5	4	3	2	1
	7	8	9	10	11	12	7	8	9	10		●Coyote Den 8 Pups 12 2 Adults
	18	17	16	15	14	13	18	17	16	15	14	13
	19	20	21	22	23	24	19	20	21	22		●Coyote Den 2 Pups 24
	30	29	28	27	26	Coyote Den ●10 Pups		29	28	27	26	25
	31	32	33	34	35	36	Deming		33	34	35	36
Township 8	6	5	Coyote Den ●7 Pups		2	1	Ranch			3	2	1
	7	8	9	10	11	●Coyote Den 6 Pups	7	8	9	10		●Coyote Den 5 Pups 12 2 Adults
	18	17	16	15	14	13	18	17	16	15	14	13
	19	20	21	22	23	24	19	20	21	22	23	24
	30	●Coyote Den 5 Pups 28 1 Adult		27	26	25	30	29	28	27		●Coyote Den 5 Pups 25
	31	32	33	34	35	36	31	32	33	34	35	36

Figure 12. Section of Elbert County, Colorado, showing remarkable concentration of coyote pup dens near source of food, consisting of poultry and young pigs raised on the Deming ranch.

wide geographic range of the animal during the spring months, were accidentally destroyed through the carelessness of some laborers. Could Sperry have made analysis of this additional material, his findings, coupled with previous field observations, would have thrown much more light on the coyote's depredations in spring, particularly upon ground nesting game birds, such as the sage grouse and others.

On making a kill of a lamb or an older sheep, or other prey, both parent coyotes will at times gorge on the meat, return to the den and disgorge portions of the food around the entrance to the den for the pups to feed upon. The disgorged meat is often mixed with a whitish fluid which in appearance and viscosity resembles pigeon milk. This habit of disgorging food, which is also done by the large wolves, begins about a month after the puppies are born and the mother's milk is disappearing. At that time also, pieces of meat and bones will be carried to the den. Coyotes have been known to carry a leg of lamb a distance of 8 miles to their young in the den.

Seton (1929: 372) states also that "Keeper Carson assures me that in the Philadelphia Zoo where the coyotes frequently breed, the mother disgorges food for them regularly, exactly as does the mother Gray-wolf."

The denning of coyotes near an assured food supply is graphically shown in Fig. 12. The illustration depicts the work of a Federal hunter who worked a section of Elbert County, Colorado, north of Kiowa. His services were sought for this area because the owners of the Deming Ranch reported severe depredations from coyotes, particularly on poultry and to a lesser extent on young Duroc pigs. Carefully surveying the area in question the hunter during June of 1924 removed a total of 53 coyotes, during which time it was ascertained that much of the food for the young in the eight dens was taken from the aforementioned ranch. Similar instances of what might be termed collective denning of coyotes was noted from time to time in Colorado during the denning seasons of the early 1920's. In some instances similar habits were noted in

Plate 23. Coyote approximately 4 months old.

Wyoming nesting areas of sage grouse, and as with the food supply from the Deming Ranch the sage grouse nests had furnished
some of the food for the coyote young. (See Plate 23a.)

Bill Hickman, of Saline County, Missouri, experienced severe
losses from a single coyote den that had become established in
a pasture adjacent to one in which Mr. Hickman was grazing
sheep and hogs, and were raising their young in that area. Losses
of 36 lambs and sheep, 25 pigs, and 100 chickens were evidence
of their presence. The female of the den was trapped on August

Plate 23(a). Sage hen nest and eggs destroyed by coyote during denning
season, (Wyoming.)

23, 1945, and the male continued the killing, and before he was
taken on September 10, he and the young coyotes had taken an
additional 3 sheep, 60 pigs, and over 100 chicks from Mr. Hickman
and his neighbors.

Coyotes at times appear, while denning, to have little fear of
man, as evidenced by the finding of two coyote dens in the spring
of 1944 under ranch buildings in close proximity to the main
ranch house on a Grand Ronde Valley ranch in Oregon. The buildings were used for storage of stock feed and were visited frequently by employees of the ranch.

INDIVIDUAL AND FAMILY TRAITS

Digging for Water

In the dry sandy country of our Southwest, including the States of Baja California and Sonora, Mexico, coyotes will often dig holes 2 to 3 feet deep in the bottom of dry washes or arroyos in search of water. They often succeed in obtaining water in this way. Nelson records such an instance as this in Arroyo de Jaraguay of Baja California. The same habit has been observed in dry sandy washes of southern Arizona and New Mexico. *C. l. mearnsi* seems more prone to do this than the other races of coyotes (Nelson, E. W., 1921: 25-26). Coyote Wells, Imperial County, California, located in what was often referred to as the Colorado Desert between Yuma, Arizona, and San Diego, California, received its name "from the fact that here the coyotes long before even white men had passed this way smelled water near the surface, and pawed in the sands until they reached it" (Green, Edward Lee, 1880). Later with the development of this part of California the Wells of the Coyotes were developed and furnished exceedingly good water to travelers visiting this section. Thus it may be said, the coyote's habit of at times digging for water resulted in at least one instance in the development of a water reservoir suitable for man in a very arid country.

Killing Prey

In the killing of some of its prey, especially the young of domestic stock, such as lambs, the coyote does this differently than does the large gray wolf. The latter approaches its victim from the rear while the coyotes works on its prey anteriorly. Thus the head and throat of the prey will show more mutilation than the rear quarters (See Plate 12).

Burying of Food

As with most dogs, and other members of the genus, coyotes often bury food they cannot consume at a single meal, and return later to the spot for another meal. Dice (1919: 10-21) mentions the case of a coyote burying all but the fore parts of a jack rabbit east of Wallula, Washington, returning the next day to the cache it had thus made. The animal has been observed to bury poisoned pork-fat baits set out for its destruction near Flagstaff, Arizona, apparently being too full of food at the time to eat further. When the hunter returned later to dig out the baits, two coyotes were found dead nearby, undoubtedly the same animals observed burying the baits the previous day. The burying of bones has also been observed, but coyotes do not seem to return to such spots except sporadically.

Freezing, Momentarily Before Springing at Prey

On numerous occasions while observing coyotes feeding in well-covered, open meadows, and mountain parks, one may note that the animals have a tendency to trot slowly and quietly along much like a setter or pointer dog. Then all of a sudden they will "freeze" momentarily, then spring on the small prey they are seeking, such as field mice and ground squirrels, invariably coming up with the victim in their mouths. Apparently they hold the prey so caught by their paws until it can be grabbed by the mouth; particularly is this true in the case of grasshoppers, crickets, and beetles.

The "freezing" habit of a coyote when detecting small rodent prey is one of the most interesting of its various hunting antics, and fortunate indeed is anyone who gets the opportunity to observe it closely.

How this animal captures a pocket gopher is not well understood, unless it is by actually outdigging the gopher seen as it pushes the dirt to the surface from an underground lateral tunnel. I observed such a performance of a coyote attempting to dig out a gopher near Monument, Oregon, during mid-summer of 1911. I was in this instance not more than 50 yards away, where a small knoll enabled me to keep hidden so that only my head showed over the top, with the wind in my favor. Before I was observed, a hole 2 feet deep was dug by this coyote into the pocket gopher's lateral tunnel, but apparently without success. The digging was rapidly done, the coyote stopping only at intervals of a second or two before starting to dig again.

Coyote Enemies, Foes and Sociability with Other Animals

Besides man, the coyote has such other enemies as the wolf, puma, and bear. Regarding this subject, Ricksecker (1890: 235, 236) nearly half a century ago, appropriately wrote:

"Every species of animal is surrounded by other species that are its foes, and eternal vigilance is the price of life; however, vigilance only serves to detect the danger—the foe itself must either be met, distanced or deceived. To avoid destruction is the first law of nature with all animals, but the methods of accomplishing this are nearly as numerous as the species themselves. As the aggressor is almost invariably superior in size and strength, it stands to reason that flight is the common resort in the moment of danger. The varying elements of cunning, strategy, deception, and mimicry, in pursurer and pursued, all play their parts in the vast game of nature, and to these same species add a powerful mal-odor or poison of bile or sting."

With respect to coyote defense in the form of flight from an enemy, E. A. Preble, in Seton (1911) records a large wolf ranging near Athabaska Landing that had a runway a distance of 70 miles. In February of the late 1880's this wolf was observed chasing a coyote, a mile below the Landing for a distance of approximately 1 mile, when it was overtaken, killed and partly devoured. Later the wolf was poisoned near the spot where the killing took place, and measured 8 ft. 4 in.

The large wolf does not treat the coyote as an equal in the wilds, nor in confinement. It seldom permits the coyote to come near it. Coyotes, however, will often follow wolves, keeping far on the flank where they will feed on wolf kills after it has finished eating and departed. The famous Custer Wolf of South Dakota was known to have two such coyote dependents that habitually trailed it to eat from prey remains this wolf abandoned from time to time.

Enmity Toward the Bobcat and Fox

In my trapping experience I have never successfully saved a trapped fox or bobcat from being killed by the coyote whenever a coyote visited a trap line ahead of me and found these animals in traps. Invariably the coyote tore them to shreds. The enmity of the coyote for the bobcat is illustrated by the following:

T. C. Creighton, a member of the government predatory animal hunting force in Arizona, reports that during December, 1945, while running his trap lines near Bowie, he observed what he thought was an owl perched on top of a telephone pole several hundred yards away, alongside the road he was traveling. As he neared the telephone pole Mr. Creighton noticed that the supposed owl was really a bobcat. In its attempts to hide, only the bobcat's ears were visible above the top of the telephone pole. After a well aimed shot from his rifle brought the bobcat to the ground Mr. Creighton began to wonder why a bobcat should be on top of a telephone pole at 9:30 o'clock in the morning. He shortly discovered that a pair of coyotes had chased the bobcat a distance of more than 80 yards before it took refuge on the telephone pole, the only point nearby where it could escape from the coyotes.

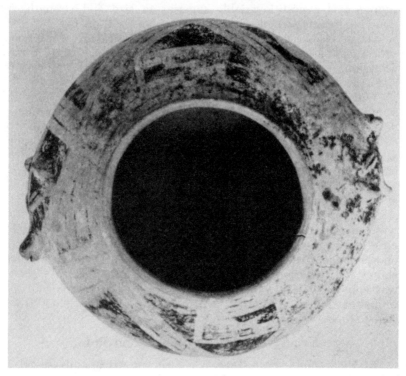

Plate 24. Casa Grandes pot—Mexico, 1000 years old, with sculptured head of badger and coyote. (See text, p. 95.) (Photo courtesy of J. Frank Dobie, Austin, Texas.)

Further evidence of the enmity between the coyote and the bobcat was observed on February 21 by Assistant District Agent Lloyd Hutchinson and Predatory Animal Hunter Arthur Morrison, of the Wyoming district, who were inspecting a coyote-getter line on the Sweetwater River near Independence Rock, Wyoming. To reach one set, it was necessary for them to walk a quarter of a mile. Just before reaching the set they noticed a large bobcat in the top branches of a poplar tree, which Hunter Morrison promptly shot.

The sign at the base of the tree showed that three coyotes had chased the bobcat up the tree and had jumped up the trunk, trying to reach it. After skinning the bobcat, it was observed that the coyotes had nipped it several times. The tooth marks showed plainly on the bobcat's hindquarters.

Many outdoorsmen of the old west have stated to me that

coyotes and badgers at times form strong friendship, and there is no indication that enmity ever exists between the two creatures.

Indicative of this friendly relationship is the type of effigy occasionally found on pre-Columbian pottery from Mexican and other ruins. J. Frank Dobie of Austin, Texas, possesses one jar from Casa Grandes showing the coyote and badger in the closest of cooperation. The vessel is believed by archaeologists to date between 1250-1300 A.D. (See Plate 24.)

In the early 80's, Aughey (1884) recounts three remarkable observations of a coyote in Wyoming accompanying a badger who were apparently boon companions. In one instance while the two were walking together, "the coyote would go in front of the badger, lay its head on the latter's neck, lick it, jump into the air, and give other expressions of unmistakable joy . . . the badger seemed equally pleased."

Approximately a quarter of a century later, A. H. Hawkins (1907) observed the same habit in southern Alberta. Concerning this observation he recorded: "During the progress of my survey in southern Alberta, I noticed on two occasions a badger and a coyote travelling in company. The same thing was observed and reported by the men who did my mounding on three different occasions, all in different localities.

"The men reported having seen the animals travelling in company in Tp. 1, R. 13, W. 4th Mer. The first time that I saw them together was in Tp. 6, R. 17, and the second time in Tp. 7, R. 17, W. 4th. This last time I had the best view. Seated one day eating our noon lunch, I noticed two animals coming towards us and drew the attention of my men to the fact. We remained perfectly quiet so that they came within 20 to 30 feet of us before seeing that we were so near. The coyote travelled ahead, and the badger followed along as fast as he could, right at the heels of the coyote.

"I could see no reason nor could I explain it in any way satisfactory to myself, and although I asked several people in the West about it, the occurrence is still a mystery to me."

Since the two animals are noted as rodent depredators may account for the apparent friendship that sometimes develops between them, and probably results in close cooperation in digging out burrowing rodents for food.

A more recent occurrence (Anon., 1947: 3) is reported from below Buck Creek in Wallowa County, Oregon, where Clayton Vauter saw "an adult coyote which had lost its right front foot, and an adult badger traveling along together . . . the best of friends."

However, during the spring of 1928, a female coyote suckling young was trapped in Wyoming. A drag was attached to her neck, and the trap removed, so she might return to the den. This she did a few days after release. The trapper traced her from the drag marks, and when he reached the den he found that a badger had taken nine pups, eaten off their heads and departed.

Numerous observations are on record of attacks on coyotes by eagles. A recent one (Anon., 1940) concerns two eagles observed by a Texas game warden, J. H. Maggard, of Amarillo. The birds chased a pair of coyotes over a plain, swooping time and again, striking them with beaks and talons so hard that the coyotes were repeatedly knocked to the ground. Had not the birds finally sighted the warden, which caused them to flap on their way, there was every indication that the eagles would have eventually killed this pair.

Coyote Attacking (Antelope) Prey

No quarter is shown the antelope, particularly the young of this game species. A vivid picture of antelope depredation is recorded as follows:

"While traveling 25 miles south of Winslow recently, A. C. Whiting, native of Arizona and resident of Holbrook, had his attention drawn to a small funnel of dust in the distance. His first thought was of running antelope, but the behavior of the dusk cloud seemed unnatural and he stopped his car.

"Nature's actors stepped on the stage and enacted a drama of life and death for him.

"An antelope fawn was fleeing from a coyote. The mother antelope was trying to protect her young. She, with superior speed and agility, dashed in and out in front of the following coyote. Desperately the mother, with flying hooves, tried to attract the predator's attention away from her offspring. But the coyote, bent on destruction, was relentless in his pursuit of the fawn.

"The trio made three complete circles about a mile in diameter. Finally the terrible race began to tell on the fawn. The young antelope began to stagger. The coyote crept closer and was within snapping distance of the fawn, running spraddle-legged in exhaustion. The mother antelope made one more desperate attempt to cut the coyote out of the race, then turned and ran over the horizon without once looking back.

"When last seen the stumbling fawn still had his distance, but the coyote was running smoothly, relentlessly, on the trail." (Anon., Arizona Wildlife and Sportsman 5 (9): 9, September 1943d.)

Coyote-Deer

Not always does the coyote chase deer when the opportunity is presented. For instance "A variant of the 'man bites dog' story was found in nature recently. Charles Vest of the Wyoming Game and Fish Commission reports seeing a big male coyote runnng at top speed with a buck deer in hot pursuit. When the deer caught up with the coyote he knocked it down with his forefeet, then jumped on it.

"After taking a hard pounding the coyote managed to crawl into a brush patch which the deer circled until he saw Mr. Vest. Then he dashed away, followed by three does that had been waiting at a distance.

"The coyote was so badly trampled that he could hardly crawl, and Mr. Vest easily put an end to him." (Science News Letter, April 1, 1944, p. 210.)

Teamwork in Obtaining Prey—Porcupine

Many field observations show that coyotes display fox-like cunningness in obtaining prey by the use of teamwork. This habit is probably more pronounced in coyotes than among the large gray wolves. Often hunting in pairs, teamwork as displayed in killing a porcupine, one of the animal's favorite foods, apparently has come about through years of painful experience. All evidence points to the conclusion that in killing the porcupine, two hunting coyotes with use of their paws first turn the animal over on its back. When they succeed in placing this prey in such exposed condition of its belly, a foreleg is grabbed by one coyote while the other grabs a hind leg; then a tug-of-war begins and lasts until the porcupine through such stretching is rendered harmless as far as use of its quills, especially those on its slashing tail are concerned when both coyotes then disembowel the victim. As a rule the porcupine's stomach, free of quills, is quite tender, and forms the most vulnerable spot in rendering this creature helpless. Coyotes in feeding from a victimized porcupine often consume this animal at a single feeding leaving as final remains only the outer skin and tail, with most of its quills intact. Apparently this creature is attacked only by old adult coyotes, without harm to them, as younger coyotes have been taken with jowls, forehead, and neck peppered with quills, showing they had yet to learn the proper manner in taking this prey without paying the usual consequences so common to other members of the none too discreet dog family. (See Plate 25.)

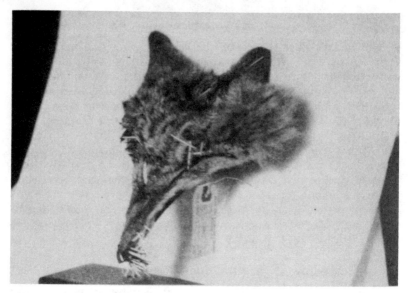

Plate 25. Head from coyote captured in New Mexico showing previous encounter with porcupine.

Gorging and Cleaning Up Prey

At times, like the large wolves, coyotes will practically clean up large prey. In Yosemite National Park, California, Garrison (1937: 16 (3): 19) records that 4 coyotes on November 10, 1936, took about 75 pounds of meat from a doe weighing approximately 100 pounds at a single meal within 30 minutes. In doing this, these predators consumed all the meat off the leg bones, the ribs and spine leaving the deer's hide completely stripped with the exception of the neck.

In the winter of February 1920 I killed a 36-lb. male coyote, 60 miles north of Roswell, New Mexico, whose stomach contents was found to comprise one solid mass of sheep-fat weighing slightly under 12 pounds. This was approximately one-third of its body weight.

Urinating on Food

At times hungry coyotes will urinate on their food before eating it—why this is done is not understood—possibly it is a claim for ownership, as each animal has its distinct scent.

Peculiarities occurring in certain individual coyotes, and examples of the recuperative power.—During the fiscal year 1940, an old adult male coyote was trapped in New Mexico that had **two** perfectly developed sets of canine teeth. Similarly a coyote with two incisor teeth in the upper righthand side of the jaw was taken on the Kaibab Forest June 1943.

In October 1931, a female coyote was taken in Michigan which had stubs for front legs, the result of previous and later healed trap injury. This malformation caused the animal to resemble a kangaroo while running. Postmortem of this female after death showed that she was carrying five unborn young.

An adult coyote (See Plate 26) trapped near Saguache, Colorado, had a missing left front and right hind foot evidently lost in traps, but the stumps had thoroughly healed. This peg-legged animal must have had a "rocking beam" like motion to its body when walking or running. The impediment, however, appeared no handicap to its existence as examination showed this creature to be in perfect physical shape.

In Idaho, B. L. Evans, assistant district predator control agent, caught a coyote which had at some time had its mouth wired shut. The hide had grown completely over the wire, as does the bark of a tree. With this impediment, the animal could only open its mouth one-half of an inch, but nevertheless it managed to obtain a living before its capture. In the same state another coyote was trapped near Howe that had its lower jaw broken, but it had set and healed again, though at an angle of 45 degrees. Both these coyotes were found to be in good physical condition at the time of capture. In a third instance of coyote capture near Howe, the animal was minus its entire lower jaw, presumably caused by a rifle bullet. The wound had entirely healed, and it had managed

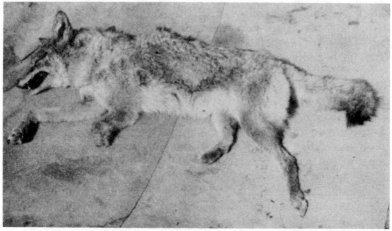

Plate 26. Peg-legged coyote captured near Saguache, Colorado.

to live partially by feeding on bits of fat pork thrown out from sheep camps with parts of buns that were not entirely consumed by sheep herders. Insects, such as grasshoppers, ants, and ground beetles gave it additional subsistence.

In New Mexico (Anon., 1945f) a coyote that was found to be a calf killer was captured which was observed to have "The right front leg off at the knee and the right hind leg off at the hock. It did not use the stubs in traveling but hopped along on the two left feet. Not able to catch any rabbits, the coyote had become a vicious killer of calves."

The catch of double peg-legged, very aged male coyote by Hunter John C. Owen in southern Texas County on May 11, 1944, stopped considerable damage for a number of Texas County farmers. This animal also ranged and ravaged in northern Howell County. Hunter Owen had taken this coyote's young mate on April 15 and its family of three pups on April 21. During about a 3-year period of depredation this old coyote was reported by Glen Mulkey to have caused him $500 worth of livestock losses. In addition, Mr. Gideon lost several lambs and Mr. Wagner suffered considerable damage.

Fred Warrix lost a calf and a number of sheep and was planning to sell out the remainder of his flock. His two brothers also were reported to have had considerable losses, including 2 calves. Floyd Baker had already disposed of his sheep and goats on account of predator losses. During trapping operations Hunter Owen observed 2 ewes, 2 goats, 1 lamb, and 1 calf, which had been killed by this old peg-leg.

This decrepit coyote weighed about 40 pounds and had lost half its tail. It had been shot in the right hind leg, crippling it so that the foot pads turned up and it had to walk on the "instep." Due to cessation of wear, hair grew out about an inch long between the toes on its foot. Its right front foot had been lost in a trap and it was by the stub of this foot that this coyote was caught in Owen's trap. Its teeth were very badly worn and one incisor and two premolars were missing. Considering the condition of this old animal it is no wonder that he had to feed on easily caught domestic livestock rather than wild game.

In western Colorado, during the mid-twenties, a coyote was trapped and killed. Removal of its pelt disclosed 4 single loop strands of hog-wire fencing was imbedded near the left hip joint. Apparently, the coyote had at one time become entangled in a hog wire fence, hung up for some time, but finally twisted loose taking the wire loop with it. In time, the strands of wire worked through the skin and into the flesh, and ultimately became covered in the healing process. Constant movement of the leg and hip joint produced a slight sideway movement of the wire strands at the joints that made the loop, so that these points were as bright as newly retorted mercury. This contraption in no way retarded this coyote in the use of any of its legs or feet.

Instances are on record of coyotes living at least a month or more after being trapped, supposedly killed, scalped (the latter for use as evidence for collecting bounties in some states and counties) and supposedly left for dead, only to recover and make a getaway. Baldheadedness caused by scalping did not seem to prevent the animal from living a normal life.

In other ways also the coyote seemingly possesses an anatomy that can withstand much in the way of shock and pain, as shown by its ability to overcome severe physical disability to the point of complete recovery. These remarkable recuperative powers may be the answer to why it can exist, persist, and extend its range in spite of the great human pressure. Apropos of this is the remarkable case of two coyotes taken in Colorado, one in western Colorado near the vicinity of Redvale, and the other near Rich Creek in Park County, 75 miles west of Colorado Springs. They convey some idea of the wonderful recuperative powers of this predator.

In the case of the coyote killed near Redvale, the illustration (See Plate 27 a, b) shows the under jaw of the animal which had been completely severed by a bullet about an inch and a half back from the lower front teeth. Following this happening a remarkable mend took place in time on the part of Mother Nature, in that the severed portion of the jaw bone held in place by the skin of the lower lip knitted at an angle of 22 degrees from the normal position of the under jaw. In the knitting of the bone, the front portion of the lower jaw at the break dropped down three-eighths of an inch from the normal horizontal position, but full recovery, nevertheless, had been made. At the time this coyote, a female, was killed, she was in fine pelage, and if she had lived would have whelped five young sometime in March. Her food was apparently taken through the left side of her jaw after recovery from her injury.

The Rich Creek coyote (See Plate 28 a, b, c), a male, had been shot through the lower jaw one-third of the distance from the front of its mouth to where the jaw sockets into the upper jaw. The lower jaw was thus smashed on its right side. The bullet, after hitting this part of the animal, ricocheted on the first molar tooth and sped across the space between the two bones forming

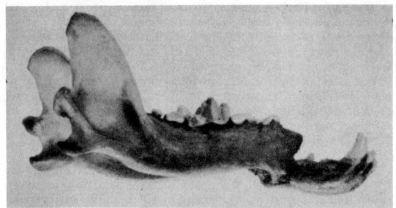

a.

b.

Plate 27. (a) Side view of Redvale coyote showing mended lower jaw near outer teeth.

(b) View of under side of Redvale coyote showing mended jaw bone and the 22 degree angle of it from the normal shape.

the lower jaw and lodged itself mushroom fashion on the left side of the lower jawbone. Again the lower lip served as a partial sling to hold the bone. As the bullet—apparently from a .22 long rifle—took this course, it carried a small splinter of the bone from one side of the coyote's lower jaw to the other. As a result Mother Nature once again—as in the case of the Redvale coyote—stepped into the picture, for a perfect bone bridging took place. In fact, it was so perfect that this coyote, after the knitting and healing of the bridge, possessed a better lower jaw than it had had normally.

One conjectures, therefore, as to how these coyotes managed to live in the interim while contending with such injured lower

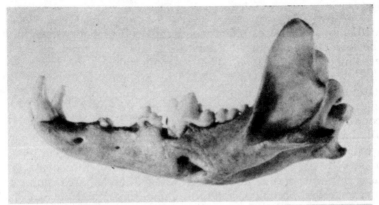

a.

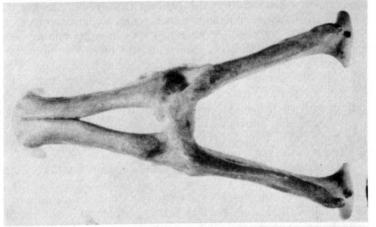

b.

c.

Plate 28. (a) Side view of Rich Creek coyote lower jawbone showing point of contact by rifle bullet near center.

(b) View of under part of Rich Creek coyote showing the bone bridging that took place after smashing injury by lead bullet.

(c) Under view of Rich Creek coyote skull showing the bridging of the lower jaw by splintered bone.

jawbones. It causes as much wonderment, for among other things, the lower jawbone in all predators is always a primary asset in obtaining essential food. The grasping power, for instance, of the lower jaw is constantly needed by predators in obtaining their natural foods. Furthermore, if soreness and slow healing of an injured bone in a carnivore approximates to any degree a similar condition known and often experienced in the genus Homo, then all the more does it puzzle the naturalist as to the manner in which an animal with such injury is able to subsist. One possible answer to the foregoing question in the case of the coyote taken near Redvale is the fact that it ranged in an area supporting many ground-nesting species of game birds, and it may have been able to subsist during the healing process by preying upon birds or swallowing sufficient insects such as grasshoppers and beetles. The Rich Creek coyote ranged an area containing at this time many domestic sheep carcasses, where there was opportunity to obtain considerable food. Feeding might have been accomplished by the coyote's gulping sufficient decomposed parts of the carcasses to sustain its needed bodily requirements while contending with such a major injury, until the jawbone could again be used normally. But in either case, how these animals really obtained sufficient food to live in the interim before recovery will always be a moot question.

In California, Merle D. Barney, field assistant for the Fish and Wildlife Service, killed a coyote with a "coyote getter" near the town of Beckwourth, Sierra Valley, Plumas County, on February 13, 1947. Half of the lower jaw was missing, apparently the result of a rifle bullet. The wound had healed completely. Examination of it at the time of the killing showed it to be unusually fat, of normal size, and in its stomach 4 *Microtus*, a jack rabbit, and deer meat, the latter being carrion (See Plate 29 a, b).

On the Kinsley Range, in northern Humboldt County, California, Hunter Guy Curliss shot a female coyote at close range. It was not killed and made its escape. Approximately one month later Hunter Curliss trapped this animal on the same range, and found the lower jaw had been shot away, and was nearly healed. The animal was found to be in fair condition.

Many female coyotes minus one or more feet have been killed from time to time carrying unborn young. Seemingly, loss of portion of the feet, legs, or both is no deterrent in the animal's ability to breed. In late March of 1926, a government hunter working a lambing range of domestic sheep between Cottonwood Creek and Paonia, Colorado, killed an old three-legged female coyote carrying nine unborn young.

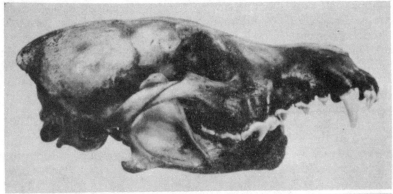

Plate 29. (a) Side view showing where half of lower jaw of California coyote is missing. (b) Underside view.

Another outstanding oddity is that reported in the following: On April 21, 1945 Hunter H. Lee Morris, stationed southeast of Tule Lake in northwestern Modoc County, California, found a coyote den on the south side of Doublehead Mountain. The mother and four pups were in the den. All of the pups were males. The mother presented one of the best examples known of how hardy and persistent is the coyote in existing and reproducing under extreme odds. This coyote had been shot, apparently with a shotgun, in both eyes and was entirely blind. She was not in really good condition but was strong. The four pups were all healthy and in good shape.

A five-footed coyote was caught by Hunter Cecil Uglow in Santa Clara County, California, on April 30, 1946. The right front leg of the coyote was divided near the ankle to form two perfect feet. The two feet were of equal length and apparently received equal use. (See Plate 30, a, b.)

Plate 30. (a) California coyote with five feet. (b) Close-up of two right front feet.

Chapter Four

Parasites and Diseases

O F ALL the larger North American carnivores, the coyote seems to have an excessive number of parasites and diseases. This may be caused by the great variety in its diet, much of which comes from its skill as a scavenger. In general, this wild fox-like dog is host to practically every parasite borne by the domestic dog. As Stiles and Baker (1935: 917) put it: "A considerable number of parasites are distributed to man and livestock and to wild animals by various carnivores. Thus hydatid disease in man and many other animals, gid in sheep and their allies, one form of pseudo-tuberculosis in cattle, hydrophobia in man and livestock, several intestinal worms in man, and a number of acarine infections in man and various other animals are disseminated by the carnivores, especially by the dog and its allies." The coyote has been found to be a host to the following parasites.

Brandegee (1890: 265-268), an early investigator of parasites affecting the wild jack rabbit showed the coyote to be one of the hosts of the *Coenurus* (tapeworm). She traced the history of this internal parasite from the time of its evacuation through the coyote's intestines to the ground to its external infestation of the jack rabbit and the completion of the cycle by the coyote preying upon the infected rabbit.

I. McT. Cowan (1948) states that in Banff National Park evidence strongly suggests that the coyote was the terminal host during the establishment of the parasite known as the granular tapeworm, *Echinococcus granulosis* in the elk herd there.

Taenis pisiformis, Multiceps multiceps (Hall, Maurice C., 1920: 79); *Opelinopsis nucleolobata* (Smith & Fox, 1908); *Amphimerus* (Barker, 1911); *Ancylostoma caninum* (Stiles & Hassell, 1894); *Rictularia splendida* (Hall, 1913); *Dermacentor venustus* (Henshaw and Birdseye, 1911) are found in the coyote.

The mange-mite *(Sarcoptes scabiei lupi)* commonly infects the coyote, being so severe at times as to cause almost complete nakedness of the body (See Plate 31). Some sheepmen aver that

Plate 31. Coyote afflicted with the mange mite.

this causes appreciable reduction in coyote abundance on some ranges, although others doubt this. It is the author's view that where sarcoptic mange exists among young pups in the den, in Colorado, Wyoming, Idaho, and Montana it does prove fatal, particularly in the case of young becoming infected during very early spring. Munro (1947) reports that the trappers of Baker Creek Valley in British Columbia believed an epidemic of mange had been the cause in reducing the local coyote population (See Hamlett, G.W.D., 1938).

According to Parker the flea *Arctopsylla setosa* (Roths.) 1906, occurs on most of the American carnivores, including the coyote (letter from Dr. R. R. Parker, Director Rocky Mountain Laboratory, Hamilton, Montana, to the author, dated July 5, 1945, in files of Fish and Wildlife Service).

In regard to the particular species of wild mammals in the Bitterroot Valley region, harboring the tick, *Dermacentor venustus*, which spreads spotted fever, Henshaw and Birdseye (1911) record the coyote as a host to adults.

The relapsing fever tick *(Orithodoras turicata)* and biting louse *(Heterodoxus longitarus)* have been found as parasites of the coyote. Similarly, the human flea *(Pulex irritans)* parasitizes the coyote (Trembley, Helen Louise, and Bishop, F. C., 1940: 701).

Brennan (1945) records the tick *(Ixodes scapularis)*, and the Gulf Coast tick *(Dermacentor variabilis)*, the latter a disease transmitting species that readily attacks man, as occurring on the coyote in the Camp Bullis area, a sub-post of Fort Sam Houston, in the hills of Bexar and Comal Counties, 18 miles north of San Antonio, Texas.

Coyotes are subject to tumors, and an extensive papilloma involving large parts of the lips and cheeks also has occurred.

District Agent Everett M. Mercer reports that examination of a coyote head taken by Hunter Leonard F. Miller in Mohave County in Arizona on April 24, 1945, revealed that the animal was suffering from a severe infection of buccal papillomata, or what is commonly known as "infectious wart."

During January and February, Mr. Miller worked as a private trapper in the district where this coyote was taken. Early in March Miller reported that from 10 to 15 percent of the coyotes he had trapped were suffering from a severe infection of the mouth. Laboratory technicians making the examination advised that although the infection is contagious to man, they have no records indicating that it may be transmitted to livestock from coyotes or domestic dogs. So far as can be determined, this is the first outbreak of the infection reported among coyotes or domestic dogs in Arizona. This malady is reported to be generally fatal to dogs.

Dog distemper, according to G. B. Grinnell (1904: 287) "played havoc with . . . . coyotes . . . . when it first came into the [western] country."

Rush (1946) tells of an observation during "one raw March day [when] Ranger Trischman and I were snowshoeing up Yellowstone River in Wyoming. We saw a blacktailed deer that walked with a peculiar jerky gait. His spine instead of being a normal straight line was curved upward. He held his head down, instead of high as he normally would have done. We shot the animal and made a field autopsy. In the muscles of his legs and back were numerous grisly bodies about the size of a grain of wheat. These were cystic larvae, the progeny of a tapeworm found in coyotes.

"The adult tapeworm lays its eggs in the coyote's intestines. Eggs pass out on the ground where in time they develop into motile larvae that migrate to blades of grass. When deer eat the grass the larvae develop further in the intestinal tract, then penetrate to the blood stream and lodge in muscle fibers. Here they encyst, that is, become covered with layers of tissue. When the deer is killed and eaten by coyotes the cyst covering is digested and the larvae liberated to develop into a mature tapeworm. The worm produces more eggs and the cycle begins again."

SALMON POISONING

That coyotes are susceptible to the salmon fluke, which is the cause of so-called "salmon poisoning," has been ascertained by scientists of the Oregon Agricultural Experiment Station (Donham, C. R., and B. T. Simms, 1927: 215-217). To what extent this serves as a check on the abundance of coyotes in the Pacific Northwest has not been definitely ascertained to date. The coyote's fondness for salmon has been noted in the Skeena River section of British Columbia during the salmon run. Here salmon canners have told me that coyotes, as with the large wolves in southeastern Alaska, either prey upon the exhausted salmon or eat salmon carrion left by bears.

Einarsen, long familiar with wildlife conditions in Washington, feels that conditions favorable to salmon poisoning to carnivores, particularly coyotes, may extend at least to the Canadian line. He is of the opinion that: "The part that salmon sickness has played in the Northwest among the canines has not been definitely mapped out in its range, according to my belief. As early as 1906 we lost a pet fox terrier, obviously the result of 'salmon sickness' on Camano Island, Island County, Washington, in September of that year. Such losses were very common throughout that range, and the usual symptom prevailed. I can recall a considerable number of losses of dogs as far north as Bellingham, Washington, although the isolation of the organisms causing the disease was not attempted. All of the usual symptoms and conditions prevailed. Although there is some room for doubt, cases were common enough between 1906 and 1932 to assume this diagnosis to be correct. Inquiry among veterinarians in that region should establish definite cases.

"There is another condition which has existed throughout the range since about 1910, according to my personal recollection. Until trails and roads started to penetrate the Cascade Mountains there were very few records of coyotes in the Skagit and Stillaguamish Valleys. With the opening of the Forest Service trails and finally automobile roads through the mountain passes, coyotes became more and more numerous; and in trapping for animals preying on domestic poultry near Cedarhome in the hills east of Stanwood, Washington, coyotes were often taken in the traps as early as 1910. A portion of this range lies along the Pilchuck river, a tributary of the Stillaguamish, which is frequented by hundreds of thousands of pink salmon, *Oncorhynchus gorbuscha*, and silver salmon, *Oncorhynchus kisutch*. The run of salmon does not begin until the first week of September and may continue until December. A phenomenon persisted in that range that is worthy of mention. Following years when water levels were normal, with an extremely good supply of water in the channels during salmon seasons, we could find an abundance of coyotes. But following a year of extremely dry weather when freshet conditions did not exist in the streams, thereby allowing the dead carcasses of the salmon to lay upon all the sand bars where they could become the daily food of carrion eaters, coyotes would be very scarce. This is noticeable throughout Washington and Western Oregon and it appears that the low coyote population on the west side of the Cascade Mountains, in both Oregon and Washington, may be influenced by taking salmon as food from the spawning beds where the fluke is found to infest the dead carcasses of these fishes. In certain portions of Eastern Washington and Eastern Oregon, many areas have become overpopulated with coyotes under conditions of less food abundance.

"Where salmon runs are on the wane, coyotes do increase. In western Oregon, along the watershed of the Alsea and the Yaquina rivers, salmon are gradually being depleted and therefore contribute less and less to the food supply of coyotes. Here, the coyote population is increasing rapidly to the point that local goat and sheep ranchers have lost as much as 90% of their lamb and kid crop each year. The situation is becoming very aggravated. Yet, at the same time on other ranges where salmon populations are holding up well, such as on the Pilchuck river, Snohomish County, Washington, predation upon farm poultry and animals by coyotes is rarely reported.

"These notes must be interpreted only as indicators to the true condition. Definite research may prove them to be of entirely different values than they seem to suggest, but the possibilities of natural limitations through the eating of infested salmon by coyotes may be very real." [1]

Tularemia, sometimes called "rabbit fever," a very prevalent disease at times among rabbits and many of the rodents, has been reported in the coyote, and according to the United States Public Health Service (Kunkel, G. M., 1930: 439) the animal "must be considered a real source of danger in the transmission of tularemia to mankind." The human affection that has occurred in one instance came as the result of a slight knife wound used in removing the pelt from an infected coyote in New Mexico.

Probably one of the most prevalent diseases found in coyotes

---

[1] Einarsen, Arthur S., Memorandum on salmon sickness in canines in the state of Washington, dated April 8, 1940, in files of Fish and Wildlife Service, Washington, D. C.

is rabies or hydrophobia, an infectious disease which terminates fatally. It is spread from animal to animal by biting. It had been known among members of the dog family dating from the earliest times. The Indians of the Great Plains were fully cognizant of the disease, and greatly feared it. The large wolves were always affected by it. The records show this disease to be widespread, and apparently at times very severe. Such was the case which resulted in a congressional emergency appropriation on March 4, 1916, for the suppression of rabies among wild animals, mainly coyotes, in an area embracing southeastern Oregon, northeastern California, the seat of the outbreak, northern Nevada, and southwestern Idaho. State cooperative funds were pledged to supplement federal funds. For instance, Nevada pledged approximately $95,000, which was expended under a State board, the Nevada Rabies Commission. (See Plate 32.)

With such a carrier as the coyote, rabies can spread far and wide in a short time. The outbreak above referred to finally spread so that by the close of 1916, it predominated over all of the country east of the Cascade Mountains in Oregon, up to the Washington line. All of the open country in southern Idaho, known as the Snake River plains, all of northern Nevada, south as far as the third standard parallel, with several isolated cases appearing in southern Nevada near Pioche, Goldfield, and Las Vegas. The three northwestern counties of Utah, Box Elder, Juab, and Tooele, were also infested. Adopting the motto "kill the coyote, and muzzle the dog" and "It is better to be seen (and alive) than sorry (and dead)," trained hunters were detailed

Plate 32. Nevada cattle dead from rabies spread by coyotes during 1915-16-17 outbreak.

to the infested areas, and slowly but gradually reduced the outbreak from plague-like proportions to sporadic and localized outbreaks by early 1919. During this peak of the outbreak, some children were guarded from feared coyote attacks on their way to and from some of the smaller rural schools.

Since the occurrence of the foregoing large outbreak, smaller outbreaks among coyotes have occurred sporadically for the past 25 years in most of the western range states. One of these in Lea County, New Mexico, occurring in February of 1933, assumed alarming proportions within a month. In one case, 18 of 22 sheep bitten by coyotes showed symptoms of rabies and were killed by the owner. Instituting of cooperative and rigorous coyote trapping and poisoning campaign for several months stamped out the epizootic.

A voluminous, but somewhat repetitious record could be given dealing with the coyote—rabies outbreaks in the old and new West affecting man, his economic interests, and the often expensive but necessary reduction that must be made in the prevailing coyote population at such times. A few characteristic episodes dealing with this disease and the coyote are given for the record. These are typical and are from various parts of Arizona.

Early in the evening of May 9, 1945, a coyote entered a farmyard near Kyrene, Arizona, in Maricopa County, and fought with a dog. The coyote was driven away by the farmer after it had severely bitten the dog. About 10:30 p. m. during the same evening, a coyote attacked a small dog at a second farm in this community and seriously injured the animal. Shortly after 5 a. m. on the morning of May 10, a coyote, thought to be the same one as above mentioned, entered the farmyard at the Hudson ranch and attacked turkeys and chickens. It also attacked a dog within a few yards of the ranch house and was driven away by a 12-year-old girl who struck it several times with a broom. The coyote was pursued and killed by the farmer who delivered its head to the State Laboratory at Phoenix where an examination revealed that the coyote had rabies.

On March 9, 1947, a rabid coyote attacked and bit Roy Ives, Chief Deputy School Superintendent for Pima County, Arizona. Ives, who was afterward treated with rabies vaccine, said there had been reports of coyotes attacking and biting cattle in the vicinity of a ranch belonging to his father-in-law, northwest of Rillito.

On the day he was bitten he was walking towards the ranch corral. A coyote rushed directly toward him and sank its teeth in his leg. Ives kicked the animal in an effort to frighten it away.

He returned to the ranch house, obtained a shotgun, and found the coyote was still roaming around the ranch buildings, and killed it.

An examination by University of Arizona of the animal's brain proved this coyote had rabies.

From the Superintendent of the San Carlos Indian Agency in Arizona, a vivid account of a rabid coyote attack occurring at that agency on August 8, 1944, adds to the record:

"Yesterday morning (August 8) a short while before daylight, Dr. Bogart, who is in charge of the breeding of the registered herd of cattle, was aroused from sleep by a commotion among his chickens. He went out of his back door to investigate and when he got about 8 feet from the door a coyote came between him and the house. The coyote attacked and bit Dr. Bogart on the thigh but he managed to jerk loose. He took a few steps toward the yard gate and the coyote jumped at his throat. Dr. Bogart instinctively threw up his arm to guard his throat and the coyote grabbed his arm. He threw the coyote to the ground and held it there by the throat until his wife killed it with a rifle. All this time the coyote kept his hold on Dr. Bogart's arm. The coyote was taken to the Laboratory Division of the Arizona State Department of Health and was found to have rabies."

On or about November 19, 1946, District Agent Everett M. Mercer of the Fish and Wildlife Service reported that a coyote suddenly made an appearance near a farm hand who was working on the Webster place in the thickly populated Arcadia district, a few miles northeast of Phoenix, Arizona. The coyote would have attacked the farm hand but was prevented from doing so by the Webster's dog, which happened to be nearby at that instant. In the fight that followed, the coyote bit the dog and then escaped into a citrus grove nearby. A local veterinarian advised the Websters to keep their dog tied and under close observation for a period of at least 3 months. His instructions were complied with, and on February 15, 1947, the dog developed rabies and it was found necessary to kill it. Almost 3 months elapsed from the time the dog was bitten by the rabid coyote until it developed the disease.

The coyote is believed to have been killed on the day that it bit the Webster's dog. On that date, a coyote that appeared to have rabies attacked three boys at a point about 2 miles north of the Webster place. One of the boys killed the coyote with a shovel.

Chapter Five

Economic Status

VALUE OF PELT AND USES

IN THE EARLY part of the 19th century coyote skins were considered to have no value. It was not until the diminution of the beaver that any particular attention was given to coyote skins. This began about 1860 when the take of coyote skins became one of the main objectives of the "wolf poisoner" on the Great Plains. In those times it brought a price of between 75 cents and $1.50 per skin.

The annual take of coyote pelts is in general constantly changing. The fickle dictates of fashion cause a minimum demand for coyote pelts in the fur industry for a season or more and a fall in prices. As a result the trapper of course has no incentive to take it. This relief from trapping pressure is one of the most important factors in coyote increases.

In the early days of the Hudson's Bay Company's fur trading, the pelts of coyotes were generally referred to as "cased wolves," because of the method in which the skin was removed from the animal. Instead of being skinned out "flat" as is the procedure for the large wolves, coyote pelts were removed much as one removes a tight fitting glove from the hand, which is the proper skinning procedure today. After removal, the skins were then turned fur side out and dried on suitable stretchers in a shady but well-ventilated spot. This is as mentioned still the usual method. (See Plate 33.) Then, as now, many skins proved to be what the Hudson Bay fur personnel termed "stagy" skins, i.e., unprime skins, or a skin with dark blue patches on the flesh side of the pelt. Later 20th century fur terminology terms such a pelt as unprime. Prime or unprime skins have therefore replaced the word "stagy" to prime or unprime, as indicating the quality and value of the particular fur.

Coyote skins are now of considerable economic importance in the fur trade, bringing a price in normal times of from $5 to $25

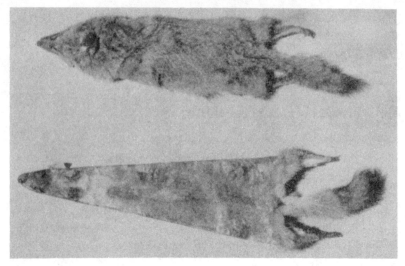

Plate 33. Proper (above) and improper (below) preparation of a coyote pelt.

per pelt, depending on the area where taken. As an example during April of 1925, the price varied from $5 to $15, depending on quality, of the pelt for those taken in the vicinity of Fort Smith, Canada. Some are used in the making of full sized garments, such as ladies' coats and jackets, scarfs or muffs, but probably find their greatest use as trimmings such as coat collars and sleeves for various women's garments. Most coyote fur can be dyed black. In this color it is then made into garments as an imitation of black fox. The aggregate annual raw fur value of coyote pelts approximated more than $1,000,000 prior to World War II. World War II had a pronounced effect on coyote skins as may be noted in the following:

"COYOTES AND THE LUXURY TAX:

"That the 20% luxury tax imposed by the Federal Government on ladies' and other fur trimmed coats has been a contributing cause of the great increase of coyotes and resultant increased loss of livestock and game might at first thought seem unreasonable. Yet, that is just what is happening

"Fur trappers won't trap for coyotes unless there is a profit in it, and certainly there is no profit in trapping when skins are at $1.19, the ridiculously low price received by the Game Department at its last fur sale. That is a great reduction from the normal price of from $5.00 to $10.00, at which price trappers can afford to work. Since low prices have prevailed for 2 years, fur trappers have about quit and the result is that coyotes have greatly increased.

"But where does the ladies' fur trimmed coat come in? It doesn't, it has gone out! Here is how it works: Coyote is classed as long fur, and is used principally for coat trimmings. On the other hand, beaver and muskrat (Hudson Seal) are short furs and used for making nice all-fur coats on which there is also a 20% luxury tax. Anyone who can afford such a coat can usually also afford to pay the tax, and those furs have held up well.

"But the man of moderate means has to be satisfied with a fur-trimmed coat for his wife or daughter, and now when he goes to buy one he hits a real snag. *The rule is that when the cost of the fur trimming equals or exceeds the cost of the fabric material, the entire coat is subject to the 20% luxury tax.* So the average coat buyer does one of two things. If he feels real prosperous he puts a little more with the price of the taxed fur-trimmed coat and buys a southern muskrat coat which costs only a little more. If he is not so prosperous he drops back to the lower price bracket and buys the wife a nice virgin wool coat *without the fur trimming.* Thus both ways the trim is eliminated and the demand for coyote and other long furs has been killed. The trade won't buy the fur-trimmed coat and pay 20% luxury tax on the whole garment because such a coat is a necessity and not a luxury. So the designers are leaving out the fur trimmed garments with the result that tens of thousands of coyote skins bought a year or two ago are stored, waiting for better prices." (*New Mexico Magazine.* From: National Fur News 17 (6): 16, July 1945.)

Coyote skins along with other long-haired furs such as the gray fox, raccoon, etc., were for several years during the recent war subjected to Office of Price Administration controls. These controls were removed on May 28, 1946, "because they have little bearing on the cost of living."

Primeness in the coyote pelt and a condition that brings its highest price in the raw fur market varies considerably within the main habitat of the coyote in North America. Markley (1945) in an examination of 1,513 coyote pelts taken from three geographic regions, viz., Southwestern, Northwestern, and Rocky Mountain States, showed the latter to be of the first in quality of prime skins, the northwestern and southwestern areas coming next in order. With the exception of the southwestern area, coyote prime skins are taken from October to early March. The southwestern area showed a much shorter period for primeness confined mainly to the months of October and November.

Table 7.–Value of Coyote Pelts 1933-1946

Year	December		January		February		March		April	
	Top	Av.	Top	Av.	Top	Av.	Top	Av.	Top	Av.
1946					6.00	1.30	5.50	2.11	6.00	2.54
1945	4.00	1.83	5.50	3.62	6.50	3.40	6.00	3.25	8.00	3.39
1944	16.00	8.66	14.00	4.79	11.00	3.00	14.00	3.85	12.25	3.11
1943	13.25	7.53	15.50	8.70	15.00	7.43	14.75	8.33	17.00	9.09
1942			12.00	6.91	13.00	7.02	12.50	5.41	12.00	5.70
1941	7.40	5.15	10.50	5.85	9.00	4.01	7.25	4.15	8.60	4.05
1940			7.20	3.89			6.50	3.10	5.75	2.62
1939	6.25	4.51	7.00	6.01	7.25	5.09				
1938	9.00	5.80	9.00		11.00	7.05	9.50	5.38	8.00	4.45
1937	15.00	8.25	13.75	9.26	13.50	9.41	13.50	8.20	12.50	8.40
1936	6.25	3.28	7.75	4.51	7.50	4.05	8.50	5.17	8.25	7.47
1935	6.25	3.62	7.25	5.07	8.00	3.48	7.75	4.37	6.75	5.02
1934	9.00	5.36	12.50	7.08	14.75	6.45	11.00	5.83	7.75	5.21
1933			7.00	3.83	7.25	4.51	6.50	3.44	5.00	3.33

According to Juan Ignacio de Armas (1888: 44) gloves were at one time made from coyote skin. At the close of the 19th century, its pelt was commonly used as sleigh robes, and now, occasionally, one may be seen, especially in the West. As such it makes an attractive robe, particularly if pains are taken to match the skins.

North Dakota produces many coyote skins that bring good prices. The average price for the years 1937-1942 inclusive was $7.22.

South Dakota skins have sold in small lots at an average price of $25.

Rand (1940: 36) states "the annual average value per pelt [in the Yukon, Canada] has varied from $5.00 (1939-40) to $17.38 (1927-28)."

For year ending March 31, 1944, 31,028 coyotes taken in Alberta, Canada, brought a total of $507,618.08 or an average of $16.36 per pelt.

For Iowa, a 16-year average 1930-46 was $3.71, the highest price being $10 per pelt in 1943-44 (Anon.: 29).

In the Canadian fur auction sales held at Montreal, Canada, on April 29, 1946, a top price of $16 per skin was given for the best of 1,100 coyotes offered.

On the Seattle fur exchange for the period 1933-1946 the highest average was $9.41 during 1937 (See Table 7).

AS HUMAN FOOD

As dog flesh is still eaten in certain parts of the World, it is apparent the coyote has also contributed to man's larder, especially in the earlier days of our western expansion. There were times when the meat of this creature became the main buffer between starvation and continued existence of individual trappers and mountain men of the old West.

A modern instance of man's attempt to sustain life by eating coyote is to be noted from the following (Anonymous, May 28, 1943):

"Barney Roussan, a Government trapper, was in a critical condition today after being pinioned by fallen rock for six days and nights in a coyote den near Meeteetse [Wyoming].

"Dr. R. C. Trueblood, who termed Mr. Roussan's ordeal 'the most gruesome I've ever heard of,' said the trapper had eaten from one to three coyote pups, raw, before the rescue and had slashed his arm and a rib 'trying to find an artery' after giving up hope of rescue.

"Mr. Roussan, about 40, crawled into the den seeking coyote pups. He was trapped by rock falling on his back and legs.

"A search was started after the man's dog returned to his home carrying Mr. Roussan's cap. The dog would not return with searchers, but two small boys found the hillside den where Mr. Roussan was trapped."

It was used in feasts by some of the plains Indians. Hoffman (1885) mentions the use of young coyotes as food by the Indians that once inhabited the San Gabriel area of Los Angeles County, California.

In taste, this animal is comparable to the meat of the large gray wolf (see Young & Goldman, 1944: 171), though the writer has found that coyote meat cooked by the method recommended for pork becomes more tender.

As with fat taken from wolves in the fall and then rendered, coyote fat was found to make a grease excellent for softening leather. I found it exceptionally good for this purpose on bridle rein particularly used in the hot, dry atmosphere of southern New Mexico and Arizona. Furthermore, this grease after being slightly salted, when lightly spread on bread, in lieu of butter, is just as tasty as ham or bacon fat drippings designated as "Flott" (pronounced in English as Flutt) by the Swedes; the latter was a common article of food in the Swedish home of my youth.

Grease, or lard, when obtainable, was much in the diet of early North American trappers, canoemen, or woodsmen. Often rendered from wild game, including wolves and coyotes, and an ingredient of pemmican, which formed one of the main items of food for expeditions between distant trading posts.

Pemmican originally made mainly from the meat of the bison, shredded and mixed with much fat, and sometimes a native fruit, was a common food used by travelers in the fur country. The disappearance of the bison, made its manufacture harder and created somewhat of a hardship as no other meat could usually be gotten in quantity. Edward A. Preble says: "On my trip with Seton, we had some modern pemmican made from beef. This was very nourishing but Seton himself could not digest it."

The largest quantity of fat ever rendered from one coyote by the author was 3 pounds 2 ounces. This animal was killed near Tennessee Pass, Colorado. The largest amount ever rendered from one coyote coming to my attention was done by U. S. Government Hunter William E. Blanchard, totaling 4 pounds 13 ounces. During World War II this hunter saved quantities of rendered coyote fat, and turned it in for so-called "Red Points." In this way he was enabled to replenish his field larder with certain food items he otherwise was denied.

CROSSING WITH DOGS

Coyotes readily hybridize with dogs, and occasionally some matings have produced offspring that readily serve man. However, hybrids of first crossings are apt to be more mischievous and unmanageable during puppyhood, less trustworthy on maturity than is the case with hybrid wolves. (See Plate 34 a, b.)

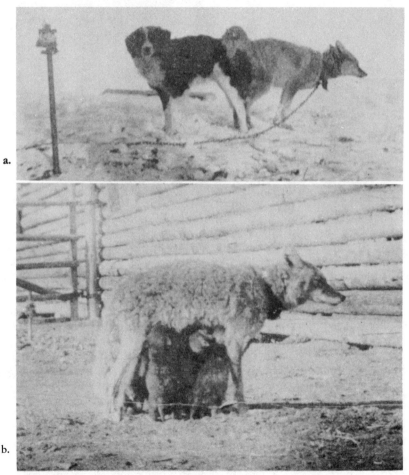

Plate 34. (a) Coyotes readily mate with domestic dogs. (b) Peculiar nursing position mother coyote sometimes assumes with hybrid young.

Plate 35. Coyote-dog hybrids. Wyoming.

Hybrid or full blood coyotes may be confiding, playful with the person who raises them (See Plate 36), but on the first sight of any strangers they become suspicious and timid, though this tendency disappears on further acquaintance. As with wolves, both sexes of coyote dog hybrids remain fertile, and they have been successfully bred through four generations. (See Plate 35.)

J. C. Cronkhite of San Bernardino, California, reported (September 27, 1941), on the mating between a female coyote and a white English bull-dog. Two young were born, one dying when 3 days old, but the other survived as a bottle-fed pup. At the time of the report, it was 4 months old. In appearance it resembled a police dog, was very shy, easily frightened, but made friends readily, barked like the dog, but not often, and was very alert to most everything. The markings of its coat was coyote gray, with white hind feet, white on belly and neck, all hair being short with the exception of fairly long, coarse bristles on the back. (From report in files Fish and Wildlife Service.)

MacFarlane (1905), writing about the wild mammals of northern Canada, says: "Indians have known of instances where both kinds of wolves [meaning one to be the coyote as distinguished from the large gray wolf] and some of their dogs have mated, and they have always found that the resultant offspring were not only prolific, but also better and stronger as beasts of burden."

Plate 36. Minnesota coyote bred to German shepherd dog that later gave birth to four hybrids.

The breeding of a female fox-hound to a 1-year-old male coyote in Montana experiments produced litters of pups that were all fighters though also friendly. Some of the female hybrids showed affection to most anyone after a few days association and care of them. In one instance a female hybrid of the coyote-fox hound cross on maturity became a good trailer of bobcats and coyotes, and was an exceptionally good killer.

O. J. Murie (1936) mated a Colorado female coyote that had been raised in Wyoming with a 40-pound dog taken from St. Lawrence Island, Alaska. Following breeding of this pair in early March, 65 days later, the coyote died while giving birth to a litter of 3 pups consisting of 2 males and 1 female. One male weighed a pound and the other 14 ounces. The female weighed a pound. Dog and coyote characters were well mixed in the foetuses.

Coyote-wolf hybrid.—In the collection of the Royal Ontario Museum at Toronto, Ontario, Canada, are two adult specimens, male and female, nos. 31.9.15.1 and 31.9.15.2 of a supposed coyote-wolf hybrid donated to the museum by the Toronto Parks Department.

According to the late E. C. Cross of the museum staff, these hybrids were successfully born, the result of coyote-wolf breeding in the Riverdale Park of Toronto.

FOOD OF THE COYOTE

Coyotes are almost as deserving of the reputation as scavengers as are the domestic goats. Carrion, lizards, toads, and snakes are frequently food for the species. Its fondness for oil often causes it to chew on leather. This trait was recognized by Francis Parkman (1872: 57), who more than 100 years ago when commenting upon the coyote of the plains that he noted along the Oregon Trail, said of the animal: "He was of the species called the prairie-wolf: a grim-visaged, but harmless little brute, whose worst propensity is creeping among horses and gnawing the ropes of rawhide by which they are picketed around the camp." In one instance a section of harness strap with a 2-inch metal buckle on it was taken from a captured coyote's stomach. The creature evidently had at one time mouthed and chewed this leather to get the oil from it and had eventually swallowed it. The unusual food seemed not to have interfered with the coyote as it was apparent that the buckle had been in the animal's stomach for a long time. Recently, coyotes have been accused of eating the insulation off the field light wires at Palm Springs, California, and thus preventing an airplane landing field from being lighted up.

In food habits coyotes are much like the large wolves except that their diet is more varied. Sheep, calves, pigs, deer, young elk, mountain sheep, grouse, quail, pheasants, nesting wild ducks, turkeys, chickens, meadowlarks, other song birds, fruit and insect-eating birds, beaver, sage chickens and birds' eggs are also frequent items of their bill of fare. They also vary their diet with wild and domestic fruits, and rodents in abundance, such as the prairie dog, pocket gopher, ground squirrel, rabbits, and all the field mice, also many insects such as grasshoppers and beetles.

In the low tropical coast of Mexico and Texas, coyotes have often been observed searching the beach for crabs, fish, and turtle eggs.

Like the large wolves, coyotes will eat human flesh whenever bodies are available. A well-known New Mexican stockman, while in the act of jacking up his car to remove a flat tire on a remote part of his cow range that he was reconnoitering suffered a heart attack, dying immediately. For several days his whereabouts was eagerly sought by his immediate family, and when his body was finally discovered, coyotes had eaten so heartily from the remains that his normal features were badly effaced.

In a less serious or gruesome way, my good friend J. Frank Dobie writes: "Will a coyote eat a dead Mexican (on account of the body being impregnated with chili)? Today I have been settling with evidence from both sides. He will, all right; I got unimpeachable evidence down in Chihuahua about ten years ago. So far as I know, this leaves the coyote's appetite absolutely catholic without a single exception." (Letter from J. Frank Dobie, Austin, Tex., dated May 12, 1947.)

Reliable information on the food of the coyote has been gathered from both the laboratory and field observations. Those of the laboratory are the first in our category.

Food Habits Laboratory

Completing study begun in 1931, Sperry's excellent publication (1941) on the food habits of the coyote, the first comprehensive laboratory study ever conducted and published is quoted in summary as follows:

In 1931 "the Biological Survey started an intensive campaign to collect coyote stomachs and established a research laboratory in Denver, Colorado, to analyze their contents and identify the food items found (Sperry 1933). It is based on the examination of the contents of 14,829 coyote stomachs obtained in all months of the year over the 5-year period 1931-35 in 17 states, including Michigan, Wisconsin, Missouri, and all the Western States except Oklahoma, Kansas, and North Dakota. Most of the stomachs were collected by the Survey's own field-men, but some were obtained from other sources, especially from the Michigan State Game Commission and the National Park Service.

"Special effort was made to get as complete a record as possible for each stomach. This comprised not only the locality and date of its collection but also the sex and approximate age of the coyote, the method of capture, including kind of bait or station used, and a comment on the immediate environment, such as 'sheep range,' 'cattle country,' 'grouse plentiful,' and 'deer common.'

"Analyses of the stomachs were made in the Denver laboratory of the Section of Food Habits of the Division of Wildlife Research. Of the 14,829 stomachs examined, 2,025 were empty, 4,368 contained debris only, and 97 were from pups that were still feeding on milk alone. This left 8,339 stomachs on which to base an appraisal of the coyote diet. All of these were used in figuring the frequency of occurrence percentages of food items but 76 of them, being nearly empty, were unfit for tabulation of volumetric percentages, which are based, therefore, on the analyses of 8,263 stomachs.

"The distribution, geographic and monthly, of the 8,339 stomachs is shown in the accompanying list. Such a good distribution for each month insures that the unusual or infrequent items of diet will be relegated to their proper position of minor importance in the total food.

Distribution of 8,339 Coyote Stomachs[1]

Geographic			Monthly		
Arizona	513	(513)	Spring, 1,224 (1,237):		
California	863	(856)	March	329	(327)
Colorado	1,101	(1,082)	April	319	(316)
Idaho	213	(208)	May	596	(594)
Michigan	88	(85)	Summer, 1,641 (1,626):		
Missouri	6	(5)	June	419	(418)
Montana	626	(623)	July	448	(445)
Nebraska	70	(69)	August	774	(763)
Nevada	145	(145)	Fall, 3,229 (3,184):		
New Mexico	1,088	(1,084)	September	975	(956)
Oregon	671	(667)	October	1,223	(1,207)
South Dakota	97	(96)	November	1,031	(1,021)
Texas	569	(566)	Winter, 2,225 (2,216):		
Utah	178	(176)	December	916	(914)
Washington	1,186	(1,179)	January	789	(785)
Wisconsin	7	(6)	February	520	(517)
Wyoming	918	(903)			
Total	8,339	(8,263)	Total	8,339	(8,263)

[1] All 8,339 stomachs were used in computing occurrence percentages; the numbers shown in parentheses totaling 8,263, are the stomachs full enough to be used in figuring volumetric food percentages.

Technique

"In amassing basic data for answering food-habits questions, the Biological Survey technique of stomach analysis assures the most complete record obtainable for each stomach. First the examiner records whether the stomach was full, partly full, or nearly empty; next he notes the nature and bulk of all nonfood items, such as dirt, gravel, and trap debris, which he sets aside; and then he analyzes food material alone, computed on the basis of 100 percent for its total bulk. Record is made of each food item identified, the number of times it occurs, and the percentage it contributes by bulk toward the whole meal. As a final precaution for accuracy, all the food items are saved and stored for ready future reference in case identifications are questioned.

"The abundance of material available throughout the year permitted the computing of bulk percentages for each of the 12 months with reasonable accuracy; and from these figures a monthly average, or year-round percentage, was obtained (See Table 8.) When, however, attempt was made to appraise the material from individual States, which is done at various points in the text, the limited number of stomachs involved in some groupings and the resultant distortions arising from insufficient data suggested the unreliability of the above procedure. In such instances calculation of percentages directly from the total stomach material available from the State without first computing monthly percentages seemed advisable. In the first method mentioned the average percentages for the several food items for each of the months became the basis for computing the yearly appraisal; in the second, the percentages for each stomach analysis were similarly used. Tabulations showed that the two methods produced approximately the same average annual percentages (See Table 9). Consequently, in figuring bulk percentages for comparing the data assembled from the different States, in order to use all available material and to give each State the greatest representation possible, the stomach was made the basic unit.

"The coyotes examined were primarily carnivorous at all times. During the first 4 months of the year they fed almost exclusively on flesh and even in August and September, when fruits and berries are most available, made animal food 96 percent of the diet.

Mammals

"The coyotes depended on mammals for more than nine-tenths of their sustenance. This mammalian food was extremely varied. . . ."

Abstracting from the complete analysis it was found that:

"Rabbits took first place in the diet throughout the year, except in mid-winter, when they were outranked by carrion. Present in 43 percent of the stomachs, they were outstanding in the coyotes' food in each of the 17 States represented. Immature rabbits were prominent in the diet of young coyotes fed by the adults.

TABLE 8.—Percentages by Volume of the Food Items Found in 8,263 Coyote Stomachs[1]

Item	January	February	March	April	May	June	July	August	September	October	November	December	Total or average
Stomachs used	785	517	327	316	594	418	445	763	956	1,207	1,021	914	8,263
	Percent	Percent	Percent	Percent	Percent	Percent	Percent	Percent	Percent	Percent	Percent	Percent	Percent
ANIMAL FOOD													
Mammals:													
Rabbits	36	34	39	41	45	35	25	28	27	29	30	30	33.25
Carrion:													
Station[2]	29	24	14	4	3	2	6	7	5	9	16	25	12.00
Other	8	11	15	16	8	12	10	13	18	18	17	12	13.17
Rodents	12	14	14	19	20	22	25	20	21	16	13	13	17.52
Domestic livestock:													
Sheep-goat	9	7	10	11	16	17	16	16	14	14	13	11	12.92
Calf-colt-pig	1	1	1	[3]	[3]	2	[3]	1	[3]	1	1	[3]	.67
Deer	2	6	4	3	2	4	5	4	3	4	3	3	3.58
Other mammals	[3]	[3]	1	2	1	1	2	2	2	2	1	1	1.06
Birds:													
Poultry	1	1	[3]	1	[3]	[3]	2	[3]	1	1	1	1	.75
Game birds:													
Upland	1	1	[3]	1	2	1	[3]	1	1	[3]	1	1	.92
Aquatic	[3]	[3]			[3]	[3]		[3]	[3]	[3]	[3]	[3]	
Nongame birds	1	1	1	1	1	1	3	2	1	1	1	1	1.25
Other vertebrates:													
Reptiles	[3]	[3]	[3]	[3]	[3]	[3]	[3]	[3]	1	[3]	[3]	[3]	.08
Amphibians	[3]						[3]		[3]		[3]		[3]
Fishes	[3]								[3]	[3]			[3]
Invertebrates:													
Insects	[3]	[3]	1	1	1	1	3	2	2	1	1	[3]	1.08
Other invertebrates	[3]	[3]		[3]	[3]	[3]	[3]	[3]	[3]	[3]	[3]	[3]	[3]
Total	100	100	100	100	99	98	97	96	96	97	98	98	98.25
VEGETABLE FOOD													
Cultivated fruit	[3]	[3]	[3]		[3]	[3]	[3]	[3]	1	1	1	1	.33
Wild fruit	[3]	[3]		[3]	1	1	3	4	3	2	1	1	1.30
Other vegetable matter	[3]	[3]	[3]	[3]	[3]	1	[3]	[3]	[3]	[3]	[3]	[3]	.12
Total	[3]	[3]	[3]	[3]	1	2	3	4	4	3	2	2	1.75

[1] In addition, 76 stomachs examined contained too little food for accurate estimate of volumetric percentages.

[2] For explanation of term see p 129.

[3] Trace.

"Carrion, the second most important food, was derived chiefly from the remains of horses, cows, coyotes, and sheep. Remains of prairie dogs, rabbits, porcupines, and other smaller animals also were classed as carrion when found in the stomachs of coyotes taken in traps [or poison stations] baited with such carcasses. The coyotes ate twice as much carrion in winter as in summer.

"Rodents occurred in one-third of the stomachs. Prominent among these were meadow mice, wood rats, cotton rats, ground squirrels, marmots, pocket mice, kangaroo rats, pocket gophers, and porcupines.

"Domestic livestock, found in one-fifth of the stomachs, was composed mainly of sheep and goat remains. Sheep losses to coyotes varied greatly in different States, but two seasonal peaks were apparent—one during the lambing season and the other just after sheep movement onto winter feeding grounds. Calf, colt, and pig remains were infrequently found.

"Big-game mammals in the diet comprised antelope, bear, bison, elk, bighorn sheep, and deer, but only the last-named (3.58 percent) is discussed in detail. It is believed that part of

TABLE 9.—Yearly Percentages, by Volume, of the Food Items Found in 8,263 Coyote Stomachs, as Obtained by Two Methods of Computation Using Different Basic Units

Food item	Basic unit Month	Stomach	Food item	Basic unit Month	Stomach
Animal Food			Animal Food—Con't.		
Mammals:	*Percent*	*Percent*	Other vertebrates—Con't.	*Percent*	*Percent*
Rabbits	33.0	32.0	Amphibians ....(1)	(1)	
Carrion:			Fishes ....(1)	(1)	
Station	12.0	13.0	Invertebrates:		
Other	13.0	13.0	Insects	1.0	1.0
Rodents	17.5	17.5	Others ....(1)	(1)	
Domestic livestock:				———	———
Sheep-goat	13.0	13.0	Total	98.0	98.0
Calf-goat-pig ..	1.0	1.0		———	———
Deer	3.5	3.5	Vegetable Food:		
Miscellaneous ...	1.0	1.0	Cultivated fruit	.5	.5
Birds:			Wild fruit	1.5	1.0
Poultry	1.0	1.0	Other vegetable matter (1)		.5
Game Birds:				———	———
Upland	1.0	1.0	Total	2.0	2.0
Aquatic ......(1)	(1)			———	———
Nongame birds ..	1.0	1.0	Total food	100.0	100.0
Other vertebrates:					
Reptiles ....(1)	(1)				

[1] Trace.

the deer remains may have been carrion. Many cases of coyotes killing deer are cited.

"Birds eaten were represented about equally by poultry, game birds, and nongame birds. The poultry consisted chiefly of chickens but included a number of turkeys and a few other fowls. The game birds were mainly upland species, grouse especially. The list of nongame bird victims was long and varied. Sparrows, meadowlarks, and magpies predominated: eggs and nestlings were rarely included.

"Invertebrates found in the stomachs were mostly insects, chiefly grasshoppers and beetles taken in summer and early fall. Occasionally a few spiders, centipedes, and crawfishes were eaten.

"Other animal matter frequently taken included skunks, weasels, shrews, moles, snakes, and lizards.

"Vegetable food consisted primarily of fruit, including both cultivated and wild varieties. The latter predominated. Grass was a frequent item in the June stomachs.

"Worms were noted in 2 percent of the stomachs. Tapeworms were rare; those found were all of the genus *Taenia*. Roundworms were represented by six genera.

"The coyotes' consumption of rabbits, rodents, carrion, insects, vegetable matter (in most cases), and miscellaneous mammals, which aggregated 80 percent of the diet, may be construed as not inimical to human interests or may even be considered beneficial; whereas their consumption of domestic livestock, poultry, deer, and wild birds, totaling 20 percent of the food, is indicative of loss and reveals the serious economic importance of the coyote.

"Within the last 12 years the coyote, whose extensive range was restricted in pre-colonial times to the open or partly open country of the West, has appeared for the first time so far as known in 13 Eastern States, so that unless checked it seems likely that it will become established throughout the East."

Food Habits—Field

Field examination of coyote stomachs were made soon after the cooperative predatory animal work of the Bureau of Biological Survey began in 1915. All hunters in its employ or under its supervision were required to examine the contents of animals taken and to report their findings to the Bureau. As summarized by Henderson (1930: 336-350), in which the author aided extensively in the compilation of this summary the findings which also took into consideration Dixon's work is recorded as follows:

"This study continued for more than 10 years and involved

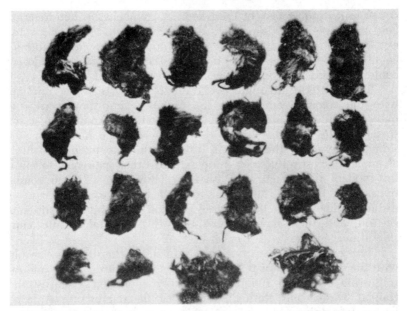

Plate 37. Remains of 20 meadow mice and 1 song sparrow taken from Oregon coyote's stomach killed in September.

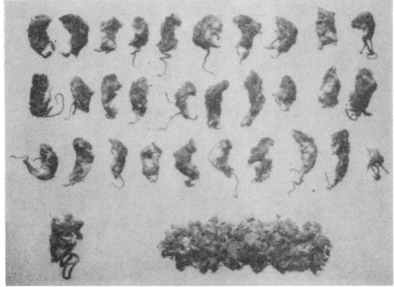

Plate 38. Remains of 30 pocket mice and 1 kangaroo rat from stomach of a California coyote killed in November.

the examination of tens of thousands of stomachs by hundreds of field men operating throughout the entire West. Many stomachs, especially of animals trapped, were found to be empty, others contained material that could not be determined, but the majority contained food material that was readily identified.

"The hunters, although not trained scientists, were familiar with the common animals of the region where they were employed. While not always able, perhaps, to determine the exact species of the animal the flesh of which was found in the coyote's stomach, generally they had no difficulty in recognizing the flesh of game, domestic livestock, rodents, and other mammals forming the food of the predators. With their knowledge of local conditions, they had one advantage over a laboratory worker at a distance: They were in a better position to recognize bait and carrion, and their reports show that this was taken into consideration.

"The examination of a coyote stomach is hardly comparable with the examination of the stomach of a small bird, where minute fragments are often found that can be identified even by the trained worker only through the use of the microscope. A large flesh-eating animal like the coyote bolts its food, and large pieces

Plate 39. Twenty-two quail eggs that had been gulped by a Texas coyote in May.

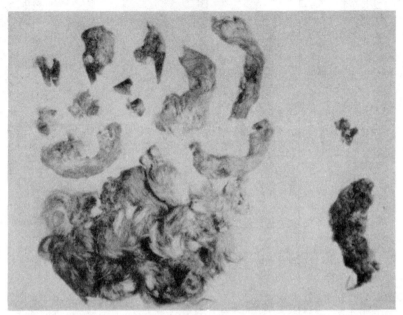

Plate 40. Deer fawn left, some mouse hair, pieces of quail egg, and a pocket gopher right hand corner eaten by California coyote in June.

of flesh, often with pieces of skin or with the head or feet of small animals attached, are found and can easily be recognized in the field. (See Plates 37, 38, 39, 40.)

"The value of a field examination of the food of predatory animals was fully recognized by Mr. Joseph S. Dixon, who, some years ago, conducted a study of the food habits of some of the predators of California. In the study of the coyote, he was assisted by field examinations conducted by 39 trappers, who were taking animals in various parts of the State. In defending the results of their findings, in an article published in the February, 1925, issue of the Journal of Mammalogy (vol. 6, no. 1, p. 37) he stated as follows:

" 'My laboratory work has been checked against the examinations made by trappers in the field and the two coincide quite closely. If all the stomachs were examined by one man, it might be claimed that he was prejudiced for or against fur-bearers. However, where there are 40 or 50 men distributed over a large State, each working entirely independently of the others and all get similar results, we can not well doubt the significance of their findings, especially when the trapper's findings check so closely with examinations made in the laboratory.'

TABLE 10.—Record of About 30,000 Coyote Stomach Examinations Made by Biological Survey Hunters 1919-1923.

Food	January	February	March	April	May	June	July	August	September	October	November	December	Total
Beef	290	195	122	122	157	152	167	229	257	337	278	211	2,517
Horse	228	181	146	90	80	48	46	55	103	142	184	197	1,500.
Sheep or goat	411	275	243	345	769	664	741	806	851	842	636	363	6,946
Pork	12	12	16	5	24	5	11	29	21	19	30	25	209
Poultry	46	41	21	38	86	91	141	224	221	189	143	65	1,306
Grouse	50	26	31	33	109	159	188	222	177	154	59	60	1,268
Waterfowl	2	1	1	4	4	39	3	7	14	9	6	4	94
Other birds	60	28	48	31	38	43	133	157	94	79	62	32	805
Deer	32	49	19	41	39	25	40	35	18	51	34	16	399
Elk	1	3	0	4	2	1	0	0	0	3	5	1	20
Antelope	3	16	0	1	3	2	4	1	1	2	4	3	40
Rabbit	674	424	290	302	554	484	587	989	1,146	1,179	723	577	7,929
Ground squirrels	6	9	49	93	189	229	218	218	59	44	28	6	1,148
Prairie dog	3	13	9	18	36	66	103	114	101	77	24	20	584
Chipmunk	1	3	4	2	1	2	11	17	15	7	1	0	65
Groundhog (marmot)	0	0	1	6	14	11	13	15	4	0	0	0	64
Mouse or rat	102	77	35	63	88	74	82	191	250	233	118	114	1,427
Bait	955	752	502	365	171	96	169	235	441	398	484	725	5,293
Carrion	195	193	175	102	154	132	145	253	248	347	234	179	2,357
Insects or worms	3	0	1	30	6	37	115	231	185	40	16	5	669
Fish, frogs, reptiles	3	1	1	3	10	22	21	44	19	6	5	3	138
Grass, sticks or berries	93	51	38	83	105	126	240	378	468	349	165	115	2,211
Totals	3,170	2,350	1,752	1,781	2,639	2,508	3,178	4,450	4,693	4,507	3,239	2,722	36,989

"His reasoning is sound. If, therefore, the results of the extensive field examinations conducted by the employees of the Biological Survey are similar to those obtained by Mr. Dixon in his study of the coyote, we must conclude that the investigations carried on by the Biological Survey were made with reasonable care and that they can not be disregarded. A summary of the results obtained by the Biological Survey for the five years ending 1923 is shown in Table 10. This covers approximately the same period during which Mr. Dixon conducted his work in California. It will be noted from an examination of this table that horse meat, which was very generally used as bait material, is reported separately; also, that a large number of items were reported as bait or carrion.

"In figure 13 is shown graphically the result of this 5-year study. It will be noted that the flesh of rodents constituted the largest single item of food found by the Biological Survey hunters

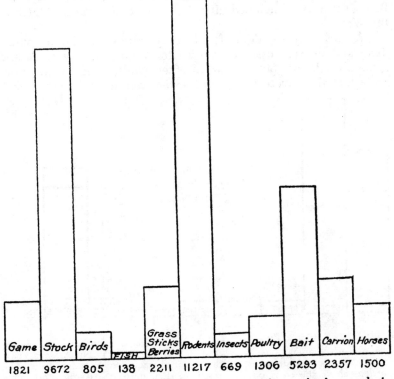

Figure 13. Record of about 30,000 coyote stomach examinations made by Biological Survey hunters 1918-1923.

in the stomachs of the coyotes taken. It will be noted also that the aggregate of domestic livestock, poultry, and game exceeds the rodent item. Mr. Dixon, in his article above referred to, published a graph showing the results of his investigation. He did not show separate items of bait, carrion, and horse meat, but rejected a percentage of each of the principal items of food to allow for bait and carrion.

"There is presented also a graph (See Fig. 14) that was prepared by Mr. Dixon, and also a graph (See Fig. 15) prepared in the same manner showing the results of the five-year study by the Biological Survey. In the Bureau's graph, bait, carrion, and horse meat have been added to the item of domestic livestock, and a reduction in this item and in the other principal items has been made, using the same percentage as that employed by Mr. Dixon. The close similarity of the net results shown by the two graphs is apparent. Closer results could hardly be expected, bearing in mind that Mr. Dixon's study was confined to one State, while that of the Biological Survey included all the principal stock-raisng States of the West.

"In each case the flesh of rodents constitutes the largest single item; and in each case the aggregate of domestic livestock and game exceeds the rodent item. In other words, both investigations show that the coyote feeds more extensively upon domestic live-

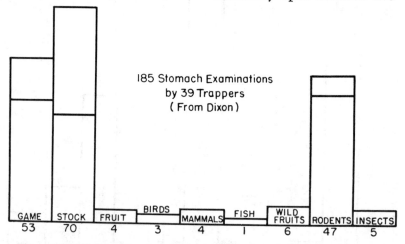

Figure 14. Diagram showing food of the coyote. One hundred and eighty-five stomach examinations by 39 trappers (from Dixon). Numerals at base indicate number of stomachs which contained game, stock and rodents. The portions above the cross lines represent carrion, thus one-half the stock, one-fourth the game and one-eighth of the rodents eaten were not killed by the coyote.

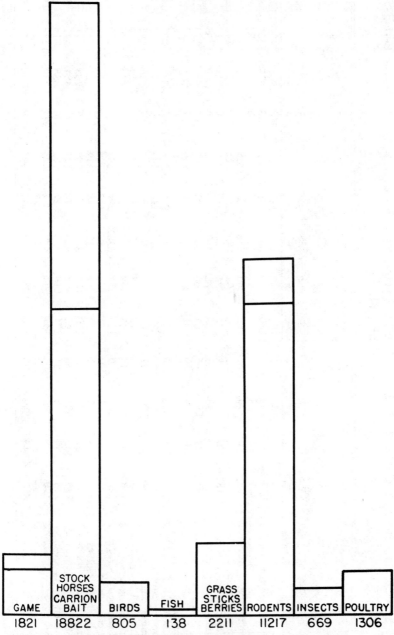

Figure 15. About 30,000 stomach examinations 1919-1923 (Government hunters).

TABLE 11.—Stomach Contents of About 50,000 Coyotes, From Field Reports. Five-Year Period—1924-1928 (Inclusive)

Food	January	February	March	April	May	June	July	August	September	October	November	December	Total
Beef	216	242	162	151	208	132	101	127	209	236	261	194	2,239
Sheep or goat	524	351	455	477	1,130	950	697	992	1,059	1,098	825	521	9,079
Pork	41	14	18	19	27	11	26	23	61	55	44	32	371
Poultry	94	75	76	66	262	250	252	385	428	415	264	138	2,705
Grouse, quail	148	146	133	123	218	404	275	334	268	219	156	147	2,571
Waterfowl	13	2	4	2	20	24	14	15	3	16	13	10	136
Other birds	44	49	43	38	79	88	140	150	93	104	99	55	982
Deer	97	129	86	95	65	63	52	85	97	165	152	123	1,209
Elk	9	9	14	16	1	0	0	2	0	7	1	13	72
Antelope	3	2	10	5	3	34	3	8	0	9	3	4	84
Rabbit	1,069	774	648	540	1,223	1,043	715	977	1,276	1,524	1,381	971	12,141
Ground squirrel	44	37	82	148	278	296	244	214	144	115	77	57	1,736
Prairie dog	4	11	20	31	32	44	66	80	87	67	46	23	511
Chipmunk	0	3	7	6	16	8	7	13	14	12	10	4	100
Groundhog	0	1	9	14	45	98	59	38	15	1	0	6	286
Mouse or rat	222	180	151	140	126	111	119	292	344	410	301	219	2,605
Insects, worms	2	1	3	0	21	28	85	197	130	54	18	3	542
Fish, frogs, reptiles	6	3	3	1	9	7	19	19	12	12	23	2	116
Grass, sticks, berries	92	61	70	120	119	154	252	586	662	618	263	141	3,138
Horse	528	405	301	150	42	48	33	76	121	351	484	471	3,010
Carrion	248	296	333	231	304	219	323	317	361	540	388	314	3,874
Bait	2,179	1,854	1,221	405	147	71	122	317	521	994	1,720	2,112	11,663
Total	5,583	4,645	3,849	2,778	4,365	4,083	3,604	5,247	5,905	7,022	6,529	5,560	59,170

stock and game than upon rodents. A summary of the results of the examinations of coyote stomachs obtained by the Biological Survey for the five-year period 1924-28, inclusive, is shown in Table 11.

"The actual economic status of the coyote, however, is not fully shown by the results of the Bureau's investigations inasmuch as coyotes are sometimes taken in regions where no livestock is found at that time of the year. It is the practice of the Biological Survey to conduct control operations on certain ranges when no livestock is present, in order that these areas may be relatively free of predatory animals when a little later the livestock are moved upon them. Consequently, the fact that the coyote has been feeding upon rodents does not necessarily indicate a preference for this variety of food. Moreover not all the rodents destroyed by coyotes are harmful. It should also be borne in mind that coyotes frequently kill animals that are not eaten. This trait, of course, can not be revealed by a stomach examination."

A recent series of observations made by Munro (1947: 120-123) in central British Columbia supports the statement that no matter where the coyote occurs its food habits are much the same. The comments made by Munro are worthy of quoting as a final closure to all of the foregoing for it adds to the Canadian findings which up to this writing are all very scanty in the literature.

Says Munro:

"In central British Columbia, as elsewhere, the [coyote] population fluctuates in numbers and there is reason to believe the fluctuations are cyclic. . . . Martin Shafer told me that coyotes are less common on the Salmon and Muskeg Rivers than in regions to the south. He reported finding evidence of one being killed and eaten by wolves and expressed the opinion that where wolves invade a district which is occupied by coyotes the latter are driven out.

"Direct observation of the coyote's feeding habits seldom was possible. One animal seen in a wet meadow on the outskirts of Quesnel was obviously hunting mice; another, observed in an open stretch of territory between a fringe of aspen woods and a sedge marsh at Goose Lake, was thought to be similarly engaged. Other observations of coyotes were limited to momentary glimpses of the animals as they disappeared into cover.

"A farmer at Dragon Lake reported the loss of three lambs, another the loss of five lambs, from coyote predation—on evidence which seemed conclusive. Many such losses are reported but not always is the predator identified with certainty.

"Only one instance of predation on birds was oberved, the prey being an adult male ruffed grouse that had been eaten at the edge of a wood road near Goose Lake.

"The study of tracks beside the dried-up carcasses of cattle, which had died in winter or early spring, showed that these were still being visited in midsummer.

"On the alplands of Rocher Deboule hoary marmots were numerous but there was no indication that coyotes had been attracted to this food; no coyotes were seen and only a single scat, an old one, was found there. Coyote pressure on hoary marmots in other mountain areas of the Province sometimes is excessive.
. . . . .

"Some information on food habits was obtained from analyzing the composition of 62 scats of which 43 were fresh, or fairly recent, while the remainder had been deposited in the winter months. The majority was composed of a single item, or a single item represented 70 to 75 percent of the total bulk. Many contained large amounts of clay, probably eaten for its mineral content, others pine needles or harsh forms of grass.

"Because the necessary equipment was lacking it was not possible in every instance to make exact determinations and volumetric percentages were only roughly estimated. The results of the examination are summarized as follows:

"*Domestic sheep:* One scat from Rocher Deboule contained a small amount of sheep's wool. There are no sheep on this mountain so this item must have been eaten elsewhere, probably in the valley below.

"*Snowshoe rabbit:* This was the sole or chief item in each of 15 winter and 21 summer scats from the Baker Creek Valley, and constituted 40 and 50 per cent respectively of the total material in two others. In one instance a rabbit's ear and in another a rabbit's foot had been passed nearly intact. At Bouchie Lake rabbit was represented in amounts ranging from 25 to 75 per cent in each of five scats examined. It formed the chief item in two from Sixteen Mile Lake and the sole constituent in another from Summit Lake. Number of occurrences—49.

"*Meadow voles:* Fur and bones of unidentified microtines formed 30 per cent of the material in each of two scats and 50 per cent of another. Two of these were from Baker Creek Valley, the third from Bouchie Lake. Number of occurrences—3.

"*Porcupine:* Porcupine hair was the sole item in one scat from Baker Creek Valley.

"*Birds:* One scat from Bulkley Lake was composed largely of grebe feathers and bones. This was the only specimen that contained bird remains.

"*Grasshoppers:* One scat from Bouchie Lake contained grasshopper fragments to the extent of 10 per cent; in another from Bulkley Lake this item represented 15 per cent of the total.

"*Blueberries:* Seeds of blueberries *Vaccinium* sp. composed 20 per cent of the total bulk of one scat from Ootsa Lake and undigested blueberries formed the chief item in three from Baker Creek Valley. Number of occurrences—4.

"*Pine needles:* Present in small amounts in eight scats from Baker Creek Valley.

"*Spruce needles:* Present in one specimen from Ootsa Lake.

"*Miscellaneous vegetation:* Vegetable matter in small amounts, and not further identified, formed a small part of six scats; coarse sedge was the chief constituent of a scat from Rocher Deboule, and one from Baker Creek Valley contained material that seemed to be dried moose dung.

"*Clay:* Clay and earth of different types was a constituent in each of 16 scats from Baker Creek Valley, in three from Bouchie Lake and in one from Bulkley Lake. In seven this material represented 50 to 70 per cent of the total bulk of each scat. Number of occurrences—20.

"In central British Columbia, as elsewhere, the coyote is omnivorous in its feeding habits, taking whatever animal food, alive or dead, is easily come by, and eating also a large amount of vegetable matter. In the Baker Creek Valley, the place represented by the largest number of scats, rabbit occurred in all but eight of the 49 specimens examined. Undoubtedly in that locality rabbit was the chief food eaten by coyotes during a period of at least six months prior to May, 1944."

AS A SEED CARRIER

Many mammals, wild and domestic, and birds are accredited with the carrying of seeds hither and yon. In some instances this assumes considerable proportions. A striking example is that concerned with domestic sheep with regard to reforestation and the spread of juniper to be noticed in the last several decades between Ash Fork and Prescott, Arizona, on both sides of the Santa Fe Railroad right of way.

Observations tend to show that the coyote often carries the seed of the cocklebur entangled in the guard hairs as noticed at times in pelts removed from coyotes in South Park, Colorado, an area over 9,000 feet in elevation. Apparently these coyotes had migrated from the lower reaches of the Arkansas River Valley where the cocklebur grows in profusion at different places.

On the Apishapa River near Thatcher, Colorado, a decomposing body of a coyote long dead from causes unknown was found to have nearly a quart of cocklebur in the hair. The seed in this instance was in an area containing suitable tilth, where it undoubtedly would make reproduction a certainty.

Occasionally the seeds of fox-tail grass will be found in the pelt, and also the ears, and it is probable the coyote does assist at times in the spread of this noxious weed.

In the pelts of coyotes removed from the animal in parts of the arid Southwest, the joint of the cholla cactus has been observed entangled, as with the cocklebur. The supposition is that the cholla joint became embedded in the guard hairs during the coyote's attempt to obtain pack rats as prey whose nests were located under this cactus. In so doing the joint was severed, and the many barbs adhering to it served a ready set of hooks for firm embedment in the guard hairs. Severe festering often takes place in the animal's skin from the cactus spines, similar to that caused by porcupine quills, but the cholla joint may be carried a long way before it is finally shaken off. This cactus reproduces itself in two ways: from seed and the "joint," so there is reason to suspect many cholla cactus of our arid Southwest has been planted not by the "hand of man," but by the "body of the coyote." Especially so, when one considers the long period coyotes have contended with the protective features of a cholla cactus under which pack rat, one of its favorite prey, makes its home.

EATING OF FRUIT

District Agent Harold E. Haecker, of the California district, reports (September 1944) that melon growers in that state are experiencing heavy losses because of coyote depredations. Mr. George Satire, a melon grower of Imperial County, recently reported that coyotes were destroying a good share of his 200 acres of melons. Investigation disclosed that 1,500 pounds of melons, which were about to turn pink, had been destroyed in about one week. These would have supplied a May market at 5½ cents a pound.

Coyotes are also fond of peaches, apricots, grapes, plums and cherries. They also eat juniper berries, manzanita berries, and the fruit of the prickly pear (Opuntia). The animal is very fond also of mesquite beans, the fruit of the well known bush of the southwestern deserts.

COYOTE-DEER RELATIONSHIP

Within certain areas, including some of the national forests of the West, coyotes become a factor in problems concerned with deer management. This, coupled with other factors in attempts to overcome or reduce over-grazing, woods burning whether by lightning or man made, often bring about need for coyote control.

In a 5-year study of coyote-deer relationship carried on in the Los Padres National Forest, Santa Barbara County, California, as well as in Madera and Fresno Counties of that state E. E. Horn (1941) summarized the finding as follows:

"Study of scats and stomachs from Santa Barbara County . . . showed that deer constituted a large part of the diet of coyotes. Removal of these predators from 160 square miles has been fol-

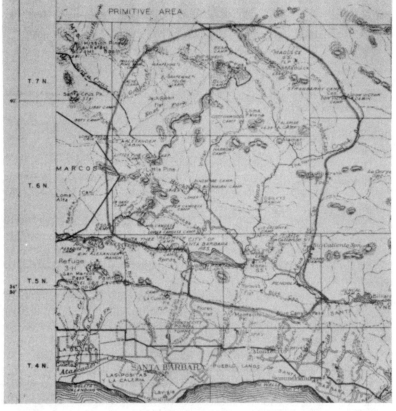

Figure 16. The Mona Basin and Los Padres National Forest, California, where coyote-deer study led by Everett E. Horn was conducted.

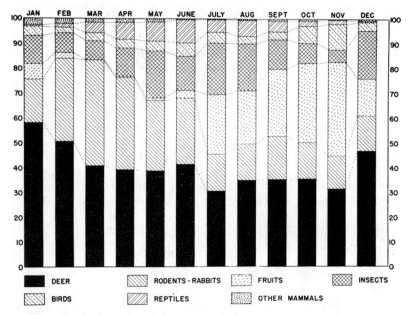

Figure 17. Graph showing findings of analyses of 6,700 coyote scats, Mona Basin, Los Padres National Forest, California.

lowed by increased survival of fawns, and by a decrease in rabbits and rodents.

"Coyotes in the foothills of Madera and Fresno Counties feed principally on squirrels and other rodents. Deer are not present. Rodents and rabbits decreased after removal of coyotes, and some species are again increasing.

"These studies indicate that coyotes play a measurable part in regulating the numbers of deer, but do not control the rodent-rabbit population. (See Figs. 16, 17.)

"Increased research on specific ecological units is essential to develop management plans that include predator control."

Horn's study, a cooperative project between the then Biological Survey, Forest Service, and later the California Division of Fish and Game, was conducted within Mono Basin of the Los Padres National Forest, formerly the Santa Barbara National Forest, California, beginning in January of 1937 and continuing to near the start of World War II. What probably was the largest coyote scat study to date (totaling 6,700) were gathered and analyzed from collecting stations established at selected spots. Before the collecting began at these stations all old scats were destroyed, so that each collecting spot was free from any previous old feces. A total of 10 men served under Horn during the study. Throughout the area nearly all forms of normal food prey of the coyote other than deer were present. War conditions during the last 2 years of the project necessitated cessation of further scat collecting, and instead study was directed to deer census and coyote trapping in addition to study of deer habitat.

In an attempt to restore deer herds in Duval County, Texas, from 1941-1946, two restoration areas approximating 67,000 and 92,000 acres were established. On these areas, a combination of closed season for 5 years, cooperation with the various oil com-

Plate 41. Remains of deer killed by coyotes on deer range of Oregon and Washington.

panies, doubling of the warden forces, conservation teaching in the public schools together with predator control to the extent of removing a total of 4,142 predators, of which 3,851 were coyotes, showed a tentative increase of 357 percent in the deer at the end of a 4-year period. In restocking the area at the beginning of the restoration attempt a total of 190 bucks and 313 does were released to supplement the 2,000 deer estimated for the entire county.

In his volume "Our Wilderness Neighbors" Yeager (1931) describes the animals of Yellowstone National Park. Accounts of the various predatory animals are included. Concerning the coyote he says: "The most dreaded enemy of the deer within the park is the coyote. The toll taken by coyotes is tremendous, especially when the snow is deep and a crust permits their walking over it. One of the Assistant Chief Rangers tells me that on a single day's patrol along the Yellowstone in 1926 he counted thirty-six deer which had been dragged down by these predatory animals." Yeager continues (p. 154) "We of the Yellowstone see the coyote in all of his 'Dr. Jekyll and Mr. Hyde' existence. As a ruthless, cunning killer, as a tame pet, following his master about like a collie, and as a wilderness animal, singing to the moon from some high ridge, for the pure joy of being alive.

"After looking at all of these angles of his varied career, we must condemn him as a murderer, yet we can not fail to appreciate his keenness and his clever side . . ." (See Plate 41.)

RELATIONSHIP TO ANTELOPE

A favorite prey of the coyote is the antelope. Coyotes working in pairs have often been observed striking down an adult buck, which often accounts for a large number of bucks killed. Buck antelope will stop to fight a coyote but while doing so, another will heel the antelope and eventually pull him down. Doe antelope seldom do this, preferring to take flight and outdistance attacking coyotes.

Chapman (1946: 23) records as follows an attack of 4 coyotes on 20 antelope as the latter attempted to cross the ice on Saskatchewan River in southern Alberta: "The antelope were strung out in single file and the last one was 50 yards off shore when the coyotes (which had been watching from the cover of bushes along the shore) broke from the screening bushes and padded swiftly across the ice.

"The patriarch of the herd, a big prong-horned buck, saw the attackers coming. He whistled a warning and whirled, then braced his feet and shook his head angrily. The rest of the antelope fled.

"The coyotes had no stomach for the buck's sharp horns. They plunged past him to where the does and fawns were slipping and falling in mad haste to escape. Here they leaped gleefully upon one of the prostrate ones and killed it quickly. Again the coyotes gave chase and another antelope died before the terrified survivors could reach the opposite shore. Then the killers began their feast.

"It happens every fall when the antelope herds migrate across the Saskatchewan. The coyotes, unable to run down the fleet-footed animals in an even chase, and unwilling to face combat use this clever trick to outwit the antelope."

The devastating effect that coyotes may have on antelope was illustrated during an attempt made to establish this animal on the National Bison Range near Moiese, Montana, during 1921. In the winter of 1921-22 from a herd of 60 it was reduced to 17. During this interval, when the range was covered with snow, coyotes drove the antelope into drifts from which they could not escape, and killed by far the larger part of the herd, an unprecedented previous loss for any refuge.

Relative to the antelope in Yellowstone Park, Yeager (1931: 85) states: "The greatest menace to the antelope in Yellowtone Park is the coyote—whatever may be said in his favor, a great deal may be said in his disfavor as far as the antelope are concerned.

No more striking come-back in numbers of antelopes is better illustrated than that area embraced where Oregon, California, and Nevada join, when by 1920 antelope herds had dwindled

Plate 42. Antelope killed by coyotes, Nevada.

to an estimated population of 1,000. Under protection and the elimination of 7,500 predators between 1915-34, 90 percent of which were coyotes, a "combination of protection and predator control" was "demonstrated by the increase in antelope . . . to approximately 10,000" by 1935 (Gabrielson, Ira N., 1935: 576). (See Plate 42.)

Nothing is a match for the swift-footed antelope when it is in the open without snow. Unfortunately, when the snow lies deep on the ground the little bands [antelope] are open to the ravages of the coyotes. And finally, Einarsen (1948: 79) in his comprehensive monograph on the antelope says: "Coyotes, uncontrolled, may be a serious limiting factor to kid crops."

Beaver and Land Otter

The beaver, predominantly a vegetarian, serves at times as food for the coyote. The role of this animal, however, in its effect on beaver population is as yet not fully known. Field observations indicate that beavers are notoriously lacking in defense of themselves when attacked by predators. This is difficult to understand when one considers the strong incisor teeth possessed by beavers with which they could inflict telling damage. Coyotes attack beavers when found on dry premises, more often at night, when working at the felling of trees or when dragging small food trees toward their aquatic homes.

Warren (1927: 149) states: "I found in the Longs Peak (Colorado) region in late August, what was left of a beaver which had been killed a few days before by a coyote or coyotes droppings of which were found close-by. All that could be found of the beaver were a few scraps of fur and of the scaly part of the tail, and part of the intestines. These were but a few feet from the lodge, which was a bank lodge, and presumably at or near the place where the victim had been surprised and killed."

Trappers employed by the State Game and Fish Department were inclined to feel that the coyote ranked first among enemies of the beaver in Colorado.

Occasionally, reports have been received that coyotes kill young otters while they are traveling overland from one watershed to another in search of new habitat.

Weasels and Skunks

In Glacier National Park, Montana, it was observed during June of 1935 that several coyotes which were attending young in dens brought to them 6 weasels they had killed, as well as a total of 13 young skunks dug out of skunk dens and killed likewise for food. (Letter from Leo L. Laythe, Regional Director, Fish and Wildlife Service, dated July 26, 1935.)

Quail

On a Texas area where stringent predator control had been carried on the previous winter, coyotes, nevertheless, were highly destructive of bobwhites, especially in the egg stage. Stomach analyses confirmed the results of field studies of the losses. Only about 5 nests in a hundred were successful in the early part of the season, but a larger proportion were productive in a later egg-laying period stimulated by heavy rains. In the fall, however, there were only 2.2 young birds to each adult; a normal proportion would have been 5.1. Additional coyote control would improve the bobwhite crop. The predators were also eating young Hereford calves. Fire ants were responsible for the destruction of about 1 percent of the quail eggs (Lehman, V. W., and W. G. Fuller: 1943).

In a study embracing 194 bobwhite quail nests during the 1942 and 1943 breeding season conducted on the W. W. Jones Wildlife Refuge in Jim Hogg County, Texas, Lehman (1946: 111-123) found heavy coyote predation on early quail nests from "late April through early June 1943." This period corresponds to the denning season of the coyote and a time when its depredations are generally extreme on poultry, livestock, and wildlife. Later available summer foods tend to cause the animal to reduce its depredations. Lehman's final conclusions in the foregoing studies are to the effect that coyote depredations as an important factor in regulating quail reproduction in southwestern Texas is exceeded only by rainfall. Coyotes in the foregoing studies accounted for "80 quail nests and about 83% of a predation."

Wild Turkey

On the morning of May 17, 1946, Clarence M. Aldous of the Fish and Wildlife Service, while engaged in field work on the Mescalero Indian Reservation, New Mexico, at about 7:30 a.m., saw a coyote come into a small grassy opening between the cabin at Turkey Well in Turkey Canyon and the edge of the timber. Six wild turkeys had been observed feeding in this area about 30 minutes prior to this time.

The coyote was watched for a few minutes before being shot. The coyote, a female, was found to have 14 porcupine quills in her nose about half of which were broken off.

The stomach was removed and the contents placed in some clean cheesecloth and allowed to dry in the shade. Because of the presence of feathers in the stomach, which were thought to be of turkey origin, the entire contents were sent to the Denver, Colorado, Laboratory of the Fish and Wildlife Service for identification. The contents were found to be as follows: Percentage of animal matter, 85; percentage of vegetable matter, 15; bones, feathers and a little flesh of *Meleagris* (apparently wild), 67; shell and membrane (fragmentary) of white egg (duck?), 3; lower jaw, other bones and fur of *Thomomys* sp., 15; 2 horsehairs, trace; and 82 seeds and fragments of rose hips, 15.

The condition of the seeds and hips of rose indicate they had been eaten by the coyote rather than by the turkey.

Aldous held the opinion that the eggshells found in the stomach contents were turkey eggs rather than those of ducks, inasmuch as there are no water areas within miles of this site where ducks could nest.

Whether or not this coyote had attacked the porcupine before eating the turkey could not be ascertained.

RODENT-INSECT RELATIONSHIP

For many years the assumption has been held by many people that any extensive control of coyotes is wrong, predicated upon the theory that because these animals eat injurious rodents they constitute an important and dependable check. The ratio of predators to animals preyed upon is what determines the effectiveness of predators as noxious rodent destroyers under normal conditions. Various parts of the range of the coyote are densely populated by jack rabbits, cottontails, ground squirrels of many kinds, prairie dogs, wood rats, kangaroo rats and mice of many species, and some or all of these animals are commonly present there in incredible numbers. All are preyed upon by coyotes, and all have a high potential, and under favorable conditions an actual, reproductive rate far beyond any possible effective check by the relatively few coyotes, even where these are present in their greatest abundance.

This relation of predators to rodents was illustrated by the late Dr. Joseph Grinnell in 1918 when he said that the general habits of ground squirrels [as occurring in California] are such that they were able to hold their own in the face of a host of natural enemies which habitually preyed upon them before the white man's event.

General observations of field conditions extending over many years in many regions have convinced me that coyotes, and probably most other predators, owing to disparity in numbers, make little impression upon the rodents under the ordinary conditions with which we have to deal; and for the same reason they are negligible in preventing mouse plagues, which are due to favorable factors, usually in combination, such as abundant food, shelter, favorable weather, scarcity of parasites, and the absence of diseases tending to become epizootic.

With reference to the lagomorphs in a recent interesting summation of a study concerned with the ecology of a cottontail rabbit (Sylvilagus auduboni) population in central California, Fitch (1947: 181) states that "On the San Joaquin Range there is no direct evidence that predation actually holds the cottontail (rabbit) to any given level." In the composition of coyote food concerned with this area which was based on the analysis of 1,173 coyote scats, cottontails headed the list with an occurrence of 377, and a "computed percentage by weight of total prey recorded" which included the ground squirrel, gopher snake, woodrat, pocket gopher, kangaroo rat, and "other (20 kinds) the latter of variable degree, of 45.4%."

In an unpublished manuscript by Fitch brought to my attention March 24, 1947, with respect to "A study of coyote relationships on Cattle Range," and concerned also with the San Joaquin Range he concluded that "the available evidence suggests that coyote predation is not a determining factor in the trends of ground squirrel, cottontail, kangaroo rat, and other gopher populations in this type of habitat, despite the fact that these small mammals comprise the bulk of the food and are taken in great numbers." He found too that: "Relations with range cattle [on this 4,600-acre range] are generally harmonious, but individual coyotes, which learn to kill small calves, may cause serious damage at times."

They may, however, seriously reduce the numbers of large game mammals or of such ground-nesting game birds as the sage hen, quail, and waterfowl, which are not usually so numerous, as they are already diminished by human occupation of land and are also subject to human toll.

Similarly, as with the rodents, some people likewise believe that the coyote and other carnivores serve as a distinct check in preventing insect plagues such as that of grasshoppers. While it is true, the coyote relishes the grasshopper in its diet, and eats this insect wherever obtainable, nevertheless there is no evidence to date that the insects eaten by all the carnivores serves as a check upon insect plagues. As with the rodents, insect plagues of vast proportions, such as the irregular periodic grasshopper outbreaks in the middle western United States, are dependent upon a combination of favorable factors, weather being one of the most important, as is also insect parasites. Their occurrence is of historic record since the beginning of early settlement and development of farming, the early 70's and 80's, and during years when an abundance of the coyote and other carnivores occurred in this area. As to the extent of the coyote population during this time the reader is referred to the yearly kill of the animal as made by the professional wolf poisoner (Young & Goldman, 1944: 323-337).

DOMESTIC LIVESTOCK PREY

Establishment of sheep and goat ranches in coyote habitat has always produced sharp clashes between the owners and this animal. As far back as the 1880-1890's, taking Texas as a typical example, it was officially reported that "the greatest and most discouraging obstacle encountered by the sheepmen of Texas is that omnipresent evil, the depredations of wild animals. From this cause alone the flockmasters suffer an annual loss of sheep and goats amounting to over $500,000. The increasing loss of calves, colts, and poultry are not considered in this conservative estimate; and yet it is a significant fact that bloodthirsty brutes are increasing in numbers from year to year—the coyote particularly. The small flockmasters in many counties are abandoning the business on account of wolves, and in such localities the land, instead of advancing in value, is at a standstill or is depreciating. It is a serious matter to the sheepmen, and it is hoped that the present agitation of the subject may result in prompt relief and stop the slaughter of live stock that is damaging the animal industry of the western ranges to an extent indeed alarming.

"The Texas wolf and bounty law is a failure. The act in force at this writing (1892) is as follows:

"That the county commissioners of the several counties within the State may issue county warrants to the person killing in any amount not exceeding $3 for every wolf, coyote, wildcat, and fox; and 5 cents for each rabbit that shall be captured and killed in the said county. No person shall be entitled to receive any bounty as set forth in section one without first making it appear by positive proof by affidavit in writing, filed with the county clerk, that the wolf, coyote, wildcat, rabbit, or fox was captured or killed within the limits of the county in which application was made. This act shall not apply to counties having a total property valuation of less than $500,000, and shall not be in force until ordered by the board of county commissioners.

"The local application of the law, together with its restrictive features, greatly interferes with the intended usefulness of the act. It will not afford protection, except in wealthy counties, where ample bounty is offered. In the sparsely settled counties, where the depredations are greatest, the law does not apply, and in no county unless it is the pleasure of the board of county commissioners; and even if they are disposed to take advantage of the act and order the law in force, they make the bounty so small, usually 50 cents per head, that unless the sheepmen themselves voluntarily increase the bounty it offers no inducement to hunt down the wolves. A movement has been inaugurated by the sheepmen to have the legislature of 1891 enact a law that will be of some service to the industry as well as increasing the taxable wealth of the State.

"To give some idea of the losses a few individual cases are cited: Ira Johnson, of Travis County, had a small flock of 300 mature sheep and 40 lambs, and out of this number he lost 30 lambs and 25 sheep from wolves and dogs. The following from the Boerne Post, a local paper in western Texas, vividly describes the situation there:

" 'We learn that a gentleman leaving his ranch on the Guadalupe River, because of the depredations of wild animals, has sold out, finding it impossible to cope with his losses. Mr. Robinson, having his ranch on the Fredericksburg road, has also sold out for the same reason, and we hear of others who are determined to sell out. Kendall, like Bandera County, will soon not have a sheepman within its bounds.' "

A. E. Shepard, ex-president of the State Wool-Growers' Association, says:

"I turned 1,500 lambing sheep into one of my pastures, and at one time counted over 500 lambs there. A short time after this I went through the flock and I had only 38 lambs left. The wolves had taken all the others; and now, from those 1,500 lambing ewes I have not more than 25 lambs left, and the wolves will soon do away with them. Besides the lambs, they pick off grown sheep every day and night.

"Eight flockmasters in Uvalde County, when asked as to their losses this season, counted up nearly 1,700 sheep. Mr. E. M. Kirkwood, of Kimble County, lost 300 out of a flock of 2,000 head, last year. These random examples represent the universal condition of the sheep industry in every part of the State.

"Almost every attempt at State legislation in behalf of the

sheep industry has failed, for the simple reason that united action on the part of all States interested can not be had. If Texas should be successful in destroying wild animals, and the neighboring States do not, the evil would soon spread again, and the destruction would continue. If all could work together there is very little room for doubt that the coyote and other destructive animals would soon be extinct. If a reasonable bounty were offered, either by the States severally or the nation, for the scalps of these destructive wild animals, they would be disposed of in less time than was required to get rid of the buffalo.

"The extinction of these destructive wild animals would reduce the cost of wool production fully one-half. It would beget confidence in the business and make sheep husbandry the most profitable industry in the West, besides saving the destruction of over $15,000,000 worth of taxable property that is now destroyed annually by wild animals" (Carman, Ezra, H. A. Health, and John Minto, 1892: 911, 912).

Lest the readers of the foregoing become confused in the thought that all of the trouble was from wolves, it must be borne in mind that the coyote was commonly called "wolf." Rarely were the two species coyote and wolf distinguished by their true names in the parlance of the rangemen.

One could write on ad infinitum concerning the sheep and goat, and at times the cattle producers' troubles with coyote depredations, all of which are more or less similar in their case against the coyote. Therefore, to avoid a tiresome and repetitious narrative, the following records from widely separated areas will suffice to express the economic role the coyote sometimes plays in livestock production.

With respect to goats, the experiences of E. P. Hilton raising goats southeast of Tucson, Arizona, is of interest. He attributes his financial success in producing goats to the study he has made over a long period of how to handle the coyote problem. He writes:

"To begin with, during the period from 1905 to 1920, in riding or driving in a wagon 15 or 20 miles in one morning, it was not unusual to see 4 to 6 coyotes on most any road, and at night they were howling on all sides. I have seen a dead cow cleaned up in one night, and at night, when camping out, they would come right up to the camp and take ropes or spurs or anything loose that they could get to eat. I have seen them take a chicken from the front yard in the day time.

"I remember about 40 years ago, I trapped a little during one winter with one trap and caught 11—most of them around dead animals. At that time, Pima County was paying $1.00 per head bounty. I also remember two or three years previous to that that two Germans trapped in the Sanford or Cienega wash, east of here, one winter, and caught 247 coyotes and 19 Lobo wolves. This was in an area about 10 by 15 miles and they only used meat bait. Today in that area, probably not over 50 could be caught with all of our modern methods and scents. However, as thick as they were, coyotes did not do the damage as of today. I never knew or heard of them killing a calf. The Lobos did, however. We ran 700 to 1200 goats from 1904 to 1912 without a herder and did not lose half what we did with herders 15 years ago. During those years, jack rabbits, cottontails and quails were very plentiful notwithstanding the coyotes. I remember around Patagonia and Canelo that most all ranch hands were given poison to put in any dead animal they found, and I have seen 5 to 8 dead coyotes around a cow. After 1920, there was a gradual marked decline in coyote numbers, but about 1925 they commenced killing calves and later deer also. Last year I found three deer that had been killed by them and not little ones at that. Along about 1930, I have known 2 or 3 coyotes to come from the river and strike a few goats left out and kill 3 or 4 out of the bunch. These coyotes probably had never seen a goat before. As to moving goats onto a new range, I cannot give any data on that except two instances. Some 12 years ago, about 900 goats were moved from the Aravaipa to the Silverbell range, where there had not been any goats before, by Sumrall Brothers. In the first week, they lost 15 head from coyotes. Also, last fall I shipped 210 does from Mayer to this ranch by rail. We trucked and turned them loose in the pasture on the west side, but through a small water gap that was washed out, 173 of these goats got out, and we did not discover the loss for three days, when we found 149 head at Barrel Springs, 3 miles west of there. As to how many were killed by coyotes, I cannot say, as we found where 5 had been eaten, but some might have been stolen as they were right on the highway; but anyway, these coyotes had never seen a goat before.

"Now to summarize it briefly, coyotes are not nearly as numerous as they were 25 years ago—probably not over 40% as many, but they are more destructive, harder to catch, and if let alone for 4 or 5 years would be as numerous as before. Also, an important factor in southern Arizona is migration from Mexico which, if it could be stopped, would eliminate several thousand each year. Another very important factor is the Papago Reservation which will produce at least 2,500 coyotes each year. From these two sources, the coyote population is increased 5,000 or more each year. Of course, these coyotes do not all stay in Pima County but drift east—probably some as far as New Mexico.

"The remedy is not by trapping a few in certain localities or depending on local trappers who catch for the fur, but a widespread and thorough poisoning of several counties for a period of two or three years. This is the most effective and economical method to control coyotes. When this ranch was opened, I poisoned and trapped the coyotes all out but it was like trying to dig a hole in the sea; they came right back again."

Similarly, Mr. Tennis C. Creighton of Bowie, Arizona, who tried to keep down coyote depredations by the use, among other things, of a coyote proof fence was finally compelled to sell out his sheep, and restock with cattle. He says:

"I will try to give you a few notes on observations made by me of coyotes on ranges in Arizona; also a few on coyotes in Texas.

"I have been reared to hate coyotes all my life. When we moved to Bowie with sheep, coyotes were already familiar with sheep, but were not really bad until after lambing. They are easy to catch on and one coyote learns from another. Coyotes, as you know, are cowards, but when cornered will fight, and when a few sheep get lost from the herd, they start on lambs. As soon as they have made a few kills, they become more familiar with sheep and they then start killing just for fun. I had one herd to leave the bed ground one night and two coyotes killed seven grown ewes. They have been known to kill just as long as sheep will run, as this is the usual method used by coyotes. Old killers kill by biting the throat. Amateurs may bite or tear holes anywhere on the side or hind quarters. I have found little difference in male or female. They both kill when they have become accustomed to sheep. I had a small female coyote to kill ten lambs in one night and to bite three more that died later. These sheep were running loose.

"I have seen coyotes den in a pasture with sheep and kill in a nearby pasture. They never kill near a den. I helped dig out four dens within a mile of each, but in different years. Coyotes, as a rule, like to den near water but several miles can be covered for water.

"One year in Texas, I bought yearling ewes and they were run loose with little fencing. No losses were found until the late fall. Killings then became more often. Dogs could be used there. Usually the coyotes were trailed away from the kill and often easily caught because of being full.

"In closing, I will say we lost about three times as many sheep the third year that we did the first."

The recent report made by the Wasco (Oregon) County Agricultural Program Planning Conference adds to the record. Herein young pigs are included along with sheep. The report says with respect to coyote depredations:

"Coyotes are definitely a problem and cause much loss to young stock.

"Sheep numbers in Wasco County, estimated now to be at 28,000 head, are the lowest in many years and compare with figures from the early history of the county. There was reported 144,000 head as recently as 1930. Sheep numbers on the whole can stand some increase to utilize ranges that are not being used. It is estimated that such ranges could provide grazing for additional thousands of sheep. However there are some sheep ranges at present that are overstocked and overgrazed.

"The large numbers of coyotes in Wasco County, that are causing losses running into the thousands of dollars annually, are a major problem among sheep men as well as other livestock growers. The coyote is more responsible for holding down sheep numbers at present than any other one factor. Ranchers are reluctant to increase sheep numbers with the predator situation as it is.

"Until recently it has been a common practice for wheat ranchers to have small bands of sheep as a sideline; but this practice has been almost entirely eliminated, principally because of the loss experienced from coyotes. Many wheat ranchers would like to keep small bands of sheep to keep the weeds down around the farm yard and to clean up scatterings of grain and roughage that otherwise often go to waste. However, it is not likely that this will be done to any great extent until coyote numbers are reduced.

"The hog production in Wasco County has always been considered a sideline activity. However, in relation to other Columbia basin counties Wasco County has produced higher than average numbers per farm. The total for the county has been around 9,000 head recently, reaching 13,500 in 1944.

"The cost of feed in 1945 and 1946 was such that it made hog production unprofitable with OPA ceilings on the price of hogs being relatively lower than cost of feed—including wheat, the principal feed used. The common practice followed in raising hogs here is to let them farrow and run at large in the wheat fields until the grain has considerable size, when it becomes necessary to pen them in until after harvest.

"Since there is always a certain amount of grain spilled during the harvesting process, the hogs are able to utilize much of this waste feed after they are turned loose again, which makes for economical production.

"There are at least two things that have interfered with this method of growing hogs in Wasco County. One is the loss experienced from coyotes, which seem to like particularly well to pick on young pigs; and the other is the problem of the operator keeping pigs on his property without fencing. All ranchers do not like hogs and few wheat ranchers have hog-tight fences. Some neighbors complain of trespassing, and this is causing several ranchers to stop hog production. Still another factor which has helped to decrease hog numbers in the southern part of the county is the lack of an available supply of milk. This used to be available for growing pigs when butterfat was sold, but is not available now since the shift to selling whole milk on dairy farms. Sideline hog production is recommended and is known to be profitable where the above factors are not too serious a problem."

Ivan E. Morgareidge and Clarence Jenks of Buffalo, Wyoming, reported on October 14, 1935, that in the spring of that year a heifer was killed by coyotes while she was calving. The coyotes, in attacking, ate on the rear quarters of the young heifer so deeply that it was necessary to shoot her as well as the calf for the front legs and head of the latter were likewise badly mutilated.

State Game Warden Elliott S. Barker (1944) rates the coyote as New Mexico's worst predator, stating it was destroying (during World War II period) 60,000 sheep and lambs, 7,000 calves, 10,000 deer, and 3,000 antelopes.

L. Doyle Matthews, junior district agent, recently reported the taking of one adult male, one adult female, and six coyote pups in Jefferson County, Idaho. The adult male coyote was a peg-leg and had been responsible for the killing of 22 lambs, 10 of them being pure bred Romneys. The sheep were killed during the past May and June. The coyotes had crossed the frozen Snake River during the winter from the desert area on the west and after the ice had broken up in the spring they became marooned in a relatively small brushy area east of the river and the killings occurred there when the sheep were turned out to pasture.

District Agent C. R. Landon, of the Texas District, reports that 5 coyotes were taken in Bastrop County, Texas, which during the year had killed 500 turkeys and 450 mutton sheep, having a market value of $2,700. During the past fiscal year coyotes killed 300 Rhode Island Reds and White Leghorn chickens on a farm near Robstown, Texas.

Mr. Landon also reports an unusual series of depredations inflicted by a lone crippled male coyote in Jeff Davis County, Texas. These started in November 1942 and continued until the coyote was captured by a Service hunter on June 29, 1943. During this period the coyote made the following kill: (1) 28 yearlings and 2 year-old buck sheep, valued at $20 each, on the ranch of M. O. Means and Son; (2) 152 yearling ewes in an adjoining pasture owned by C. A. Means; the yearling ewes were valued at $10 each; (3) Practically a complete destruction of a lamb crop from 450 ewes. This occurred during the April, 1943, lambing season.

Although this coyote was continually chased by dogs and sought by amateur trappers, its depredations continued until at the request of the ranchmen concerned, predatory animal hunter Guy West, working outside his assigned territory, placed 7 traps in the area and caught the animal.

According to a report of the Agricultural Statistician, in charge of the Bureau of Agricultural Economics office in North Dakota, livestock losses as the result of wild animal predation amounted to $1,014,000 in that State during the calendar year 1944. The estimated loss was based on data obtained through a questionnaire sent to a sample of some 2,000 North Dakota livestock producers. Since the large wolves are now practically extinct in that State, the coyote which now predominates must be counted as the foremost predator in this State.

The survey indicated that coyotes killed approximately 5,800 calves, valued at $151,000. The number of sheep killed was estimated at 12,500, with an estimated total value of $109,000; lambs, 18,000 head, valued at $153,000. Chicken losses reached the surprising total of 328,000 head, probably attributable to other predators, as well as coyotes. These were valued at $279,000. Turkey losses, estimated at 92,000 head, added another $322,000 to the total losses caused by coyotes and other predators. On the basis of these estimates, the total value of all livestock killed or destroyed during 1944 amounted to the surprising total of $1,014,000.

Many livestock producers at the time of sending in their reports expressed serious concern at the mounting losses, especially of lambs and turkeys, and stated that unless some widespread control measures were adopted, production of lambs and turkeys would continue to decline.

The livestock losses during 1944 caused by predators, may be made more realistic by calling attention to the fact that if the livestock destroyed had reached maturity and gone to market, approximately 7,800,000 additional pounds of meat would have been available to consumers.

A release on the subject of "Losses of Meat Animals and Poultry in Missouri—Year 1943" by the Federal and State departments of agriculture, constituting the Federal-State Crop Reporting Service, issued by the Office of Agricultural Statistician, Columbia, Missouri, gives the numbers and kinds of livestock and poultry lost during 1943 together with the percentages of the various attributed causes of loss. These figures are based on 800 replies received from questionnaires mailed to 6,611 crop reporters in Missouri. With values based on reports of averages by the U. S. Department of Agriculture for 1943, the losses by predation were computed by the Missouri Conservation Commission and with their permission are here summarized:

Losses Attributed to Red Wolves and Coyotes

LIVESTOCK (all ages)	Number	Value
Cattle and calves	1,358	$ 91,967.00
Sheep and lambs	43,959	439,590.00
Hogs and pigs	52,720	1,091,304.00
Total	98,037	$1,622,861.00
POULTRY		
Chickens (all ages)	576,933	$ 492,762.00
Turkeys (over 3 months)	522	2,453.00
	577,455	$ 495,215.00

Losses Attributed to Foxes

LIVESTOCK (under 6 months)	Number	Value
Lambs	14,520	$ 145,200.00
Pigs	52,480	1,086,336.00
Total	67,000	$1,231,536.00
POULTRY (all ages)		
Chickens	2,824,629	$2,319,215.00
Turkeys	103,170	286,874.00
	2,927,799	$2,606,089.00

While these figures as computed may somewhat exaggerate the picture of predation in Missouri, they nevertheless indicate that a real problem does exist. Here again the coyote predominates.

To conclude the dissertation on this problem the following is more national in scope.

According to some leading livestock statisticians sheep in the

United States were in liquidation beginning in early 1942, shortly after our entry into World War II. This reduction was estimated at about 7 percent a year to 1946, when it was ascertained to be nearly 9½ percent. In response to letters as to the reason for this sent out by Geo. A. Montgomery, Associate Editor of Capper's *Farmer*, published at Topeka, Kansas, a tabulated summary of the forthcoming replies from sheep producing areas gave as reasons: (1) Labor shortage; (2) coyote depredations; (3) shortage of ammunition; (4) lack of hunters; and (5) the rapid increase of coyotes.

Destructiveness of Renegade Coyotes

As with the large gray wolves, in widely separated parts of the western range have occurred many individual coyotes that were considered of the renegade type because of individual peculiarities in their depredations on domestic livestock. In time each drew such attention that it was especially singled out for elimination. As an example, a description of the capture of that coyote dubbed "Old Three Toes Super-Coyote of Caddo County, Oklahoma" will indicate what the presence of certain individual killer coyotes mean to a livestock farming community.

Old Three Toes and his co-killers were a hard-boiled lot, whelped in a region where the length of a coyote's life depended a good deal upon the length of his legs and on the same dimension in his head. They belonged to a superior breed, developed by the very methods that had been designed for their undoing, and Old Three Toes was the strongest, fleetest, and wisest of the clan. For 6 years he spread destruction among the herds and flocks in an 18-mile area in Caddo County, Oklahoma, outwitting packs of expensive dogs that killed off his slower and weaker relatives. Only the fittest survived. The weaklings and dullards were culled before they had the opportunity to reproduce their inferiority.

The people of the Lookaba community had sustained losses from coyotes amounting to many thousands of dollars, and, after spending $1,000 for a pack of stag hounds, had failed to bring the animals under control. On account of a superabundance of dogs in the locality, many of which were still referred to as "valuable dogs," the use of traps was resorted to in capturing Three Toes.

After looking over the largest pasture in the neighborhood, where coyotes were said to have committed depredations for the last 6 years or more, it was concluded that coyotes were not unusually abundant but their tracks were unusually large and indicated that most of them were large, heavy animals. In fact, the people there stated that all the slower, weaker specimens had been caught with dogs and that the survivors were all large, rangy animals and that a race of super-coyotes was being produced in Caddo County. Much was heard of Old Three Toes, an extra large coyote or wolf, that has been chased with dogs for the past 6 years. At first, the government hunter detailed to capture Three Toes did not look especially for his tracks, but the first tracks he found were rather large, even for a very large coyote, measuring 3¾ inches long and 2¼ inches wide, with one toe missing from the right fore foot. In shape they were typical coyote tracks. He found the same tracks in three different parts of the pasture, two or three miles apart, and thought possibly this animal might be a coyote-dog or a wolf hybrid.

After 29 days of strenuous activity devoted to the Caddo County project, a total bag of 19 coyotes was recorded. All of them were large, rangy old coyotes that had outrun the dogs, refused to be enticed with bait or scent, and committed depredations against livestock to the extent of at least $10,000.

In the final report on this assignment the hunter on the job stated:

"It is too bad that you could not have stayed another day and had a good look at Old Three Toes, who hit the two traps with the short stakes we set together. The very last night he roamed the woods was the night you left. He was not a wolf or coyote-dog hybrid as had been rumored, but an extra large coyote, as was indicated by his tracks. We did not weigh him until Saturday evening, when we took him to town to give the people a chance to see him; that is, the few who had not heard of his capture and come to our camp. There has been a crowd here ever since he was caught, one person coming 17 miles. Five days after his capture Old Three Toes weighed exactly 39 pounds, which means that he must have weighed at least 45 pounds when caught. There is no doubt in the minds of the people here that he is the offender they have been chasing all over the county for the past six years."

POPULATION TRENDS

Nearly two decades past, the late Dr. Chas. T. Vorhies, one of our most ardent conservationists in the Southwest, in speaking of a certain area while camped in Texas said: "I have never heard so many coyotes in one night . . ." (Taylor, Walter P., July 31, 1931: 92.)

The trend in wildlife management, among other things, has been the attempts to arrive at definite conclusion as to population densities. One of the most perplexing population trends to fathom is with predators, and particularly, the coyote. One is confronted with so many little understood factors found in the usual coyote habitat that often the most laborious attempts to arrive at some near correct figures for coyote population per square mile, in final analysis turn out to be figures that are far below the actual numbers involved, often gross underestimates. Some students become so enthused over working out population trends that their resultant algebraic equations leave the poor layman in a maze of confusion. I wonder sometimes if these students are not left likewise.

The extent of coyote infestation always has a direct economic bearing in determining required control, if any, on most of the livestock producing lands. Recent developments in control technique as exemplified by the use of the so-called "Coyote go-getter" which is described further on in the text is bringing to light more definite statistics concerning the animal than has been heretofore possible.

Referring to the statement made by Doctor Vorhies in the foregoing, a recent take of coyotes in Maverick County, Texas, would have caused a similar remark as that made by him by anyone who might have visited said county prior to the coyote reduction instigated during October 1946.

Maverick County is primarily cattle country, though some sheep and goats are raised in the northern portion of it. A good portion of it is heavily covered with black brush, huajilla, running mesquite, and pricklypear or cactus. Pack rats and mice exist in abundance. Quail and deer are likewise well represented, together with a goodly population of javelinas. Prior to October 1946, no organized predator work had been done in Maverick County for several years.

During the month of October 1946, A. B. Bynum, of the Fish and Wildlife Service, with the aid of 325 coyote go-getters baited with a food bait made up from decomposed prairie dog meat and fat to which was added a small amount of artificial musk and beaver castor took 536 coyotes from 240,000 acres upon which he worked. He estimated that he had killed an additional 75 coyotes during this interval which he was unable to find because of the density of thick brush.

He returned to the area in January of 1947, and worked on 164,000 acres within the 240,000 acre area he had worked the previous October; 340 coyotes were killed, his biggest catch was made on January 23 when he ran line No. 2 (See Fig. 18) approximately 35 miles in length that contained 150 "getters" from

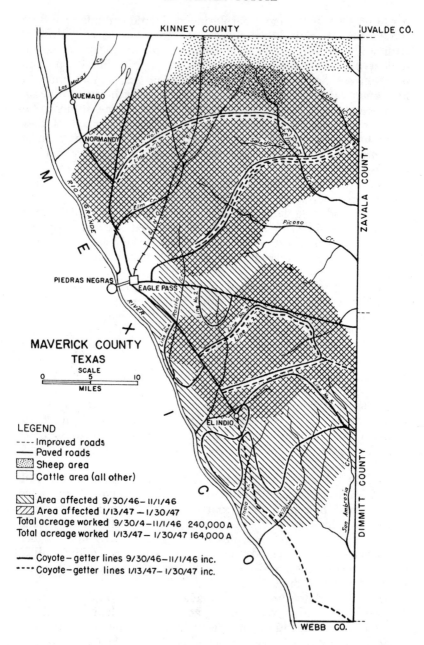

Figure 18.

which he took 57 coyotes. During October 1946, 190 coyotes were taken from the same area, making a total of 247 coyotes killed on line No. 2.

From the actual kill counted in October, and not taking into consideration the additional 75 coyotes, Bynum felt positive he had killed, the 240,000 acres of land contained .7 coyote per square mile. The January take from 164,000 acres represents .75 coyote per square mile.

From all indications it was evident that the abundance of food foremost of which were packrats, caused the coyote, like other of the carnivores, to increase and maintain its numbers in direct proportion to the available food supply, and no doubt caused some coyote drift following the October reduction.

The total cost of the take of coyotes during October was a little less than $1.30 per animal.

Another instance that brings to light similar astounding coyote population, as exemplified in the foregoing, concerns a week's work in McMullen County, Texas. During the period from April 10 to 14, 1947, inclusive, Bynum, assisted by Noble E. Buell, also of the Fish and Wildlife Service, took 105 coyotes with the aid of 175 "coyote-getters," 56 of these coyotes were taken out of two pastures, one of which contained 2,200 and the other 1,000 acres. This kill represents more than 10 coyotes to the square mile. Had it not been for the fact that all the dense shrub growth was fully leafed out which made recovery of dead coyotes exceedingly difficult, more than 105 coyotes would have been found on the 3,200 acres, for 20 "getters" had been fired from which

---

Figure 18. Showing the 240,000 and 164,000 acres of land from which were removed a grand total of 876 coyotes during the single months of October 1946 and January 1947. (Courtesy of Noble Buell, Fish and Wildlife Service.)

Coyote-getter line No. 1—9/30/46-11/1/46, Burr ranch, maximum getters 196, coyotes taken 96.

Coyote-getter line No. 2—9/30/46-11/1/46, Weyrich ranch, maximum getters 38, coyotes taken 9.

Coyote-getter line No. 3—9/30/46-11/1/46, Singleton ranch, maximum getters 190, coyotes taken 202.

Coyote-getter line No. 4—9/30/46-11/1/46, George ranch, maximum getters 52, coyotes taken 25.

Coyote-getter line No. 5—9/30/46-11/1/46, Cage ranch, maximum getters 245, coyotes taken 204.

Coyote-getter line No. 1—1/13/47-1/30/47, Burr ranch, maximum getters 195, coyotes taken 204.

Coyote-getter line No. 2—1/13/47-1/30/47, Singleton ranch, maximum getters 225, coyotes taken 136.

no recovery was made, and sign indicated at least 15 additional coyotes had caused the firing. Another lure used successfully by Bynum, other than that mentioned, in bringing the coyote to the "go-getter" had as the base: ground up armadillo, cow-hide, and at times burro meat.

Population trends of coyotes as noted in various parts of Arizona obtained by the use of traps and in some instances by poison add to the record. In conference during February 1947, with the author, Everett M. Mercer, District Agent of the Fish and Wildlife Service, stationed at Phoenix, commented upon first the work of U. S. Government Hunter Leonard F. Miller for the period April 9, 1945, to April 8, 1946, inclusive, stating that:

"Mr. Miller entered on duty with the Service on April 9, 1945, and commenced to set traps on that date in the Hualpai Valley northeast of Kingman, Arizona, Mohave County. Traps were used from that date until early in November when some poison stations were placed. He had unusually good success with strychnine baits and discontinued trapping in December. Coyotes taken from that time until April 8, 1946, were picked up around decoy stations where strychnine drop baits had been placed. During the twelve months period of operations with traps and poison Mr. Miller scalped or skinned 458 coyotes that he took in the Hualpai Valley. Many of the coyotes that he recorded were taken with poison and it is believed that he took a goodly number of the animals by this method that traveled a considerable distance from decoy stations before being killed. It is certain that he killed some coyotes with poison that were not found and therefore not recorded in his catch. Also, from April 9, 1945, until the first of November of that year, it is known that buccal papillomata was present among coyotes in that district and some of the animals undoubtedly died from the infection.

"That part of the Hualpai Valley that Mr. Miller worked during this period, or we might say the part of the Valley where his work would have an influence on coyote populations comprised approximately 25 townships, or 900 sections of land. He actually recorded 458 coyotes from an area of approximately 900 sections of land. We have chosen this area because natural barriers in the way of mountain ranges undoubtedly have an influence on the regular movements of coyotes in the Valley and in the country on the other side of the mountains that border the Valley. The Hualpai Valley is bounded on the east by the Grand Wash Cliffs. Coyotes can readily migrate from the Hualpai Indian Reservation down these mountains to the valley below. The Hualpai Mountains and some unnamed peaks are at the south end of the valley. The Cerbat Mountains are along the west side of the valley. To the north the valley extends to the Colorado River or Mead Lake. Mr. Miller worked no farther north than Gold Basin.

"Roads were so situated as to permit him to travel from the vicinity of Hackberry, Arizona, northwest to Gold Basin, or from the vicinity of Kingman, Arizona, to the same point. It was seldom that he conducted control work immediately along the edge of the valley, except at a few points on the west side. Stock tanks and springs supply water for livestock, and coyotes wherever they happened to be ranging visited these waters regularly. Most of the coyotes he recorded were taken in the vicinity of tanks and springs.

"At one point nine miles east of Kingman, where coyotes were attracted to a dump ground on an Army Airport, and a stock tank just outside the airport, Mr. Miller located and scalped 59 poisoned coyotes on one section of land over a period of two and one-half months. Coyotes came in for miles around to visit this point and at the conclusion of the period covered by this report no coyote sign could be noted around this point. He had equal success at other points near water in the valley. The area was visited and inspected by Mr. Howard J. Martley at the end of the program and he saw only three or four different coyote tracks in the entire area where Mr. Miller's work would have had some effect on coyote populations. The program resulted in almost exterminating coyotes in the Hualpai Valley and I would like to point out that it was commenced at a time of year when coyotes are at their lowest point in numbers and ended at the same period.

"The Hualpai Valley is a desert type of country. Rabbits were scarce during the time covered by this report. Woodrats were plentiful. Kangaroo rats and ground squirrels were moderate. The coyote population was average at that time for similar areas in Arizona. Coyotes were not nearly as plentiful at that time as they were in the same country from 1938 to 1942, inclusive."

Continuing with the aid of his field notes and other official statistics kept through the years, Mercer further stated the following concerning population trends in southern Arizona.

"On December 18, 1943, Mr. Vurland F. Crook, Junior District Agent in Arizona, placed seven decoy stations on the Franco Ranch about 15 miles southeast of Tucson, Arizona. This ranch comprised 36 sections or one township of land but was "L" shaped instead of being a square township. Six of the stations were near stocktanks and the offal of the horse butchered for station material served as the seventh station. By February 3,

1944, or 48 days later, Mr. Crook had scalped 93 poisoned coyotes on this ranch. None of the coyotes scalped were more than 220 yards from a decoy station. He made no attempt to look farther away for dead coyotes. Two skunks and seven foxes were poisoned around these stations.

"This ranch lays in the valley southeast of Tucson, Arizona, and north from the Santa Rita Mountains. The entire area is covered with a heavy growth of Cholla cactus, prickly pears and mesquite. Resident coyotes on the Franco Ranch were practically exterminated by February 3, 1944, and the effects of Mr. Crook's work was noted on adjacent ranges. In fact poisoned coyotes were reported in considerable numbers within a reasonable distance on surrounding ranches. I inspected the area on February 3 and coyote sign was scarce along the road I traveled until I got three miles from the Franco Ranch. There was no evidence that Mr. Crook's work had had any effect on coyote populations after I got six miles from the Franco Ranch. It is known that Mr. Crook did not find and scalp nearly all the coyotes that he poisoned on the Franco Ranch.

"On November 15, 1943, Mr. Crook placed six decoy stations on the Bob Locke Ranch in the Altar Valley Southwest of Tucson, Arizona. The following day he placed five decoy stations on the King Bros. Ranch which is also located in the Altar Valley. By February 3, 1944, he had scalped 78 poisoned coyotes on the Locke Ranch and 70 on the King Bros. Ranch. Thirty-seven of the coyotes taken on the Locke Ranch were picked up within 220 yards of one tank. As in the case of the Franco Ranch Mr. Crook did not look for poisoned coyotes more than 220 yards from a tank. Stockmen checking the work he did on their ranges reported that there were as many, or more dead coyotes scattered along between tanks as there were around the tanks. The areas covered by his operations on the Locke and King Bros. Ranches comprised about one township of land in each case. Mr. Crook's work had some effect on coyote populations for a few miles outside the particular area where he worked, but Douglas W. Fanning poisoned coyotes on the King Bros. Ranch commencing in December, 1945, and recorded kills equal to those made by Mr. Crook before the project was terminated in the spring of 1946. Some idea of the density of coyotes in this area may be had by noting that Mr. Fanning recorded 300 coyotes in a little over three and one-half months. Most of the coyotes he accounted for were taken in the Altar Valley but some were taken in the country around Arivaca, Arizona and just south of the Sierrita Mountains southwest of Tucson, Arizona."

And finally, using statistics pertaining to Pinal County, the Fort Apache Indian Reservation, and the so-called "Strip," north of the Grand Canyon, Mercer concluded by saying:

"During the month of January, 1946, Mr. Freeman H. Taber, a hunter employed by the Service scalped 75 coyotes on a ranch comprising about four townships and located in Pinal County, Arizona. This ranch is located a short distance north of the Santa Catalina Mountains out of Tucson, Arizona. He was still taking coyotes from this area in February.

"During December and January of the present fiscal year Hunter Henry M. Mausser scalped 145 poisoned coyotes on an area comprising approximately 270 square miles in the Cibecue-Grasshopper District on the Ft. Apache Indian Reservation in Arizona. This is one of the heaviest concentrations of coyotes that has been called to my attention during recent years. Coyote control has not been carried on in that country in the past. The area in particular is rough mountainous country cut by canyons and covered with a heavy growth of juniper and oak. It is doubtful if Mr. Mausser got one out of three coyotes that he poisoned in this country. Such a dense population of coyotes is by no means found in all parts of the Ft. Apache Reservation, we estimate however, that the animals will average one to a section of land for the entire reservation.

"Mr. Howard J. Martley, Assistant District Agent, in Arizona has spent considerable time on the Arizona Strip during the past two years. In the fall of 1945 Mr. Martley estimated that coyote populations on the "Strip" during the fall and winter months will average one coyote to each section of land."

In such places as enumerated in the foregoing much of the nation's livestock is endangered by unchecked coyotes. The margin between success and failure in the livestock and poultry industry is often very narrow and the inroads of coyotes may be the deciding factor. Under modern conditions practical considerations demand the most effective management of wildlife everywhere. This means that such a predator as the coyote must be checked whenever it becomes too numerous or injurious to human interests.

Chapter Six

Measures Used in Coyote Hunting and Control

THERE is probably no North American predator that exceeds the coyote as regards the variety of schemes and devices brought into use by man for its control. Though practically all of these are used mainly for the protection of domestic stock, the public health, or for the taking of its fur, one method—coursing with hounds—generally constitutes a form of sport, and has been practiced in many parts of the West for the past three quarters of a century.

Some of the more common measures and methods now in use may be described as follows:

THE GOVERNMENT HUNTER

A full account of the control of predators, including the coyote, by the government hunters is discussed in the *Wolves of North America* (Young and Goldman, 1944) and the *Wolf in North American History* (Young, 1946).

Suffice it to say further, however, in just recognition of the work these men do, that they make up one of the most interesting groups in governmental service. To be successful, they must have the fundamental virtues of reliability, ability, and energy. With this is needed a pleasing personality for they may be called upon to confer with State or other officials, or to appear before committees of the legislatures, to address stockmen's associations, county commissioners, and to maintain a friendly cooperative footing with individual stockmen and farmers. In addition they must be familiar with their territory and the ways of stock-killing predators infesting the area, as they are often called upon to train newly employed hunters or cooperating farmers and stockmen (See Plate 43). The difficulties these men must contend with at times is vividly portrayed in the following incident.

In the California District, a pair of especially destructive

Plate 43. Government hunter and camp.

coyotes were taken during the month of April, 1946, by Government hunter, William Yeager, from the Rancho Los Amigos in Los Angeles County. The female was trapped on Easter morning, April 21, and the male on April 25. Both animals were old and mangy, with worn teeth. From all indications, the female was suckling eight pups which could not be located. The two coyotes had killed eight pure bred Hampshire sheep on the Rancho, valued at $60 each. According to reports from neighboring households, these two coyotes had inflicted damages amounting to over $1,500 during the past year in this densely settled area. Rancho Los Amigos is completely surrounded by paved streets and modern city improvements. Apparently these coyotes had become accustomed to city life!

In this assignment the hunter demonstrated an unusual degree of diplomacy and persistence because he often left camp at 4 o'clock in the morning to cover his line, which would interfere with pet dogs running at large during the day.

Successful hunters in the Federal State service are virile, hard-working men, some possessing the best characteristics of the early pioneer hunters and trappers. They are called upon continually to exercise all their resourcefulness and hardihood in the great expanses of wild western country in which they operate. Not only must they endure the scorching heat of desert regions in summer, but in winter, in the north they must endure conditions arising when blizzards sweep the ranges and temperatures drop to zero or often below.

Farmer cowboys and young men from ranches often develop a special aptitude for coyote control, due to their love of life on the broad open ranges. Numerous graduates of colleges, some from the east, have been attracted by the adventurous character of coyote control work. A number have been so apt in learning it that they have successfully advanced to leadership in the States, and to administrative places at the main headquarters in Washington and elsewhere.

As Vorhies (1931: 112-113) stated: "The impression derived from close observation of the work of these men and the other leaders met on the trip is of exceptional competence and high efficiency. It seems that no hours are too long nor any obstacle too great to keep them from giving their best efforts to the performance of their official work. We do not believe we have ever met any body of Government men or outsiders who were performing their duties more conscientiously or creditably." And finally, with regard to both field administrators and the hunters supervised by them Vorhies (ibid., 113-114) further stated "one of the puzzles in the whole situation is how such good men as are now on the job both as leaders and hunters can be secured and held at the miserably low pay which is given them." Then concluding his impression of the leaders, he observed that "Here are men capable of handling a considerable number of subordinates successfully, transacting business with thousands of cooperators, caring for government property worth many thousands of dollars, and maintaining harmonious and effective relations with multitudes of politically appointed State and County officials. On the outside these abilities would undoubtedly commend three or four times as much in the way of pay as the men are now getting." Through the succeeding years, there has been a betterment in the financial status of these men, but there is still much room for improvement in this situation. (Plate 44.)

The number of hunters employed in the Federal and State cooperative control work varies seasonally, and to a lesser degree

Plate 44. (a and b) Den hunting equipment of one very successful hunter in Oregon. Trailer is used for hauling horses from one part of range to another, as a shelter and for cooking purposes, as well as conveying minor essential equipment.

by years; the funds available likewise affects the total, but is always above 200, and at times has exceeded 600.

Lately Missouri has tried out the so-called extension trapper plan, involving the services of the government trapper, which has been used sporadically throughout the Range States for the past quarter of a century. It is effective where funds are scarce, the territory to be worked is large, and depredations occurring that seem to call for a trapper being in two places at the same time. (See Plate 45 a, b, c, d.) This extension procedure, so admirably summed up by Sampson and Bennett (1948), "First tried in September, 1945, the method employed by these men grew out of the government-trapper plan. The most successful government trappers were those who responded to calls most promptly; such men usually found the animals present and active. Promptness was impossible when one man had all of the trapping to do, but by working closely with a farmer, the trapper could establish a workable trapline in a day or two, showing the farmer how to locate good sites and make sets. The trapper could then move to another area and repeat the process. Often, upon his return to the first area, the farmer had made a catch, or had a good idea where the animals were, and this saved the trapper time in starting another line. From this procedure came the idea of helping the farmers help themselves, which is at the root of all agricultural extension service.

"Two extension trappers are now employed, the Commission paying the salary and expenses of one while sharing with the U. S. Fish and Wildlife Service the cost of the other. Farmers buy their own equipment and requests for assistance are cleared through the county agents, who arrange local demonstrations. Often the local wildlife conservation agent assists.

"All-day demonstrations are conducted, preferably with not over a dozen farmers. Among the subjects treated are trapping equipment and techniques adapted to use by busy farmers; habits of wolves, coyotes, and foxes; location of "sign," trapping sites, and sets. The farmers make most of the sets themselves. If the predators are active the traps are left set, and under favorable conditions a catch may be made by at least one farmer within a week—sometimes the first night.

"If the farmers cannot find suitable traps locally, a minimum number purchased with a revolving fund sponsored by the Missouri Sheep and Wool Growers' Association are made available at cost. A small quantity of commercial natural-urine scent is furnished, and the farmers are shown how to prepare more.

(a)

(b)

Plate 45. (a) Cooperative hunter demonstrating traps and their mechanism to farmers. (Photo courtesy of Missouri Conservation Department.)

(b) Hunter points to coyote track in mud. (Photo courtesy of Missouri Conservation Department.)

(c) Hunter introduces art of bedding traps. (Photo courtesy of Missouri Conservation Department.)

(d) Hunter coaches farmer in trap-setting. (Photo courtesy of Missouri Conservation Department.)

(c)

(d)

"The results of 22 months of extension trapping (to June 30, 1947) show an average cost of $15.92 per animal taken, excepting foxes; including foxes, which are often as important to farmers as the other predators are, the average cost per animal has been $6.99. This is the most economical of all the procedures except the less selective bounty system. The cost might appear still lower if it were possible to get complete reports from all farmers. Most of these data came from a questionnaire that yielded only a 34 per cent return.

"All counties requesting extension-trapper service have received it, in nearly all cases within four weeks. Formerly a county often had to wait several months, if indeed it received assistance at all. Prompt and effective action under the extension program has reduced the number of complaints received by the Commission almost to zero.

"Farmers trained under the extension-trapper program have spent an average of 2.01 man-days per catch (excepting foxes); the corresponding time spent by the two extension trappers has averaged 1.42 man-days per catch. Thus both together spent only 3.43 man-days per catch, which is less than half of the 7.54 man-days spent by the government trappers.

"An advantage of this plan is that once farmers in an area of damage are trained as they can apply control measures when these are needed, without waiting for someone to act for them. Also, farmers in Missouri enjoy more legal privileges than did the government trappers. For example, a farmer may kill any animal (except a beaver or bald eagle) found damaging his property, while the government trapper had to release any predator that was on the protected list.

"It has been well shown, in Missouri and elsewhere, that extermination is neither financially possible nor biologically wise. At the same time, it has been shown that satisfactory control of damage (as contrasted with the more killing of many animals) is practicable through the elimination of the individual 'criminals.' This is best done by concentrating the trapping within the range of these individuals."

The reader of the foregoing may feel the author somewhat prejudiced in favor of the government hunters, but after being one himself, later leading them in various States, and finally, directing the activities of hundreds of them, I am sure any fair critic will agree with what I write, particularly if time in the field could be spent viewing their activities. The choosing, developing, and training of government hunters in adopting and practicing sane policies and methods that are based on every consideration

Plate 46. World War II made possible use of the "Jeep" on coyote trap lines enabling hunter to go anywhere and cover large territory.

of the selectivity, safety, humaneness with respect to the control of harmful species of wildlife as we find them today paralleled the trials and tribulations of the builders of our western railroads in earlier times. At the time, the railroad contractor contended with situations where he often had one crew leaving that he had just fired, one on the ground, and finally one on its way to take the place of those about to be dismissed. As a result, there came a time when he had a trustworthy crew that could build the railroad any place under any conditions as exemplified in the astounding engineering accomplishments as our rails crossed the western mountains. So today we find the government hunters as a group capable of coping in a most satisfactory manner with any vexing predator problem that may arise. (See Plate 46.)

COOPERATIVE DIANAS OF THE RANGE

Beginning and continuing onward from World War I, a number of women have become federal predatory animal hunters, generally wives of government hunters. They often run their own traplines. A description of two will suffice, as their cases parallel that of the other women. Our first lady weighing less than 100 pounds who was humorous, talkative and energetic had lived for years with her one child, the nomadic life of her hunter-husband. In addition to doing the cooking and other camp work she assisted on the traplines, and had become a good driver of their four-horse team, saddled and rode horses skilfully, used a rifle well, and was competent to meet any conditions that might arise under the primitive conditions of life in the open. One day she asked the Federal State leader in charge of predator control to be placed on the pay roll as a government hunter under the condition that if she failed to make good she was to receive no pay. Somewhat doubtfully her request was granted and during the 2 years she remained in the service, her catch of coyotes and bobcats about equaled that of her husband, while she continued to keep the camp in excellent condition, and assisted in the packing and moving of it when the occasion demanded.

These dianas also have just as many hair-raising episodes in dealing with the denizens of the wild. Our lady number two witnessed a most unusual incident that occurred on July 15, 1946: While Mrs. Iva Young, Government predatory animal huntress was inspecting her trapline in New Mexico, she found a young bear weighing approximately 75 pounds in one of her coyote traps. Although she was accompanied by her husband, who is not very active, release of the bear (when known to be non-predatory and a government hunter procedure wherever possible) presented quite a problem. She drove her pick-up close to the trap location and the bear ran under it and wrapped the trap chain around the rear axle. She then succeeded in getting a rope around the bear's neck and pulling him out from under the pick-up. Jumping up into the pick-up bed, she pulled the bear's head up against the bumper and held him while her husband released the bear's foot from the trap. The bear then attempted to climb into the pick-up with her and she fought him out with a shovel and again he ran under the vehicle. Mrs. Young then quickly cut the rope about a foot from his neck and the bear scooted up a tree, much to her relief. Since there was a slip loop around the bear's neck, he soon freed himself from the rope and is presumably enjoying his freedom in the mountains.

Throughout the past 25 years heated controversy has arisen as to the efficacy of the government hunter's control of the coyote compared to the bounty system. Seldom is an annual meeting of the stock interests held anywhere in the West but what this question is invariably debated. Prior to the Federal Government's entry into cooperative predatory control by actual appropriations from the Federal Treasury in 1915, most of the States, in addition to the counties, had sanctioned various bounty acts for many years (the first one for wolf control previously noted was enacted by the colonial government of Massachusetts in 1630). The majority of the bounty acts in the West against the coyote were attended by disastrous financial results, and had brought but little relief. Many authorities have considered the bounty acts legalized fraud; and many of their operations proves this.

As a result of patch work defense of the western bounty system there occurred at the turn of this century an attempt to bring into being a unified bounty plan for all the western states, the so-called "west wide" plan. This proposal formed one of the main topics at the annual convention of the American Livestock Association held in Denver, Colorado, during January 1899. The proposal favored not only uniformity for all western and territorial bounty laws, but a reward "sufficiently large to be effective" (Palmer, T. S., 1899: 65). Accordingly four States, Colorado, Montana, Minnesota, and Wyoming, attempted a new bounty law, but all attempts failed.

The "west wide" bounty plan, though first conceived nearly a half century past, and having in that interval died several natural deaths for want of unified action, nevertheless demands for the bounty to replace the cooperative work of the federal hunter still echo from the western range states. Sproat (1943: 27-28) whose sincerity and long experience as a range man qualifies him as an authority on coyote controls puts it the following way with respect to the bounty vs. the government hunter:

"Practically every issue of the (National) *Wool Grower* mentions an increase in the coyote population all over the western ranges. Decided differences of opinion are expressed by sheepmen regarding the control of this varmint. Some advocate a bounty, some swear by the Fish and Wildlife Service, and some favor a combination of both methods, with bounties being paid during the denning season and professional hunters carrying on the year round.

"At the risk of bringing up a heated controversy, I herewith flatly state that the bounty system is totally useless in the control of the coyote. When the bounty is mentioned, its advocates always fall back on the cost per head per animal killed. Very well, let's say a section has a hundred coyotes infesting it. We go after them under the bounty system and get 80 percent or better in a comparatively short time. Eighty coyotes at a $2 bounty looks like good work, but is it? Those eighty animals are the young and almost harmless of the species. They have not yet learned to be killers and do not exceed 10 percent of the damage, and are easily caught. Many of your bounty hunters will then pull their line of traps and seek more favorable localities. Just what have they accomplished? Practically nothing so far as control of the killing coyote is concerned. Even should they stay and get 15 percent more, they still would be far from cleaning the range. The last 5 percent does 90 percent of the damage and when you get them you have done something, but not if figured on a cost-per-head basis.

"I have had the unfortunate experience of having to provide sustenance or, to say it a little more plainly, feed for a real killer this spring.

. . . .

"When you find one lamb partly eaten, another with the side torn open and only the stomach gone (that is an especial tidbit for real killers—the warm milk which the lamb has suckled from his mother) and then five or six more, bitten through the head and not killed, maybe just able to give a mournful little bleat, you rather lose control and express yourself much more forcefully than politely.

"This section has been lucky to have had, during the winter, a trapper from the Fish and Wildlife Service. He has made a good kill but has been handicapped in the use of poison as the locality is a farming one and there may be one or two trapwise old residenters who stay close enough to the ranches to be safe except from traps, which means immune almost from anything except a rifle shot, and they are clever enough to keep out of sight of even that. Now just what is that coyote worth to me, I mean his carcass? On a cost basis that coyote has done $500 worth of killing and that is not an estimate, it is cold fact from the count of lambs. Figure that fellow on a cost basis and the bounty men have you whipped but I hope I have three celebrations coming —when we whip Hitler and Hirohito and when we kill that damn coyote.

"I have condemned the bounty system. What have I to offer? Just who are most interested in coyote destruction? Wool growers first, game men next. Right here I want to insert a statement that the game men never have given the wool growers credit for their work in coyote control. Take the wool men's contribution to coyote destruction out of the picture and in a few years there would not be enough game left to bother with. Finally we have the Federal Government, which could spend a lot more money on coyote destruction and be doing a lot more good than it is with lots of other expenditures. Many states have laws allowing the sheepmen to act themselves to provide funds for predatory animal destruction. Some game departments voluntarily contribute or keep their own men in the field.

"My idea of the way to control the coyote is to combine all those efforts under one head, and I prefer the Fish and Wildlife Service. If the man in charge is not of the cooperative type, get him out, but someone has to be at the head of things and these men have the experience. Then district the states, if possible, so making the districts that control work can go on the year round. Beat the sheep into the mountains and use poison baits which a few warm days render harmless to the herder's dogs. The same in the fall on the winter ranges, be either ahead or behind the sheep. Pay the trapper a good wage, and cooperate with him when he is on your range. A lone trapper is a rather helpless individual in many instances if on his own entirely, but you can do him and yourself a lot of good by a little bait, a little hay, the use of a pasture or even grub. All furs should be sold and the proceeds go into the pot. I do not believe in letting the trapper have the furs. In conclusion, let me say that I am a great believer in poison as a means of getting the coyote, but the man who uses it must know his business. Preferably he should keep the sheepman informed of where it is being used, perhaps the herders also. Traps come next but a good rifle in the hands of a man who can use it is not to be sneezed at.

"I know I am going to find opposition to my plan, but I am not just talking through my hat. I have been 44 years on the range and have seen most every method of coyote destruction tried. I can remember when the sheepmen would employ a few good riders to bring the wild burros from the Snake River plains into the foothills where they would be shot and filled full of strychnine when warm. We used to make tremendous kills that way. It was sort of hard on the jackasses, though, and they finally petered out. Some of my readers may think they are not quite all gone.

"The best kills I ever saw made were made by the Fish and Wildlife Service (then the Biological Survey) supervising my efforts at poisoning. One job was done in the fall before the sheep hit the fall range. We use the leaf system of straight pork fat, the poison being inserted between two thin slices. Never lost a dog but we did clear that section of the range for that fall anyway. The other time was in late winter before the sheep left the feed yards. The same method was used as in the spring except that I tied an old skinned ewe on behind the car with a chain and dragged her over the frozen snow till there was nothing but the bones of the two hind legs left and not much bone either. There were just enough pieces of flesh left on the hard snow to intrigue the coyotes along and every little ways a bait was dropped. We never found many but we got them just the same. When one carcass was used we fixed up another and away we went. I ran on to a Basque operator on the range the next spring. I struck him for a little assistance to pay for the gasoline I had used—that was before rationing—and he whipped out his check book, 'How much?' I said a couple dollars. 'You ask ten,' he said, 'I give you it. You ask twenty, I give it. Last year I lose a hundred lambs out of two bands. This year never hear coyote holler, dead ones I see lots. And that's the way I like them.'"

Tindall (1942: 6, 14), writing of the work of the cooperative federal hunter, adds further to the record as established in Missouri, stating: "The men are termed cooperative trappers, and wisely so. Local organizations or groups, including county courts, farm bureaus, and livestock associations, pay about half of the salaries of the trappers. The remainder is divided between the Federal Fish and Wildlife Service and the Missouri Conservation Commission. The traps and other supplies are provided by the federal agency. . . .

"Few services are appreciated more than those of our wolf trappers."

Similar comments have been continually voiced in all the other livestock producing states of the western United States, all tending to seek more extended federal cooperation from its hunters in coyote control. Generally this is in the form of requests for increased appropriations for the hiring of more trained hunters.

TRAPPING

The trapping of coyotes is a popular and often profitable form of recreation for many farm boys, private professional trappers, or those seeking a short respite in the out-of-doors. Coyote trapping technique among amateur and professional trappers is as varied as in the case of trapping the large wolves. Basically, however, after all the pros and cons for the various techniques practiced are boiled down, it will be found that the following recommendations parallel or duplicate most of the present-day techniques. It is the procedure followed by the majority of the Federal-State hunters. Furthermore, the descriptions and techniques used such as in trapping and den hunting may convey additional information about the natural history of the coyote that may have been inadvertently omitted in all of the foregoing.

As coyotes at times make serious inroads on the stocks of sheep and lambs, cattle, pigs, and poultry, as well as on the wild game mammals and the ground-nesting and insectivorous birds of the country good control can be accomplished many times by trapping. Wherever the coyote occurs in large numbers, it is a source of worry and loss to stockmen, farmers, and sportsmen because of its destructiveness to wild and domestic animals. The coyote is by far the most persistent of the predators of the western range country; and moreover, it is a further menace, as previously noted, because it is a carrier of rabies, or hydrophobia. This disease as previously noted was prevalent in Nevada, California, Utah, Idaho, and eastern Oregon in 1916 and 1917, and later in Washington and in southern Colorado. Since this widespread outbreak, sporadic cases of rabid coyotes have occurred each year in the Western States. Likewise it has been noted the coyote has also been found to be a carrier of tularemia, a disease of wild rabbits and many rodents that is transmissible and sometimes fatal to human beings.

Much of the country inhabited by coyotes is purely agricultural and contains vast grazing areas, and a large percentage of the food of the animals of those areas consists of the mutton, beef, pork, and poultry produced by the stockman and farmer, and the wild game that needs to be conserved. It is a matter of great importance, therefore, to the Nation's livestock-producing sections, as well as to the conservationist's plan of game protection or game propagation, that coyotes be controlled in areas where they are destructive.

Every wild animal possesses some form of defense against danger or harm to itself. With coyotes this is shown in their acute sense of smell, alert hearing, and keen eyesight. To trap this animal successfully, one must work to defeat these highly developed senses when placing traps, and success in doing so will come only with a full knowledge of the habits of the predator and after repeated experiments with trap sets. Individual coyotes possess great cunning, particularly old animals that have been persistently hunted and trapped with crude methods.

Most any foul smelling odor will always attract the coyote to any point. It is this trait that trappers mainly depend upon in concocting various scents for use in trapping the animal. Recent remarkable occurrences showing this trait were recently reported from southwestern Arizona and brought to the attention of Arthur F. Halloran, Manager of the Kofa Game Range. It appears that the maintenance men serving the newly constructed 26-inch natural gas line that extends from New Mexico to California and crosses the Kofa Game Range of Arizona claim that coyotes find the leaks in the line.

At the pipe joints small leaks are occasionally present. The escaping gas seeps up through the soil, thus creating a slight odor at the surface. Coyotes attracted by the odor dig down through the soft, powdery soil to the source at the pipe. When the repairmen find the coyote diggings, they know that they have located the leak.

The steel trap, in sizes 3 and 4, for coyotes is recommended for capturing this predator. Steel traps have been used in this country by many generations of trappers, and although deemed by many persons to be inhumane, no better or more practical device is yet available to take their place.

On the open range coyotes have what are commonly referred to as "scent posts," or places where they come to urinate. The animals usually establish these posts along their runways on stubble of range grasses, on bushes, or possibly on some old bleached-out carcasses. Where ground conditions are right for good tracking, these scent posts may be detected from the toenail scratches on the ground made by the animal after it has urinated. This habit of having scent posts and of scratching is similar to that noted in dogs. As coyotes pass over their travel ways, they generally stop at these posts, invariably voiding urine and occasionally excreta also.

Finding these scent posts is of prime importance, for it is at such points that traps should be set. If such posts cannot be found, then one can be readily established, if the travel way of the coyote has been definitely ascertained, by dropping scent of the kind to be described later on a few clusters of weeds, spears of grass, or stubble of low brush. The trap should then be set at this point. Any number of such scent stations can thus be placed along a determined coyote travel way.

Time consumed in finding a coyote scent post is well spent, for the success of a trap set depends upon its location. Coyotes cannot be caught unless traps are set and concealed where the animals will step into them. If traps are placed where the animals are not accustomed to stop on their travel ways, the chances are that they will pass them by on the run. Even if a coyote should detect the scent, the fact that it is in an unnatural place may arouse the suspicion of the animal and cause it to become shy and make a detour. Often the fresh tracks of shod horses along the coyote runways are sufficient to cause the predator to leave the trail for some distance.

Travel ways of coyotes are confined to open and more or less broken country. In foraging for food over these runways the animal may use trails of cattle or sheep, canyons, old wood roads, dry washes, low saddles on watershed divides, or even highways in thinly settled areas. Any one of these places, or any combination of them, may be a coyote runway.

Places where carcasses of animals killed by coyotes, or of animals that have died from natural causes, have lain a long time offer excellent spots for setting traps; coyotes often revisit these carcasses. It is always best to set the traps a few yards away from the carcasses at weeds, bunches of grass, or low stubble of bushes. Other good situations are at the intersection of two or more trails, around old bedding grounds of sheep, and at water holes on the open range. Ideal places for coyote traps are points 6 to 8 inches from the bases of low clusters of weeds or grasses along a trail used as a runway.

Setting the Traps

Traps used should be clean, with no foreign odor. In making a set, a hole the length and width of the trap with jaws open is dug with a trowel, a sharpened piece of angle iron, or a prospector's pick. While digging, the trapper stands or kneels on a "setting cloth," about 3 feet square, made of canvas or of a piece of sheep or calf hide. If canvas is used, the human scent may be removed by previously burying it in an old manure pile. The livestock scent acquired in this process is usually strong enough to counteract any scent later adhering to the setting cloth and likely to arouse suspicion. The dirt removed from the hole dug to bed the trap is placed on the setting cloth. The trap is then dropped into the hole and firmly bedded so as to rest perfectly level.

Instead of using digging tools, some hunters bed the trap where the ground is loose, as in sandy loam, by holding it at its base and with a circular motion working it slowly into the ground even with the surface, and then removing the dirt from under the pan before placing the trap pad to be described later. An important advantage of this method is that there is less disturbance of the ground around the scent post than when tools are used, for the secret of setting a trap successfully is to leave the ground as natural as it was before the trap was concealed. A double trap set, as shown in Plate 47 may be used and is often preferred to a single set for coyotes.

The trap may be left unanchored or anchored. Either drag-hooks may be attached to a chain (preferably 6 feet long) fastened by a swivel to the trap base or to a spring, and all

Plate 47. Double steel trap set on coyote runway bedded before using trap pan covers and final burial. Coyote scent post is old bone shown in upper left corner.

buried underneath, or a steel stake pin (See Plates 48, a, b) may be used, attached by a swivel to a 6-foot chain fastened to the base or a spring of the trap. If a stake pin is used, it should be driven full length into the ground near the right-hand spring of the trap, with the trigger and pan directly toward the operator. Anchoring the trap is the preferred method, because animals caught are obtained without loss of time and because other animals are not driven out of their course by one of their kind dragging about a dangling, clanking trap, often the case where drag hooks are used.

The next stage (See Plates 49 and 50) is the careful burying of the trap and building up of a so-called shoulder around and under the pan. This should be so built that, when it is completed, the shape of the ground within the jaws of the trap represents an inverted cone, in order to give a foundation for the pan cover, commonly called the "trap pad." The trap pad may be made of canvas, of old "slicker cloth," or even of a piece of ordinary wire fly screen cut into the shape shown in Plate 51. The trap pad to be effective must contain no foreign odor that might arouse the suspicion of the coyote.

In placing the trap pad over the pan and onto the shoulders of the dirt built up for carrying it, the utmost care must be taken to see that no rock, pebble, or dirt slips under the pan, which would prevent the trap from springing. With the trap pad in place (See Plate 51), the entire trap is carefully covered with the remaining portion of earth on the setting cloth (See Plate 52).

Traps should be covered at least half an inch deep with dry dust if possible. It is well to have the covered surface over the trap a little lower than the surrounding ground, for a coyote is then less apt to scratch and expose the trap without springing it. Furthermore, the animal will throw more weight on a foot

Plate 48. (a and b) Photos showing use of stake pins.

Plate 49. Building up shoulder around and under trap pan.

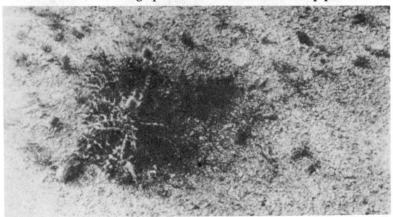

Plate 50. Trap completely buried.

placed in a depression, and thus is more likely to be caught higher on the leg and with a firmer grip. All surplus earth on the setting cloth not needed for covering the trap should be taken a good distance away and scattered evenly on the ground.

Scenting

A few drops of scent are now applied (See Plate 53) to the weed, cluster of grass, or stubble used as the scent post. A scent tested and successfully used by Government hunters is made as follows:

Put into a bottle the urine and the gall of a coyote, and also the anal glands, which are situated under the skin on either side

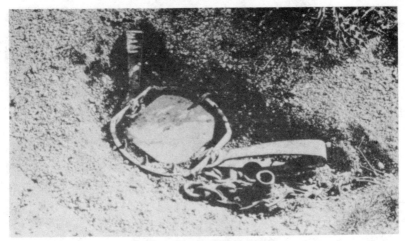

Plate 51. Trap pad and its use.

Plate 52. Use of earth on setting cloth.

of the vent and resemble small pieces of bluish fat. If these glands cannot be readily found, the whole anal parts may be used. To every 3 ounces of the mixture add 1 ounce of glycerin, to give it body and to prevent too rapid evaporation, and 1 grain of corrosive sublimate to keep it from spoiling.

Let the mixture stand several days, then shake well and scatter a few drops on weeds or ground 6 or 8 inches from the place where the trap is set. The farther from the travel way the trap is set, the more scent will be needed. A little of the scent should be rubbed on the trapper's gloves and shoe soles to conceal the human odor.

Plate 53. Coyote scent is placed on side of brush or weed that is nearest the buried trap.

If the animals become "wise" to this kind of scent, an effective fish scent may be prepared in the following way:

Grind the flesh of sturgeon, eels, suckers, carp, or some other oily variety of fish in a sausage mill, place in strong tin or iron cans, and leave in a warm place of even temperature to decompose thoroughly. Provide each can with a small vent to allow the escape of gas (otherwise there is danger of explosion), but screen the aperture with a fold of cloth to prevent flies depositing eggs, as the scent seems to lose much of its quality if many maggots develop. This scent may be used within 3 days after it is prepared, but it is more lasting and penetrating after a lapse of 30 days. It is also very attractive to livestock, and its use on heavily stocked ranges is not recommended, as cattle are attracted to such scent stations and will spring the traps.

An excellent system for a hunter to follow is to commence with a quantity of ground fish placed in large iron containers, similar to a milk can. As the original lot is used on the trap line, it should be replenished by adding more ground fresh fish. The addition from time to time of new material seems to improve the quality of the scent mixture.

Where no moisture has fallen, rescenting of scent posts need be done only every four or five days. In wet weather every third day is good practice. For dropping the scent it is best to use a 2- to 4-ounce shaker-corked bottle.

The actual trapping of a coyote by the method here described occurs when the animal comes over its runway and is attracted to the "post" by the scent that has been dropped. In approaching the spot for a smell the animal invariably puts a foot on the concealed pan; the jaws are thus released and the foot is securely held. The place where a coyote has thus been caught affords an excellent location for a reset after the animal has been removed from the trap. This is due to the natural scent dropped by the animal while in the trap.

It is advisable always to wear gloves while setting traps and to use these for no other purpose than for trap setting.

DEN HUNTING

One of the best methods of keeping down the increase of coyotes is to destroy the newly born whelps before they leave the dens to shift for themselves. A little time spent in April, May and June in locating dens and destroying the young coyotes will save months of strenuous effort trying to rid the range of the predators after they have reached maturity.

Coyotes are particularly destructive during the denning season because of the need of extra food both for themselves and for their young. Lambing bands of sheep on open ranges suffer the heaviest losses. Coyotes that kill lambs during April and May generally have dens, and when the dens are located and the whelps destroyed, the sheep killing usually stops. Some coyotes show great cunning in refraining from killing lambs near their dens and will pass by a band of sheep herded directly over a den to raid another several miles distant. They have been known to carry a leg of lamb as far as 8 miles to their young in the den. Contrary to the belief of stockmen and others, the male coyote is as destructive as the female, and special attention to fresh kills at lambing time has shown that the tracks of male coyotes are more in evidence than those of females.

The most essential qualifications of a den hunter are keen observation, persistence, and familiarity with the habits of coyotes. He can probably become more skilled in den hunting than in any other phase of coyote control. The denning habits of coyotes are similar in most sections, and the same general methods of den hunting can be applied in humid mountainous sections as in semi-arid deserts.

"Den signs" are indications of denning activity and the den

hunter should always watch for them. They may consist of tracks, a well worn path leading to and from a den, or holes freshly cleaned out. Holes made by coyotes in digging out squirrels or rabbits should not be confused, however, with those prepared for dens. A good hunter will overlook no likely place and will investigate every hint, for dens are often found where least expected. He should look for den signs in every locality where animals are frequently seen. He should keep in mind the places used by pairs of coyotes and visit all old dens known, as signs may often be discovered there at whelping time. Holes may be cleaned out in one canyon and the den be just over the hill in another. Sheep herders on a range usually can give information concerning locations of dens.

The equipment of a den hunter should include at least two gentle saddle horses, a small shovel, a pair of field glasses, a rifle of not less than .25 caliber, and a dog. Coyotes are not so much afraid of a man on horseback as of one on foot. A rider, therefore, can get many good shots, and in heavy sagebrush he can more easily see and track coyotes from his vantage seat upon a horse.

The proper time for hunting coyote dens is from April 5 to June 15. If too early a start is made, before some of the coyotes have whelped, the territory will have to be covered again. Where signs indicate a late den, however, a follow-up visit to it should be made.

Den hunting should be systematic and thorough. Where the soil is sandy the movements of coyotes can be readily determined by means of tracks and other signs characteristic of the whelping season. The general location of a den may occasionally be learned by hearing the howling of the coyotes, but other means must be employed to find the exact spot. It may be located by tracking, by watching the movements of the old coyotes, or by riding the range looking for holes, but systematic tracking insures the best results.

A good time to hunt dens by tracking is just after a rain. Another is the day after a severe windstorm, as storms restrict the activity of the coyotes.

Water holes and springs in the desert are excellent places from which to start in hunting dens. The den hunter should circle the water hole, noting the direction of the tracks and giving special attention to those of pairs and to their relative freshness, for when fresh tracks of a pair are noted, they are generally close to the den. When sign is found, it should be back-tracked to a point where there are tracks going both ways; the tracks begin to form a trail within a quarter of a mile from the dens. Near the den, unless the ground is too hard, many tracks will be found going and coming in every direction. Finding the den is then an easy matter. Sometimes, however, tracks lead to a den from only one direction.

Loose hairs and distinctive tracks are often observed in the mouth of a used coyote den.

When a female leaves the den for water she nearly always travels in a direct line, probably not deviating over a hundred yards from it in a distance of several miles. Coyotes do not always water at the same place each time, however, nor return to their den direct from the watering place unless the den is a long distance from water. Sometimes the male will remain near the den while the female is away, but more often the two travel together, the female holding a little more to a true course than the male. The tracks often indicate that they travel side by side for some distance, the male then wandering away several hundred yards but later returning to his mate.

Coyotes with dens have regular hunting grounds to which they usually travel on a nearly straight course, whether near or several miles distant, but they do not travel back to the den on a direct line again until after they have made their kills.

When the den is in danger of being discovered coyotes act in a nervous manner. Some will circle about it at a distance when the hunter is near; the old female may be seen in one direction and after disappearing, may later be seen peering over a hill in another quarter. When a female with a den first sees a person, she looks at him for a moment, then almost invariably toward the den, sometimes turning completely around to do so.

A den is usually located within a radius of approximately a mile of freshly cleaned-out holes. An experienced hunter can tell by the appearance of a den and by signs nearby whether it is occupied, without dismounting from his horse. When a den is found, if the whelps are roaming a considerable distance away, the searcher should circle it, making much noise to frighten them into returning. They should not be rushed, however, as they will then scatter and run into any accessible hole and extra effort in digging them out will be required.

As a rule, one will not find many live rabbits near a den; so that in a rabbit-infested district a scarcity of rabbits may be an indication of a nearby den.

The digging necessary to capture pups depends largely on the nature of the soil and the location of the den (Plate 54). Some dens are so shallow that little digging is required; others cannot be dug out; and some burrows lead straight into a bank or under a hardpan ledge. Much work can be avoided by running a shovel handle or long stick as far as possible into the hole to ascertain its direction and then digging a pit down to the den instead of following the burrow. Where digging is extremely difficult, the animals can be destroyed by the use of calcium cyanide gas as later described. If pups can be seen back in a den but cannot be reached in digging, a forked stick or a wire so twisted as to catch in their fur has been employed to save labor; but if the den or burrow branches and turns, such an instrument is never wholly satisfactory, as some of the whelps are likely to be missed. (See Plate 55.)

Before digging is begun, the den entrance should be blocked to prevent the escape of the mother coyote, should she be inside the den. When the pups are of suckling age she is often in the den with them, but when they are old enough to play and be fed outside she seldom goes into it. It is difficult to tell her whereabouts by her tracks, as she backs out of the den unless disturbed and the tracks all appear as if made in entering.

Pups are wobbly on their legs when only 2 or 3 weeks old so if a pit 18 inches deep is dug just outside the mouth of the den, they will fall into it when they attempt to crawl out of the den and can easily be captured.

Plate 54. Digging required to capture coyote pups depends on the nature of the soil and location of the den.

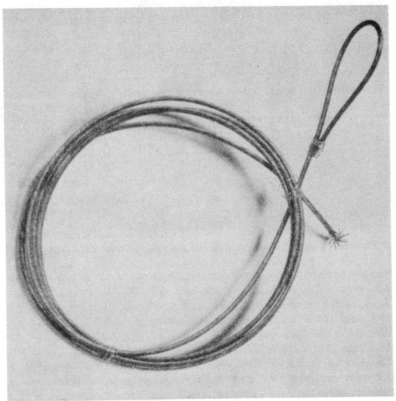

Plate 55. Wire cable (one-quarter-inch diameter), handle loop at one end and rosette of sharpened wires one-half inch long at the other, used (by twisting in the fur) in pulling coyote pups from the den.

Smoking the young out of the den is not satisfactory as a rule, but is sometimes successful. A good smoker can be made by soldering a half-inch hose coupling to the spout of a bellows-operated bee smoker and using sulphur and pieces of burlap as fuel. A piece of garden hose about 10 feet long can be attached and worked down into the den close to the pups, preferably behind them. The operator should stand back from the mouth of the den, armed with a club to dispatch the pups as they come out. Throwing a handful of calcium cyanide into a den and stopping the hole with dirt is an effective method of fumigation, but this chemical must be handled with extreme care—as a rule by experienced workers only—as it is also dangerous to man.

A small dog trained to go into dens and bring out the whelps is useful. Such dogs are scarce, but with careful handling, the

Plate 56. Wire-haired terrier dog and male coyote resting between rounds.

proper breed (wire-haired fox terrier or other terrier) soon learns and enjoys this work (See Plate 56). Any dog, however, is a great help, as the parent coyotes become much alarmed if it nears their den and often set up a howl or series of barks and yelps thus betraying the fact that a den is near. A small dog is preferable, and one that runs rabbits and hunts several hundred yards from the hunter is better than one that follows at the horse's heels. Coyotes are likely to give wide berth to a large dog, but will sometimes fight and chase a small one, thus presenting a good target for shots, particularly when the coyote goes some distance from the den to fight the intruder. For several days after the den has been destroyed females that have lost their whelps frequently fight or chase any dog that comes near.

A 12-gauge pump shotgun loaded with BB shot is good for hunting pups that have left the dens but are still together. They may be found lying under sagebrush or among the rocks and are more easily hit with a shotgun than with a rifle when they start to scatter.

Trapping and Shooting Adults

A hunter should leave as few traces as possible of his visit to a den. He should carry several traps, with which to try to capture the old coyotes. It is well to set a few traps "blind"— that is, without bait or scent—in the trails leading to the den, although some coyotes never return to a den after a hunter has visited it. A good set can be made by burying a dead whelp, leaving one foot exposed, and setting traps nearby. Holes that have been cleaned out for dens make excellent places for trap sets, particularly for catching females as they go in or out before whelping. In such a situation, two traps should be set blind, one on each side of the entrance or mound. Other favorable sites are the beds where old coyotes lie, presumably on guard. These beds may be close to the den or on a hillside or canyon rim half a mile away.

When coyotes are sighted near their dens they are usually quiet, and some good shots may be possible. A hunter should never dismount from his horse when a coyote stops to watch him, but should wait until it starts moving and then dismount on some high spot and be ready to shoot the instant it stops again. If it does not stop of its own accord, a low whistle will often halt it long enough to afford the hunter a good target.

FENCING

Fencing against coyote depredations has long been experimented with.

In the author's opinion, prevention of coyote depredation by the construction of a coyote proof fence involving large acreages is not economical or practical. Where smaller enclosures are required it can be made fairly effective in small pastures that are located near farm buildings for the protection of sheep, young lambs, poultry, and pigs.

In the early 1890's, a sheep ranch of 5,000 acres near Petaluma, California, fenced a field to keep out dogs and coyotes. Even for those times it must have been expensive for this fencing consisted of "split redwood pickets 5 feet long, 1½ inches thick, and 3 to 4 inches wide, driven into the ground at the lower end about 2 inches apart, spaced the same direction apart at top and woven into strands of wire by the machine made for the purpose. At intervals of 10 feet a post is set securely, standing 5 feet out of the ground, and to these posts the wires sustaining the pickets are secured by staples. A barbed wire is stretched 8 inches above the top of the pickets to make it dog proof, and another is stretched 2 feet from the ground to make it bull proof. Either dog or coyote getting into the field has an experience that deters future attempts. They are generally found seeking a way out. Two greyhounds are kept for the purpose of finishing them when necessary. The catch on this farm during the year 1891 was eighteen dogs, and ten coyotes. . . . The necessity for and the value of these arrangements to catch and kill the enemies of the sheepfold will be understood from the statement that the farm was devoted to the breeding of Red Polled cattle, polled Merino and Shropshire sheep. High grade ewes valued at $50 per head had but recently been brought to this ranch by importation and the importer was ready at all times to give $10 for killing a coyote on his land" (Carman, E. A., 1892).

During 1907 and 1910, the Forest Service of the Department of Agriculture initiated experiments with coyote proof fences surrounding certain lambing grounds known as Billy Meadows, located on the Wallowa National Forest of northeastern Oregon. Later experiments were conducted on the south fork of Carnero Creek, and the west fork of Cochetopa Creek, on the Cochetopa National Forest in Colorado. The findings were published in three circulars and one bulletin by the Forest Service numbered Circular 156, 1903, 32 pp., illus.; 160, 1909, 40 pp., illus.; 178, 1910, 40 pp., illus.; and Bulletin No. 97, 32 pp., illus. To the best of my knowledge, the findings in these experiments were never followed through by the Federal Government or national forest grazing permittees in actual wide acreage enclosure for the protection of livestock.

Over large acreage of sheep and goat grazing lands of west Texas, coyote proof fences have been constructed, but are not especially effective, for coyotes either dig under the wire, climb over it, or hunt for weak spots in the fencing as where it must often cross dry creek beds or arroyos that offer access inside these large pastures. Once in, coyotes often live, den, and depredate inside the pastures for years. I saw one large fenced pasture rounded up for coyotes that resulted in a kill of 23 that had succeeded either in digging under or had climbed over the wire.

Within the past decade, the practicability of using the so-called electrical fence, containing a live wire as a deterrent to coyote inroads to pastures or lambing grounds, has been advocated. With some domestic animals such a fence has proven its worth, but no knowledge at this writing has been obtained as to its application as a preventative means against coyotes. In areas where it might best be used, installation and maintenance expense would probably bar its practical use.

Often local control of depredating coyotes on a very limited scale can be obtained by certain management practices especially where poultry is involved. Jackson (1931) cites an instance on the Salt Plain area of Oklahoma where coyotes, aided by the tall maize as cover, laid in wait for chickens as they fed from an adjoining ranch during early morning. The owner had suffered a loss of as many as 10 chickens by a single coyote in one morning.

However, this was finally obviated by keeping his chickens enclosed until 11 a. m. before letting them out to forage.

USE OF SNARES

Snares are successfully used on coyote runways through brush and dense undergrowth or under woven wire fences, or through holes in wooden fences. Being of light wire construction, compact, and easy to set, they are considered by many trappers as a valuable supplement to traps. The snares that seem preferable to most coyote hunters are equipped with an automatic locking device that tightens and holds the animal, but does not cut the snare.

The technique of snare setting for the coyote calls for shaping the snare into a loop from 7¼ to 8½ inches wide and 8½ to 10½ inches long, all depending on the character of the set. Such a loop is lightly hung between two bushes in the trail the coyote is using. The bottom of the snare loop is kept 12 to 18 inches from the natural ground level. Some hunters use a temporary fastening of stovepipe wire to support the upper part of the snare loop, in addition to a small piece of wire fastened to the opposite supporting bush which causes the snare to hang the desired looseness in the center of the trail or runway. The end of the snare is securely fastened around a substantial tree or to a well-placed stake-pin. Often fine brush, dead weeds, and grass are used to camouflage the snare at its bottom and sides. Where convenient brush is not available for anchoring the sides of the snare, hunters use two supporting side sticks. Often from three to six snares are used along a single coyote runway, spaced according to the particular liking of the individual hunter.

COURSING WITH DOGS

The domestic dog and its use in the chase dates many centuries B.C. On some reliefs discovered by archaeologists in Egypt and elsewhere, hunting scenes are depicted showing the chariot drawn by horses in full speed in company with a racing hound-like dog. Apparently the gazelle, then a part of the Nile Valley fauna, was coursed and eventually captured much as was the coyote and wolf in later times wherever habitat permitted. The evolution of this form of sport unfolds an intriguing story, the minute details of which are too extensive to be used in this text. Suffice it to say, however, that running dogs of the greyhound, Russian wolf hound, and Scottish deer hound type have served many masters at times on our great plains as a method of coyote control, but more often merely as a form of sport. Often these dogs, referred to by their owners as "running dogs" were and are still used in certain parts of the West, to course jack rabbits as well as coyotes. (See Plate 57.)

Plate 57. A seasonal result of coursing coyotes with dogs. (Courtesy of South Dakota Dept. of Game, Fish and Parks. Photo occurs in June 1946 issue of South Dakota Conservation Digest, p. 11.)

At times coyote killing by this method became rather striking. Typical was the case of a hunter using 11 "running hounds" near Great Falls, Montana, in the fall and early winter of 1929-30, when in the course of 68 days he killed 162 coyotes. He used an especially equipped automobile capable of traveling 65 miles an hour from which he turned loose his 11 hounds after a coyote was once spotted. In 7 years this hunter had killed a total of 660 coyotes.

This sport, however, at the present writing is not as popular on the Great Plains as in former times because of barbed wire fences and the settlement of the country. During the heyday of coyote coursing seldom was any ranch to be found that did not own a pack of "running hounds." And, it is said every excuse was used by the respective owners "to let them follow their horses as they pursued their ranch duties." Thus throughout the plains in the latter part of the past century, and during the first decade of the present, one might often see "several hounds matching their strides against a flying bundle of animated fur which made great holes in the atmosphere as the long-eared jack rabbit or streaking coyote bounded in escape, and often won too. Hard on the heels of the dashing animals rode the excited ranchers, reveling in the full pleasure and thrill of the chase." . . . "with his brush whipped straight back in the breeze, his ears flat against his hard skull, his tough toes pushing the ground behind him as he raced from the gaping jaws of the lean hounds hot on his trail, the coyote offered his pursuers a sporting race seldom equaled in the annals of hunting."

Within the last several years, the airplane has been brought into use to support "running dogs" with their hunters, and in some coyote habitat subjects the animal to one more hazard with which it was heretofore unfamiliar during the intervals when pioneer coursing first got underway. A hunt that illustrates the proportions that this sport may assume was conducted over a 2-square mile grassy field 18 miles southeast of Elk City, Oklahoma, on March 21, 1945. Here it is recorded that while he was "Watched by a crowd of 1,000 curious onlookers, British Ambassador Lord Halifax today rode to the hounds in a coyote hunt staged for his benefit.

"The English diplomat, a devotee of the chase in his own country, termed the bizarre American show 'all very jolly.' Because the aim was to kill predatory animals he said he considered the sport 'an appropriate pastime in wartime.'

"Ten airplanes equipped with two-way radios raced above the hunting field throughout the chase to give the hunters and dilettantes 'spotter' information about the quarry.

"A cavalcade of about 50 persons rode in the hunt. For some time before the Halifax party arrived the airplanes had been flushing coyotes from surrounding territory and herding them into the field where the doughty hunters could find them.

"A slight hitch developed. The tall, spare Ambassador's legs were too long for the saddle stirrups on the horse he was to ride. A news photographer asked him to get on anyway to show how short the stirrups were but Halifax declined, smilingly: 'I know you're really hoping I'll fall off.' But finally the saddle was changed, the stirrups fit and the 'tally ho' for the big hunt was given.

"Barking dogs were released from the four sides of the field. The planes roared overhead. The hunting party surged forward at a leisurely walk. The hunt was in the English style, consequently, not a shot was fired.

"The dogs apparently were the only hunters to get close to a coyote. They caught two, the full bag of the hunt, and killed them before the horsemen reached them.

"The hunters were astride their horses little more than an hour before the show ended" (Anonymous, 1947).

During certain periods of the past century, bounties that were offered for dead coyotes by the ranchers caused numerous so-called "hound men" to devote their entire time toward coursing and killing coyotes. Thus the job of professional coyote killing for a time became a paying one, for the bounties offered by the ranchers were in most instances supplemented by bounties from the various counties and some States in the west.

COYOTE-GO-GETTER

In recent years a device known by the name of "The Humane Coyote-Getter," "Getter," or "Coyote-Go-Getter" has been invented and used on some western stock ranges as an adjunct but not a substitute for the steel trap as far as its use by government hunters is concerned. When ground conditions are unfavorable and thus hinder the efficacy of steel traps, or where an area needing coyote control is too extensive for using traps, this device serves a more useful and economic procedure in obtaining necessary control. The go-getter is a small set-gun that shoots a cyanide loaded shell. In the hands of an expert, it can be so used that it usually is more selective than the steel trap in controlling the coyote. As previously mentioned, Bynum's astounding take of coyotes in Maverick County, Texas, during October, 1946, was done by the sole use of the "go-getter."

Before the "go-getter" was used in coyote control on an operational basis by federal and cooperating personnel it was given an extensive field trial all of which was admirably reported upon by Weldon B. Robinson (1943) of the Wildlife Research Laboratory, Fish and Wildlife Service, Denver, Colorado.

The advantages of this device are its simplicity, requiring a minimum of trained hunters; its adaptability to use on ranges grazed by livestock or game; and its humane effectiveness against trapwise coyotes.

Parts of the coyote-getter.—The coyote-getter consists of the following parts: (1) the stake or barrel (See attached illustrations in Fig 19), the cartridge holder and chemical cartridge (2), and the firing pin unit (3). A setting tool (4) is furnished by the manufacturer. In addition it is necessary to have extra cartridge holders and cartridges and baits so that discharged coyote-getters may be reset.

Coyote-getter set locations.—The coyote-getter set locations are much the same as those used in trapping—that is, the device should be placed where the coyote can readily find it. Natural coyote runways, trails, bone piles, etc., are good sites. Whenever possible it is advisable to choose locations where the dead coyote

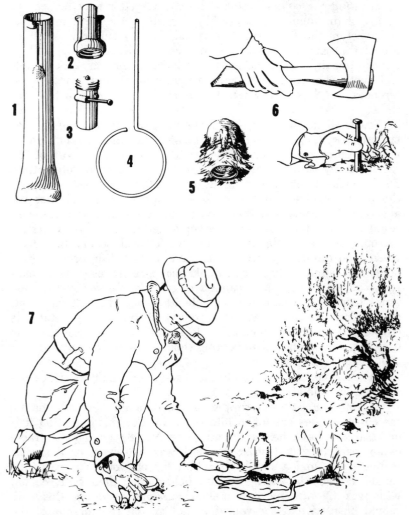

Figure 19. (1) Stake or barrel of coyote-getter; (2) cartridge holder with chemical cartridge in place; (3) firing pin unit; (4) setting tool for firing device; (5) the bait, consisting of the mounted cartridges covered with fur and then waxed to which the scent is applied; (6) method of driving the stake into the ground by use of inserted bolt; (7) method of handling a "set" coyote-getter to avoid danger from accidental discharge.

can easily be found. Although most of the animals are recovered within 100 yards of the set and many of them within 50 yards some will die as far as a quarter of a mile or more away, and thus it is desirable to choose locations that will permit the recovery of the quarry with a minimum of hunting.

Scenting the coyote-getter.—The coyote-getter may be scented in any of the following ways: (1) by putting the scent inside the stake before the firing pin is inserted, (2) by smearing scent on top of the bait, or (3) by putting scent inside the stake and on top of the bait. Any of the above methods appears to work equally well with the possible exception that rodent and insect interferences are lessened when the scent is put only within the stake.

Scents should be chosen with the view of arousing the coyote's curiosity or hunger and thus inducing it to take the bait in its mouth. Lures which cause coyotes to make a scent post of the set or merely to prowl around it are ineffective on coyote-getters. Since much of the success in using coyote-getters depends upon the proper choice and use of scents, operators should first use a variety of scents and then choose the ones that give the best results. Scents that are effective in a certain area, or a certain season, may be ineffective in others. Typical scents that have given good results at various times have bases of fish, beef, mutton, horse meat, prairie dog meat, mink, snake, rotten eggs, bone marrow, canned salmon, and canned dog foods. Beaver castors and skunk secretions often make valuable additions. Many of the scents may be used fresh as well as decomposed, but as a general rule coyote-getter scents should be less fetid than those used in trapping. The periods of rescenting should be governed by weather conditions as in trapping.

In the pioneer usage of the "go-getter" hunters were instructed as follows:

Making the baits.—A supply of baits should be made before the coyote-getters are taken into the field. For this operation it is necessary to have heavy thread (size No. 8) or light, durable twine, paraffin wax (either paraseal wax, parowax, or a similar sealing wax), and a supply of rabbit fur or wool. The cartridge should first be inserted into the holder and then both coated with wax by dipping into melted paraffin. In doing this care should be used that the wax does not get on the threads of the holder or on the primer of the cartridge. This initial waxing operation may be dispensed with, but it appears worth while in that it helps eliminate odors and holds the cartridge more firmly in the holder. Baits may be covered with rabbit fur or wool; either appears to work equally well. If mice are particularly troublesome, wool baits may give better results. In making rabbit fur baits, a square of fur about an inch on the side, should be placed over the top of the cartridge so as to cover all parts of the cartridge and holder and then tied securely with thread or twines. If wool baits are made, the wool should be wrapped around the cartridge and holder in such a manner as to completely cover them and then securely tied. There should be no excess of fur or wool at the bottom of the bait which would allow the coyote to grab something other than the part which will effectively discharge the device. The partially completed rabbit fur or wool bait should then be dipped in melted paraffin wax and the rough bait smoothed with the finger or an appropriate tool (5). In some instances, particularly in winter, it may be necessary to weaken the top of the bait with a knife, either before or after the waxing, so as to permit free passage of the poison.

In some localities and during some seasons baits can also be made of pieces of fat, prairie dog or rockchuck fur, feathers, or similar materials.

Setting the coyote-getter.—An iron rod or bolt, of a size to fit loosely inside the coyote-getter stake, should be used in driving the stake into the ground (6). Pounding the top of the stake itself should be avoided since it may dent the edge and retard the action of the firing pin unit. About an inch of dirt should be placed in the bottom of the stake so that the iron rod will not lodge there. The stake can then be driven into the ground by striking the rod with a hammer until the top of the stake is flush with the ground. Be sure that the stake is firmly anchored so that an upward pull on the bait will discharge the device rather than pull out the stake. In soft soils it may be necessary to drive a spike downward through the bottom of the stake to give it additional anchorage. The firing pin unit may be set by placing the trigger in a downward position, forcing the firing pin down with the setting tool, and then raising the trigger and releasing the firing pin. It should then be inserted into the top of the stake with a very thin layer of wool between it and the stake. This layer of wool, which will take out any rattles that might occur in the contact of the two metal parts, should be thin enough that it does not bind and retard the action of the firing pin unit. During cold weather it is advisable to moisten this layer of wool with mineral oil or glycerin to prevent the formation of ice around this vital working part. The prepared bait should then be attached by screwing it on to the top of the firing pin unit and by pushing downward at the same time to prevent discharge.

Whenever the bait must be changed or the coyote-getter taken up, the top should first be unscrewed, a downward pressure being maintained to prevent accidental firing.

Cautions in settng the device.—It is *absolutely essential* that the operator *exercise extreme caution* in working with the coyote-getter when the loaded cartridge is inserted. He should ascertain, without the bait and cartridge attached, just how much of an upward pull is necessary to release the firing pin and must realize that, with the bait attached, slight upward pull is likely to discharge it. The following safety rules should be observed:

(1) Gloves should always be worn while attaching and detaching the bait.

(2) No part of the body, with the possible exception of the gloved hand, should be exposed directly above the device (7).

(3) The operator should work on the up-wind side of the coyote-getter so that the poison is not blown in his face in the event of an accidental discharge.

(4) The operator preferably should form the habit of working with the bait from the side so that no part of his hand (or body) is directly above the device (7). However, if this method is too awkward, as is often the case, and it is necessary to have the hand above the device, then the gloved hand should be "cupped" in such a manner that in the event of an accidental discharge the poison does not strike the hand directly but at an angle and also is deflected away from his face and not into it.

The above cautions may seem unnecessary, but sooner or later practically every trapper who has used this device has had one explode accidentally. Some have been struck in the face and on the bare hands with the poison and, although no serious accidents have occurred, it must be realized that a serious injury or even a fatality is not an impossibility. The operator must appreciate the potential dangers of this implement and protect himself accordingly by forming safe operating habits.

Continued improvements are being made in this contraption and the techniques in its use, especially those concerned with protection of human beings, domestic stock, valuable dogs and fur bearers. As mentioned previously its main use is concerned with areas where trapping or other methods are not feasible.

The stealing of coyotes from coyote-getter lines has become a serious problem in some areas. It has been found that the addition of a small amount of aniline dye to the cyanide will permit the identification of coyotes killed by those cartridges. The dye will color the mouth of every coyote, and in many cases the coloration will extend to the fur around the mouth. Thus the employment of aniline dye only in cartridges supplied to government hunters makes possible conviction in the courts of fur thieves prone to follow the field activities of hunters and steal from their lines.

An eye witness account of a female coyote and the resulting antics following the explosion of the "getter" near Priest Lake, located 6 miles southeast of Choteau, Montana, on February 22, 1944, states that when the cartridge exploded in its mouth, it jumped 4 feet off the ground, then ran hard for approximately 77 yards and dropped dead.

As a means for safety, legislation has been passed forbidding the use of the cyanide gun except under the supervision of the State Game and Fish Department. Oklahoma passed such a law in its 1947 legislature.

AERIAL COYOTE HUNTING

Within the past 15 years killing coyotes with an automatic shotgun loaded with BB or No. 4 buckshot from the air over a flat, open country as found in the Dakotas, Nebraska, Idaho, and other western states, and to a limited extent in Alaska has become quite common, and in some instances has produced some heavy kills. The airplane is used to some extent also in spotting coyote dens to be later destroyed by men returning to den sites afoot.

This scheme of hunting involves the use of a hedgehopping airplane flown at ceilings of 300 feet, and sometimes slightly lower in the controls of a good pilot in company with a good marksman. At times it is most hazardous, and throughout the West smash-ups with resultant death to the participants have occurred. Besides low flying with all sorts of expert maneuvering and "gimlet twisting" to avoid hitting low hills, trees or buttes, the main technique requires the manipulating of the airplane, after a coyote has been spotted, so that the animal will be broadside to the marksman who generally sits directly behind the pilot, or alongside of him. As the coyote of course is handicapped when trying to outdistance the plane, once it has been spotted the resulting broadside target that it makes is sure murder whenever a coyote is maneuvered into this position, no matter how hard it tries to make its escape. Airplane hunting is generally begun with the breaking of dawn on a clear day.

In the beginning this form of hunting was mainly for sport, but in recent years it has assumed such large proportion that some states have been forced to regulate procedures that must be followed. Typical is North Dakota, and because it shows the trend of the times, this state's regulations are recorded as follows:

STATE REGULATIONS

"Pursuant to authority vested in the State Game and Fish Commissioner under Chapter 20-0108 of the North Dakota Revised Code of 1943, the following regulations are hereby prescribed for the use of aircraft in the hunting, killing and taking of predatory animals upon which the State of North Dakota pays a bounty.

"1. A permit to use aircraft in the hunting, killing, and taking of predatory animals may be granted for a limited period in any year to any person who complies with the following regulations and shall be valid only for the period stated in the permit and for the hunting of the predatory animals specified.

"2. Application for a permit shall be made to the Game and Fish Commissioner on forms prescribed by him and shall be verified.

"3. The application must be accompanied by a cash bond in the sum of $250.00, two hundred and fifty dollars, which shall be forfeited to the State of North Dakota if the holder of the permit is found guilty of violating the laws relative to hunting with aircraft or these regulations.

"4. The applicant must be at least 21 years of age and a resident of the State of North Dakota and shall be a duly licensed airplane pilot who has complied with all requirements of Federal and State laws, and regulations to entitle him to operate the airplane covered by the permit during the term and within the area covered by the permit, involving low flying, landing on ground other than established flying fields, trespass upon private property and other operations incident to such flying.

(In order to insure the safety of the pilot and for the protection of the general public, Rule No. 5 is prescribed upon recommendation and with the approval of the Director of the North Dakota Division of Aeronautics.)

"5. The applicant shall have at least 400 hours of total logged flying time as an airplane pilot of which at least 200 hours shall have been devoted to flying an airplane or airplanes of substantially the same type as the airplane to be used under the permit, and at least 30 hours shall have been devoted to flying the airplane to be used under the permit within six months immediately preceding the beginning of the term of the permit.

"6. Application for permit must show pilots license number and C.A.A. number and type of aircraft to be used.

"7. The number of the aircraft hunting permit must be painted on both sides of the plane fuselage so as to be readable from the ground while plane is in flight.

"8. Permits to hunt fox with airplane shall be valid only during the months of December, January, February and March.

"9. The granting of a permit to use aircraft in coyote and fox hunting does not grant the privilege of trespassing on private land. Such permission must be secured from the land owner or operator.

"10. Holders of permits to hunt predatory animals with aircraft must, prior to July first of each year, make a complete report to the Game and Fish Commissioner of all animals killed while operating under such permit.

"11. The permit shall be valid only for the use in such hunting of a specified airplane belonging to or under the control of the applicant, of such type and in such condition as to be suitable and safe for such use. The application shall state the name and address of the applicant, his interest in the airplane, the name and address of any other person having an interest therein and the nature of such interest, the N. D. license number, general description, make, model, color and distinguishing markings of the airplane and the number and location of the airport where it is based."

This order has been examined and approved as to form and execution this 4th day of October, 1946, by Nels G. Johnson, Attorney General of North Dakota. (Anonymous, November 1946: 9.)

Experiments in airplane hunting of the coyote in North Dakota during December of 1945 in which a Piper Cub plane was used a total of 104½ hours of flying time at $12.50 per hour resulted in a kill of 87 coyotes, and 49 foxes.

Hjelle (1946: 6) summarizing the hunting activities of 68 permit holders authorized by the North Dakota Game and Fish Department to take fox and coyote during winter of 1945-46 (November-March) shows a total of 3,290 coyotes were taken, or an average of 48 coyotes per permittee from airplane. These 68 permittees spent a total of 5,506 flying-hours, and averaged 0.60 coyote per flying-hour. The largest daily kill of coyotes were by two individual permittees who bagged 23 and 22 respectively. Cost per animal is not given.

As with other western states, Oregon has through its State Game authorities taken a try at controlling the coyote by use of the airplane. In a recent comment (Anonymous, 1946: 2) it is reported that:

"Sky hunting for coyotes this season (1945-46) produced results for the period of flying sponsored by the Oregon State Game Commission, according to the final report just compiled. During the fall and winter months the Commission paid for 373.20 hours of flying time and the hunters reported an actual kill of 804 coyotes plus a probable kill of 94. Total cost to the Commission was $4,722.71.

"Fliers employed were Roe and Oscar Davis of Burns; Dick Ballantine of Redmond and Al Tilse of Bend. The area covered included Lake, Klamath, Malheur, Harney, Deschutes, Grant, and Jefferson counties.

"Conditions for hunting were good during the winter because the coyotes bunched up in the open areas on account of the deep snow. The best kill of the season was made in South Warner Valley by Al Tilse, whose report on that particular trip reads: 'We got 48 in South Warner Sunday morning from 7:30 until 11:00. Scored 24 in the first 45 minutes of hunting. Only reason the gunner had to keep his eyes open when shooting was to keep from hitting a cow. The ranchers thought the Piutes [Indians] were attacking.' Wheat fields in that area serve as feeding grounds for ducks and geese, and at times the concentrations of waterfowl were so large that the shooting had to be delayed until the birds were through feeding and had returned to their resting grounds.

"The figures quoted here cover only the work done with game funds. Considerable aerial hunting has been financed by private individuals and county grazing boards and is being continued by those agencies." (Oregon State Game Commission Bulletin 1 (2): 2, May 1946.)

An Associated Press dispatch dated April 26, 1944, stated that two vacationing hunters who tried this scheme of coyote hunting for 35 days in eastern Oregon sagebrush country near Burns, Harney County, bagged 278 coyotes that netted a total of $2,432 from the sale of the pelts.

Some enthusiasts in hunting the coyote by airplane maintain elaborate equipment as in the case of two hunters of Atchison County, Missouri. These men at the time of writing possessed 3 jeeps, 2 Piper Cub planes, a plane to truck radio communication, plus 16 stag and greyhounds. When a coyote is spotted from the air, radio contact with the nearest truck following the plane carrying hounds brings a load of dogs pell-mell to the scene which are turned loose after the spotted coyote.

USE OF POISON

Use of various poisons, foremost of which has been strychnine, has long been directed against predators, rodents, and some birds as an instrument for ridding certain areas of these creatures when deemed detrimental, or for the taking of fur bearers. Use of poison for the latter should be discouraged by every means possible.

Poisoning operations for the control of the coyote beyond the limits of competent supervision, without full measure of precaution, or loosely conducted under various methods, can only result in condemnation of the method as a whole. Such was the case with regard to the poison exposed for killing coyotes, and other beasts, previously mentioned during the quarter of a century 1860-1885. Its like will probably never be duplicated or paralleled again in North America. This made a clean sweep of or greatly reduced numerous harmless species inhabiting the Great Plains.

On the other hand, intelligent use of poison under proper regulation and approved technique can so far remove or control objectionable features as to make the method entirely creditable to those using it as well as a most important means of solving the coyote problem in certain areas where it supplements other control methods. When properly used, poison should not be more destructive to other species than the use of traps, and in some cases it has been found to be even less harmful and more humane. This method is especially suitable for winter use against the coyote on some of the great stock ranges of the West, as it can then be employed with little or no danger to useful life. The cost of the same measure of control by any other known means would be practically prohibitive.

In the author's opinion, based on long field experience, only certain men become expert in the technique involving the use of lethal baits for coyote control. For this reason, the long descriptive hints explanatory of the proper use of this method of control had best be omitted. The interested reader can obtain full information from State and Federal agencies fully and expertly familiar with the subject. Poisoning, as a means of control, has been inserted at this point for the record simply to indicate that it is, and long has been in use as a method for killing certain so-called noxious animals. And, whenever its use is deemed advisable, this method should be entrusted only in the hands of experts.

BOUNTY SYSTEM

The exact period when man first began the practice of paying a bonus or gratuity provided by law or decree for the killing of so-called noxious mammals or birds is buried in the mists of antiquity. There is, however, a fairly clear record that can be traced over the past 2,700 years beginning with the Greeks about the year 600 B.C., and continuing on throughout various countries to the present time.

In the United States bounty legislation developed during a period of more than 300 years dating from the colonial act of 1630 in Massachusetts, but this legislation did not concern the coyote. It was not until the beginning of Territorial and the later formation of state and county in the Great Plains area, or generally speaking, not before the settlement of the vast region west of the Mississippi River to the Pacific Coast and from the Canadian to the Mexican borders that coyote bounty in the United States had its real start. Bounty legislation for control of the coyote therefore, is approximately a century old. Within that interval, millions of dollars have been paid in North America by bounty legislation of one sort or another for the riddance of coyotes. Generally speaking, administration of the bounty system wherever and whenever in vogue for killing this animal has been notoriously loose. Many who have studied the plan with an open mind are in agreement that the bounty system is legalized fraud—good benevolence, but poor business.

That well directed control of the enemies of livestock and game based on clearly defined facts is necessary is generally conceded. However, a depredation of a hawk or other predator is often so conspicuous that undue importance is usually attached to it, and an uninformed public is too often led to believe that if effective and complete predator control is practiced game may be produced in almost limitless numbers, and a whole species, such as the coyote, will be wiped out. As a consequence, predator control has been overly popular in some quarters. Because of its appeal, the bounty system has been repeatedly practiced. In North America practically every state, province, and territory has attempted it in some form or other, and in the aggregate appalling sums have been expended. All sorts of bounty schemes have been advocated. A modern instance concerns an effort to reduce the coyote population within the borders of a western state. As a means to accomplish this certain state sportsmen advocated a control measure for adoption by its State Game Department the following: That the department trap coyotes, ear tag them, and release three coyotes in each of the state's counties. Each tagged coyote killed would be worth $100 per animal, thus this scheme, it was declared, would cause a greater impetus to sportsmen for the killing of coyotes everywhere as they hoped to be rewarded eventually by an ear-tagged animal worth $100.

In considering the bounty problem as it applies to the coyote, or any species upon which it has been tried, it would seem the part of wisdom to consider the probable costs and benefits and also all possible negative factors. A venture of such proportions calls for sound business principles, and those responsible for its adoption should consider it as sanely as they would if it were a personal business proposition.

First, consider how long the bounty system has been in operation. The bounty system as mentioned has been in vogue a surprisingly long time. In Britain, it had been practiced for centuries, and in America (Massachusetts) since 1630—a period well over 300 years. Almost every state has tried it in some form or other and, in the aggregate, millions of dollars of public funds have been spent. At the present time, many states and territories have some such law on their statute books. Many of these are largely inoperative because adequate funds have not been provided. With other states, the law is on a county basis, and is therefore at the discretion of the county or township officials. In almost every instance, the bounty is paid only on a limited number of species, be it coyote or otherwise.

In general, justices of the peace, local game wardens, or county treasurers frequently officials unfamiliar with the species concerned must pass on the validity of claims. It is not surprising, therefore, that flagrant fraud and deception have characterized many of the attempts at control by bounty. Duplicate payments have been frequent, while payments on countless numbers of unidentified predators have been the rule in many states. Reports indicate, for example, that during the 5 years preceding 1927, Virginia had paid claims on 9,000 goshawks, yet there is only one authentic record of this species having been found within the commonwealth!

Bounties on predators are paid ostensibly: (1) to increase the game supply, and (2) to protect domestic livestock. But to what extent have these objectives been attained through payment of bounties on their supposed enemies?

States that have had the most experience with bounties find

no definite improvement in game or livestock conditions through such expenditures. It is of course difficult to analyze fluctuation numbers of game species and evaluate the causes. The factors affecting abundance of game species are numerous and not easily singled out. Nevertheless, it is significant that no state or county has yet proven that bounty payments are effective in increasing and improving game or livestock conditions.

Seth Gordon (American Game Association News Service, Washington, D. C., March 5, 1932), long one of America's more ardent conservationists, expressed his opinion as follows: "The trend of Game Departments today is away from the bounty system of predatory animal control because of the frauds and the intentional or ignorant destruction it has always inspired." This expression born of experience reflects in a few words the matured conclusion of the great majority of game officials throughout the country. The bounty system after having been tried in practically every state in the Union at some time has almost universally failed to fulfill the objectives for which it was established. Even in Pennsylvania, where the bounties have long been considered to justify huge expenditures of game funds this hope has been disproved. A carefully organized bounty system on coyotes in Michigan has been disappointing both to the game officials and farmers alike. A statement by J. VanCoevering (The Detroit News, March 21, 1937, p. 7, Sport Section), a Michigan wildlife columnist, crystallizes· thought on the situation as follows: "It must be admitted that the bounty system operates in a rather hit-and-miss fashion. Bounty trappers go where the harvest is likely to be best, which is natural enough. If the trapper is in the game for a living, he is not averse to turning loose a female coyote, either, for obvious reasons. Sheep men complain that the bounty trapper does not pay attention to the single coyotes that raise havoc with their flocks."

Jacobsen (1945) long and prominently familiar with rodent and predator conditions in California has this to say: "At no time in our 30 years of direct and indirect association with predatory animal control work in the Western States have we encountered any bounty payment plan which of itself has successfully brought about the reduction of predators [meaning mainly the coyote] when and where needed."

Sampson and Bennett (1948), after a meticulous study of the bounty system as affecting Missouri, conclude that "The bounty system is the cheapest way to assure the destruction of large numbers of predators. However, such destruction is indiscriminate and reduces neither the material damage nor the number of complaints. In Missouri, eleven years of bounty figures offer no evidence that the population of wolves and coyotes has been reduced thereby."

Here might be added the meaty comments of D. W. Douglas and A. M. Stebler (1946) who say:

"Many advocates of the bounty system apparently assume that it is something new and untried by the state of Michigan, and that if it were only given a fair trial, it would quickly prove itself. The fact is that a state bounty is very nearly as old as the state itself. In 1838, one year after Michigan became a state, the Legislature authorized the payment of a bounty of eight dollars on adult wolves and four dollars on wolf pups less than three months old. Half the cost of the bounty was paid by the state, half by the county. In this first year, the state paid out only $218 for wolf bounties, but the figure jumped to $1,245 in 1839 and to $1,938 in 1840. For nearly 60 years the 1840 expenditure was not exceeded in any year. Minor changes were made in the law from time to time, but no significant alterations were made until 1897. In that year, the Legislature established a bounty of $15 on adult wolves and $7 on pups under six months old; it also placed a bounty on lynx and bobcat. The bounty on an adult wolf became $25 in 1903.

"Annual payments began to rise (although not in a steady progression) to reach $7,156.50 in 1909 and $10,022.50 in 1915. In 1917, the bounty on wolves became $35 for adults, $15 for pups, and fox, owls, hawks, and weasels were placed on the bounty list. Woodchucks and crows were added in 1919. In the period following World War I bounty racketeers began to operate on a large scale, and payments skyrocketed, as here shown:

```
1917  ...............................$10,160.00
1918  ...............................  13,441.00
1919  ...............................  32,260.25
1920  ...............................  54,713.02
1921  ............................... 159,871.58
```

"During these 'bountiful' years there developed a flourishing business of importing pelts of 'wolves' (mostly coyotes, which were not distinguished from timber wolves in the bounty payments) from western and southwestern states. It wasn't a bad investment, buying Dakota coyote pelts for around $3 and selling them to the state of Michigan for $35. One pair of operators submitted 248 pelts to western Northern Peninsula counties for payment, and collected $8,880 for nine months' trafficking. . . . . State bounties since 1934 have been confined to wolves, coyotes, and Northern Peninsula bobcats. Present bounties of $15 on male coyotes or wolves, $20 on females, and $5 on bobcats in the

COYOTES, WOLVES AND BOBCATS BOUNTIED

Michigan, 1936-1945

Year	Wolves	Coyotes	Bobcats	Cost
1936	22	2,904	980[*]	$ 33,625
1937	37	2,573	500[*]	42,795
1938	49	2,593	...	46,000
1939	33	2,066	...	36,665
1940	33	1,866	4	33,165
1941	42	1,610	309	30,425
1942	43	1,501	290	28,690
1943	35	1,905	362	35,975
1944	44	2,869	582	53,915
1945[**]	23	3,278	626	60,510
Totals	361	23,165	3,653	$401,585

[*] Bounties paid in both peninsulas.
[**] Totals through November.

Northern Peninsula, are modest compared with the rates in the heyday of 1917-1921.

"Regulations covering payments apparently have prevented the serious abuses of importation and multiple payment, but it doesn't look as though the system has had much effect on the timber wolf population, while the coyote crop has declined and come back just as it probably would have done anyhow.

"The one incontrovertible fact is that bounty payments cost a lot of money, have cost the state of Michigan considerably over one and one-half million dollars since 1838. . . ."

Michigan State Conservation authorities aptly put the question (Anon., 1948, 17 (3): 14) by saying, "In the 10 years the bounty pay scale has remained constant, the number of coyotes bountied has gone up and down according to a regular curve of abundance and scarcity."

These foregoing comments about the Michigan situation can be applied to the majority of other States and Canadian Provinces.

Legalized Fraud

A study of the bounty plan in each century of its use brings to light countless examples of fraud. And the whole history of bounty payments shows that they tend to perpetuate rather than eradicate the animal they are supposed to destroy. Human nature being what it is, as soon as an objective (killing of predators) is made a source of income (by payment of bounty) the prevailing idea becomes one of propagating rather than eradicating.

Numerous examples and incidents could be cited. Scalps of domestic dogs and of coyotes are presented as wolf scalps. Female wolves or coyotes are deliberately turned loose after capture so that the species will continue and thus afford more revenue when whelps taken later bring in bounty money.

Unscrupulous hunters and others ship skins and scalps across state, provincial, or international boundaries to districts where the bounty payment is higher. Another common practice is to present the same skins at different (or even the same) bounty office twice or more times to step up the profits. (At the Game Department's expense.) Cases of this last nature have been discovered just recently (1947) in British Columbia according to Game Commissioner Cunningham.

Another swindle practiced frequently is that of "farming" predators. An example of this fraud is that of a case in a western state where more than 300 coyote pups were taken alive from many dens, put into a wire enclosure and fed on horse meat until they reached adult stage when they were killed and turned in for the higher bounty adult animals bring. At an increased value of over $10 an animal this particular fraud was up in the grand larceny class. Naturally this case was an extreme instance of its type but by no means unusual in design.

Impractical and Expensive

Besides being the point where "politics" enter into the question of wildlife management, the bounty system is awkward, costly and inefficient. As a control measure it is expensive even where honest efforts are made to carry out its provisions.

For one thing, huge sums are paid out for predators in remote areas where their presence is not a menace or even a genuine problem. Further, much money is paid out which might well have been directed to other conservation measures for predators that would have been killed even had there been no bounty.[1]

It has been demonstrated that the bounty method is a haphazard and unscientific means of control. In most cases, it has not resulted in the control of the predators at which it was aimed, and it has left confusion among stockmen, sportsmen, and conservationists alike, and perhaps more than any other single factor, is responsible for dividing the ranks of the friends of wildlife, and caused

---

[1] Apropos of this is the case, one among hundreds where a citizen wrote to a state auditor saying "When will it [the bounty] be on, or if you have any idea when it will be payed. I have 20 to 30 [coyotes] in a pen and would like to get some idea how long I have to keep them alive.

"Answer soon as you can so I will now what to due."

many a bitter battle in stockmen meetings. If we are to have sound game management or intelligent control of predator destruction on livestock we must build on the experience of the past and prevent costly duplication of mistakes. When confronted with a bounty issue, stockmen, sportsmen and conservationists should demand the facts as to how this method of control has worked, what the costs have been, and what results have been obtained.

There are many species of wild animals which are classed as predators. Some are destructive under certain conditions, others are of little economic consequence one way or another, and still others are almost wholly beneficial. In everyday operation the bounty results in indiscriminate destruction of these various classes of so-called "vermin." The average individual does not know the differences even in some of the most common birds of prey. Many do not have the time or inclination to learn them. As a result, countless numbers of useful or harmless varieties are destroyed with no benefit whatsoever to game. It is little wonder that there is indignation and resentment against such unselective control. Campaigns of this sort are responsible for developing radically opposed groups on the matter of the need for control. Sane and practical programs of control, based on actual knowledge of local conditions, are therefore difficult of attainment.

By way of illustrating the consequences of an indiscriminate bounty law, the experience of county authorities in one of our western states might be given. The cycle of events leading up to the establishment of the bounty in this instance was typical. Continued local demands from hunters for "vermin" extermination forced the county commissioners to appropriate the necessary funds for bounty payments. A variety of animals were listed upon which awards would be paid, amongst which was a twenty-five cent bounty that was designated for hawks. There was no tangible evidence that the hawks were doing any significant damage, but they were considered predators, and as such were eligible for the bounty. Here was opportunity to obtain some valuable information on the operation of a bounty law, and through arrangement with the local game warden it was possible to obtain the stomachs of many of the hawks which were submitted to the commissioners. These stomachs were carefully examined for food content to ascertain what damage, if any, was being done by these birds. The results are interesting in that they shed some light on what kinds of birds were being affected by this regulation and also present a picture of what the predators were feeding on.

KIND	FOOD						
	Number of individuals	*Ground squirrels*	*Mice*	*Rabbits and hares*	*Game birds*	*Song birds*	*Snakes and lizards*	*Insects and other small animals*
		Percent	Percent	Percent	Percent	Percent	Percent	Percent
Sharp-shinned hawk (*Accipiter velox*)	2*					100		
Red-tailed hawk (*Buteo borealis*)	26	82	4	10		1	3	
Swainson's hawk (*Buteo swainsoni*)	47	87	4		trace		4	5
Sparrow hawk (*Falco sparverius*)	41	5	13			2	17	63
Great horned owl (*Bubo virginianus*)	3	50		50		trace		
Screech owl (*Otus asio*)	2		25			50		25

* 1 empty.

In less than two months, 308 hawks were presented for payment of the twenty-five cents award. A total of 121 were received in Washington for examination. A detailed report of these examinations is not necessary here. A brief summary of what was found in the stomachs of these birds, however, will indicate the results that were obtained as shown on accompanying chart.

On the basis of this evidence, it was quite clear that relatively few of the destructive sharp-shinned hawks and great horned owls were being taken by bounty hunters. Those species most affected were almost entirely beneficial in this section. When supplied with these data, the commissioners immediately repealed the bounty law.

A similar story is told in the examination of the birds of prey which were turned over to the Department of Conservation of the State of Ohio for bounty payments in 1931-1932. In this case, also, the bounty law was repealed when the details concerning the food of the birds were made known.

A great many of the animals offered for bounty rewards would be destroyed regardless of whether a bounty law was in force or not. Destruction by predators does not cease when bounty payments are stopped. It continues on and not infrequently as vigorously as before. A significant portion of bounty funds goes to rewarding stockmen, farmers and poultrymen for protecting their property, which they would do anyway. A hawk or coyote approaching a chicken yard is not spared because the poultryman happens to recall that there is no bounty for its scalp. Payment of bounties on all predators which are killed to protect personal property constitutes a wasteful spending of game or other funds.

In Pennsylvania, one bounty summary showed that more than two million dollars has been spent in paying bounties and in administration costs. Over half of this expenditure has gone for weasels alone, most of which were taken when their fur was prime, and for which the bounty was obviously a secondary consideration. It is significant also that during this period the trend of the annual cost of the bounty system has been upward, proving that the objective of control has not been accomplished.

At one period, a lot of least weasels which prey almost entirely on *Microtus* and other small rodents, and so slender that it readily follows their burrows anywhere, were paid for. E. A. Preble saw dozens of such skins, but the number bountied could not now be learned.

The futility of paying bounty on a wide-ranging migrant species which, as a rule, are often only temporary visitors within a state, may be shown from Pennsylvania's experience in paying bounties of $5.00 per bird on goshawks taken between November 1 and May 1. During the 1936-37 season more birds were taken than in the six preceding years combined. Gerstell (1937) at the time in the employ of the Pennsylvania Game Commission concludes that "obviously, the payment of bounty for the destruction of goshawks within the State of Pennsylvania has not, and never will, result in the control of the species within the Commonwealth."

The officials who have had the closest and widest contact with the bounty system are those associated with State Game Departments. In Maryland, the late former Chief Warden E. Lee LeCompte (Chambliss, Peter C., 1932), viewed his experience as follows: "One of the worst features of the bounty system is that it creates crooks. From 1920-1927 the Maryland law relative to bounties provided bounty should be paid to any person producing a hawk head or heads to a Justice of the Peace, who should certify to the presentation and collect fifty cents from this Department for each and every hawk. I found the Justices of the Peace were using the law to collect moneys for their own personal benefit."

The Assistant Secretary of State of Wisconsin in 1916 wrote (Roberts, Thos. S., 1917): "I have had ten years' experience in auditing bounty claims, and the result convinces me that the system in vogue is not only ineffective but wasteful and in a large measure, harmful."

E. C. Cross (1932) writing in *Rod and Gun in Canada*, stated that during the past 10 years some 33,000 wolves were taken under the bounty system at a cost of half a million dollars and with no evidence of any reduction in the timber wolf population, while at the same time there has been an actual increase of the brush wolves [coyotes]. The author concludes that "numbers are controlled by a complex of factors, of which the predator is but one and by no means the most important . . . If the money spent in 'wolf control' were to be used in finding out what our natural resources in fur and game need, and meeting that need, it would return dividends instead of deficits."

D. F. Switzenberg (1948: 14) was told by one state that the bounty was "the silliest and most uneconomic method of control known to man."

SUMMARY

State game departments and conservationists in general have almost unanimously concluded that the bounty system is not satisfactory as a method of controlling predatory animals. The results obtained from bounty control have not only been negative insofar as improving game supplies or protecting poultry and other domestic animals are concerned, but the system has been destructive to general wildlife interests in that it encourages indiscriminate killing of valuable forms of wildlife. Many of the species on the bounty lists are valuable fur bearers, the unguided destruction of which results in considerable economic loss to the state. It has proved everywhere exorbitantly expensive to operate and, as commonly practiced, it is highly productive of fraud. It results in bringing many irresponsible gunners into the field during the closed season and encourages, therefore, violation of gunning regulations. And finally and most significantly as far as the field of game management is concerned the bounty through usurpation of game funds impedes progress in more productive phases of game management, such as game protection, refuge development, and food and cover improvement work, which, in the final analysis, are as important, if not more important, than predator control.

In the actual operation of bounty laws some of their most

glaring faults are as follows: Skins are fraudulently shipped across State and international boundaries to be presented for bounty in a State other than the one in which taken.

Breeding areas are produced for which the professional bounty hunter is responsible. Instances are known where female coyotes and wolves have been constantly trapped and liberated with the idea of educating them against traps and thus making them extremely difficult of capture by this method. This is apparently done to insure that these animals and their young may be trap-wise, and thus become a constant source of revenue to bounty hunters.

Bounty hunters often present to inexperienced officials for bounty payment skins of one species purported to be another. This is particularly true regarding dog and other scalps turned in as coyote or wolf.

Bounties do not bring relief in the higher rugged mountain areas, such as found on practically all of the national forest summer ranges. The bounty hunter will not as a general rule, work in this kind of country because of the hardships it forces on the individual trapper, whereas attention to this type of country is often essential to the protection of stock, particularly from July to October; work on these summer ranges is sometimes of vast importance to wild game. Very often the economic importance of control of coyotes that is necessary on such ranges has a direct bearing on their use for grazing livestock such as sheep and goats, particularly because an open herd does better than one that is close herded. Frequently, only three or four coyotes on a grazing unit allotment will cause a sheepman great trouble and loss in course of the grazing months, and if not trapped and removed will force them to close herd. Bounty hunters will not expend the time necessary to trap out a comparatively slight but troublesome predator infestation of this kind.

While no true conservationist would like to think that the time could come when the large predators of North America had gone the route of the passenger pigeon and the bison, all are agreed that rigid control is a vital issue. But bounty payments, which in operation tend to perpetuate themselves because often the most objectionable individual predators and their offspring go free while the most easily obtained are being destroyed, is not an answer to the matter. Experience has taught many of the states that the answer does lie in the employment of trained predator hunters. Nothing better has yet come forward to take their place.

CONCLUSION

From civilized man's selfish point of view, predators are commonly looked upon as pests or outlaws with almost every hand raised against them. In fairness to these animals, it should always be kept in mind that their destructive habits cannot be due to any criminal intent, but are due wholly to their efforts to gain a livelihood by the only means that nature has provided through untold ages of evolution. From this just point of view any one, except perhaps those who have recently suffered heavy losses from their depredations, must be impressed by the skill with which they carry on the fight for existence, which with the single exception of the coyote, is a steadily losing battle. The best of the hunters who spend their lives in their pursuit are often obliged to put in months of intense work before they can outwit some of the "outlaw" animals that have made extraordinary records in many parts of North America.

Predatory animals which once lived solely on native game and rodents very promptly learned that the clumsy and in most instances stupid domestic animals introduced in their territory by man were a more certain and easier prey than the wild things that were always on guard against them. Thus, they followed the lines of least resistance in gaining a livelihood through the same mental processes that man would have used under similar conditions. The apparently wanton killing of many more poultry, sheep or other livestock during a raid by a wolf, coyote or other carnivore than are necessary for food is not of course the result of a criminal instinct, but is really due to the play of impulses similar in general character to that which animates some humans who get pleasure from bagging far more game than their personal needs require. Probably most of the mass killing by any predatory animal indicates that it is in the height of its vigor and thus kills through sheer physical exuberance. Certain of the Eskimos and Indian tribes so history shows have had at times the same lust for killing when occasion offered, and it is not wholly absent from men higher up the scale today.

Those visiting the West for the first time I am sure will concur in the words of the immortal Bret Harte who, long ago, wrote about the coyote:

> "Blown out of the prairie in twilight and dew
> Half bold, and half timid yet lazy all through;
> Loath ever to leave, and yet fearful to stay
> He limps in the clearing, an outcast in grey."

And then willing to do his bit in perpetuating this "wanderlust of the plains" Harte went on to sing

"Well, take what you will—though it be on the sly,
    Marauding, or begging—I shall not ask why;
But will call it a dole just to help on his way
    A four footed friar in order of grey."

In summary and final conclusion, therefore, it seems to this author that the coyote, when not an economic liability and therefore requiring local control, has its place as a wilderness animal among North America's fauna. Even the coyote's bitterest enemies amongst men, I feel would admit this, if for no other than an esthetic desire to hear its yap with the setting of the western sun. The West would never be the West, should this Gothic-like creature, all in points, become entirely extirpated. Because of its versatile natural attributes, it is extremely doubtful that it ever will entirely disappear from the landscape, in spite of so many hands with improved devices for killing it constantly turned against it.

THE CLEVER

Coyote

PART II

Classification of the Races of the Coyote
By HARTLEY H. T. JACKSON

Chapter Seven

Introduction

THE COYOTE *(Canis latrans)* is strictly an American mammal, and in fact might well be termed strictly North American since so far as is known it occurs nowhere south of Costa Rica. It has close relatives in the Eastern Hemisphere, particularly in the jackals which it resembles somewhat in structure and habits. In fact, on account of this close resemblance the coyote has frequently been referred to as the American jackal by the early explorers and naturalists. Less wary than its big brother the timber wolf and always more abundant in most of its range, it became more familiar to the early settlers of the Plains than the true wolf. Where both species occurred in the eastern part of the coyote's range as, for example, in the upper Mississippi Valley, the coyote was generally known as the brush or prairie wolf, in contrast to the name timber wolf for the true wolf. Coyote was a Spanish name for the animal that was later applied by explorers and naturalists after they came in contact with the southwestern Spanish settlements. An attempt has been made by the present reviser to retain a semblance of this early name brush wolf for the coyote by naming the coyote of the upper Mississippi Valley *Canis latrans thamnos,* the Greek word *thamnos* meaning literally a bush or shrub.

The great amount of individual variation in color, size, and cranial characteristics causes one to hesitate about "splitting" the group into too many subspecies. If the present reviewer has erred, he believes it will have been on the side of conservatism. Where geographic variations appear to occur, yet insufficiently constant to warrant subspecific recognition, it has been brought to the attention of the reader in the text. Life zones or other biotic areas or factors other than dense forestation seems to play little part in the distribution of coyotes. Coyotes of a given subspecies may occur in life zones from the deserts of the Lower Sonoran to timberline of the Boreal.

The actual limits of the geographical range of any of the subspecies can not be indicated by sharp and fast lines, but by

229

average characteristics or those of a majority of the specimens, characteristics that may blend almost imperceptibly over a broad distributional area from one subspecies to another, and in which area frequently single individuals may be found that may be almost typical representatives of either bordering subspecies. The present reviewer can say with Grinnell, Dixon, and Linsdale that "review of our material leaves us with a feeling that the coyotes display a greater range of variability without geographic coordination than does any other group of mammals we have studied" (Grinnell, Dixon, and Linsdale, 1937: 498).

The present revision of the coyotes recognizes 19 subspecies of *Canis latrans.* The study is based mainly on the extensive collection of coyote specimens brought together especially in connection with predatory animal control operations conducted since 1915 by the Fish and Wildlife Service, of the U. S. Department of the Interior, formerly the Biological Survey, of the U. S. Department of Agriculture, and other collections in the U. S. National Museum, now numbering 3,894 specimens of coyotes. Many of these are skulls without skins, and a few are skins without skulls. These specimens have been augmented by 611 from other American museums, making a total of 4,505 examined (See Acknowledgments, p. VII). Type specimens have been examined of all of the 16 forms for which type specimens exist, and essentially topotypes have been studied of the 3 forms for which no type specimen was designated. This wealth of material so extensive and massive as to be cumbersome at times to handle has made possible the solution of many problems.

Chapter Eight

History

THE HISTORY of the dog family (Canidae) as shown by fossil records extends back through many ancestral types and variants to the Miocene. The phylogeny of dogs has been treated by Matthew who says that "wolves, coyotes and foxes represent the family Canidae today in North America, and all of them are found as fossils in the Pleistocene, apparently much like their living descendants (Matthew, 1930: 131). Concerning a specimen of the genus *Canis* from the Pleistocene of Cumberland Cave, Maryland, Gidley says:

"A skull fragment with part of P^3 and P^4 on the right side and the root portions of M^1 and M^2 on the left shows the presence in the fauna of a coyote near *Canis latrans*. The anterior portion and the right side of the muzzle are incomplete, but the cranium and left zygoma are well preserved. The skull is very close in size to that of *C. latrans* but is slightly more robust, particularly in the region of the frontals. The small, very slender, sharp-cusped character of P^3 and the fragment of P^4 further substantiates reference of the form to the coyote group. Direct comparison with *C. priscolatrans* Cope from the Port Kennedy deposit in Pennsylvania or with *C. reviveronis Hay* from Florida is not satisfactory, because of the different nature of the materials. The reference of the Cumberland Cave form to *C. priscolatrans* is based on the somewhat more robust character of the Maryland form as compared with living coyotes" (Gidley, 1938: 23). In connection with this it might be mentioned that the living eastern coyote *(Canis latrans thamnos)* has cranial features somewhat more robust than those of typical *Canis latrans latrans*.

Two races of canids, *Canis ochropus orcutti* J. C. Merriam and *Canis andersoni* J. C. Merriam, have been described from the asphalt beds of Rancho La Brea, California, as being coyote-like (Merriam, J. C., 1912: 255). It is not possible fully to appraise these canid forms from the descriptions and illustrations. It is not entirely outside the range of possibility, however, that the specimens represent living races, and that possibly when more material is available both names may fall synonyms to *Canis latrans ochropus,* or that *Canis ochropus orcutti* may fall synonym to *Canis latrans ochropus,* and *Canis andersoni* fall synonym to *Canis latrans clepticus.*

The first of the living coyote species was described from Engineer Cantonment, Nebraska, as *Canis latrans* by Thomas Say in Long's "Expedition to the Rocky Mountains" in 1823, though "little wolves," "prairie wolves," or "brush wolves" were known by early explorers to exist probably a full century before Say published his description. The next one to be named was *Canis ochropus* from Sacramento River valley, California (Eschscholtz, 1829: 1), now recognized under the name *Canis latrans ochropus.* The Mexican coyote, *Canis latrans cagottis,* was next in order to be described from Rio Frio, Mexico, under the name *Lyciscus cagottis* (Hamilton Smith, 1839: 164). The name *Canis frustror* (Woodhouse, 1851: 147) was next to appear and was applied to an animal called the "American jackal," and which Merriam (1897: 26) correctly included with the coyotes. Bailey (1905: 175) concluded the type specimen was a wolf, and for several years the name was applied to the red wolf of eastern Oklahoma. Goldman has pointed out that the type specimen is that of a coyote and not a big wolf (Young and Goldman, 1944: 396).

The first revision of the coyotes was the paper "Revision of the coyotes or prairie wolves, with descriptions of new forms" by C. Hart Merriam (1897). Although Merriam uses the word "forms" in the title, actually he recognized no subspecies and gave each "form" specific rank. He arranged them into three groups, namely:

1. Latrans Group
   Canis latrans Say   Council Bluffs, Iowa.
   pallidus   Johnstown, Nebraska.
   lestes   Toyabe Range, Nevada.
2. Frustror Group
   Canis cagottis H. Smith Rio Frio, near City of Mexico.
   frustror Woodhouse   Fort Gibson, Indian Territory.
   peninsulae   Cape St. Lucas, Lower Calif.
3. Microdon Group
   Canis microdon   Mier, Tamaulipas, Mexico.
   mearnsi   Quitobaquito, Pima Co., Ariz.
   estor   San Juan River, Utah.
   ochropus   Esch. 'California' (San Joaquin Valley).

   vigilis   Manzanillo, Colima, Mexico.

Merriam's classification, and particularly his recognition of each "form" of coyote as a distinct species brought forth considerable criticism of his species concept. This soon developed into a discussion at the meeting of the Biological Society of Washington, May 8, 1897, when according to Society reports the program consisted of:

"C. Hart Merriam: Suggestions for a New Method of Weighing Species."

By invitation, Hon. Theodore Roosevelt, Assistant Secretary of the Navy, presented an address on the same subject.

Members now living still enjoy the memory of that ardent discussion between two friends of diverse opinions as to the specific rating of various forms of coyotes.

There has been no revision of the entire group of coyotes since Merriam's until the present study. Many excellent papers have appeared on coyote habits, ecology, economics, and the like, and several technical and taxonomic accounts have appeared in which ten new forms recognized as subspecies in the present monograph have been published. These are all listed in their proper sequence in the chapter on *Canis latrans* and its subspecies.

Several names have been erroneously or questionably applied to coyotes which need clarification. The name *Canis mexicanus* (Linnaeus, 1766: 61) was shown by G. M. Allen (1920: 478) to apply to the Mexican hairless dog. The *Canis nigrirostris* Lichtenstein (1930: 106) has been considered as possibly a coyote, but the original description precludes that possibility. According to the description the animal had a black muzzle and short pointed ears, which might fit a gray fox or a raccoon, but certainly not a coyote.

The name *Lyciscus* Hamilton Smith was revived as a subgenus by Gidley (1913: 101).

Heller probably had not seriously studied specimens of coyotes when he wrote "The jackals and their American representatives the coyotes are separable from the true wolves, which are typical of the genus *Canis,* by several constant dental characters which seem to justify the recognition of the group under the generic name *Thos* first proposed by Oken in 1816 for the Indian jackal, *Canis aureus.*" Later this name *Thos* was reduced to subgeneric rank by Miller (1924: 150). In our opinion the characteristics that separate coyotes from true wolves are not sufficiently important or stable to warrant subgeneric recognition for the group.

Chapter Nine

Explanations

EXTERNAL MEASUREMENTS

ALL EXTERNAL measurements of coyotes are in milli-meters, and unless otherwise stated in the text are those made by the collector from the animal in the flesh. Many of the specimens were collected by predator hunters and trappers and usually in such cases original flesh measurements were given in inches. All such have been transposed to millimeters. The weights given are in pounds. On account of the small number of individuals of which the external measurements and weights were available, more dependence as to relative sizes of the animals can be placed on the measurements of skulls. The following external measurements have been used:

Total length.—Tip of nose to end of terminal tail vertebra.

Tail vertebrae.—Base of tail at superior surface to end of terminal tail vertebra.

Hind foot.—Posterior border of heel to apex of longest claw.

CRANIAL MEASUREMENTS

Cranial measurements unless otherwise stated, were made with vernier and dial calipers by the author with the assistance of William H. Stickel, who made many of the measurements independently. The following have been employed:

Condylobasal length.—Antero-posterior diameter of skull from above base of first incisor to most posterior point of occipital condyle of same side.

Palatal length.—Antero-posterior diameter between anterior-most point on posterior border of the palate to anterior base of first upper incisor of same side. (Taken with curved-jaw calipers.)

Squamosal constriction.—Lateral diameter across squamosals at least constriction of squamosal shelf posterior to zygomata. (Taken with caliper having jaws 3.5 mm. wide so true measurement is slightly less than that given.)

Zygomatic breadth.—Greatest lateral diameter across zygomata. (In coyotes, greatest breadth of skull.)

Interorbital breadth.—Least lateral diameter between the orbits at top of skull.

Maxillary tooth row.—Antero-posterior diameter of upper tooth row from anterior border of canine to posterior of second molar measured at cingulum in line parallel to long axis of skull.

Upper carnassial length.—Antero-posterior diameter of upper carnassial (fourth upper premolar) measured on outer side parallel to long axis of tooth from most anterior point of cingulum to posterior base of tooth just above alveolar margin.

First upper molar length.—Antero-posterior diameter of first upper molar measured at cingulum with tips of caliper placed anteriorly at inner side of contact between fourth premolar and first molar, and posteriorly at outer side of contact between first molar and second molar.

First upper molar breadth.—Greatest lateral diameter of first upper molar measured at cingulum in line perpendicular to long axis of skull.

Lower carnassial length.—Antero-posterior diameter of lower carnassial (first lower molar) measured at cingulum from anterior tip of tooth to outer side of contact with second molar.

SEX AND MATURITY OF SPECIMENS

It is very easy in research on coyotes or any other group of mammals to select only such specimens as fit readily into prescribed identification channels as represented by one or more characteristics. Often true characteristics and relationships may be hidden in specimens of which the age or sex of the animal may not have been properly determined. Series of specimens might be measured en masse without regard to sex, yet preponderance of either sex in the series where there is pronounced sexual differences of characteristics or size, such as occur in the coyotes, would throw possibilities of diagnosis or identification far out of alignment. Likewise it is important that in making comparisons the age of the animals be known in general terms, and that measurements be made of animals essentially adult, and comparisons made of specimens of animals of approximately the same age. This applies particularly to cranial measurements, and for this reason separate measurements of skulls are given for males and females. Furthermore cranial measurements are given only for skulls of animals classed as young adult, adult, and old adult. In the general descriptions under each subspecies measurements of younger animals are sometimes given when young adults or older were not available. Most of the cranial measurements were made by William H. and Lucille Stickel.

COLORS

The pelage of coyotes, like that of most other mammals with banded hairs, presents blended colors difficult to segregate, compare, and describe. The names of colors employed in this revision insofar as is possible are from "Color Standards and Color Nomenclature," by Robert Ridgway, 1912. They represent the closest approximation to color tones possible, but are frequently supplemented by generally understood, modifying or comparative terms.

SPECIMENS EXAMINED

All specimens examined unless otherwise indicated are in the United States National Museum, including the Biological Surveys collection which contains by far the major portion of material studied.

USE OF DISTRIBUTION MAP

No attempt has been made to present a key to the subspecies of the coyote. It is believed that the making of keys to closely related and intergrading subspecies is not satisfactory, and it is suggested that recourse to the paragraph on *Diagnostic Characters* under each subspecies in the text and to the distribution map (Figure 28) will afford more reliable means to the identification of specimens.

Chapter Ten

General Characters

THE PRESENT revision includes only the coyotes or prairie wolves, members of the species *Canis latrans,* the so-called true wolves, *Canis lupus,* and the red wolves, *Canis niger,* of North America having been well covered in "The Wolves of North America" (Young and Goldman, 1944). Coyotes are all smaller than any of the true or the red wolves, but are larger than any of the foxes of the genera *Vulpes, Urocyon,* and *Alopex,* which are the only other living representatives of the family Canidae in North America. The dog family (Canidae) on the whole is a rather compact taxonomic group, the members of which are closely similar anatomically, although there are some aberrant genera such as *Icticyon,* the bush dog of South America. All members of the genus *Canis* have glands on the upper basal part of the tail, usually marked by a narrow patch of black-tipped bristly hairs which are somewhat shorter and stiffer than the hairs of adjacent areas. The mammary glands are normally ten. There are four toes on each hind foot and five on each front foot, the first short and rudimentary but bearing a well-developed claw. The claws are non-retractile and rather blunt. A prominent callosity is present near the outer side on the posterior surface of the lower part of the forearm. The cranium is elongate and tapers anteriorly, the posterior processes of the frontals and the zygomata are short, leaving a wide opening between them.

The dental formula in *Canis* is typically

$$\text{I. } \frac{3\text{-}3}{3\text{-}3}; \quad \text{C. } \frac{1\text{-}1}{1\text{-}1}; \quad \text{P. } \frac{4\text{-}4}{4\text{-}4}; \quad \text{M. } \frac{2\text{-}2}{2\text{-}2}.$$

The coyote *(Canis latrans)* has large pointed ears facing forward, quite movable and able to be directed so as to catch sound vibrations. The eyes are round, the iris yellow. The coyote is smaller than the wolf though large individuals of the coyote *Canis latrans frustror* sometimes approach in size small individuals of the wolf *Canis niger rufus*. The nose pad (rhinarium) is smaller, average diameter being about 1 inch or less in the coyote as against 1¼ inches or more in the wolf. The forefoot of the coyote is much smaller, the diameter of the heel pad being less than 1¼ inches whereas in the wolf the diameter of this pad is more than 1½ inches.

The skull of the coyote in any subspecies is smaller and weaker than that of the smallest wolf (age for age and sex for sex). The teeth offer several essential differences. In the coyote the canines are actually of less diameter at the base, being less than .4 inch or 11 millimeters in antero-posterior diameter as against more than .5 inch or 12 millimeters for the wolf. The canines in the coyote also are relatively longer and in an anterior view of the skull with lower jaw attached the tips of the upper canines fall below a line drawn through the anterior mental foramina (Figure 20), whereas in the wolf (Figure 21) and the dog (Figure 22) the tips of the upper canines fall well above a line drawn through the anterior mental foramina. The canine of the domestic dog is usually relatively even shorter and thicker than that of the wolf. Also in this anterior view the incisors of the coyote show

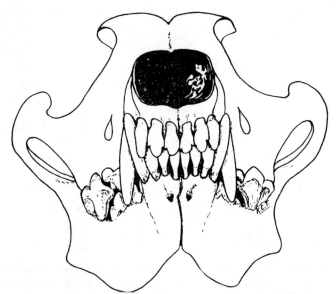

Figure 20. Southeastern Coyote, *Canis latrans frustror* (male). Anterior view of dentition. Natural size. Note small incisors, long and narrow canines, the tips of the upper ones coming below line drawn through anterior mantel foramina.

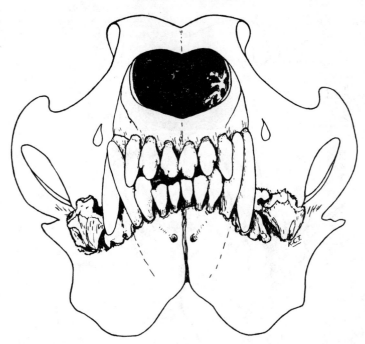

Figure 21. Mississippi Valley Red Wolf, *Canis niger gregoryi* (male). Anterior view of dentition. Natural size. Note large incisors, and the rather short and broad canines, the tips of the upper ones coming above line drawn through anterior mantel foramina.

much smaller than those of the wolf, and usually also much smaller than those of the domestic dog. The differences in size of the canines and incisors respectively in coyotes, wolves, and dogs are also noticeable in lateral views of the rostra. Here also may be noted the wide spacing between the premolars, both upper and lower, in the coyote (See Figure 23) as compared with relatively narrow spacing in the wolf (See Figure 24) and in the domestic dog (See Figure 25). The teeth of coyotes are all relatively narrower and less robust than in the wolves, while the carnassials are distinctly weaker. As pointed out by Gidley in the lower carnassial of the coyote (See Figure 26) as compared with that of the wolf (See Figure 27) the "heel is less reduced, with the two principal cusps more trenchant and more nearly subequal; the metaconid is more prominent; the paraconid shorter; and the bodies or columns of the paraconid and protoconid are less full and rounded, leaving the cutting blades of the trigonid much sharper. The P_4 has two posterior tubercles and a posterior basal

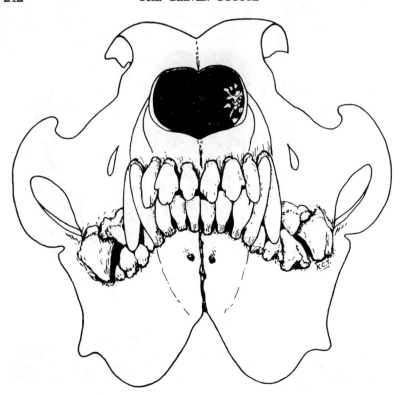

Figure 22. Domestic Dog, *Canis familiaris* (male). Probably near German Shepherd breed. Anterior view of dentition. Natural size. Note large incisors, and the short, broad canines, with rather blunt tips, those of the upper ones coming well above line drawn through anterior mantel foramina.

cingulum" (Gidley, 1913: 101). While these differences do hold in many skulls the present reviser finds that they can not be relied upon always inasmuch as these particular tooth characters break down frequently in *Canis latrans*.

Recently it has been attempted to measure proportionally and explain statistically the average broader and shorter rostrum of the domestic dog as compared with that of the coyote. "This index or ratio is the *palatal width* (between inner margins of alveoli of upper, first premolars) *divided by the length of the upper molar tooth-row* (anterior margin of alveolus of first premolar to the posterior margin of the last molar alveolus). To identify a skull in the field and without a ruler, the reciprocal of this ratio is used; the length of the upper molar tooth-row divided by the palatal width between the upper first premolars. If the molar tooth-row is

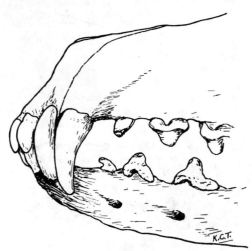

Figure 23. Southeastern Coyote, *Canis latrans frustror* (male). Lateral view of dentition. Natural size. Note small incisors, and long, narrow canines, and wide spaces between premolars, particularly between P₂ and P₃.

3.1 or more times that of the palatal width, the specimen is coyote; but if it is less than 2.7 times it is a dog. Skulls can be differentiated even when flesh is present" (Howard, W. E., 1949, p. 171). Howard's method would probably accurately separate about 95 percent of the dog and coyotes skulls. It would be more nearly accurate in some sections of the country than in others. In northern Cali-

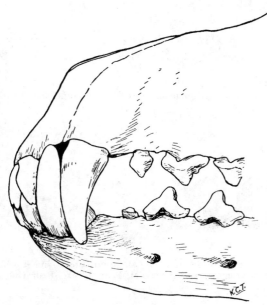

Figure 24. Mississippi Valley Red Wolf, *Canis niger gregoryi* (male). Lateral view of dentition. Natural size. Note large incisors, rather short, thick canines, and narrow spaces between premolars, particularly between P₂ and P₃.

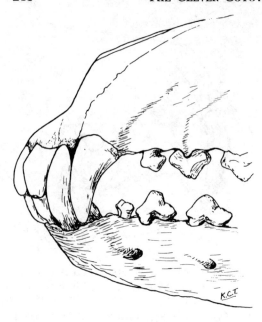

Figure 25. Domestic Dog, *Canis familiaris* (male). Probably near German Shepherd breed. Lateral view of dentition. Natural size. Note large incisors, short, thick canines, and narrow spaces between premolars particularly between P_2 and P_3.

Figure 26. Coyote, *Canis latrans*. Intero-lateral and superior view of right lower fourth premolar and carnassial. Natural size. Redrawn after Gidley.

Figure 27. Wolf, *Canis lupus*. Intero-lateral and superior view of right lower fourth premolar and carnassial. Natural size. Redrawn after Gidley.

fornia where the native coyote *(C. l. ochropus)* has an especially relatively long and narrow rostrum the method might accurately separate close to 100 percent of the animals. In the Great Lakes States where the native coyote *(C. l. thamnos)* has a relatively short and broad rostrum it would probably not accurately separate more than 80 or 90 percent of the skulls. Skulls of dogs of the collie and Russian wolf hound breeds frequently may fall within the prescribed coyote limitation. Among the narrower canid skulls in the immense Biological Surveys collection is one from southern Indiana of a mongrel dog (No. 243,405, U. S. Nat. Mus.) showing collie affinities that has a molar tooth row more than 3.7 times the palatal width (between the first molars) and has a B/A X 100 ratio of only 26.

Chapter Eleven

Pelage and Molt

THE PELAGE in the coyote as in many mammals consists of a soft and comparatively short underfur, and much longer and coarser guard hairs. The pelage, also as in many species, is longer and denser in the northern than in the southern subspecies, and in some of the Mexican and Central American forms becomes so coarse as to be almost hispid. The pelage is also much denser to the north, the feet and ventral parts of some of the extreme southern forms being sometimes almost void of hair.

In the coyotes there is only one molt each year, which may be somewhat irregular but usually starts early in the summer and continues over a rather long period, but is usually completed by early in the autumn. In the extreme southern parts of the range of coyotes the time of molt may be more irregular, and may occur either later or earlier than the normal starting time of about June. Before molting begins, late in winter and early in spring, the full pelage of the animal generally becomes greatly worn and often faded, so that the color, usually duller and more grayish does not have the appearance of the full fresh autumn pelage. Likewise the fresh incoming pelage early in autumn may be short and lack some of the flush of full pelage. The colors of most coyotes are brightest in full fresh winter pelage which is at its prime usually from the last of November until well into February.

Chapter Twelve

Variation

GEOGRAPHIC VARIATION

COYOTES, similar in the more essential taxonomic features and believed to intergrade through their extensive range in North and Central America, are here included in one species, *Canis latrans*. The subspecies composing this species are taxonomic expressions of similarities and differences of geographic variation in size, proportions, color, cranial features, and other details of structure. In the case of the coyote these geographic variations are not considerable and in most cases occur more or less constant over wide areas with broad, overlapping regions between variation types (subspecies). Pictured as a group the eastern subspecies *(thamnos* and *frustror)* are large, dark animals. There is a gradual paling of color and reduction in size to the westward and northward *(texensis, latrans, lestes, incolatus)*, a brightening of the ochraceous tones towards the Pacific coast *(ochropus, umpquensis)*; a reduction of size in southwestern United States *(microdon, mearnsi)*, and a general trend towards reddish and dark color, and a short rostrum, in the Mexican and Central American subspecies.

INDIVIDUAL VARIATION

The term individual variation has reference to the extent of divergence from a mean or average in a series of specimens from a given locality. In the coyotes this range of variation is excessive, and frequently specimens from near the center of range of one or another subspecies more closely fit another subspecies outside of the range. These variations apply not only to size and color of the animal, but to cranial characters and dentition. In explaining these individual variations it has been said: "There is a possibility suggested here, that in the last 50 years or so populations of coyotes have been abnormally mixed. Invasion of individuals out-of-bounds might well follow not only deforestation but the extermination of populations locally as a result of pest-control campaigns; a coyote-freed area would be open for invasion by animals from an adjacent faunal area where no such unnatural factor had operated to the same extent" (Grinnell, 1933: 113). This is good theory and possibly good philosophy. It does not meet the facts of the case, however, because the same variation applies to specimens collected by early naturalists nearly a century ago. The plain truth is that coyotes display an individual variation possibly greater than any other species of North American mammal, and certainly equaled by few. Cognizance of this variation has been made in studying the group.

SEXUAL VARIATION

Male coyotes are on the average distinctly larger than females. The skulls of males average correspondingly larger than those of females, are more angular, have the sagittal crest and other suture ridges more developed, and have heavier dentition.

AGE VARIATION

Coyote pups have a fuzzy, woolly pelage, the upper parts dark cinnamon grayish, the head paler more brownish, muzzle and back of ears snuff brown; under parts somewhat paler, with a whitish elongate spot on throat and one on chest; tail scantily haired, tapering, same color as back; rhinarium black. When the young coyote reaches the age of about 5 or 6 months it begins to acquire the color of the adult.

The skull of a coyote goes through a continuous development that we have divided into six more or less artificial stages, namely, juvenile, immature, young, young adult, adult and old adult.

The skull of the *juvenile* as from an animal about 4 months old has most of the sutures more or less open, the coronal suture being much arched posteriorly, the milk dentition is being dropped and the first of the permanent dentition is starting to push out.

The skull of the *immature* as from an animal about 6 or 7 months old, has the sagittal and coronal suture fairly anastomosed, the coronal suture has moved forward somewhat leaving a less pronounced arch posteriorly, the maxillo-nasal suture open, sutures at the base of the skull (posterior nares) open; dentition complete, unworn, the canines not fully out of their sockets.

Skull of the *young* as from an animal about 10 months old, has the sagittal and coronal sutures closed, and the sagittal ridge beginning to develop, the coronal suture has moved farther forward and is less arched posteriorly, the maxillo-nasal suture has begun to close, sutures at the base of the skull beginning to close, dentition complete, unworn, the canines not quite fully out.

The skull of the *young adult* as from an animal about 12 to 18 months old has the sagittal suture completely closed and the sagittal ridge developed, coronal suture closed and the posterior arch only slightly developed or not evident, the maxillonasal suture closed, sutures at the base of the skull closed but not completely anastomosed, dentition unworn or slightly worn, the canines fully out.

The skull of the *adult* as from an animal probably between 18 months and 3 years old has the coronal and sagittal sutures anastomosed and the sagittal ridge well developed, the maxillonasal suture is tightly closed, sutures at the base of the skull tightly closed, dentition slightly worn to moderately worn, canine fully out and usually slightly worn.

The skull of the *old adult* as from an animal probably more than 3 years old has the coronal and sagittal sutures anastomosed, the sagittal ridge well developed and widening, the maxillo-nasal suture anastomosed, as are also the sutures at the base of the skull, and most other sutures; dentition usually much worn.

The above descriptions are based on skulls of males. Skulls of females show less development of sagittal ridge, and there is some evidence that they mature at an earlier age than those of males. In making measurements of skulls we have endeavored wherever possible to use only skulls of *young adult, adult,* and *old adult.*

Chapter Thirteen

List of Subspecies of Coyotes, With Type Localities

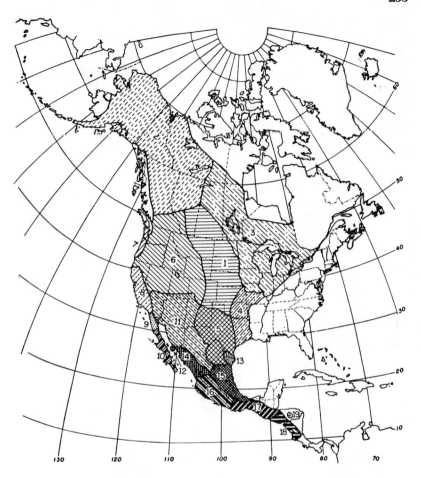

Figure 28. Distribution of subspecies of *Canis latrans*.

1. *Canis latrans latrans*
2. *C. l. incolatus*
3. *C. l. thamnos*
4. *C. l. frustror*
5. *C. l. texensis*
6. *C. l. lestes*
7. *C. l. umpquensis*
8. *C. l. ochropus*
9. *C. l. clepticus*
10. *C. l. peninsulae*

11. *C. l. mearnsi*
12. *C. l. jamesi*
13. *C. l. microdon*
14. *C. l. impavidus*
15. *C. l. cagottis*
16. *C. l. vigilis*
17. *C. l. goldmani*
18. *C. l. dickeyi*
19. *C. l. hondurensis*

Chapter Fourteen

Descriptions of Subspecies of
Canis latrans

Canis latrans latrans Say

Plains Coyote

Canis latrans Say, in S. H. Long and E. James Expedition to the Rocky Mountains, 1: 168, 1823.

Lyciscus latrans Hamilton Smith, In Naturalist's Library, vol. 18, edited by William Jardine, Dogs, 1: 162, 1839 (2nd issue, 1846).

Lupus latrans J. C. Fisher, Proc. Acad. Nat. Sci. Philadelphia 5 (1850-1851): 148, June 30, 1851.

Canis pallidus Merriam, Proc. Biol. Soc. Washington 11: 24, March 15, 1897.

Canis nebracensis Merriam, Science n.s. 8: 782, December 2, 1898.

Canis (hyscins latrans) Gidley, Proc. U. S. Nat. Mus. 46: 100, August 23, 1913.

Canis latrans latrans Jackson, Journ. Mammal. 1 (2): 62, March 2, 1920.

Canis latrans nebracensis Bailey, North Amer. Fauna no. 49, p. 157, January 8, 1927.

Canis latrans nebracensis Blair, Amer. Midland Nat. 22 (1): 107, July 1939.

Type specimen.—None now known to exist.

Type locality.—"Engineer Cantonment," about 12 miles southeast of the present town of Blair, Washington County, Nebraska, on the west bank of the Missouri River.

Geographic range.—Southeastern Alberta and southern Saskatchewan, Montana, Wyoming, and Colorado east of the Rocky Mountains, and northeastern corner of New Mexico; extreme southwestern corner of Manitoba, North Dakota except northeastern quarter; South Dakota, Nebraska; Kansas, except southeastern quarter; northwestern Oklahoma, and northern Panhandle region of Texas.

Diagnostic characters.—A medium-sized coyote, on the average palest and most grayish of the species, with little or no blackish on the forelegs; skull medium in size, moderately elongate, little depressed frontally, with moderate dentition. Compared with *C. l. incolatus, C. l. latrans* is also pale but distinctly more grayish (less cinnamon colored), and also has no or very little blackish on forelegs; the frontal and post-rostral region of the skull is less concave (less depressed) and the rostrum is relatively narrower and longer than in *C. l. incolatus*. The subspecies *latrans* is about the size of *C. l. thamnos* or slightly smaller, much paler in color with less black intermixed on the face, back, and tail, and muzzle and back of ears paler, more nearly cinnamon buff; skull relatively narrower with frontal region less dished; dentition somewhat weaker. Compared with *C. l. lestes,* the subspecies *latrans* averages slightly smaller, much paler in general color tone, the muzzle, ears, and leg color being near pinkish buff to pinkish cinnamon or cinnamon as contrasted with near cinnamon to sayal brown or darker (almost snuff brown) of *lestes*; skull slightly smaller than that of *lestes,* usually with somewhat weaker dentition. Smaller and contrastingly paler and less rufous than *C. l. frustror,* with smaller skull and weaker dentition. The subspecies *latrans* is about the size of *C. l. texensis,* but is much paler, has less or no black on the forelegs, and weaker dentition.

Color.—Winter pelage (fresh; December to February): Muzzle pinkish cinnamon to cinnamon; forehead and cheeks pale pinkish cinnamon mixed with gray, the forehead sometimes with a vinaceous fawn cast; crown more mixed with cinnamon buff or clay color, becoming pinkish buff to cinnamon buff on nape; back of ears pinkish buff to cinnamon buff; general tone of body upper parts pinkish buff, sometimes to near cinnamon buff, extending ventrad on the flanks, and on outer sides of fore and hind legs. Back more or less mixed with gray and blackish, producing on midline and rump a darker area; tail as in back, somewhat paler below; forelegs pinkish buff to cinnamon buff, seldom with trace of blackish line or patch on front surface; under parts between pale pinkish buff and light buff. *Summer pelage:* Much like winter pelage, averaging somewhat paler and a shade more yellowish.

*Skull.—*Medium large in size and moderately elongate; frontal region little depressed (dished) as compared to the relatively deep frontal concavity of *C. l. incolatus* and *C. l. thamnos;* dentition comparatively not heavy, the molariform teeth and carnassials, both upper and lower, being noticeably smaller and less swollen than in *thamnos*.

*Measurements.—*Adult male (essentially topotype) from Beemer, Cuming County, Nebraska: Total length, 1,250; tail vertebrae,

337; hind foot, 212; weight, 36 pounds. Three adult males from Laramie, Albany County, Wyoming, respectively: Total length, 1,210, 1,205, 1,255; tail vertebrae, 330, 370, 380; hind foot, 195, 195, 195. Three adult females from Laramie, Wyoming, respectively: Total length, 1,125, 1,160, 1,150; tail vertebrae, 317, 330, 330; hind foot, 180, 190, 195. *Skull:* Adult male (essentially topotype) from Beemer, Cuming County, and young adult male (type specimen of *Canis pallidus* Merriam) from Johnstown, Brown County, Nebraska, respectively: Condylobasal length, 193.9, 183.8; palatal length, 100.6, 94.1; squamosal constriction, ——, 58.1; zygomatic breadth, 105.0, 98.6; interorbital breadth, 36.4, 33.3; maxillary tooth row, 91.3, 86.5; upper carnassial length, 19.8, 19.8; first upper molar length, 13.4, 13.4; first upper molar breadth, 18.2, 16.9; lower carnassial length, 22.7, 22.7. Two adult males from Laramie, Albany County, Wyoming, respectively: Condylobasal length, 187.8, 185.7; palatal length, 96.4, 96.8; squamosal constriction, 60.8, 61.0; zygomatic breadth, 102.5, 103.3; interorbital breadth, 32.3, 32.3; maxillary tooth row, 88.4, 86.9; upper carnassial length, 20.8, 21.6; first upper molar length, 12.3, 13.2; first upper molar breadth, 17.1, 16.9; lower carnassial length, 22.2, 23.0. Two adult females from Laramie, Wyoming, respectively: Condylobasal length, 176.2, 178.1; palatal length, 93.5, 92.1; squamosal constriction, 56.6, 56.1; zygomatic breadth, 97.1, 95.8; interorbital breadth, 31.5, 32.0; maxillary tooth row, 83.2, 83.3; upper carnassial length, 20.2, 19.5; upper molar length, 12.6, 12.9; first upper molar breadth, 15.9, 16.4; lower carnassial length, 22.1, 22.1. Average of 35 skulls of young adult and adult males (Alberta, 2; Colorado, 3; Montana, 5; Nebraska, 5; New Mexico, 2; North Dakota, 1; Oklahoma, 1; South Dakota, 4; Wyoming, 12): Condylobasal length, 187.0 (175.5-202.0); palatal length, 97.0 (91.5-103.1); squamosal breadth, 60.2 (57.3-64.0); zygomatic breadth, 101.1 (92.6-105.9); interorbital breadth, 33.4 (30.0-38.3); maxillary tooth row, 88.3 (82.9-94.3); upper carnassial length, 19.8 (18.1-21.6); first upper molar length, 12.9 (11.6-14.4); first upper molar breadth, 17.0 (15.5-18.5); lower carnassial length, 22.6 (21.2-24.3). Average of 26 skulls of young adult and adult females (Colorado, 3; Montana, 1; Nebraska, 6; New Mexico, 1; Oklahoma, 1; South Dakota, 3; Wyoming, 11): Condylobasal length, 175.2 (163.7-181.6); palatal length, 91.4 (85.2-95.5); squamosal breadth, 56.9 (54.0-59.6); zygomatic breadth, 94.9 (91.9-100.1); interorbital breadth, 31.1 (28.0-33.7); maxillary tooth row, 82.9 (78.6-87.1); upper carnassial length, 18.7 (16.9-20.4); first upper molar length, 12.4 (11.5-13.8); first upper molar breadth, 16.3 (15.2-17.4); lower carnassial length, 21.6 (20.0-23.5).

Remarks.—Say's important camp on the Missouri River that was known as "Engineer Cantonment" and which became the type locality of so many of his animal species, including *Canis latrans*, has been variously located as having been at Council Bluffs, Iowa (Merriam, 1897: 20, 23; and Swenk, 1908: 64); vicinity of Council Bluffs, Pottawattamie County, Iowa (Miller and Rehn, 1901: 208; Elliot, 1905: 460); five miles below Council Bluffs, on west bank of Missouri (Weiss and Ziegler, 1931: 71); near present town of Blair, Washington County, Nebraska (Miller, 1912: 79; 1924: 151).

"The position selected for the establishment of winter quarters for the exploring party, was on the west bank of the Missouri, about half a mile above Fort Lisa, five miles below Council Bluffs, and three miles above the mouth of Boyer's river. At this place we anchored on the 19th September [1819], and in a few days, had made great progress in cutting timber, quarrying stone, and other preparations for the construction of quarters.

"Cliffs of sparry limestone rise in the rear of the site we had selected, to an elevation of near three hundred feet. At times of low water, strata of horizontal sandstone, are disclosed in the bed of the Missouri. These pass under and support the limestone. . . ." (Long, S. H., and E. James, 1823: 146).

". . . This spot presented numerous advantages for the cantonment of a small party like ours. Here were abundant supplies of wood and stone, immediately on the spot where we wished to erect our cabins, and the situation was sheltered by the high bluffs from the northwest winds. The place was called Engineer Cantonment. On the 26th of September, Mr. Say and Mr. Jessup, arrived . . ." (loc. cit., p. 153).

The location of Engineer Cantonment could not possibly be 3 miles above the mouth of the Boyer River and 5 miles below the present city of Council Bluffs, since the city is some 12 miles below the mouth of the Boyer River. It seems probable to the writer that the "Council Bluff" mentioned by Long was a bluff at some more northerly location than that of the present city, and that "west bank of the Missouri, about half a mile above Fort Lisa . . . and 3 miles above the mouth of Boyer's river" fairly well describes the location. Elsewhere in an appendix the location of Engineer Cantonment is given as 41° 25′ 04″ N. Lat. and 95° 43′ 53″ W. Long. (Long and James, 1823, vol. 2, p. xlii), which latitude would locate it close to 3 miles above the mouth of the Boyer River, although the longitude would place it a considerable distance to the east of the Missouri. The placement at about half a mile above Fort Lisa is clear. Writing about Manuel Lisa, Douglas says "The first expedition of the new company set out in two barges, one of which sailed on 2 May 1812, and the other four days later. . . . It was on this expedition that Fort Lisa was built eleven miles by land above the present city of Omaha. . . ." (Douglas, W. B., 1911: 369). Again, "Fort Lisa, 45 miles above the River Platte, on the Missouri. . . ." (loc. cit., p. 379). If we follow the bends of the Missouri River northerly from the mouth of the Platte, we locate at almost the identical spot described as 11 miles north of Omaha, and 3 miles above the mouth of the Boyer River. All of these descriptions place Engineer Cantonment as having been about 12 miles southeast of the present town of Blair, Washington County, Nebraska, on the west bank of the Missouri River.

In his original description of *Canis pallidus* from Johnstown, Brown County, Nebraska (Merriam, 1897: 24), which form he later renamed *Canis nebracensis* (Merriam, 1898: 782), Merriam compared his central Nebraska specimens with specimens from Elk River, Sherburne County, Minnesota, as representing typical *Canis latrans* described from Engineer Cantonment, Nebraska. As has elsewhere been pointed out (Jackson, 1949: 31) the coyote of the Great Lakes region, including all of Minnesota, represents another subspecies, *C. l. thamnos* Jackson, and Merriam's two names *pallidus* and *nebracensis* fall as synonyms of *Canis latrans latrans*. Specimens from the type region of *Canis latrans* are indistinguishable from specimens from Johnstown, Nebraska. Say's name, therefore, applies to the coyote of the Great Plains region. The subspecies seems to be more constant in characters, particularly as to color, over a large geographic range than most other subspecies of coyotes. Nevertheless in its peripheral range there is the usual broad band of intergradation with the adjacent subspecies and subspecific determination of specimens from these borders may be difficult or a matter of personal judgment. The subspecies *latrans* can generally be recognized as the palest and grayest of the coyotes.

Specimens examined.—Total number, 414, as follows:

Alberta: Buffalo, 1[1]; Lacombe, 1[2]; Red Deer, 3; Red Deer River, 3[1]; Walsh, 1[1].

Colorado: Brush, Morgan County, 1; East Pinneo, Washington County, 2; Estelene (25 miles northwest of), Baca County, 4; Estelene (13 miles northwest of), 3; Kuhn's Crossing, Logan County, 1; Pawnee Buttes, Weld County, 1.

Kansas: Fort Larned, Pawnee County, 1; Gove, Gove County, 2; Lakin, Kearny County, 1; Meade, Meade County, 1; Trego County, 6.

Montana: Big Porcupine Creek, 7[3]; Billings (Canyon Creek, 15 miles west

---

[1] Nat. Mus. Canada.
[2] Royal Ontario Mus. Zool.

of), Yellowstone County, 17; Breder Creek, Powder River County, 1; Broadus (Powder River valley near), Powder River County, 2; Brunelda, Dawson County, 1; Cache Creek, Powder River County, 3; Cottonwood Creek (36 miles northeast of Stacy), Custer County, 1; Delphia, Mussel-shell County, 6; Dry Creek (10 miles north of Graham), Powder River County, 2; Fort Conrad (now Conrad), Pondera County, 2; Glendive, Dawson County, 5; Hysham, Treasure County, 3; Ingomar, Rosebud County, 7; Lodge Grass, Big Horn County, 1; Miles City, Custer County, 9; Musselshell River, 2[3]; Powderville, Powder River County, 3; Piney Buttes, Garfield County, 1; Pumpkin Creek, Custer County, 6; Stone Shack, Custer County, 4; Sula, Ravalli County, 3.

Nebraska: Beemer, Cuming County, 4; Fort Kearney, Buffalo County, 17[4]; Johnstown, Brown County (type locality of *Canis pallidus* Merriam), 28.

New Mexico: Clayton, Union County, 16; Des Moines, Union County, 2.

North Dakota: Fort Union, Williams County, 4; Killdeer, Dunn County, 1; Medora, Billings County, 3; Palace Buttes (6 miles north of Cannon Ball, Sioux County), Morton County, 1; Shell Creek, Mountrail County, 1.

Oklahoma: Anthon, Custer County, 5; Arnett, Ellis County, 1; Boise City, Cimarron County, 12; Butler, Custer County, 1; Cooperton, Kiowa County, 1; Frederick, Tillman County, 20.

Saskatchewan: Cypress Hills, 1[2]; Govenlock, 3[2]; Indian Head, 2[2]; Maple Creek, 7[3]; Melfort. 1[2]; Prince Albert National Park, 1[1]; Windthorst, 5[1].

South Dakota: Belvidere, Jackson County, 1; Crow Creek Reservation, Buffalo County, 1; Custer County, 1; Dewey, Custer County, 6; Eagle Butte, Ziebach County, 1; Faith (15 miles northeast of), Ziebach County, 1; Fort Randall, Gregory County, 13; Fort Pierre, Stanley County, 1; Twilight, Butte County, 2.

Texas: Amarillo (70 miles west of Oldham County), 1[5]; Canadian, Hemp-hill County, 5.

Wyoming: Arvada (20 miles north of), Sheridan County, 2; Aurora, Carbon County, 1[3]; Bear Lodge Mountains, Crook County, 3; asper, Natrona County, 1; Chugwater, Platte County, 1; Converse County, 3; Douglas, Converse County, 10; Federal, Laramie County, 15; Fort Laramie, Albany County, 1; Grand Canyon (near Sundance), Crook County, 1; Hamp-shire, Weston County, 12; Horse Ranch Pass (near Jelm), Albany County, 1; Howard, Weston County, 7; Jelm, Albany County, 1; Laramie, Albany County, 36; Manville, Niobrara County, 16; Medicine Bow Range (near Jelm), Albany County, 3; Moss Agate Creek, Converse County, 1; Natrona County, 2; Newcastle, Weston County, 2; Rattlesnake Canyon (near Sun-dance), Crook County, 1; Red Mountains, Albany County, 1; Shirley, Carbon County, 1; Sundance, Crook County, 2; Upton, Weston County, 2.

Canis latrans incolatus Hall

Northern Coyote

Canis latrans incolatus Hall, Univ. California Publ. Zool. 40 (9): 369, November 5, 1934.

Type specimen.—No. 43,898, Museum of Vertebrate Zoology,

---

[3] American Mus. Nat. Hist.
[4] One in collection of Carnegie Mus.
[5] Carnegie Mus.

University of California; female adult, skin and skull; collected October 23, 1928, by T. T. and E. B. McCabe; original number 201.

Type locality.—Isaacs Lake, 3,000 feet altitude, Bowron Lake region, British Columbia.

Geographic range.—Northern Alaska from north of the Arctic Circle (Kotzebue; Point Barrow) south to latitude 61° N. (Eagle River); Yukon, except extreme northern part; western Mackenzie (Mackenzie River region); northern and central British Columbia, south to latitude 51° N. on the west and 52° N. in eastern British Columbia; northern and central Alberta, south to latitude 52° N. in western Alberta and to latitude 55° N. in eastern Alberta.

Diagnostic characters.—A medium large pale cinnamon-colored coyote with no or rarely a trifle of black on forelegs, and skull with depressed (dished) frontal region and relatively short rostrum. Compared with *C. l. latrans*, *C. l. incolatus* is also pale, but more cinnamon (less gray), and also has no or very little blackish on forelegs, the frontal and post-rostral region of the skull is more concave (depressed) and rostrum relatively broader and shorter than in *C. l. latrans*. More cinnamon color, no or scarcely a trace of blackish or grayish, particularly on legs, than in *C. l. lestes*, with skull averaging slightly larger, rostrum relatively broader and shorter, frontal region more deeply depressed (dished), and zygomatic breadth relatively broader. Averaging somewhat smaller and much paler with distinctly less black or none, particularly on back and legs than in *C. l. thamnos*, the skull relatively narrower and longer, particularly in the rostral region.

Color.—*Winter pelage* (fresh; October): Muzzle, avellaneous to pinkish cinnamon, rarely approaching sayal brown; forehead and cheeks light pinkish cinnamon or pinkish buff, much grizzled; crown more mixed with cinnamon buff, becoming cinnamon buff on nape; back of ears cinnamon buff to sayal brown; general tone of body upper parts light pinkish cinnamon to pinkish cinnamon, extending down on the flanks and on outer sides of fore and hind legs. Back more or less grizzled, somewhat darker in midline or even slightly blackish; tail as in back, somewhat paler below; forelegs whitish and pinkish cinnamon, generally without any trace of black; under parts whitish, tinged with pale pinkish cinnamon. *Summer pelage:* Much like winter pelage, possibly averaging somewhat paler.

Skull.—Medium large in size and relatively broad, with depressed (dished) frontal region; broad, short rostrum; tooth rows as measured from outside margins of upper fourth premolars wide apart relative to length.

Measurements.—Type specimen and topotype (adult females),

respectively: Total length, 1,099, 1,072; tail vertebrae, 255, 307; hind foot, 181, 178. Adult female from Murdock Creek, Wood Buffalo Park, Alberta: Total length, 1,310; tail vertebrae, 360; hind foot, 220. *Skull:* Type specimen and topotype (adult females), respectively: Condylobasal length, 172.6, 174.5; palatal length, 89.4, 90.4; squamosal constriction, 55, 59.9; zygomatic breadth, 97.2, 100.5; interorbital breadth, 29.2, 32.8; maxillary tooth row, 80.6, 79; upper carnassial length, 18.5, 18.5; first upper molar length, 11.7, 11.5; first upper molar breadth, 15.4, 15.1; lower carnassial length, 20.4, 20.9. Two adult males from Big Delta, Alaska, respectively: Condylobasal length, 188.7, 192.7; palatal length, 100.3, 100.8; squamosal constriction, 58.8, 57.2; zygomatic breadth, 94.3, 102.1; interorbital breadth, 31.8, 35.9; maxillary tooth row, 87.6, 91.1; upper carnassial length, 19.8, 20.8; first upper molar length, 12.4, 13; first upper molar breadth, 17, 17.6; lower carnassial length, 22.2, 23.6. Two adult females from Big Delta, Alaska, respectively: Condylobasal length, 178.7, 187.7; palatal length, 92.9, 97.8; squamosal breadth, 57.9, 60.9; zygomatic breadth, 95.7, 98.7; interorbital breadth, 32.8, 32.8; maxillary tooth row, 84.5, 87; upper carnassial length, 20, 20.3; first upper molar length, 12.4, 12.8; first upper molar breadth, 15.8, 16.8; lower carnassial length, 22.1, 22.2. Two adult males from Athabaska Landing, Alberta, respectively: Condylobasal length, 187.7, 191.3; palatal length, 97.3, 98.9; squamosal constriction, 59.6, 63; zygomatic breadth, 98.8, 104.4; interorbital breadth, 31.8, 32.9; maxillary tooth row, 89, 88.7; upper carnassial length, 20.6, 20.1; first upper molar length, 13.2, 13.3; first upper molar breadth, 17.2, 16.8; lower carnassial length, 23.4, 23.2. Two young adult males from Stuart Lake (Fort Saint James), British Columbia, respectively; Condylobasal length, 185.2, 191.9; palatal length, 95, 99.2; squamosal constriction, 60.7, 59.8; zygomatic breadth, 95.2, 96.9; interorbital breadth, 32.5, 32.5; maxillary tooth row, 87.8, 89.3; upper carnassial length, 19.8, 19.6; first upper molar length, 12.6, 12.3; first upper molar breadth, 16.5, 16.6; lower carnassial length, 22.8, 21.9. Average of 25 skulls of young adult, adult, and old adult males Alaska, 13; Alberta, 4; British Columbia, 7; Yukon, 1): Condylobasal length, 189.2 (182.2-194.4); palatal length, 98.4 (95.0-101.5); squamosal breadth, 60.3 (57.2-66.0); zygomatic breadth, 101.1 (94.3-106.6); interorbital breadth, 33.7 (29.4-36.3); maxillary tooth row, 88.7 (86.5-91.4); upper carnassial length, 20.3 (18.3-21.8); first upper molar length, 12.8 (11.8-14.2); first upper molar breadth, 17.1 (16.2-18.4); lower carnassial length, 22.3 (20.1-23.6). Average of 15 skulls of adult females (Alaska, 7; Alberta, 1; British Columbia, 5; Yukon, 2): Condylobasal length,

180.8 (171.7-189.8); palatal length, 94.7 (89.4-100.3); squasmosal breadth, 58.5 (54.5-61.2); zygomatic breadth, 96.3 (89.4-101.0); interorbital breadth, 31.7 (29.2-33.9); maxillary tooth row, 84.7 (79.0-88.6); upper carnassial length, 19.3 (18.1-20.4); first upper molar length, 12.4 (11.2-13.3); first upper molar breadth, 16.4 (15.1-17.4); lower carnassial length, 21.9 (20.1-23.0).

Remarks.—The northern coyote *(Canis latrans incolatus)* is a fairly well-marked subspecies showing for a coyote comparatively little variation over an extensive range. The original describer mentions a character "distance from orbit to anterior opening of infraorbital canal amounting to less than 41 per cent (except in animals of extreme age) of the distance across the fourth upper premolars" (Hall, E. R., 1934b: 370) that to the present author seems too evasive and intangible to be reliable, and one that depends upon careful analysis of age and sex of the specimen. When coyote skulls, even of animals of comparable age are not segregated into their respective sexes, any measurements made therefrom are of little value for comparative purposes.

As in the case of many of the coyotes, the type locality for *Canis latrans incolatus* has been located near the border of the range of the subspecies, in this case near the southern border. In the main, skull features that segregate *incolatus* are accentuated in specimens from more northwesterly localities, so that we find in skulls from Alaska the extreme of the type. Some of the Alaska skins (from Fairbanks, Matanuska, and more especially the one from Kotzebue) show more blackish in the dorsal region than typical *incolatus*, and the one from Kotzebue is more grayish and has less cinnamon color. The muzzles in some of the Alaska specimens are also a shade darker than in typical *incolatus*. A very few of these skins show a bare trace of a blackish overcast on the forelegs, but occasionally a specimen of *incolatus* from the general type-region shows slight traces of blackish on the forelegs, particularly in summer pelage. Inasmuch as all of these Alaskan specimens are "cased" skins, and not flat tanned skins or stuffed scientific skins, the blackishness along the dorsal area in them at first glance appears exaggerated, and stretching the skin slightly noticeably reduces the darkness.

The intensification of the skull characters of the subspecies *incolatus* in specimens from Alaska leads one to the belief that coyotes have been very long resident there, and that the comparatively recent increase in coyote populations there is not as from an invading army, but rather from an uprising within the native coyote population.

Specimens examined.—Total number, 115, as follows:

Alaska: Big Delta River, 15; Chitina River (Hubrick's Camp), 1[1]; Copper River Flats (20 miles from Cordova), 2; Delta River, 1; Eagle River, 7; Fairbanks (near), 5; Healy, 1; Indian (near Anchorage), 2; Jarvis Creek (mouth of), 1; Kenai Lake, 2; Kotzebue, 1; Matanuska, 5; Mount Hayes, 4; Portage Creek (tributary to Susitna River), 1; Tanana, 1; Wonder Lake (Mount McKinley region), 1[2].

Alberta: Athabaska Landing (20 miles south of), 6; Athabaska River, 2[3]; Buffalo Prairie (15 miles south of Henry House), 1; Jasper House, 2; Murdock Creek (Wood Buffalo Park), 1[1]; "Northern Alberta," 1[1]; Whitemud, 2.

British Columbia: Anahim Lake, 11[2]; Beaver Pass (Barkerville region), 1[2]; Bowron Lake (region of), 3[2]; Bowron River, 1[2]; Cottonwood, 6[4]; Driftwood River, 1[5]; Indian Point Lake (Barkerville region), 4[2]; Isaacs Lake (type locality; Barkerville region), 2[2]; Klenna Kleene, 1[2]; Lightning Creek (Barkerville region), 1[2]; Little Prairie (Peace River), 1[5]; One-eye Lake (expansion of Klinaklini River), 1[2]; Ootsa Lake, 1[5]; Red River (30 miles north of Hudsons Hope), 1[3]; Spruce Mountain, 2[2]; Stoney Lake (Barkerville region), 1[2]; Stuart Lake (Fort Saint James), 6; Stuie (junction Atnarko and Whitewater Rivers), 2[1]; Sustut River, 1[5]; Takla Lake, 1[5].

Mackenzie: Fort Smith, 2[6]; Providence (near), 1[1]; Tuktuyaktok (Mackenzie Delta), 1[1].

Yukon: Champagne Landing (Alsek River), 1[8]; Grouse Creek (between Atlin and Teslin), 1[2]; Tepee Lake (west of Kluane Lake), 1[1]; Teslin Lake, 1[2]; White River, 8[7]; Yukon River, 4[8].

Canis latrans thamnos Jackson
Northeastern Coyote or Brush Wolf

Canis latrans thamnos Jackson, Proc. Biol. Soc. Washington, 62: 31, March 17, 1949.

Type specimen.—No. 233,034, U. S. National Museum, Biological Surveys collection; male young adult, skin and skull; collected September 4, 1919, by Harry H. Sheldon. Original number 1073.

Type locality.—Basswood Island, Apostle Islands, Ashland County, Wisconsin.

Geographic range.—East-central Saskatchewan south of 54° N. and north of 51° N., Manitoba except extreme southwestern corner, extreme eastern North Dakota, Minnesota, Iowa, northern Missouri

---

[1] Nat. Mus. Canada.
[2] Mus. Vert. Zool., Univ. California.
[3] Amer. Mus. Nat. Hist.
[4] Five in Mus. Vert. Zool., Univ. California; one in Royal Ontario Mus. Zool.
[5] Prov. Mus. British Columbia.
[6] One in Nat. Mus. Canada.
[7] Seven in Royal Ontario Mus. Zool.; one in Mus. Vert. Zool., Univ. California.
[8] Three in Royal Ontario Mus. Zool.; one in Mus. Vert. Zool., Univ. California.

(north of Missouri River), easterly through western Ontario, Michigan, Wisconsin, northern and central Illinois, northern Indiana, southern and eastern Ontario, to extreme southern Quebec (near Luskville, Eardley Township).

Diagnostic characters.—A large, heavy-set, rather dark coyote, with broad skull, short rostrum and heavy dentition. About the size of *Canis latrans latrans* or larger; darker with more blackish intermixed on the face, back, and tail, the blackish on foreleg more distinctly pronounced, the muzzle and backs of ears a deeper shade, more fulvous; skull relatively broader and rostrum relatively more dished. Darker and larger than *Canis l. incolatus*, with black streak on forelegs; skull relatively broader, dentition heavier. Possibly somewhat smaller than *Canis l. frustror*, the cinnamon and fulvous shades less brilliant, black streak on foreleg narrower and less diffused; skull relatively shorter and broader, rostrum relatively shorter and more depressed (dished) frontally.

Color.—*Winter pelage* (fresh; October and November): Muzzle, sayal brown to snuff brown, occasionally near cinnamon-brown; forehead and cheeks somewhat paler, much mixed with gray and some black; crown more mixed sayal brown to ochraceous-tawny, becoming sayal brown or ochraceous-tawny on nape; back of ears sayal brown sometimes approaching ochraceous-tawny; upper parts from nape to tail coarsely mixed buffy gray and black, the general tone being gray to cinnamon gray, with more blackish down the midline; tail as in back, tipped with black, and paler below sayal brown or paler, with little or no black; color of upper parts extending down fore and hind legs; forelegs and feet deeply lined with black on upper (anterior) surface; under parts pinkish buff more or less stained with cinnamon, mixed with deep gray and a few blackish hairs on the throat; chin grayish. *Summer pelage:* Much like winter pelage, but usually slightly more buffy.

Skull.—Closely resembling that of *Canis l. incolatus* in general features, but usually larger, relatively broader, with heavier dentition. Relatively broader, with rostrum more depressed posteriorly than in that of *C. l. latrans*; relatively shorter and broader, with rostrum relatively shorter and more depressed posteriorly (dished in frontal region) than in that of *C. l. frustror*.

Measurements.—Type-specimen: No external measurements for animal in flesh available. Hind foot (measured from dry skin), 180. An adult male from Ironwood, Michigan, and an adult male from Baudette, Minnesota, respectively: Total length, 1,320, 1,200; tail vertebrae, 380, 300; hind foot, 220, 218; weight, 34, 34 pounds. *Skull:* Type specimen (young adult male): Condylobasal length,

192.8; palatal length, 99.6; squamosal constriction, 62.0; zygomatic breadth, 108.4; interorbital breadth, 35.6; maxillary tooth row, 87.3; upper carnassial length, 21.2; first upper molar length, 13.5; first upper molar breadth, 18.6; lower carnassial length, 23.6. Two adult males from Gogebic County, Michigan, respectively: Condylobasal length, 191.9, 189.5; palatal length, 98.3, 96.1; squamosal constriction, 60.9, 59.7; zygomatic breadth, 106.4, 103.2; interorbital breadth, 33.5, 32.5; maxillary tooth row, 89.1, 86.2; upper carnassial length, 20.2, 20.0; first upper molar length, 12.8, 13.3; first upper molar breadth, 17.6, 17.5; lower carnassial length, 23.6, 22.2. One adult female from Henry, Illinois, and one young adult female from Negaunee, Michigan, respectively: Condylobasal length, 181.4, 177.6; palatal length, 93.9, 92.2; squamosal constriction, 60.1, 59.2; zygomatic breadth, 99.5, 99.9; interorbital breadth, 32.8, 34.4; maxillary tooth row, 84.5, 82.8; upper carnassial length, 18.7, 19.9; first upper molar length, 13.1, 12.4; first upper molar breadth, 16.6, 17.3; lower carnassial length, 21.2, 22.4. Average of 34 skulls of young adult and adult males (Illinois, 4; Indiana, 3; Iowa, 1; Michigan, 8; Minnesota, 12; Missouri, 1; Ontario, 3; Wisconsin, 2): Condylobasal length, 190.8 (180.0-198.3); palatal length, 98.1 (91.6-102.0); squamosal breadth, 61.7 (57.2-65.0); zygomatic breadth, 104.0 (96.4-109.4); interorbital breadth, 34.9 (32.2-39.6); maxillary tooth row, 87.8 (83.4-92.8); upper carnassial length, 19.8 (18.4-21.4); first upper molar length, 13.2 (11.6-14.5); first upper molar breadth, 17.4 (15.9-18.6); lower carnassial length, 22.8 (20.9-25.1). Average of 24 skulls of young adult and adult females (Illinois, 1; Indiana, 2; Manitoba, 1; Michigan, 5; Minnesota, 5; Missouri, 3; North Dakota, 2; Ontario, 4; Wisconsin, 1): Condylobasal length, 181.4 (163.0-190.6); palatal length, 93.6 (86.9-99.0); squamosal breadth, 59.0 (55.7-62.0); zygomatic breadth, 97.9 (92.2-106.6); interorbital breadth, 32.6 (29.2-35.7); maxillary tooth row, 84.3 (78.7-91.1); upper carnassial length, 18.9 (16.8-21.5); first upper molar length, 12.7 (11.2-13.9); first upper molar breadth, 16.7 (15.5-17.8); lower carnassial length, 21.9 (20.1-24.2).

Remarks.—When C. Hart Merriam described the coyote *Canis pallidus* (Merriam, C. Hart, 1897: 24) from Johnstown, Brown County, Nebraska, and which he later renamed *Canis nebracensis* (Merriam, C. Hart, 1898: 782), he used as comparative material representing typical *Canis latrans* Say specimens from Elk River, Sherburne County, Minnesota. The type locality of *latrans* is Engineer Cantonment, west bank of Missouri River, Nebraska, and specimens from that region cannot be distinguished from specimens from the type region of *nebracensis*. Specimens from Elk

River, Minnesota, do differ noticeably from those from Nebraska, since they represent the form we now know as *thamnos* from the Great Lakes region. The coyote was known to the early settlers of this region sometimes as the "prairie wolf," but more often as the "brush wolf," hence the scientific name *thamnos*, I have given to it, meaning brush or shrub. It is a large dark coyote but is quite in contrast with the huge timber wolf of the Great Lakes country, though many of the adult individuals weigh more than 30 pounds each.

The geographical area of demarcation and intergradation between *Canis l. thamnos* and *C. l. latrans*, while covering a distance of one or two hundred miles, on the whole is fairly clear cut for a subspecies of coyote. Inconsistencies are mostly a matter of color, the cranial characteristics on the whole being more nearly uniform. Thus a specimen of a youngish animal from Wall Lake, Iowa, is dark color and in every way typical of *thamnos*, whereas one in worn winter pelage from Rockford, Iowa, 180 miles to the east-northeast, is paler dorsally than typical specimens, though having comparatively dark legs and muzzle. The specimen from Babcock, Wisconsin, is paler than normal for Wisconsin specimens. One faded March skin from Henry, Illinois, is almost as pale on head and muzzle as specimens of *C. l. latrans* from central Nebraska, but has the normal amount of blackish on the forelegs and back of typical *thamnos*. Another skin from Henry, Illinois, is quite typically the color of *thamnos*. Mid-May skins from Mc-Coysburg, Indiana, are somewhat paler and smaller than average. All of the specimens examined from Manitoba are large with heavy dentition of the *thamnos* type. A large skull of a male from Parry Sound, Ontario, seems to be relatively a little longer in proportion to width than typical *thamnos*.

Specimens examined.—Total number, 234, as follows:

Illinois: Bradfordton, Sangamon County, 1[1]; Cook County Forest Preserve, 1[1]; Douglas County, 1[1]; Frederick, Schuyler County, 1[1]; Galesburg, Knox County, 1[1]; Henry, Marshall County, 2; Kelley Township, Warren County, 1[1]; Le Roy, McLean County, 1[1]; Macoupin County, 1[2]; Mahomet, Champaign County, 1[3]; Warsaw, Hancock County, 1[2]; Willow Springs, Cook County, 1[1].

Indiana: Kankakee River Bottom, Newton County, 6; McCoysburg, Jasper County, 2.

Iowa: Decatur County, 1[4]; Missouri Valley, Harrison County, 1[4]; Peosta, Dubuque County, 1[5]; Rockford, Floyd County, 1; Wall Lake, Sac County, 1.

[1] Illinois State Nat. Hist. Survey.
[2] American Mus. Nat. Hist.
[3] Mus. Nat. Hist. Univ. Illinois.
[4] Iowa State College.

Manitoba: Aweme, 3[6]; Carman, 4; Duck Mountain, 3; Kenville, 3[7]; Portage Plains, 1[2]; Shoal Lake, 5[8]; Treesbank, 1[7].

Michigan: Alger County, 1[9]; Amasa, Iron County, 1[9]; Bark River, Delta County, 4[10]; Bessemer Line, Gogebic County, 1[9]; Brimley, Chippewa County, 2[9]; Daggett, Menominee County, 1; Floodwater (7 miles northwest of Michigamme River), Dickinson County, 5; Gogebic County, 1[9]; Grand Island, Lake Superior, 1; Ingalls, Menominee County, 1; Ironwood, Gogebic County, 1[9]; Isle Royale, Houghton County, 14[9]; Keweenaw County, 2[9]; Manistique, Schoolcraft County, 1; Marquette, Marquette County, 1[9]; Miners River, Alger County, 3; Mohawk, Keweenaw County, 1[9]; Montreal River, Gogebic County, 1[9]; Nadeau, Menominee County, 1; Negaunee, Iron County, 2; Rapid River (14 miles northeast of), Delta County, 1; Rudyard Township, Chippewa County, 1; Schoolcraft County (R. 16 W., T. 46 N., Sec. 6), 1[9]; Shingleton, Schoolcraft County, 1[2]; South Pond, Iron County, 1[9]; Stephenson, Menominee County, 1; Trout Lake Township, Chippewa County, 1; Wilson, Menominee County, 1[9]; Yalmar, Marquette County, 1[9].

Minnesota: Badger, Roseau County, 5[2]; Baudette, Lake of the Woods County, 1[11]; Beltrami County, 11[11]; Burntside Lake, Saint Louis County, 1[11]; Castle Danger (a few miles northeast of Two Harbors, on shore of Lake Superior, Lake County, 1[11]; Clearwater County, 1[11]; Duluth, 3[2]; Duquette, Pine County, 1[11]; Elk River, Sherburne County, 18; Fernberg (17 miles east of Winton), Lake County, 1[11]; Hibbard County, 1[11]; Koochiching County, 2[11]; Lake of the Woods County, 7[11]; Madison, Lac qui Parle County, 1; Pine County, 1[11]; Roosevelt, Roseau County, 1[11]; Thief River Falls, Pennington County, 2[11].

Missouri: Blue Mound, Livingston County, 1; Bogard, Carroll County, 1; Carrollton, Carroll County, 2; Ethel, Macon County, 2; Higbee, Randolph County, 1; Livingston County, 1; Lovelake, Macon County, 1; New Cambria, Macon County, 1; Spencerberg, Pike County, 1; Tarkio, Atchison County, 1; Tina, Carroll County, 1.

North Dakota: Grafton, Walsh County, 4; Grand Forks, Grand Forks County, 2; Sullys Hill National Park, Benson County, 2.

Ontario: Dunrobin (about 25 miles west of Ottawa), 1[8]; Ghost Narrows (Lac Seul), 1[7]; Honey (Baxter Township), 1[7]; Lakefield ("Northcote"), Peterborough County, 1[8]; Langton (near), Norfolk County, 1[7]; Oxdrift, 2[7]; Parry Sound (Monterth County), 1[7]; Pine wood, 1[7]; Sifton Township, Rainy River District, 1[7]; Smoky Falls, 1[7]; Sparrow Lake (18 miles north of Orilla), 4; Tannin, 3[7]; Thedford (north of), Lambton County, 1[8]; Silver Islet P. O., Fenn's Bay, Thunder Cape, 1[8]; Quetico, 4[11].

Quebec: Luskville (Eardley Township, about 16 miles north of International Bridge), 1[8].

---

[5] Received at National Zoological Park, February 10, 1903; one year old April 28, 1903; died May 17, 1905.
[6] Collection of Stuart Criddle.
[7] Royal Ontario Mus. Zool.
[8] Nat. Mus. Canada.
[9] Univ. Michigan Mus. Zool.
[10] Two in Coll. Univ. Michigan Mus. Zool.
[11] Minnesota Mus. Nat. Hist.
[12] Univ. Wisconsin, Dept. of Zoology.
[13] Milwaukee Public Museum.
[14] Chicago Nat. Hist. Mus.

Wisconsin: Babcock, Wood County, 1[12]; Baraboo (6 1/2 miles south of), Sauk County, 1[12]; Basswood Island, Apostle Islands, Ashland County (type locality), 1; Barron County, 1; Clark County, 1[2]; Delavan, Walworth County, 1; Douglas County, 2[12]; Eagle River, Vilas County, 3; Jackson County, 1[12]; Kelley Brook, Oconto County, 1[13]; Lake Saint Germain, 1; Moquah National Forest, Bayfield County, 8[2]; Prairie du Sac, Sauk County, 1[13]; Pembine, Marinette County, 1[14]; Saint Croix County, 1; Sauk County (between Reedsburg and Wisconsin Dells), 2[12].

Canis latrans frustror Woodhouse
Southeastern Coyote

Canis frustror Woodhouse, Proc. Acad. Nat. Sci. Philadelphia 5 (1850-1851): 147, June 30, 1851.

Canis frustrator (sic) Black, 30th Bien. Rept. Kansas State Board Agr. 1935-1936, p. 169, 1937.

Type specimen.—No. 4105, U. S. National Museum; male juvenile young (about 4 months old); skin only; collected in August, 1850, by Dr. S. W. Woodhouse.

Type locality.—Red Fork of Arkansas River probably near 97° west longitude near the present town of Perkins, Payne County, now Cimarron River, Oklahoma, about 100 miles west of Fort Gibson, Oklahoma (see Lyon and Osgood, 1909: 217).

Geographic range.—Southeastern and extreme eastern Kansas; Oklahoma mostly east of 99° west longitude; Texas east of 99° west longitude north of 30° north latitude and east of Nueces Bay, 97° west longitude, south of 30° north latitude; Missouri, south of the Missouri River and west of 91° west longitude; extreme northwestern and western Arkansas.

Diagnostic characters.—Averaging the largest coyote; dark colored with pronounced cast of fulvous or rufous mixed with black on upper parts, and with rich fulvous and rufous on both fore and hind legs, the forelegs with heavy streak or patch of black on front; skull large, not greatly depressed, rostrum relatively somewhat elongate; dentition heavy. Compared with *C. l. texensis,* *C. l. frustror* averages larger, is rich colored and darker, with the black on the forelegs more intense and more extensive; the skull averages larger, and the rostrum relatively longer; dentition somewhat weaker than in *frustror*. Compared with *C. l. thamnos,* the subspecies *frustror* averages larger and is a much richer colored fulvous or rufous, with the black overcast usually more pronounced; the skull of *frustror* is larger, relatively narrower, and more flattened (less depressed frontally). The subspecies *frustror* is a much darker and richer colored animal than the pale *C. l. latrans,* and has decidedly more black on the forelegs; the skull of *frustror* is larger and with longer palate than that of *latrans*.

Color.—*Winter pelage* (fresh: October and November): Muzzle, ochraceous tawny to cinnamon rufous, sometimes near snuff brown; forehead and cheeks ochraceous buff to orchraceous tawny, considerably grizzled; crown more mixed with cinnamon buff, clay color, or cinnamon, becoming more cinnamon on the nape; back of ears sayal brown, ochraceous tawny, to almost cinnamon brown; general tone of body upper parts ochraceous buff to ochraceous tawny, extending down on the flanks and on outer sides of fore and hind legs, becoming deeper and clearer color on lower parts of legs. Back heavily mixed with black tipped hairs, producing a very dark appearance and a distinct blackish or dusky mid-area down entire back; tail as in back, somewhat paler below; forelegs sayal brown to ochraceous tawny or darker, with heavy black marking down front of leg; under parts pale ochraceous buff to light ochraceous buff. *Summer pelage:* Essentially like winter pelage, possibly averaging somewhat paler.

Measurements.—Adult male and young adult male from Calumet, Canadian County, Oklahoma, respectively: Total length, 1,251, 1,207; tail vertebrae, 368, 318; hind foot, ——, ——. Two young adult males from Deerfield, Vernon County, Missouri, respectively: Total length, 1,295, 1,270; tail vertebrae, 330, 330; hind foot, 197, 191; weight, 33 pounds, 32 pounds. Two adult females from Calumet, Canadian County, and Red Fork, Tulsa County, Oklahoma, respectively: Total length, 1,226, 1,251; tail vertebrae, 364, 368; hind foot, 169, ——. Two young adult females from Vernon County, Missouri, respectively: Total length, 1,194, 1,041; tail vertebrae, 267, 330; hind foot, 184, 178; weight, 35 pounds, 28 pounds. *Skull:* Two adult males from Calumet, Canadian County, and Tahlequah, Cherokee County, Oklahoma, respectively: Condylobasal length, 193.7, 189.2; palatal length, 99.2, 95.9; squamosal constriction, 61.3, 59.2; zygomatic breadth, 104.6, 103.8; interorbital breadth, 31.7, 34.8; maxillary tooth row, 91.0, 89.5; upper carnassial length, 19.2, 19.6; upper first molar length, 13.0, 13.5; upper first molar breadth, 17.7, 18.2; lower carnassial length, 22.7, 23.0. Two adult females from Mannford, Creek County, and Red Fork, Tulsa County, Oklahoma, respectively: Condylobasal length, 182.3, 174.0; palatal length, 96.7, 89.0; squamosal constriction, 56.9, 57.6; zygomatic breadth, 99.3, 95.5; interorbital breadth, 35.4, 32.0; maxillary tooth row, 84.7, 82.0; upper carnassial length, 16.8, 17.5; first upper molar length, 12.6, 13.2; first upper molar breadth, 16.7, 16.3; lower carnassial length, 21.1, 21.0. Average of 32 skulls of young adult and adult males (Arkansas, 3; Kansas,

4; Missouri, 8; Oklahoma, 10; Texas, 7): Condylobasal length, 193.9 (183.8-203.5); palatal length, 100.8 (96.3-106.7); squamosal breadth, 61.7 (58.4-66.5); zygomatic breadth, 103.3 (97.2-112.8); interorbital breadth, 34.0 (29.3-37.4); maxillary tooth row, 89.6 (85.4-96.3); upper carnassial length, 19.7 (18.1-20.8); first upper molar length, 13.1 (12.1-14.7); first upper molar breadth, 17.2 (15.8-18.8); lower carnassial length, 22.6 (20.5-24.5). Average of 29 skulls of young adult and adult females (Arkansas, 2; Kansas, 7; Missouri, 6; Oklahoma, 10; Texas, 4): Condylobasal length, 182.3 (172.1-190.9); palatal length, 94.4 (87.2-100.4); squamosal breadth, 57.9 (53.6-63.3); zygomatic breadth, 96.0 (89.0-105.9); interorbital breadth, 31.7 (27.5-35.4); maxillary tooth row, 84.3 (79.8-92.6); upper carnassial length, 18.3 (16.2-21.2); first upper molar length, 12.8 (11.3-14.1); first upper molar breadth, 16.5 (14.6-18.4); lower carnassial length, 21.5 (18.9-24.2).

Remarks.—Woodhouse, when he named *Canis frustror* from Cimarron River, about 100 miles west of Fort Gibson, Oklahoma (Woodhouse, 1851: 147), recognized his animal as not being a wolf by describing it as the American jackal. In comparing his new form with *Canis latrans* Say, he apparently had a confused picture of the relationship of *latrans* to the true wolves, since all coyotes might well be described as "American jackals." The point is that Woodhouse recognized his animal as one of the coyote type, and not one of the big wolves. Merriam (1897: 26) in his "Revision of the Coyotes or Prairie Wolves, with Descriptions of New Species" included *frustror* as a coyote, giving it full specific rank, as he did to every coyote in his treatment of the group. Merriam, however, considered specimens from Padre Island, Texas, as representative of *frustror*, which specimens are identified by the present author as belonging to *C. l. texensis*. In a footnote to his original description of *Canis nebracensis texensis*, Bailey concluded that *frustror* was a wolf in his statement that "A series of topotypes of *frustror* secured since [i.e., since Merriam's revision] at Red Fork, Ind. T. shows it to be a widely different species, more nearly related to *Canis rufus*. The coyote of southern Texas is thus left without a name, and its nearest relative proves to be the pale *nebracensis* of the more northern plains" (Bailey, 1905: 175). Goldman carefully studied the type specimen and concluded that it was a coyote in words that "more critical comparison of this skin with those of red wolves and coyotes of similar age has convinced me that it is that of a coyote" (Young and Goldman, 1944: 396).

The present writer also has examined again the type specimen and recognizes it as without question a coyote. The specimen is that of a very young animal about four months old and less than one-third grown. At the time of its collection in August it had molted its first juvenile pelage of plain dusky or sooty brown and had acquired the first pattern pelage of adult. The specimen had been mounted and on exhibit for many years, and has faded so that its color may be misleading. In many essential characters, however, such as size of feet, size and shape of nose pad (rhinarium), and size of ears, it is characteristically coyote.

The subspecies *frustror* is the largest of the coyotes, and is dark colored, often with much black on the back, usually with a deep fulvous cast, and in typical specimens always with conspicuously fulvous or rufous feet, the fore feet heavily marked with black on the front. As coyotes go *frustror* is a well marked form that intergrades throughout wide intervening range with *C. l. texensis* its nearest, but smaller and paler ally. Intergradation with *C. l. latrans* is clearly marked, as for example in skins from Douglas and Miami Counties, Kansas, some of which are considerably paler and some slightly smaller than typical *frustror*, thus showing a trend toward the subspecies *latrans*. A very few specimens from the Ozark region of Arkansas and Missouri superficially hint that there may be possible hybridization, but probably not intergradation, with the Mississippi Valley red wolf, *Canis niger gregoryi* Goldman, in that region. All such specimens, however, have on the basis of careful study of primary characters fallen into their respective species.

Specimens examined.—Total number, 249, as follows:

Arkansas: Ashdown, Little River County, 1; Cherokee City, Benton County, 3; Mull, Marion County, 1; Siloam Springs (8 miles southeast of), Benton County, 2; Springtown, Benton County, 1; Summers, Washington County, 2; Three Brothers, Baxter County, 2; Umpire, Howard County, 1; Wedington, Washington County, 3.

Kansas: Eudora, Douglas County, 4[1]; Hamilton, Greenwood County, 3[2]; Hillsdale, Miami County, 5[1]; Paoli, Miami County, 4[1].

Missouri: Hercules Tower, Teney County, 4; Barren, Carter County, 2; Deerfield, Vernon County, 6; Eve, Vernon County, 3; Highlandville, Christian County, 1; Madisonville, Rall's County, 1; Mitchell Ranch, Texas County, 1; Nevada, Vernon County, 2; Ozark, Christian County, 1; Randolph County, 1; Rolla, Phelps County, 8; Rueter, Teney County, 1; Tyrone Texas County, 2.

Oklahoma: Calumet, Canadian County, 5; Chattanooga, Comanche County, 4; Cimarron River (type specimen; 100 miles west of Fort Gibson), Payne

---

[1] Univ. Kansas Mus. Nat. Hist.
[2] One in Univ. Kansas Mus. Nat. Hist.; two in Carnegie Mus.
[3] Texas Cooperative Wildlife Research Unit.
[4] One in collection Texas Cooperative Wildlife Research Unit.

County, 1; Fairfax (11 miles southeast of), Osage County, 1; Mannford, Creek County, 1; Cache, Comanche County, 3; Noble, Cleveland County, 5; Red Fork, Tulsa County, 4; Tahlequah, Cherokee County, 1; Wichita Mountains Wildlife Refuge, 69.

Texas: Aransas National Wildlife Refuge, 15; Baby Head, Llano County, 1; Blanco, Blanco County, 1; Bloomington, Victoria County, 4; Burnet County, 1; Castell, Llano County, 4; Cherokee, San Saba County, 2; Dayton, Liberty County, 2; Fruitland, Montague County, 1; Frelsburg, Colorado County, 1; Genoa, Harris County, 2; Graford, Palo Pinto County, 1; Hearne (between Hearne and Wheelock), Robertson County, 1[3]; Humble, Harris County, 2; Hye, Blanco County, 2; Jack County, 2; Jacksboro, Jack County, 3[4]; Jean, Young County, 5; Llano, Llano County, 14; Marysville, Cooke County, 1[3]; Marble Falls, Barnet County, 7; Murray, Young County, 1; Palo Pinto County, 1; Port Lavaca, Calhoun County, 2; Round Mountain, Blanco County, 6; Rudd, Burnet County, 2; Tivoli, Refugio County, 2; Valley Springs, Llano County, 2; Van Zandt County, 1[3]; Woodsboro, Refugio County, 1.

Canis latrans texensis Bailey

Texas Plains Coyote

Canis nebracensis texensis Bailey, North American Fauna 25: 175, October 24, 1905.

Canis latrans texensis Bailey, North American Fauna 53: 312, March 11, 1932.

Type specimen.—No. 116,277, U. S. National Museum, Biological Surveys collection; male young (about 10 months old), skin and skull; collected December 14, 1901, by J. M. Priour; original number 2, Biological Surveys miscellaneous No. 3478X.

Type locality.—Forty-five miles southwest of Corpus Christi, at Santa Gertrudis, in Kleberg County, Texas.

Geographic range.—Texas west of the Gulf of Mexico coast region at 97° west longitude (Nueces Bay) in the south, except extreme southern Texas in lower Rio Grande region, west of 99° west longitude in the north and south of the Panhandle region (about 34° north latitude); New Mexico east of the Rio Grande and south of about 35° 30′ north latitude; northern Coahuila; and extreme northwestern Tamaulipas.

Diagnostic characters.—A medium-sized coyote, rather richly colored; medium-sized skull averaging somewhat flattened; dentition moderate, the carnassials and molars usually relatively weak. Compared with *C. l. frustror* to the east, *C. l. texensis* averages smaller, and is usually somewhat paler and duller, though having a fulvous cast; skull averages smaller with relatively shorter rostrum; dentition weaker. About the size of *C. l. latrans,* but darker, brighter colored, with much more fulvous in underfur, and usually distinct blackish markings on foreleg; teeth weaker than in the subspecies *latrans*. Darker and more fulvous in color than *C. l. lestes*, somewhat smaller, with correspondingly smaller skull and somewhat weaker dentition. Darker and more fulvous than most specimens of *C. l. mearnsi*, larger, with more massive skull; dentition heavier.

Color.—Winter pelage (fresh; December): Muzzle, cinnamon buff to clay color; forehead and cheeks, pale pinkish buff to pinkish buff, much mixed with gray and black; crown more mixed with cinnamon, becoming near cinnamon or slightly darker on nape; back of ears cinnamon buff, cinnamon or frequently ochraceous tawny or near sayal brown; general tone of body upper parts light pinkish buff to pinkish buff, sometimes almost cinnamon buff, extending down on the flanks and on outer sides of forelegs; hind legs cinnamon buff or clay color. Back much grizzled, with considerable mixture of blackish-tipped hairs, usually more blackish on rump; tail as in back, paler below; forelegs cinnamon buff or clay color, frequently near ochraceous tawny, with a distinct elongate black blotch or line on front; under parts near pinkish buff or light buff. *Summer pelage:* Much like winter pelage, usually a little duller.

*Skull.—*Intermediate in size and many characters between that of *C. l. frustror* and that of *C. l. mearnsi*. Considerably smaller than that of *frustror*, tending to be narrower; dentition weaker, the carnassials and molars averaging somewhat smaller and less swollen. Distinctly larger than that of *C. l. mearnsi*, skull and dentition heavier; teeth, particularly carnassials and molars larger.

*Measurements.—*Type specimen (young male): Total length, 1,143; tail vertebrae, 356; hind foot, 180 (measured from dry skin). Adult male from San Andres Mountains, Dona Ana County, New Mexico: Total length, 1,295; tail vertebrae, 368; hind foot, 190. Two adult females from Salinas Peak, San Andres Mountains, Socorro County, New Mexico, respectively: Total length, 1,175, 1,165; tail vertebrae, 340, 305; hind foot, 194, 190. *Skull:* Type specimen (young male): Condylobasal length, 178.0; palatal length, 92.2; squamosal constriction, 59.6; zygomatic breadth, 93.4; interorbital breadth, 30.6; maxillary tooth row, 81.6; upper carnassial length, 20.0; first upper molar length, 13.1; first upper molar breadth, 17.1; lower carnassial length, 21.9. Two young adult males from Frio Town, Frio County, Texas, respectively: Condylobasal length, 194.1, 187.9; palatal length, 99.6, 98.3; squamosal constriction, 60.0, 60.8; zygomatic breadth, 104.9, 98.3; interorbital breadth, 33.8, 31.2; maxillary tooth row, 89.2, 87.2;

upper carnassial length, 19.3, 18.2; first upper molar length, 12.9, 12.7; first upper molar breadth, 17.0, 15.5; lower carnassial length, 22.8, 20.8. Two adult females (topotypes) from 45 miles southwest of Corpus Christi, in Kleberg County, Texas: Condylobasal length, 179.9, 175.0; palatal length, 94.6, 90.2; squamosal constriction, 61.4, 58.1; zygomatic breadth, 98.5, 94.8; interorbital breadth, 32.0, 32.1; maxillary tooth row, 84.5, 78.5; upper carnassial length, 17.5, 16.9; first upper molar length, 11.9, 11.3; first upper molar breadth, 16.1, 16.2; lower carnassial length, 21.2, 20.6. Average of 19 skulls of young adult and adult males (New Mexico, 1; Texas, 18): Condylobasal length, 188.3 (184.0-194.1); palatal length, 97.8 (91.8-103.7); squamosal breadth, 60.0 (57.8-62.0); zygomatic breadth, 100.6 (92.8-106.9); interorbital breadth, 32.9 (29.0-35.7); maxillary tooth row, 87.6 (83.8-93.5); upper carnassial length, 19.1 (18.2-20.3); first upper molar length, 12.6 (11.8-13.6); first upper molar breadth, 16.5 (15.0-18.1); lower carnassial length, 21.8 (19.0-24.5). Average of 15 skulls of adult females (Coahuila, 1; New Mexico, 4; Texas, 10): Condylobasal length, 176.5 (168.1-183.2); palatal length, 91.3 (88.4-96.2); squamosal breadth, 57.6 (55.8-61.3); zygomatic breadth, 94.2 (88.4-96.2); interorbital breadth, 31.6 (27.7-33.4); maxillary tooth row, 82.7 (78.5-85.4); upper carnassial length, 18.0 (16.9-19.9); first upper molar length, 12.3 (11.3-14.0); first upper molar breadth, 16.0 (15.1-17.7); lower carnassial length, 21.0 (19.8-23.6).

Remarks.—When Bailey (1905: 175) described *Canis nebracensis texensis*, he used it as a substitute description for the coyote of eastern Texas, until then known as *Canis frustror*, but which Bailey considered a wolf on the basis of specimens he had examined from Red Fork, Oklahoma. Recent study of the type specimen of *Canis frustror* shows it to be a juvenile coyote. Had Bailey selected a type locality for his *texensis* 150 miles to the northeast of where he did, he would have made a synonym of *texensis* for *frustror*. It so happens that the topotype series of *Canis nebracensis texensis* lies within the border of a recognizable form of coyote different from *frustror* and occupying a range throughout western Texas and southeastern New Mexco.

The form *C. l. texensis* is clearly an intergrade between *C. l. mearnsi* and *C. l. frustror*, and the ideas expressed by Merriam (1897: 20) and Bailey (1905: 175) that *mearnsi* and *frustror* and *mearnsi* and *texensis* belong to distinct groups, and the later expressions of Bailey (1932: 321) that *mearnsi* is a distinct species, are not borne out by facts presented in the present study of the vast number of specimens now available. The subspecies *texensis* also integrates with *microdon,* and certain borderland specimens are not easily referable to one form or the other. In other words there is not the clear cut overlapping of ranges of two "species" as mentioned by Bailey (1905: 178).

There is some indication of intergradation between *texensis* and *mearnsi* at various localities all along the Rio Grande above the Big Bend country (103° west longitude) both in Texas and New Mexico. One of the specimens from the southern end of the San Andres Mountains, Dona Ana County, New Mexico, approaches *mearnsi* very closely in all essential characters, yet four other specimens from the San Andres are very close to *texensis.* The four specimens from El Paso, Texas, have been referred by Bailey (1905: 177) to *mearnsi,* but the present reviewer considers them more nearly like *texensis.* These El Paso specimens are all of young animals and have smaller skulls and weaker dentition than adult specimens of *texensis.* The series of nine specimens from Los Ratones, Zapata County, Texas, although collected only some 35 or 40 miles from Mier, Tamaulipas, the type locality of *Canis latrans microdon,* shows some approach toward *microdon* but in general skull characters and particularly in size of carnassials and molars is nearer to *C. l. texensis.*

A single specimen, an adult male, from 10 miles southeast of Vernon, Wilbarger County, Texas, is large enough to be referred to *Canis l. frustror,* and has cranial measurements that might fit that subspecies. In color, however, it is more like *C. l. texensis* or even paler, and since other specimens from not far distant are referable to *texensis* the Vernon specimen is so classified.

Specimens examined.—Total number, 466, as follows:

Coahuila: Muzquiz (25 miles northwest of, near Hacienda de La Palma), 1; Muzquiz (110 miles northwest of), 1.
New Mexico: Carlsbad, Eddy County, 3; Carthage, Socorro County, 2; Cienega, Otero County, 5; Cowles (Pecos River), San Miguel County, 2[1]; Fort Sumner, De Baca County, 1; Gallo Canyon (40 miles southeast of Corona), Lincoln County, 4; Isleta, Bernalillo County, 1; Jicarilla Mountains, Lincoln County, 1; Lamy, Sante Fe County, 1; Lincoln National Forest, Otero County, 21; Manzano Mountains, Torrance County, 3; Mesa Jumanes (Ruins of Grand Quivera), Torrance County, 1; Organ Moun-

---

[1] Carnegie Mus.
[2] Three in collection Texas A. & M. College.
[3] Texas A. & M. College.
[4] Texas Cooperative Wildlife Research Unit.
[5] Two in collection Texas Cooperative Wildlife Research Unit.
[6] Three in Carnegie Mus.
[7] Eleven in collection of Texas Cooperative Wildlife Research Unit; one in Texas A. & M. College.

tains, Dona Ana County, 6; Pecos, San Miguel County, 2; Salt Creek, Socorro County, 1; Salt Valley (north end Guadalupe Mountains), Eddy County, 3; San Andres Mountains, Dona Ana County, 2; San Andres Mountains (Salinas Peak), Socorro County, 3; Santa Rosa, Guadalupe County, 1; Tajique, Torrance County, 1; Tucumcari, Quay County, 1; Tularosa, Otero County, 2.

Tamaulipas: Nuevo Laredo, 1.

Texas: Alice, Jim Wells County, 1; Alpine, Brewster County, 5[2]; Arden, Irion County, 1; Big Lake, Reagan County, 8; Brady, McCulloch County, 2; Brewster County, 1; Callan (12 miles northeast of Menard), Menard County, 1; Cameron County (50 miles north of Brownsville), 1; Carlsbad, Tom Green County, 7; Christoval, Tom Green County, 13; Clayton Ranch, Borden County, 1; Coleman (16 miles north of), Coleman County, 1; Corpus Christi (30 to 45 miles southwest of, in Kleberg County; type locality), 45; Corpus Christi (24 miles west of), Nueces County, 2; Cotulla, La Salle County, 2; Crystal City, Zavala County, 2[3]; Dawson County, 1; Del Rio, Val Verde County, 1; Doole, McCulloch County, 1; Eagle Pass, Maverick County, 1; El Paso, El Paso County, 4; Encinal, La Salle County, 1[4]; Fort Clark, Kinney County, 1; Fort McKavett, Menard County, 1; Frio Town, Frio County, 31; Frontera, El Paso County, 1; Gillespie County, 2; Grand Falls, Ward County, 1; Juno (15 miles north at Hudspitt Ranch), Val Verde County, 1; Kent (23 miles northwest of), Culberson County, 1[3]; Kerrville, Kerr County, 6; Laredo, Webb County, 1; Los Angeles, La Salle County, 1[4]; Los Ratones, Zapata County, 9; Menard, Menard County, 13; Monahans, Ward County, 3; Nueces Bay, Nueces County, 3; Ozona, Crockett County, 23; Padre Island, 2; Pasche, Concho County, 1; Pearsall, Frio County, 22; Rankin, Upton County, 28[5]; Robert Lee, Coke County, 2; Sabinal, Uvalde County, 5; Samuels, Terrell County, 2; San Angelo, Tom Green County, 47; San Antonio, Bexar County, 6[6]; Sanderson, Terrell County, 8; San Diego, Duval County, 1; Sheffield, Pecos County, 1; Sherwood, Irion County, 3; Sonora, Sutton County, 9; Sterling City, Sterling County, 6; Throckmorton County, 6; Van Horn, Culberson County, 12[7]; Vernon, Wilbarger County, 1; Water Valley, Tom Green County, 34.

Canis latrans lestes Merriam

Mountain Coyote

Canis lestes Merriam, Proc. Biol. Soc. Washington 11: 25, March 15, 1897.

Canis latrans lestes Grinnell, Univ. California Publ. Zool. 21 (10): 315, January 27, 1923.

Type specimen.—No. $\frac{24552}{32347}$, U. S. National Museum, Biological Surveys collection; male adult, skin and skull; collected November 21, 1890, by Vernon Bailey; original number 2223.

Type locality.—Toyabe Mountains, near Cloverdale, Nye County, Nevada.

Geographic range.—Southern British Columbia south of about latitude 52° north, except coast region; southwestern Alberta;

Washington and Oregon east of Cascade Mountains; Idaho, western Montana, western Wyoming; northern Colifornia north of about latitude 40° north, except coast region to about latitude 41° north; eastern California in Sierra Nevada south to about latitude 36° north; Nevada and Utah north of about 37° 30′ north latitude except in eastern Utah where it extends south to about 38° 30′ north latitude; mountainous regions of western Colorado, except extreme southwest corner south of 38° 30′ north latitude and west of about 107° west longitude; mountain region of northern New Mexico between 105° and 107° west longitude, and north of about 35° 30′ north latitude.

Diagnostic characters.—Size rather large, averaging about that of *C. l. latrans* or possibly larger; darker than *latrans*, showing more black hair tips over the back, darker muzzle, ears, and feet, the forefeet showing more tendency to deeper and more extensive black markings. More grayish (less cinnamon), darker, more black hair tips than in *C. l. incolatus,* with skull averaging about same size or slightly smaller, and less depressed (flatter) through frontal region; zygomatic breath relatively narrower, rostrum relatively narrower and longer. Larger than *C. l. umpquensis,* paler and less brilliant color on legs; skull larger, dentition heavier. Somewhat larger and paler than *C. l. ochropus,* duller less rufous coloration; ears smaller; skull larger, rostrum relatively broader; dentition heavier. Compared to *C. l. mearnsi,* the subspecies *lestes* is larger, usually has more blackish on back and shoulders, and is less reddish; skull larger, and dentition heavier than in *mearnsi.*

Color.—*Winter pelage* (fresh; November and December): Muzzle between ochraceous tawny and Sudan brown; forehead and cheeks pinkish buff to pinkish cinnamon, much mixed with pale gray; crown more mixed with cinnamon buff, becoming near cinnamon buff on nape; back of ears pinkish cinnamon to cinnamon, or slightly darker; general tone of body upper parts pinkish buff to almost warm buff, extending down on the flanks and on outer sides of fore and hind legs. Back much grizzled, considerably darker in midline, usually having a pronounced blackish cast from black-tipped hairs; tail as in back, paler below; forelegs pinkish buff or warm buff, often clay color, and sometimes almost ochraceous tawny, with trace of black line or blotch on front; under parts near pale pinkish buff. *Summer pelage:* Much like winter pelage, averaging somewhat paler, usually with less of the blackish overcast from black-tipped hairs.

Skull.—Medium large, relatively moderately narrow, rather flat and little depressed frontally; rostrum medium broad; dentition moderate, carnassials smaller and less swollen than in *C. l. thamnos* or *C. l. frustror*. Skull averaging much larger than that of *mearnsi*, the rostrum wider, and dentition heavier. Slightly larger than that of *C. l. ochropus*, with relatively broader rostrum, and heavier dentition. Larger than that of *C. l. umpquensis* with heavier dentition.

Measurements.—Type specimen (adult male) and adult male from Fallon, Churchill County, Nevada, respectively: Total length, 1,116, 1,282; tail vertebrae, 320, 394; hind foot, 200, 190. Adult female from Tarryall, Park County, Colorado: Total length, 1,092; tail vertebrae, 318; hind foot, 178. *Skull:* Type specimen (adult male): Condylobasal length, 180.0; palatal length, 91.5; squamosal length, 60.4; zygomatic breadth, 102.3; interorbital breadth, 33.9; maxillary tooth row, 82.3; upper carnassial length, 20.7; first upper molar length, 12.4; first upper molar breadth, 17.4; lower carnassial length, 23.1. Two adult males from Carlin, Elko County, Nevada, respectively: Condylobasal length, 195.1, 187.8; palatal length, 102.1, 97.4; squamosal constriction, 61.6, 60.6; zygomatic breadth, 101.4, 101.0; interorbital breadth, 36.8, 34.8; maxillary tooth row, 93.1, 90.6; upper carnassial length, 21.0, 20.6; first upper molar length, 13.2, 12.9; first upper molar breadth, 18.6, 17.4; lower carnassial length, 23.6, 23.2. Two adult females from Marble, Nye County, Nevada, respectively: Condylobasal length, 171.9, 164; palatal length, 88.1, 84.0; squamosal constriction, 56.0, 56.4; zygomatic breadth, 94.0, 94.4; interorbital breadth, 29.6, 30.6; maxillary tooth row, 83.3, 75.8; upper carnassial length, 19.1, 18.7; first upper molar length, 12.9, 12.6; first upper molar breadth, 17.0, 16.9; lower carnassial length, 22.5, 22.9. Average of 111 skulls of young adult and adult males (Alberta, 3; British Columbia, 4; California, 5; Colorado, 17; Idaho, 11; Montana, 6; Nevada, 12; Oregon, 9; Utah, 16; Washington, 17; Wyoming, 11): Condylobasal length, 187.1 (176.2-199.0); palatal length, 97.2 (89.8-105.0); squamosal breadth, 60.2 (55.0-65.0); zygomatic breadth, 99.5 (93.1-106.4); interorbital breadth, 33.4 (29.4-37.3); maxillary tooth row, 88.1 (82.1-94.0); upper carnassial length, 19.6 (17.4-22.2); first upper molar length, 12.7 (11.3-14.1); first upper molar breadth, 16.7 (15.0-18.3); lower carnassial length, 22.5 (20.3-25.8). Average of 82 skulls of young adult and adult females (Alberta, 1; British Columbia, 1; California, 3; Colorado, 13; Idaho, 9; Montana, 4; Nevada, 10; Oregon, 7; Utah, 11; Washington, 12; Wyoming, 11): Condylobasal length, 176.1 (164.4-189.9); palatal length, 91.5 (84.0-99.6); squamosal breadth, 57.2 (54.4-60.3); zygomatic breadth, 94.2 (88.4-99.8); interorbital breadth, 31.5 (27.6-34.9); maxillary tooth row, 83.1 (75.8-89.3);

upper carnassial length, 18.4 (16.6-20.0); first upper molar length, 12.3 (11.1-14.1); first upper molar breadth, 15.9 (14.1-17.4); lower carnassial length, 21.3 (19.6-23.4).

Remarks.—The mountain coyote, *Canis latrans lestes,* is probably the best known in the wild of any of the races. It occupies an extensive range, parts of which are sparsely inhabited by humans. In many regions it is by no means scarce and at times actually common, and is less seclusive than are coyotes in regions more densely settled by humans. Over its extensive geographic range, like all coyotes, it is subject to wide variation in size and color, yet on the whole it maintains its characteristics fairly constantly for the species. Sometimes these fluctuations in size, color, or even slight cranial characters appear to be significant of subspecific tendencies, but the variations are usually very localized, and break down through the extent of individual variation when series of specimens are available.

The subspecies *lestes* shows clear intergradation with all races adjoining it distributionally, and often borderline specimens are difficult to determine over a considerable range. Thus certain of the specimens from western Montana (National Bison Range, Little Belt Mountains, and as far west as Philipsburg) show in color a trend toward *C. l. latrans.* Some of the specimens from southern British Columbia could about as well be referred to *C. l. incolatus* as to *lestes,* but the dominance of characters and number of specimens carrying them from the region indicates best classification with *lestes.* Specimens from northeastern Washington also showed affinities with *C. l. incolatus,* so much so that Dalquest has provisionally referred the coyote of that region to *incolatus* (Dalquest, 1948: 230-231). Intergraduation with *C. l. umpquensis* occurs in the Klamath region, Oregon, and with *C. l. ochropus* in northern California and along the west slopes of the Sierra Nevada in Colifornia.

Specimens examined.—Total number, 2,068, as follows:

Alberta: Banff, 1; Calgary, 4[1]; Eagle Pass, head of James River, 1[2]; Heemsdale P. O., 10[2]; Iddesleigh, 1[3]; New Oxley, 4; Waterton Lakes National Park, 2[2].

British Columbia: Chezacut, 1[4]; Keremeos, 1[2]; Okanagan, 1; Roche River, 4; Shuswap, 1; Spence's Bridge, 2; Sunday Creek (near Roche), 1.

California: Adin, Modoc County, 1; Alturas, Modoc County, 6; Beckwith Pass, Lassen County, 1; Benton, Mono County, 1[5]; Beswick, Siskiyou County, 1; Bieber, Lassen County, 2; Brownell, Siskiyou County, 3; Burney, Shasta County, 1; Cassel, Shasta County, 3; Cedarville, Modoc County, 1; Cinder Cove, Lassen County, 1; Clipper Gap, Placer County, 1; Clover Swale (near Canby), Modoc County, 2; Davis Creek, Modoc County, 4; Deep Spring Lake, Inyo County, 2[5]; Doyle, Lassen County, 2; Eagle Lake,

Lassen County, 2; Eagleville, Modoc County, 1; Edgemont, Lassen County, 3; Fort Crook, Shasta County, 2; Glade, Tehama County, 1; Gottville, Siskiyou County, 1; Lake City, Modoc County, 1; Mammoth, Mono County, 1[5]; McCloud (Pilgrim Creek, 12 miles northeast of), Siskiyou County, 2; Merrillville, Lassen County, 3; Milford, Lassen County, 1; Montague, Siskiyou County, 1; Montgomery Creek, Shasta County, 3; Pine City, Mono County, 4; Prattville, Plumas County, 2; Ravendale, Lassen County, 1; Round Mountain, Shasta County, 1; Shasta Valley, Siskiyou County, 1; Smoke Creek, Lassen County, 3; Tecnor, Siskiyou County, 1; Tioga Lake, Mono County, 1[6]; Tule Lake, Modoc County, 4; Wawona, Mariposa County, 1; Winthrop, Shasta County, 1; Yosemite Valley, 4.

Colorado: Arkins, Larimer County, 8; Austin, Garfield County, 9; Battlecreek, Routt County, 12; Baxter Springs, Rio Blanco County, 1; Boulder, Boulder County, 6; Bountiful, Conejos County, 1; Buena Vista, Chaffee County, 1; Cedaredge, Delta County, 1; Cenicro, Conejos County, 5; Clark Ranch, Cochetopa Pass, Saguache County, 1; Coventry, Montrose County, 6; Craig, Moffat County, 11; Crevasse, Mesa County, 1; Douglas Creek, Rio Blanco County, 5; Dragon (23 miles east of), Rio Blanco County, 1[7]; East Salt Creek, Garfield County, 6; Glade Park, Mesa County, 8; Gore Range (near Kremmling), Grand County, 1; Grand Mesa, Mesa County, 2; Greystone, Moffat County, 1[7]; Kremmling, Grand County, 9; Ladore, Moffat County, 1; La Jara, Conejos County, 12; Laramie District National Forest (western), Larimer County, 5; Lily (Yampa River, 7 miles north of Elk Springs), 5,500 feet, Moffat County, 2[7]; Lay, Moffat County, 2; Little Snake River, Moffat County, 4; Loveland, Larimer County, 3; Medano Ranch, Saguache County, 6; Meeker, Rio Blanco County, 1; Mesa, Mesa County, 9; Monte Vista, Rio Grande County, 48; Montrose, Montrose County, 2; Piceance, Rio Blanco County, 20; Rangeley (15 miles west of), Rio Blanco County, 1[7]; Rifle, Garfield County, 1; Rio Grande, Conejos County, 2; Russell Springs, Rio Grande County, 15; Salida, Chaffee County, 1; Salt Creek, Garfield County, 2; Sargents, Saguache County, 2; South Park, Park County, 5; Spicer, Jackson County, 2; Spinney, Park County, 1; Steamboat Springs, Routt County, 5; Tarryall P. O., Park County, 16; Troublesome, Grand County, 1; Unaweep Canyon, Mesa County, 1; Walden, Jackson County, 1.

Idaho: Almo, Cassia County, 3; Alridge (10 miles east of Blackfoot), Bingham County, 7; Arco, Butte County, 1; Arrow Rock, Elmore County, 1; Bannock County, 3; Birch Creek, Butte County, 1; Black Pine, Oneida County, 1; Bliss, Goodnow County, 6; Boise, Ada County, 2; Bowmont, Canyon County, 15; Burley, Cassia County, 1; Caribou Mountains, Bonneville County, 3; Cerro Grande, Bingham County, 12; Challis National Forest, Custer County, 3; Chesterfield, Bannock County, 2; Cottonwood Creek, Idaho County, 1; Custer County, 2; Deer Creek Ridge, Idaho County, 1; Dickey, Custer County, 2; Dubois, Clark County, 1; Fairylawn, Owyhee County, 3; Forest, Lewis County, 2; Fort Hall, Bingham County, 4; French, Payette County, 3; Fritz Creek, Clark County, 1[8]; Gooding, Gooding County, 3; Grandview, Owyhee County, 2; Grangeville, Idaho County, 4; Grassmere, Owyhee County, 1; Hill City, Camas County, 1; Hot Springs, Owyhee County, 7; Humphrey, Clark County, 1; Idaho National Forest, Valley, 1; John Gray's Lake, Bonneville County, 1; Juniper, Oneida County, 2; Ketchum, Blaine County, 1; Kilgore, Clark County, 2; King Hill, Elmore County, 3; Leadore, Lemhi County, 4; Leesburg, Lemhi County, 1; Lemhi National Forest (Antelope Valley), Lemhi County, 1; Malad, Oneida County, 1; Mayfield, Ada County, 6; McCammon, Bannock County, 3; Medicine Lodge Creek, Clark County, 4; Mont-pelier, Bear Lake County, 2; Nora, Latah County, 1; Oakley, Cassia County, 13; Owinza, Lincoln County, 1; Payette, Payette County, 5; Pegram, Bear Lake County, 8; Picabo, Blaine County, 1; Pioneer, Butte County, 6; Pocatello, Bannock County, 7; Preusse Mountains, Caribou County, 4; Priest River, Bonner County, 4; Rice Creek, Idaho County, 8; Riddle, Owyhee County, 5; Rupert, Minidoka County, 1; Salmon, Lemhi County, 5; Salmon River, Lewis County, 2; Sawtooth National Forest, Blaine County, 4; Schnoors, Boundary County, 1; Shoshone, Lincoln County, 5; Shoshone Falls, Twin Falls County, 2; Snake River (Minidoka Dam), Cassia County, 2; Soda Springs, Caribou County, 1; Stites, Idaho County, 5; Sugar City, Madison County, 1; Sunnyside, Elmore County, 1; Three Creek, Owyhee County, 22; Thurman, Elmore County, 6; Timber Creek, Bannock County, 2; Tygee Basin, Bannock County, 2; Victor, Teton County, 1; Westlake, Lewis County, 9; West Targhee National Forest, Fremont County, 2[8]; West Warrior Creek (Boise National Forest), Boise County, 1; White Bird, Idaho County, 7.

Montana: Alder, Madison County, 1; Beaver Creek (6 miles northwest of Wallis), Wheatland County, 1; Belfrey (11 miles north of), Carbon County, 1; Big Blackfoot River (12 miles west of Lincoln), Powell County, 4[7]; Big Elk Creek (North Fork), Wheatland County, 3; Bridger, Carbon County, 8; Cardwell, Jefferson County, 1[7]; Corvallis, Ravalli County, 3; Deer Lodge, Powell County, 1; Dillon, Beaverhead County, 5; Florence, Ravalli County, 2; Gardiner, Park County, 14; Glacier National Park (Camas Creek), Flathead County, 1; Lakeview (12 miles north of), Beaverhead County, 1; Lima, Beaverhead County, 9; Little Belt Mountains, Cascade County, 10; Luther, Carbon County, 3; Midnight Canyon (5 miles north of Dean), Stillwater County, 1; Monida, Beaverhead County, 7; National Bison Range, Moise, Lake County, 9; Nye, Stillwater County, 1; Philipsburg, Granite County, 33; Pipestone Hot Springs (20 miles south-east of Butte), Jefferson County, 1[7]; Red Lodge, Carbon County, 5; Red Rock, Beaverhead County, 8; Stevensville, Ravalli County, 3; Wallis, Wheatland County, 5; Warm Spring Creek (head of Ruby River, 10 miles southeast of Homepark), Madison County, 1; White Sulphur, Meagher County, 11; Whitetail Creek (15 miles west of Whitehall), Jefferson County, 1[7]; Wisdom, Beaverhead County, 35[7]; Wise River (15 miles northwest of), Deer Lodge County, 1[7].

Nevada: Adelaide, Humboldt County, 1; Austin, Lander County, 7[10]; Beo-wawe, Eureka County, 5; Big Smoky Valley, Nye County, 1; Blair, Esmer-alda County, 5; Buffalo Creek, Washoe County, 1; Calico Mountains, Humboldt County, 2; Carlin, Elko County, 26; Cottonwood Range, Hum-boldt County, 2; Currie, Elko County, 1; Darrough's Hot Springs, Nye County, 3[9]; Deeth, Elko County, 7; Desert Ranch (T. 40 North, R 50 East, 100 miles northeast of Golconda), Elko County, 1; Dun Glen, Pershing County, 1; Elko, Elko County, 13; Fallon, Churchill County, 3; Flowing Spring, Humboldt County, 1; Gerlach, Washoe County, 22; Golconda, Humboldt County, 7; Halleck, Elko County, 2; Hilltop, Lander County, 2[11]; Humboldt, Pershing County, 1; Humboldt River (North Fork), Elko County, 4; Imley, Pershing County, 7; Jungo, Humboldt County, 25; Little Humboldt River (Bull Head Ranch, 45 miles north of Golconda), Humboldt County, 4; Lovelock, Pershing County, 1; Marble, Nye County, 5[11]; Mary's River, Elko County, 5; Massacre Lake, Washoe County, 1; Midas, Elko County, 1; Millett P. O., Nye County, 5[9]; Montello,

Elko County, 1; Morgan Hill (15 miles northeast of Elko), Elko County, 3; North Fork, Elko County, 6; Palisade, Eureka County, 3; Paradise Valley, Humboldt County, 12; Pueblo Valley (3 miles from Denio, Oregon), Humboldt County, 1; Quinn River Crossing, Humboldt County, 1[s]; Quinn River Valley, Humboldt County, 2; Rebel Creek, Humboldt County, 1; Red House, Humboldt County, 13; Red Rock, Washoe County, 1; Reno, Washoe County, 3; Roop, Washoe County, 1[s]; Rye Patch, Pershing County, 1; Silver Peak Mountains, Esmeralda County, 3; Steamboat, Washoe County, 1; Tecoma, Elko County, 1; Toyabe Mountains (near Cloverdale), (type of *Canis lestes*), Nye County, 1; Trout Creek (near Battle Mountain), Lander County, 2; Vya, Washoe County, 1; Wells, Elko County, 1; Willow Point, Humboldt County, 1; Winnemucca, Humboldt County, 29.

New Mexico: Abiquiu, Rio Arriba County, 2; Alcalde, Rio Arriba County, 1; Costella River, Taos County, 1; Embudo, Rio Arriba County, 7; Espanola, Rio Arriba County, 3; Hall's Peak, Mora County, 1; Martinez, Colfax County, 1; Pojuaque, Santa Fe County, 1; Provenir (30 miles northwest of), San Miguel County, 1; Santa Fe Forest, Santa Fe County, 4; Twining, Taos County, 3; Velarde, Rio Arriba County, 7.

Oregon: Andrews, Harney County, 7; Arlington, Gilliam County, 2; Bend, Deschutes County, 2; Big Butte Creek, Morrow County, 1; Blitzen Creek, Harney County, 1; Bly, Klamath County, 3; Burns, Harney County, 3; Cecils, Morrow County, 8; Christmas Lake, Lake County, 1; Cord, Malheur County, 9; Crooked Creek, Malheur County, 1; Disaster Peak, Malheur County, 2; Echo, Umatilla County, 5; Field (south of Alvord Lake), Harney County, 3; Fort Klamath, Klamath County, 3; Fremont, Lake County, 2; Hampton, Crook County, 4; Hardman, Morrow County, 2; Harney, Harney County, 4; Harriman, Klamath County, 4; Hay Creek, Jefferson County, 6; Heppner, Morrow County, 1; Horse Ridge, Crook County, 1; Ione, Morrow County, 2; Ironside, Malheur County, 1[s]; Jamieson, Malheur County, 1; Juniper Canyon (12 miles south of Wallula, Washington), Umatilla County, 3; Klamath Falls, Klamath County, 1[s]; Lake Alvord, Harney County, 1; Lakeview, Lake County, 2; Lena, Morrow County, 6; Lone Rock, Gilliam County, 3; Lost River (Klamath), Klamath County, 1; McDermott, Malheur County, 1; Medical Springs, Baker County, 1; Minsin National Forest, Union County, 1; Mooreville (15 miles south of), Malheur County, 1; Mount Warner, Lake County, 6; North Fork, Umatilla County, 1; Paisley, Lake County, 1; Pine Creek, Harney County, 2; Rock Creek Sink, Harney County, 3; Rome (Owyhee River), Malheur County, 1; Shirk, Harney County, 1; Sink, Sherman County, 1; Skeleton Cave (14 miles southeast of Bend), Deschutes County, 1; Spray, Wheeler County, 7; Stauffer, Lake County, 4; Sycan Marsh, Klamath County, 1; Thorn Creek (near Medical Springs), Union County, 1; Tupper Ranger Station (east of Fossil, Umatilla National Forest), Wheeler County, 1; Van Sycle, Umatilla County, 1; Vale, Malheur County, 1.

Utah: Altonah (10 miles north of), Duchesne County, 5; Beaver (20 miles northeast of), Beaver County, 14; Beaver Mountains (Puffer Lake), Beaver County, 1; Beech Canyon, Box Elder County, 1; Black Mountain, Tooele County, 2; Bowen's Spring, Duchesne County, 1; Boxelder, Duchesne County, 1; Box Elder County, 1; Buckskin Valley, Iron County, 1; Cedar Creek, Box Elder County, 1; Cedar Springs, Box Elder County, 1; Cedar Valley (near Fairfield), Utah County, 11; Cherry Creek, Juab County, 3;

Coal Canyon (15 miles west of Fruitland), Wasatch County, 1; Cotton-wood Canyon (about 20 miles south of Duchesne, Uinta National Forest), Duchesne County, 3; Currant Creek, Wasatch County, 1; Dark Valley (15 miles southwest of Teasdale), Wayne County, 1; Dave Creek, Box Elder County, 7; Day Springs (10 miles southwest of Milford), Beaver County, 1; Deep Creek, Tooele County, 3; Delle, Tooele County, 4; Duchesne, Duchesne County, 4; Etna, Box Elder County, 2; Fairfield, Utah County, 2; Fish Lake, Sevier County, 1; Fish Spring, Juab County, 6; Fruitland (15 miles southwest, on Strawberry River), Wasatch County, 3; Fulmer Springs (15 miles northwest of Nada), Beaver County, 4; Gandy, Millard County, 1; Garrison, Millard County, 2; Grouse Creek, Box Elder County, 1; Hay Springs (4 miles northeast of Nada), Beaver County, 5; Hunts-ville, Weber County, 1; Ibapah, Tooele County, 4; Indianola (14 miles east of), Sanpete County, 4; Kamas, Summit County, 3; Kelton, Box Elder County, 10; Laketown, Rich County, 1; Lampo, Box Elder County, 2; Low, Tooele County, 8; Lucin, Box Elder County, 1; Manila, Utah County, 1; Meadowville, Rich County, 1; Meeks Hollow (15 miles west of Fruit-land), Wasatch County, 3; Minersville, Beaver County, 1; Morgan, Morgan County, 1; Mountain Home, Duchesne County, 2; Myton, Duchesne County, 3[7]; Ogden, Weber County, 1; Panguitch, Garfield County, 2; Paro-wan, Iron County, 10; Pine Grove Valley (25 miles southwest of New-house along Pine Creek), Beaver County, 3; Pine Valley, Beaver County, 3; Pleasant Grove, Utah County, 3; Pleasant Valley, Juab County, 3; Post Canyon (Book Cliffs, 75 miles south of Ouray, Uintah County), Grand County, 1[7]; Reeves Ranch (near Seco, 14 miles east of Kelton), Box Elder County, 1; Roosevelt, Duchesne County, 2[7]; Rosette, Box Elder County, 3; Rush, Tooele County, 3; Shingle Creek (18 miles southwest of Sevier), Summit County, 4; Simpson Springs, Tooele County, 1; Six Mile Canyon, Sanpete County, 1; Snowville, Box Elder County, 2; South Eden, Weber County, 2; Tabby, Duchesne County, 1; Tremonton, Box Elder County, 1; Uintah County, 90[7]; Vernal, Uintah County, 1; Wah Wah Pass, Beaver County, 3; Wanship, Summit County, 1; Wendover, Tooele County, 3; Willow Creek (20 miles southeast of Heber), Wasatch County, 3; Yost, Box Elder County, 2.

Washington: Alden Creek, Chelan County, 2; Anglin, Okanogan County, 4; Badger, Benton County, 19; Baird, Douglas County, 1; Boyds, Ferry County, 2; Burbank, Walla Walla County, 2; Carlton, Okanogan County, 4; Cashmere, Chelan County, 3; Chattaroy, Spokane County, 1; Chelan, Chelan County, 1; Chewelah, Stevens County, 2; Cloverland, Asotin County, 1; Coffin Range, Yakima County, 1; Coldcreek (12 miles north in Grant County), 45; Colville, Stevens County, 1; Conconully, Okanogan

---

[1] Three in Amer. Mus. Nat. Hist.
[2] Nat. Mus. Canada.
[3] Royal Ontario Mus. Zool.
[4] Provincial Mus., Victoria, British Columbia.
[5] Collection Donald R. Dickey.
[6] Mus. Vert. Zool., Univ. California.
[7] Carnegie Mus.
[8] Amer. Mus. Nat. Hist.
[9] Two in Carnegie Mus.
[10] Three in Royal Ontario Mus. Zool.; three in Mus. Vert. Zool., Univ. California.
[11] One in Mus. Vert. Zool., Univ. California.

County, 5; Corral Creek (near Benton City), Benton County, 1; Coulee City, Grant County, 1; Cowiche, Yakima County, 2; Creston, Lincoln County, 1; Danville, Ferry County, 2; Dayton, Columbia County, 1; Ellensburg, Kittitas County, 3; Ephrata, Grant County, 10; Goldendale, Klickitat County, 3; Hanford, Benton County, 4; Hooper, Adams County, 8; Horse Heaven, Benton County, 2; Keller, Ferry County, 1; Kennewick, Benton County, 5; Lake Chelan, Chelan County, 8; Longmire Range, Yakima County, 1; Loomis, Okanogan County, 8; Malo, Ferry County, 1; Malott, Okanogan County, 10; Manning, Whitman County, 1; Marlin, Grant County, 1; Moses Coulee, Douglas County, 2; North Yakima, Yakima County, 1[8]; Okanogan, Okanogan County, 1; Okanogan County, 1; Oroville, Okanogan County, 3; Othello, Adams County, 2; Park Rapids, Stevens County, 1; Peach, Lincoln County, 1; Penawawa, Whitman County, 1; Plymouth, Benton County, 28; Rattlesnake Hills, Yakima County, 5; Ritzville, Adams County, 1; Rockford, Spokane County, 1; Rockland, Klickitat County, 1; Rye Grass, Franklin County, 3; Tampico, Yakima County, 1; Tekoa, Whitman County, 1; Tieton (near Ephrata), Grant County, 1; Touchet, Walla Walla County, 2; Trinidad, Grant County, 9; Usk, Pend d'Oreille County, 3; Wallula, Walla Walla County, 3; Washtuena, Adams County, 5; Wauconda, Okanogan County, 3; Wilbur, Lincoln County, 1; Yakima (20 miles southwest), Yakima County, 1.

Wyoming: Afton (27 miles east of), Lincoln County, 6; Big Creek P. O., Carbon County, 15; Big Horn (Shell Creek Basin), Big Horn County, 4; Big Piney, Sublette County, 1; Cody, Park County, 7; Cokeville, Lincoln County, 1; Crystal Creek, Lincoln County, 1; Elk, Lincoln County, 5; Evanston, Uinta County, 1; Fort Bridger, Uinta County, 4[9]; Jackson, Teton County, 2; Kelly, Teton County, 7; Kendall, Fremont County, 13; Kirby Creek, Hot Springs County, 1; Longs Creek, Fremont County, 2; Moran, Teton County, 2; Opal, Lincoln County, 27; Pinedale, Fremont County, 3; Pinyon Ridge, Fremont County, 1; Pole Creek, Sublette County, 1; Rock Springs, Sweetwater County, 3; Rongis, Fremont County, 3; Sheep Range (north of Afton), Lincoln County, 1; Shell Creek, Big Horn County, 14; Shell Creek (25 miles south of Bitter Creek), Sweetwater County, 1[7]; Sweetwater River, Fremont County, 15; Valley, Park County, 1; Yellowstone National Park, 115.

Canis latrans umpquensis Jackson

Northwest Coast Coyote

Canis latrans umpquensis Jackson, Proc. Biol. Soc. Washington 62: 31, March 17, 1949.

Type specimen.—No. 216,537, U. S. National Museum, Biological Surveys collection; female young adult, skin and skull; collected March 11, 1916, by W. L. Tison. Original number 16; Biological Surveys miscellaneous number 15,880X.

Type locality.—Five miles southeast of Drew, Douglas County, Oregon.

Geographic range.—West of the Cascade Mountains, in Oregon and Washington.

Diagnostic characters.—A small, usually rufous-tinged, dark-colored coyote, with distinct black markings on the forelegs, and deep fulvous or rufous on both hind and forelegs, usually with distinct cast of rufous on the rump; ears relatively large; skull comparatively small, moderately elongate, with weak dentition. Smaller than *Canis l. lestes*, darker and deeper rufous color on legs, muzzle, and ears; skull smaller and dentition weaker. Smaller and darker than *C. l. ochropus*, deeper rufous on the legs, ears, and muzzle; ears smaller; skull averaging smaller than in *ochropus*.

Color.—*Winter pelage* (full and little worn; January and February): Muzzle, sayal brown to snuff brown, rarely approaching cinnamon; forehead and cheeks cinnamon buff, grizzled and mixed with grayish; crown more mixed with sayal brown, becoming more nearly cinnamon on nape; back of ears sayal brown, sometimes approaching snuff brown; general tone of body upper parts usually cinnamon to pinkish cinnamon, sometimes near light pinkish cinnamon or cinnamon buff, usually more rufous on the rump extending ventrad on the flanks and on upper outer sides of fore and hind legs; back with distinct blackish overcast, particularly in midline; color of tail as in back, somewhat paler below; forelegs clay color to cinnamon buff, with distinct blackish line down front; under parts paler, light cinnamon buff to light pinkish cinnamon. *Summer pelage:* Much like winter pelage, but averaging slightly paler and more grayish.

Skull.—Comparatively small in size, relatively moderately broad, with frontal region but slightly depressed, and rostrum somewhat elongate and narrow; dentition comparatively weak.

Measurements.—Adult male from Forks, Clallam County, Washington: Total length, 1,247; tail vertebrae, 358; hind foot, 207; ear from notch, 122; weight, 27¼ pounds. *Skull:* Type specimen and topotype (young adult females), respectively: Condylobasal length, 171.1, 173.2; palatal length, 86.4, 86.5; squamosal constriction, 57.5, 57.2; zygomatic breadth, 94.0, 90.8; interorbital breadth, 29.5, 31.0; maxillary tooth row, 78.5, 79.7; upper carnassial length, 17.3, 19.0; first upper molar length, 11.9, 11.8; first upper molar breadth, 16.1, 15.9; lower carnassial length, 20.0, 21.1. Two young adult males from Sequim, Clallam County, Washington, respectively: Condylobasal length, 178.8, 181.5; palatal length, 91.4, 96.4; squamosal constriction, 58.1, 59.2; zygomatic breadth, 94.8, 97.6; interorbital breadth, 31.0, 30.3; maxillary tooth row, 83.2, 85.4; upper carnassial length, 18.7, 18.0; first upper molar length, 11.9, 12.3; first upper molar breadth, 16.5, 16.0; lower carnassial length, 22.1, 21.7. Average of 8 skulls of young adult and adult males (Oregon, 3; Washington, 5): Condylobasal length, 182.7 (173.1-191.0); palatal length, 95.8 (91.4-102.0); squamosal breadth, 59.9 (56.3-63.0); zygomatic breadth, 98.1 (94.8-103.2); interorbital breadth, 32.0 (26.8-34.7); maxillary tooth row, 85.5 (80.6-88.6); upper carnassial length, 18.5 (17.0-19.4); first upper molar length, 12.4 (11.9-12.9); first upper molar breadth, 16.2 (15.3-16.8); lower carnassial length, 21.8 (19.8-23.1). Average of 9 skulls of young adult and adult females (Oregon, 6; Washington, 3): Condylobasal length, 170.0 (162.0-174.1; palatal length, 87.9 (83.9-91.4); squamosal breadth, 56.8 (55.1-57.5); zygomatic breadth, 93.4 (90.8-95.8); interorbital breadth, 31.0 (28.9-33.1); maxillary tooth row, 79.2 (76.4-82.2); upper carnassial length, 17.8 (16.3-19.0); first upper molar length, 11.8 (11.2-12.5); first upper molar breadth, 15.6 (14.8-16.1); lower carnassial length, 20.3 (18.8-21.3).

Remarks.—So far as is known *Canis latrans umpquensis* is confined to those parts of Oregon and Washington west of the Cascade Mountains. Specimens are not available to show whether or not it is the subspecies found in the extreme northwestern corner of California, but it would seem probable that *umpquensis* intergrades wth *C. l. ochropus* in that part of California. Specimens from the Klamath region (Fort Klamath, Harriman, Klamath Falls, Sycan Marsh), Klamath County, Oregon, although showing some approach to *umpquensis* both in size and in deeper rufous on legs than in average *C. l. lestes* as well as in cranial characteristics are more like *lestes*, to which they are referred.

There is as one might expect considerable variation in the amount and intensity of fulvous or rufous coloration in the hair on the back, but in most specimens any reduction of this color is replaced by black, so that these specimens have a dark dorsal aspect. There is also some variation in intensity of the rufous color on the legs, but the deepest leg coloration in specimens of *C. l. lestes* from Nevada and eastern Washington is a shade paler than the palest rufous on the legs of nearly all specimens of *C. l. umpquensis*. There seems to be a general tendency towards a reduction of the rufous toward the northward, which may indicate an influence of *lestes* as an intergrading subspecies in that region. In fact, most of the specimens of *umpquensis* examined from the State of Washington show some of this reduction in the reddish cast, which reduction appears to reach its maximum in the skin of a male from 5 miles north of Forks, Soleduck River, Clallam County, Washington. The skulls of two males collected April 13, 1928, 11 miles northeast of Lewis, Lewis County, Washington, are wider across the zygomata than normal specimens of *umpquensis*, and the skins also have less intense rufous and more blackish than typical *umpquensis*, as does also the skin of female collected at the same locality, April 5, 1928. The skull of this female, however, is near average *umpquensis* in characteristics.

Specimens examined.—Total number, 45, as follows:

Oregon: Agness, Curry County, 1; Ashland, Jackson County, 1; Blue River, Lane County, 4; Drew (type locality), Douglas County, 6; Estacada, Clackamas County, 4; Kerby, Josephine County, 1; Marmot, Clackamas County, 1; Oakridge (20 miles southeast of), Lane County, 1; Pyramid Rock (on Pistol River, 12 miles from mouth), Curry County, 1; Rogue River, Jackson County, 3; Stockyards Camp (on Pistol River, 14 miles from mouth), Curry County, 1.

Washington: Forks, Clallam County, 1; Johnson Creek (West Fork), Thurston County, 1; Joyce, Clallam County, 1; Kapowsin, Pierce County, 1; Lewis, Lewis County, 3; Nooksack River, Whatcom County, 1; Renton, King County, 1; Sequim, Clallam County, 1; Snoqualmie (10 miles northeast of), King County, 3; Tenino, Thurston County, 1; Thompson Creek (8 miles southeast of Tenino), Thurston County, 1; Thurston County, 1; Trout Lake, Klickitas County, 4; Washougal, Skamania County, 1.

Canis latrans ochropus Eschscholtz

California Valley Coyote

Canis ochropus Eschscholtz, Zool. Atlas 3: 1, 1829.

Canis latrans ochropus Nelson, Proc. Biol. Soc. Washington 45: 224, November 26, 1932.

Type specimen.—None now known to exist.

Type locality.—Sacramento River valley, not far south of the present city of Sacramento, Sacramento County, California.

Geographic range.—California west of the high Sierra Nevada and south of about 40° north latitude except in coast region where its range extends north to 41° north latitude; south through central California to about 34° north latitude and in the western coast region nearly to 33° north latitude.

Diagnostic characters.—A medium sized, rather dark, usually highly colored coyote, with relatively large ears, medium sized, rather elongate skull, with relatively long and narrow rostrum, and relatively small teeth. Somewhat smaller and darker than *C. l. lestes*, brighter and more rufous or buffy coloration; ears larger and relatively longer; skull smaller, rostrum relatively narrower, dentition weaker. Larger and a shade paler than *C. l. umpquensis*, the rufous on the legs not so dark, but usually more brilliant; ears larger; skull averaging larger than in *umpquensis*. About the size of *C. l. clepticus* or slightly larger, with skull noticeably relatively longer and narrower, the rostrum particularly relatively narrower and longer; color usually more mixed with black and gray, than in *clepticus*. Larger than *C. l. mearnsi*, more rufous in coloration, skull larger, and relatively longer and narrower, particularly in the rostral region; dentition slightly heavier.

Color.—*Winter pelage* (fresh; January): Muzzle, cinnamon to sayal brown; forehead and cheeks pinkish buff, much grizzled; crown more mixed with sayal brown or ochraceous tawny, becoming more sayal brown or cinnamon on nape; back of ears near ochraceous tawny; general tone of body upper parts pinkish buff to warm buff, heavily mixed with black; buff of upper parts extending down on the flanks and on outer sides of fore and hind legs; tail as in back, usually less black, somewhat paler below; forelegs clay color to deep ochraceous buff, sometimes almost ochraceous orange, with distinct blackish broad line running down front; under parts between pinkish buff and cinnamon buff. *Summer pelage:* Usually much like winter pelage but often much paler and more grayish brown on account of worn pelage.

Skull.—Medium in size, relatively very narrow, particularly anteriorly, moderately flat and little depressed frontally; rostrum relatively long and narrow; dentition comparatively weak, premolars widely spaced, the carnassials and molars smaller than in *C. l. lestes*.

Measurements.—Two adult males from Alila, Tulare County, and Fremont Peak, Gabilan Range, Monterey County, California, respectively: Total length, 1,269, 1,220; tail vertebrae, 331, 390; hind foot, 205, 206. Two adult females from Alila, Tulare County, and Tracy, San Joaquin County, California, respectively: Total length, 1,281, 1,181; tail vertebrae, 326, 290; hind foot, 188, 191. *Skull:* Adult male from Alila, Tulare County, and young adult male from Tracy, San Joaquin County, California, respectively: Condylobasal length, 194.8, 186.7; palatal length, 99.1, 98.5; squamosal constriction, 59.3, 59.7; zygomatic breadth, 98.6, 93.7; interorbital breadth, 34.8, 29.8; maxillary tooth row, 89.2, 88.4; upper carnassial length, 19.2, 18.5; first upper molar length, 12.2, 12.0; first upper molar breadth, 15.6, 15.4; lower carnassial length, 21.5, 21.4. Adult female from Alila, Tulare County, and young adult female from Tracy, San Joaquin County, California, respectively: Condylobasal length, 183.9, 179.3; palatal length, 90.7, 91.5; squamosal constriction, 56.6, 58.6; zygomatic breadth, 91.0, 91.6; interorbital breadth, 29.4, 28.9; maxillary tooth row, 84.3, 83.6; upper carnassial length, 17.8, 17.3; first upper molar length, 11.0, 11.8; first upper molar breadth, 15.1, 15.7; lower carnassial length, 20.6, 21.1. Average of 9 skulls of young adult and adult males from California: Condylobasal length, 190.4 (180.6-199.6); palatal length, 98.3 (92.4-105.3); squamosal breadth, 60.2 (57.4-64.1); zygomatic breadth, 100.3 (93.7-107.8); interorbital breadth, 32.7 (29.5-38.1); maxillary tooth row, 89.2 (85.5-93.8); upper carnassial length, 19.2 (17.4-21.9); first upper molar length, 12.3 (11.8-13.9); first upper molar breadth, 16.1 (15.4-17.7); lower carnassial length, 21.9 (20.7-25.1). Average of 12 skulls of young adult and adult females from California: Condylobasal length, 179.4 (172.3-191.7); palatal length, 92.2 (86.5-99.5); squamosal breadth, 57.8 (55.6-60.8); zygomatic breadth, 94.0 (91.0-97.6); interorbital breadth, 29.6 (27.6-33.4); maxillary tooth row, 83.5 (78.8-86.6); upper carnassial length, 18.1 (16.2-21.7); first upper molar length, 11.8 (10.5-12.7); first upper molar breadth, 15.6 (14.2-16.4); lower carnassial length, 21.1 (19.3-22.3).

Remarks.—The California Valley coyote was collected by Dr. Friedrich Eschscholtz while he was the naturalist on Kotzebue's second voyage around the world. Kotzebue visited the Russian settlement of Ross, California, by way of San Rafael and Bodega, and remained some time collecting plants and other natural history material. According to Kotzebue's narrative he made a hunting trip during November 18 to 24, 1824, by boat from his anchorage in San Francisco Bay through Suisun Bay and up the Sacramento River to a point about directly east of the present town of Davis (Kotzebue, 1830: 137-148). Eschscholtz accompanied Kotzebue on this trip. The narrative gives an interesting light on the abundance of game in the region. Deer, elk, and wildfowl were seen apparently in abundance. Large gray wolves as well as coyotes were seen at various times, and writing of their last night in camp on the Sacramento River, Kotzebue records that "we were again disturbed by the little wolves so common here: they stole a piece of venison" Kotzebue, 1830: 147). The main hunt of the trip appears to have been made at this upper camp, which may reasonably be considered the locality where Eschscholtz procured the coyote upon which he based the description of *Canis ochropus* (Eschscholtz, 1829).

There is the usual considerable individual variation in color in *C. l. ochropus,* and a tendency for the fur to become somewhat more grayish in summer because of the wearing of the black tips, and thus cause the summer fur to more nearly approach that of *C. l. lestes* in color during that season of the year. Most specimens, however, are quite in contrast to *lestes* in color, and the longer palate, more widely spaced premolars, and smaller teeth are quite diagnostic.

Specimens examined.—Total number, 257, as follows:

California: Alcalde, Fresno County, 3; Alila, Tulare County, 8; Berkeley, Alameda County, 1[1]; Blocksburg, Humboldt County, 1; Bodega, Sonoma County, 1; Buena Vista Lake, 1[2]; Buttonwillow, Kern County, 1; Caliente, Kern County, 1; Cameron, Kern County, 1; Campo, San Diego County, 1; Carlotta, Humboldt County, 2[2]; Chico, Butte County, 2; Chino, San Bernardino County, 3; Cuyama Valley, Santa Barbara County, 3; Delano, Kern County, 1; Del Monte, Monterey County, 2; Etiwanda, San Bernardino County, 2[2]; Fort Tejon, Kern County, 4; Freeman Canyon, Kern County, 1[2]; Fremont Peak, Monterey County, 1; Garberville, Humboldt County, 2; Goshen (west of Visalia), Tulare County, 11; Hayward, Alameda County, 1; Jolon, Monterey County, 5; Lockwood, Monterey County, 2; Los Olivos, Santa Barbara County, 1; Maple Creek, Humboldt County, 1; Mariposa County, 2; Montecito, Santa Barbara County, 1[2]; Mount Diablo, Contra Costa County, 2[1]; Onyx, Kern County, 1; Orosi, Tulare County, 21; Palo Alto, Santa Clara County, 3[3]; Pescadero, San Mateo County, 2[1]; Portola Lake, San Mateo County, 1[1]; Punta Gorda, Ventura County, 1; Redlands, San Bernardino County, 11; Sacramento, Sacramento County, 1; San Bernardino, San Bernardino County, 1; San Felipe, Santa Clara County, 1; San Francisco, San Francisco County, 1; San Jacinto, Riverside County, 1; San Lorenzo Creek, Monterey County, 1[1]; San Luis Obispo, San Luis Obispo County, 1; Santa Barbara, Santa Barbara County, 1[2]; Santa Clara County, 1[1]; Santa Rosa Island, Santa Barbara County, 1; Tracy, San Joaquin County, 120; Trinity County, 1[2]; Volta, Merced County, 2; Walnut Creek, Contra Costa County, 2[1]; Warrens Well, San Bernardino County, 1; Westley, Stanislaus County, 6[1]; West Riverside, Riverside County, 1; Wheatland, Yuba County, 1[1]; Willow Springs, Kern County, 5.

Canis latrans clepticus Elliot

San Pedro Martir Coyote

Canis clepticus Elliot, Field-Columbian Mus. Publ. No. 79, Zool. ser., vol. 3, p. 225, June, 1903.

Canis latrans clepticus Nelson, Proc. Biol. Soc. Washington 45: 224, November 26, 1932.

Type specimen.—No. 10,919, Chicago Natural History Museum; female adult, skin and skull; collected September 26, 1902, by Edmund Heller. Original number 1667.

Type locality.—Vallecitos, San Pedro Martir Mountains, altitude 8,500 feet, Baja California.

Geographic range.—Northern Baja California north of 30° north latitude except northeastern part north of 31° 31' north and east of 116° west longitude; southwestern California, mostly confined to San Diego County.

---

[1] Mus. Vert. Zool., Univ. California.
[2] Collection of Donald R. Dickey.
[3] Amer. Mus. Nat. Hist.

Diagnostic characters.—A medium sized coyote; average color noticeably reddish, particularly so in summer pelage, but often varying to much mixed with grayish or blackish; particularly in winter, when its color is but slightly less blackish and more reddish than *C. l. peninsulae;* ears relatively large. Skull short and broad, with especially rounded cranium and short broad rostrum, dentition moderate.

Color.—Somewhat variable, but in the majority of specimens examined the general tone is a rusty or cinnamon rufous color. Generally the rusty tones are similar to *Canis latrans peninsulae,* but averaging paler, and the black greatly reduced. The rusty tones somewhat more yellowish than in *C. l. ochropus,* and the black slightly reduced.

Skull.—Relatively shorter and broader, more rotund, with relatively shorter rostrum, and on the average smaller teeth than *Canis l. peninsulae.* Smaller and shorter, with contrastingly shorter rostrum, and relatively larger teeth than in *C. l. ochropus.*

Measurements.—Two young adult males from La Grulla and San Felipe Bay, Baja California, respectively: Total length, 1,088, 1,180; tail vertebrae, 275, 367; hind foot, 188, 186. Two young adult females from La Grulla and San Felipe Bay, Baja California, respectively: Total length, 1,032, 1,100; tail vertebrae, 305, 305; hind foot, 178, 176. *Skull:* Two young adult males from La Grulla and San Felipe Bay, Baja California, respectively: Condylobasal length, 170.2, 175.1; palatal length, 88.0, 91.2; squamosal constriction, 57.2, 57.7; zygomatic breadth, 102.3, 93.8; interorbital breadth, 31.8, 32.1; maxillary tooth row, 76.6, 79.8; upper carnassial length, 16.6, 17.8; first upper molar length, 11.7, 11.8; first upper molar breadth, 15.1, 14.5; lower carnassial length, 20.3, 20.9. Two young adult females from La Grulla and San Felipe Bay, Baja California, respectively: Condylobasal length, 169.2, 169.1; palatal length, 87.9, 88.2; squamosal constriction, 57.2, 56.7; zygomatic breadth, 97.1, 89.7; interorbital breadth, 30.2, 31.6; maxillary tooth row, 76.7, 81.5; upper carnassial length, 16.3, 18.1; first upper molar length, 11.3, 12.1; first upper molar breadth, 14.4, 16.3; lower carnassial length, 19.2, 20.9. Average of 5 skulls of young adult and adult males (Baja California, 4; California, 1): Condylobasal length, 172.6 (170.2-175.1); palatal length, 89.4 (88.0-91.2); squamosal breadth, 57.6 (56.6-58.5); zygomatic breadth, 96.7 (93.8-102.3); interorbital breadth, 32.7 (31.8-34.5); maxillary tooth row, 80.3 (76.6-84.4); upper carnassial length, 18.1 (16.6-19.6); first upper molar length, 11.9 (11.1-12.8); first upper molar breadth, 14.9 (14.5-15.4); lower carnassial length, 20.8 (20.3-21.7).

Remarks.—The San Pedro Martir coyote is a large coyote and very clearly a connecting subspecies between *Canis latrans ochropus* on the north and *Canis latrans peninsulae* on the south. It also intergrades with *Canis l. mearnsi* towards the northeast, and many specimens are difficult to determine as to closest subspecific affinity. There is considerable variation in color. Specimens from Alamo have a broad band of bright ochraceous extending down the back and shading into a paler buff on the sides. These colors extend back over the tail, where in one it becomes a zinc orange. In specimens with excessively worn and faded pelage, as in certain ones from Vallecitos and La Grulla collected in May and June, the general color may become a dingy gray with only slight rustiness on the outside of the thighs and legs, a dull rusty fawn color that evidently has faded from the stronger rusty color of full pelage.

Specimens from California referred to *Canis latrans clepticus* nearly all show a trend away from the typical *clepticus* color and cranial characters, and are intergrades with *C. l. ochropus* to the north, or with *C. l. mearnsi* to the east.

Specimens examined.—Total number, 59, as follows:

Baja California: Alamo, 8[1]; Concepcion (San Pedro Martir Mountains; altitude 6,000 feet), 1[2]; La Grulla (San Pedro Martir Mountains, altitude 7,500 feet), 5[3]; Parral, 1[4]; Poso Vicente, 1; San Felipe, 15[5]; San Quintin, 5[6]; San Ramon (mouth of San Domingo River), 1[2]; Santa Eulalia, 1[4]; Santa Rosa, 1[4]; San Telmo (altitude 600 feet), 2[1]; Trinidad Valley, 1; Vallecitos (San Pedro Martir Mountains; altitude 8,500 feet; type locality), 5[7]; Valle Trinidad (altitude 2,500 feet), 2[2].

California: Jacumba, San Diego County, 1; Julian, San Diego County, 1[8]; La Jolla, San Diego County, 1[9]; La Puerta Valley, San Diego County, 1[2]; San Diego, San Diego County, 3; San Marcos, San Diego County, 3.

---

[1] Six in San Diego Nat. Hist. Mus.; two in Chicago Nat. Hist. Mus.

[2] Mus. Vert. Zool., Univ. California.

[3] Two in Mus. Vert. Zool., Univ. California.

[4] Chicago Nat. Hist. Mus.

[5] Five in Chicago Nat. Hist. Mus.; two in Mus. Vert. Zool., Univ. California; one in Amer. Mus. Nat. Hist.

[6] Two in Chicago Nat. Hist. Mus.; two in Mus. Comp. Zool., Harvard College.

[7] One in Chicago Nat. Hist. Mus.; three in Mus. Vert. Zool., Univ. California.

[8] Collection of Donald R. Dickey.

[9] San Diego Nat. Hist. Mus.

Canis latrans peninsulae Merriam

Peninsula Coyote

Canis peninsulae Merriam, Proc. Biol. Soc. Washington 11: 28, March 15, 1897.
Canis latrans peninsulae Nelson, Proc. Biol. Soc. Washington 45: 224, November 26, 1932.

Type specimen.—No. 74,245, U. S. National Museum, Biological Surveys collection; male adult, skin and skull; collected May 15, 1895, by J. E. McLellan. Original number 1354.

Type locality.—Santa Anita, Cape Saint Lucas, Baja California.

Geographic range.—Peninsula Baja California south of 30° north latitude.

Diagnostic characters.—A medium sized, rather dark and richly colored coyote, with distinctly large ears; skull medium size, relatively broad and short, with relatively broad rounded cranium and short broad rostrum; dentition medium. Similar to *Canis latrans clepticus,* but a shade darker and more black on the back; skull somewhat larger than that of *clepticus;* dentition heavier, particularly carnassials and molars.

Color.—(Greatly worn winter pelage; March and April): Muzzle, sayal brown, or a shade darker; forehead and cheeks cinnamon or pale sayal brown, much grizzled; crown and nape more mixed with sayal brown; back of ears ochraceous tawny; general tone of upper parts buffy ochraceous, much mixed with black; tail as in back, somewhat paler below; fore and hind legs ochraceous tawny or paler, the black markings on forelegs not conspicuous; under parts near cinnamon buff.

Skull.—Medium size, relatively broad and short; rostrum broad, particularly basally; dentition moderate, a bit heavier than in *C. l. clepticus,* particularly the carnassials and molars.

Measurements.—Type specimen (adult male) and adult male from Magdalena Island, Baja California, respectively: Total length, 1,100, 1,132; tail vertebrae, 310, 345; hind foot, 180, 183. Two young adult females from Matancita, Baja California, respectively: Total length, 1,073, 1,030; tail vertebrae, 325, 297; hind foot, 178, 181. *Skull:* Type specimen (adult male) and young adult male from Cape Saint Lucas, Baja California, respectively: Condylobasal length, 177.8, 175.8; palatal length, 93.2, 88.6; squamosal constriction, 56.7, 54.2; zygomatic breadth, 98.9, 95.5; interorbital breadth, 34.6, 30.2; maxillary tooth row, 84.0, 82.8; upper carnassial length, 20.4, 20.6; first upper molar length, 13.6, 13.2; first upper molar breadth, 17.1, 16.2; lower carnassial length, 22.2, 22.8. Two adult females from Cape Saint Lucas, Baja California, respectively: Condylobasal length, 171.0, 166.3; palatal length, 85.3, 85.2; squamosal constriction, 57.0, 53.5; zygomatic breadth, 95.6, 89.2; interorbital breadth, 32.6, 29.3; maxillary tooth row, 79.7, 78.8; upper carnassial length, 17.5, 18.1; first upper molar length, 12.1, 11.6; first upper molar breadth, 15.5, 14.9; lower carnassial length, 20.4, 20.1. Average of 7 skulls of adult males from Baja California: Condylobasal length, 176.6 (172.5-181.0); palatal length, 90.1 (86.6-93.2); squamosal breadth, 58.2 (54.2-60.9); zygomatic breadth, 98.6 (92.7-106.8); interorbital breadth, 32.2 (30.0-37.1); maxillary tooth row, 82.9 (80.0-86.8); upper carnassial length, 19.1 (16.8-20.8); first upper molar length, 12.2 (10.0-13.2); first upper molar breadth, 15.8 (13.5-17.1); lower carnassial length, 21.6 (19.5-23.0). Average of 11 skulls of young adult and adult females from Baja California: Condylobasal length, 166.6 (161.2-173.2); palatal length, 85.1 (82.2-88.4); squamosal breadth, 56.8 (52.7-67.7); zygomatic breadth, 91.6 (85.4-95.6); interorbital breadth, 30.3 (28.2-33.1); maxillary tooth row, 78.5 (76.6-82.3); upper carnassial length, 17.9 (17.1-18.7); first upper molar length, 11.7 (11.2-12.2); first upper molar breadth, 15.1 (14.5-15.8); lower carnassial length, 20.7 (20.0-21.9).

Remarks.—The Peninsula coyote is made conspicuous by its large ears, giving the animal somewhat of a foxlike appearance. These large ears are a continuation of a character common to all the Pacific Coast coyotes particularly to *C. l. ochropus, C. l. clepticus,* and *C. l. peninsulae.* The subspecies is fairly constant in characters for a coyote throughout its range south of 30° north latitude in Baja California. Specimens from Playa Maria Bay, collected in August, 1896, are in worn and pale pelage. Three skulls from San Bartolome Bay are somewhat heavier than average skulls of *peninsulae,* which expresses itself in the wide squamosal constriction. Since these specimens are otherwise normal the variation may be considered as individual.

Specimens examined.—Total number, 43, as follows:

Baja California: Calmalli, 8; Campo Los Angeles, 1[1]; Cape Saint Lucas, 7; Magdalena Island, 3; Matancita, 4; Mezquital, 1[1]; Mulege, 1; Playa Maria Bay, 2; San Andres, 1; San Bartolome Bay, 3[2]; San Cristobal Bay, 5; San Ignacio (20 miles west of), 1; Santa Anita (type locality), 1; Santa Rosalia Bay, 4; Santo Domingo, 1.

---

[1] San Diego Nat. Hist. Mus.
[2] Amer. Mus. Nat. Hist.

Canis latrans mearnsi Merriam

Mearns Coyote

Canis mearnsi Merriam, Proc. Biol. Soc. Washington 11: 29, March 15, 1897.

Canis estor Merriam, Proc. Biol. Soc. Washington 11: 31, March 15, 1897. (Type locality Noland's Ranch, San Juan River valley, San Juan County, Utah.)

Canis ochropus estor Grinnell, Univ. California Publ. Zool. 12 (4): 254, March 20, 1914.

Canis latrans estor Bailey, North Amer. Fauna 53: 318, March 1, 1932.

Canis latrans mearnsi Nelson, Proc. Biol. Soc. Washington 45: 224, November 26, 1932.

Type specimen.—No. 59,899, U. S. National Museum; male young adult, skin and skull; collected February 5, 1894, by Dr. Edgar A. Mearns. Original number 2925.

Type locality.—Quitobaquito, Pima County, Arizona.

Geographic range.—Extreme southwestern Colorado (San Juan County), Utah and Nevada south of about 37° north latitude; southeastern California south of 37° north and mainly east of 118° west longitude; northeastern Baja California, Arizona, New Mexico west of Rio Grande; most of Sonora and Chihuahua.

Diagnostic characters.—Excepting only *Canis latrans microdon* which occupies a limited range in the lower Rio Grande valley, *Canis latrans mearnsi* is the smallest coyote in the United States. It is variable in color, but usually in fresh pelage its coat is bright and colorful, particularly the contrasting deep cinnamon shades on the legs; skull and teeth small, the carnassials and molars being on the average the smallest of any of the coyotes except those of *C. l. microdon* and *C. l. vigilis*. On the whole *mearnsi* does not differ greatly in color from *C. l. lestes,* but has as a rule deeper ochraceous on the legs and feet, and the black marking on the foreleg is usually more pronounced; the skull and teeth are much smaller. The subspecies *mearnsi* is paler and smaller than *C. l. texensis,* with which it intergrades in the upper Rio Grande valley.

Color.—Winter pelage (fresh; December, January, and February): Muzzle, sayal brown or darker to cinnamon buff; forehead and cheeks pale pinkish buff to pinkish buff or darker, much grizzled; crown cinnamon buff to pinkish buff, sometimes almost olive buff; back of ears clay color to sayal brown, sometimes near ochraceous tawny; general tone of upper parts pinkish buff to cinnamon buff, more or less grizzled and mixed with black, occasionally heavily marked with black; legs pinkish buff to cinnamon, the forelegs usually marked on front with blackish stripe, not pronounced; tail as in back, somewhat paler below; under parts pinkish buff to cinnamon buff, sometimes near pale pinkish buff or light buff.

Skull.—Skull small, with moderately depressed frontal region and rather short rostrum; dentition weak. Similar to that of *Canis latrans microdon* but a little larger, with heavier dentition, particularly the carnassials and molars.

Measurements.—Young adult male from Antelope Spring, Navajo County, Arizona, and adult male from Tule Tanks, Yuma County, Arizona, respectively: Total length, 1,215, 1,230; tail vertebrae, 372, 370; hind foot, 200, 203; weight, 27 pounds,—. Type specimen of *Canis estor,* adult female, from Noland's Ranch, San Juan County, Utah, and adult female from Tule Tanks, Yuma County, Arizona, respectively: Total length, 1,052, 1,057; tail vertebrae, 300, 340; hind foot, 203, 177. *Skull:* Type specimen (young male): Condylobasal length, 170.9; palatal length, 90.8; squamosal constriction, 53.5; zygomatic breadth, 82.8; interorbital breadth, 29.9; maxillary tooth row, 80.2; upper carnassial length, 17.7; first upper molar length, 11.1; first upper molar breadth, 15.1; lower carnassial length, 19.6. Topotype (old adult male) and adult male from Gila Mountains, Yuma County, Arizona, respectively: Condylobasal length, 175.0, 176.5; palatal length, 90.9, 89.9; squamosal constriction, 58.3, 59.9; zygomatic breadth, 95.4, 93.9; interorbital breadth, 33.1, 29.9; maxillary tooth row, 82.6, 82.6; upper carnassial length, 17.8, 18.6; first upper molar length, 11.8, 12.3; first upper molar breadth, 16.9, 15.7; lower carnassial length, 21.3, 21.9. Two adult females from Tinajas Altas, Yuma County, and Tule Tanks, Yuma County, Arizona, respectively: Condylobasal length, 164.9, 163.6; palatal length, 86.3, 82.5; squamosal constriction, 52.8, 53.4; zygomatic breadth, 89.0, 87.0; interorbital breadth, 28.2, 30.8; maxillary tooth row, 76.6, 78.3; upper carnassial length, 17.6, 18.0; first upper molar length, 12.2, 12.1; first upper molar breadth, 15.6, 15.8; lower carnassial length, 20.7, 20.2. Average of 51 skulls of young adult and adult males (Arizona, 18; Baja California, 5; Chihuahua, 7; Colorado, 3; Nevada, 1; New Mexico, 13; Utah, 4): Condylobasal length, 181.7 (169.7-190.4); palatal length, 94.0 (83.4-100.8); squamosal breadth, 58.0 (54.4-61.8); zygomatic breadth, 97.4 (91.2-103.4); interorbital breadth, 32.7 (29.8-36.2); maxillary tooth row, 85.5 (76.3-90.2); upper carnassial length, 18.8 (17.4-20.9); first upper molar length, 12.4 (11.3-14.4); first upper molar breadth, 16.2 (14.7-18.4); lower carnassial length, 21.8 (19.6-25.2). Average of 30 skulls of young adult and adult females (Arizona, 9; Baja California, 2; Chihuahua, 4; Colorado, 1; New Mexico, 8; Sonora, 1; Utah, 5): Condylobasal length, 172.2 (160.2-182.5); palatal length, 89.5 (80.7-98.0); squamosal breadth, 55.1 (52.5-58.5); zygomatic breadth, 91.4 (87.0-98.8); interorbital breadth, 30.2 (27.7-34.2); maxillary tooth row, 80.9 (74.8-86.8); upper carnassial length, 18.0 (16.3-19.9); first upper molar length, 12.2 (11.5-13.1); first upper molar breadth, 15.7 (13.2-17.0); lower carnassial length, 20.9 (18.7-22.7).

Remarks.—In placing *Canis latrans estor* Merriam as a synonym of *Canis latrans mearnsi* Merriam, I do so with full cognizance of the marked differences in color between the two type specimens. The type of *estor*, however, does not accurately represent the color of many coyotes from the region of San Juan Valley, Utah, nor does the type of *mearnsi* from Pima County, Arizona, act as a fair representative of southern Arizona coyote coloration. The individual variation in coyotes over the geographic range of *Canis l. mearnsi* as here recognized is so great that to separate them into subspecies would add only confusion. Moreover, skulls from the *mearnsi* and *estor* regions are more nearly uniform in subspecific characters than are skull of some other subspecies within their respective ranges. Skulls of *C. l. mearnsi*, including of course those of its synonym *C. l. estor*, average more than 5 percent smaller than skulls of *C. l. lestes* or *C. l. latrans*, and usually can be separated without much difficulty.

Besides the individual variation in *Canis latrans mearnsi* there is the usual geographic variation that makes assignment to a subspecies of specimens from the border of the range a matter of judgment on average characters. Thus specimens of *mearnsi* from Florida River, La Plata County, Colorado, could with about equal propriety be referred to *Canis latrans lestes*. Many of the specimens from southwestern New Mexico are not strictly typical of *mearnsi* in every detail but are on the average nearer to that subspecies than to *C. l. texensis* with which it intergrades.

Some of the specimens of *C. l. mearnsi* from Baja California show intergradation with *C. l. clepticus*, but many are as clearly *mearnsi* as are specimens from southern Arizona.

Specimens examined.—Total number, 498, as follows:

Arizona: Adonde, Yuma County, 1; Anderson Mesa (30 miles southeast of Flagstaff), Coconino County, 1; Antelope Spring, Navajo County, 1; Beal's Spring (2 miles northwest of Kingman), Mohave County, 3; Bill William River, Yuma County, 1; Bright Angel Spring, Coconino County, 3; Canyon Diablo, Coconino County, 1; Chiricahua Ranch (Ash Flat), Graham County, 1; Cibecue (20 miles northwest of), Navajo County, 1;

Dolan Spring, Mohave County, 1; De Motte Park (Kaibab Plateau), Coconino County, 3; Flagstaff, Coconino County, 3; Fort Apache, Navajo County, 9; Fort Defiance, Apache County, 1; Fort Lowell (near Tucson), Pima County, 2[1]; Fort Valley (9 miles northwest of Flagstaff), Coconino County, 1; Fort Verde, Yavapai County, 13[2]; Fredonia, Coconino County, 11; Ganado, Apache County, 1; Gila Mountains, Yuma County, 1; Globe, Gila County, 1; Grand Canyon (Hopi Point), Coconino County, 2; Grand Canyon (Hualpai Indian Reservation), Coconino County, 1; Growler Valley, Pima County, 1; H Bar Ranch (10 miles south of Payson), Gila County, 1; Jacob Lake, Coconino County, 2; Jepson's Ranch (8 miles south of Fredonia), Coconino County, 1; Kaibab National Forest, Coconino County, 3; Little Spring (18 miles northwest of Flagstaff), Coconino County, 1; Marsh Lake (White Mountains, 9,000 feet), Apache County, 1; Morales, Pima County, 1; Mud Springs, Mohave County, 1; Natanes Plateau (25 miles northeast of Rice; San Carlos Indian Reservation, 5,800 feet), Gila County, 1; North Canyon (20 miles south of Utah line, 60 miles southeast of Kanab, Utah), Coconino County, 1; Oak Spring (65 miles southeast of Kanab, Utah), Coconino County, 1; Parker, Yuma County, 8; Phoenix, Mariposa County, 3; Quitobaquito (type locality), 3; Ryan, Coconino County, 5; Saint Johns (10 miles north, altitude 5,600 feet), Apache County, 1; San Francisco Mountain, Coconino County, 2; Santa Catalina Mountains (east slope), Pima County, 1; Santa Rita Mountains, Pima County, 1; Springerville, Apache County, 2; Springerville (15 miles southeast, altitude 7,600 feet), Apache County, 26; Springerville (25 miles northeast, altitude 6,800 feet), Apache County, 2; Tinajas Altas, Yuma County, 2; Trumbull Mountains (Trumbull Spring), Mohave County, 1; Tuba, Coconino County, 7; Tucson (15 miles north of), Pima County, 1; Tule Tanks, Yuma County, 3; White Mountains, Apache County, 1; Winslow, Navajo County, 1; Zuni River, Apache County, 1.

Baja California: Carriso Arroyo (east base of Laguna Hanson Mountains), 1; Gardner's Laguna, 5; Hardy River (head of), 3; Laguna Hanson (Sierra Juarez), 7[3]; Laguna Pascualitos (14 miles southeast of Mexicali), 4; Laguna Salada (15 miles south of International Boundary), 1; Mesquite Lagoon (15 miles southeast of Mexicali), 1; Mexicali, 1; Mexicali (17 miles south of), 5; Mexicali (80 miles south of), 2; Mount Mayor (Cocopah Mountains), 1; Palmer Arroyo (east base Laguna Hanson Mountains), 1; Tres Posos, 5; Volcano Lake, 1.

California: Amargosa River, Inyo County, 1; Barstow, San Bernardino County, 2; Chuckawalla Spring, Riverside County, 1; Coso, Inyo County, 1; Death Valley, Inyo County, 2[4]; Ehrenberg (25 miles southwest of), Riverside County, 1; Furnace Creek (Death Valley), Inyo County, 3; Granite Springs, San Bernardino County, 1; Hesperia, San Bernardino County, 1[5]; Imperial Dam Headquarters, Imperial County, 1; Independence, Inyo County, 1; Inyo Mountains, Inyo County, 1; Lone Willow Spring (Panamint Valley), Inyo County, 1; Ludlow, San Bernardino County, 1; Mohave Desert, San Bernardino County, 1; Oro Grande, San Bernardino County, 1; Panamint Mountains, Inyo County, 1; White Mountains, Mono County, 2[4].

Chihuahua: Colonia Diaz (near Casa Grande), 8; Colonia Garcia, 4; Colonia Juarez, 1; Guzman, 1; Lake Palomas, 2; Lake Santa Maria, 1; Mosquito Springs, 1; Sierra en Media, 1.

Colorado: Animas River, La Plata County, 1; Dolores, Montezuma County, 5; Durango, La Plata County, 11; Florida River, La Plata County, 16;

McElmo, Montezuma County, 2; Pagosa, Archuleta County, 2; Pine River, La Plata County, 5; Rio la Plata (near Durango), La Plata County, 2.

Nevada: Colorado River (head of Black Canyon), Clark County, 2; Oak Springs, Nye County, 1[5]; Pahrump Valley, Nye County, 3; Vegas Valley, Clark County, 1.

New Mexico: Animas Mountains (Indian Canyon), Hidalgo County, 1[5]; Animas Valley, Hidalgo County, 10; Aragon, Catron County, 1; Barker's Canyon (40 miles south and a little west of Durango), San Juan County, 4; Black Range (50 miles north of Silver City), Grant County, 1; Blanco, San Juan County, 1; Blue Water, Valencia County, 1; Canyon Blanco, San Juan County, 1; Central, Grant County, 2; Chloride, Sierra County, 9; Chuska Mountains, San Juan County, 6; Cois Ranch (35 miles northwest of El Paso, Texas), Dona Ana County, 1; Coppermines, Grant County, 2; Copperton, Valencia County, 1; Datil Mountains, Catron County, 1; Dona Ana County (Mexican Boundary Line, 15 miles west of El Paso, Texas), 1; Dulce, Rio Arriba County, 1; El Vado, Rio Arriba County, 3; Fort Wingate, McKinley County, 1; Fruitland, San Juan County, 2; Gallup, McKinley County, 1; Gila National Forest, Grant County, 35; Hatchet Ranch (16 miles south of Hachita), Grant County, 1; Hermosa, Sierra County, 1; Hidalgo County (Lat. 31° 47′ N.), 2; La Jara Lake (7,600 feet), Sandoval County, 1; La Plata, San Juan County, 3; Largo, San Juan County, 1; Lee Ranch, Hidalgo County, 2; Liberty, San Juan County, 11; Lordsburg, Hidalgo County, 1; Luna, Catron County, 5; Magdalena, Socorro County, 14; Magdalena Mountains, 12; Monument 15 (Mexican Boundary line), Dona Ana County, 1; Old Fort Tularosa, Catron County, 1; Playas Valley, Hidalgo County, 1; Pratt, Hidalgo County, 10; Quemado, Catron County, 1; Ramah, McKinley County, 1; Redrock, Grant County, 1; Reserve, Catron County, 3; San Bernardino Ranch, Hidalgo County, 3; San Luis Mountains, Hidalgo County, 2; San Luis Springs, Hidalgo County, 3; San Mateo Mountains, Socorro County, 2; San Rafael, Valencia County, 1; Sapillo Creek (Gila National Forest), 1; Stinking Springs Lake, Rio Arriba County, 3; Turkey Spring, Hidalgo County, 1[5]; Wingate, McKinley County, 3; Zuni Mountains, Valencia County, 4.

Sonora: Costa Rica Ranch, 1[6]; Hermosillo, 6[7]; Pinacate Mountains, 1; San Luis (47 miles south of, Rio Colorado), 1[4]; Sierra Seri, 2.

Utah: Blanding, San Juan County, 2; Chadburn's Ranch, Washington County, 1; Dry Valley (near La Sal), San Juan County, 9; Heart Draw (near Monticello), San Juan County, 4; Henry Mountains (Mount Ellen), Garfield County, 1; Kanab, Kane County, 2; La Sal, San Juan County, 3; New Castle, Iron County, 2; Noland's Ranch (type locality of *Canis estor* San Juan River), San Juan County, 1.

---

[1] One in collection of Donald R. Dickey.
[2] Amer. Mus. Nat. Hist.
[3] One in Mus. Vert. Zool., Univ. California; two in Amer. Mus. Nat. Hist.; four in San Diego Nat. Hist. Mus.
[4] Collection of Donald R. Dickey.
[5] Carnegie Mus.
[6] Mus. Comp. Zool., Harvard College.
[7] One in Mus. Comp. Zool., Harvard College.

Canis latrans jamesi Townsend
Tiburon Island Coyote

Canis jamesi Townsend, Bull. Amer. Mus. Nat. Hist. 31 (13): 130, June 14, 1912.
Canis latrans jamesi Nelson, Proc. Biol. Soc. Washington 45: 224, November 26, 1932.

Type specimen.—No. 198,402, U. S. National Museum; male, young adult, skin and skull; collected April 13, 1911, by H. E. Anthony.

Type locality.—Tiburon Island, Baja California.

Geographic range.—Known only from the type locality.

Diagnostic characters.—Apparently paler and more grayish than average *Canis latrans mearnsi;* ears longer than in typical *mearnsi;* skull about as in *mearnsi,* the molariform teeth apparently somewhat heavier.

Measurements.—Type specimen (young adult male): Total length, 1,143; tail vertebrae, 330; hind foot, 192; ear from crown, 118. *Skull:* Type specimen (young adult male): Condylobasal length, 173.2; palatal length, 90.2; squamosal constriction, 57.8; zygomatic breadth, 92.0; interorbital breadth, 30.3; maxillary tooth row, 80.1; upper carnassial length, 18.5; first upper molar length, 12.4; first upper molar breadth, 16.6; lower carnassial length, 21.2.

Remarks.—At best in the light of available material *Canis latrans jamesi* is a very weakly marked subspecies, and whether it should receive permanent recognition can be decided only when more specimens are available from Tiburon Island. It does appear to be unusually grayish in region where the general tendency is towards a development of ochraceous coloration.

The type specimen was originally No. 31987, American Museum of Natural History, and was so listed in the original description of *jamesi* (Townsend, 1912: 130). It was transferred to the U. S. National Museum in June, 1914.

Specimen examined.—Total number, 1, as follows:
Baja California: Tiburon Island, 1.

Canis latrans microdon Merriam
Lower Rio Grande Coyote

Canis microdon Merriam, Proc. Biol. Soc. Washington 11: 29, March 15, 1897.
Canis latrans microdon Nelson, Proc. Biol. Soc. Washington 45: 224, November 26, 1932.

Type specimen.—No. 27555, U. S. National Museum, Biological

39654

Surveys collection; male adult; collected April 28, 1891, by William Lloyd; original number 478.

Type locality.—Mier, on Rio Grande, State of Tamaulipas, Mexico.

Geographic range.—Lower Rio Grande region, extreme northeastern Nuevo Leon, extreme northern Tamaulipas, and extreme southern Texas in southern parts of Cameron, Hidalgo, and Starr counties. Southern limits of range in Tamaulipas unknown.

Diagnostic characters.—Size so far as known smallest of the coyotes, color dark with much rufous and ochraceous, and a liberal showing of black-tipped hairs on back and sometimes dusky shading on throat, chest, and abdomen, the upper surface of hind foot sometimes near whitish; skull small, relatively rather short and broad; dentition weak, the carnassials and molars averaging smaller than in any other coyote.

Color.—Sometimes very little different from the color of *Canis latrans texensis,* but averaging in all parts a shade darker, with a tendency for more blackish in the upper parts, particularly on the rump, more ochraceous on the neck and nape, and more frequently with a broad band of dusky or grizzled ochraceous extending from upper parts over throat, chest, and abdomen.

Skull.—In its typical form smallest of the coyotes, relatively short and broad, with short and relatively broad rostrum, and short palate; teeth smallest of the coyotes, the carnassial and molars particularly being small. Compared with that of *Canis l. mearnsi* the skull of *C. l. microdon* averages smaller, relatively shorter and broader, with correspondingly shorter palate and broader palatal notch; dentition averaging weaker than in *mearnsi,* the carnassials and molars smaller.

Measurements.—Type specimen (adult male) and young male from Camargo, Tamaulipas, respectively: Total length, 1,070, 1,180; tail vertebrae, 320, 350; hind foot, 186, 192; weight, 28 pounds, ——. Adult female from Bagdad, Tamaulipas: Total length, 1,165; tail vertebrae, 334; hind foot, 189. *Skull:* Type specimen (adult male) and young adult male from Brownsville, Cameron County, Texas, respectively: Condylobasal length, 169.5, 174.1; palatal length, 86.4, 89.9; squamosal constriction, 55.4, 56.6; zygomatic breadth, 93.5, 95.9; interorbital breadth, 32.0; 30.3; maxillary tooth row, 77.4, 79.3; upper carnassial length, 16.3, 17.6; first upper molar length, 10.8, 11.7; first upper molar breadth, 14.6, 15.7; lower carnassial length, 18.8, 19.9. Adult female from Bagdad,

Tamaulipas: Condylobasal length, 179.7; palatal length, 90.0; squamosal constriction, 56.0; zygomatic breadth, 93.7; interorbital breadth, 31.8; maxillary tooth row, 81.7; upper carnassial length, 18.4; first upper molar length, 12.4; first upper molar breadth, 14.5; lower carnassial length, 20.2.

Remarks.—Although in its extreme form as represented by the type specimen from Mier, Tamaulipas, *Canis latrans microdon* is distinctly characterized from all other coyotes, nevertheless it seems to have a restricted range and intergrades with *Canis l. texensis* to the northward and probably with *Canis l. mearnsi* or *C. l. impavidus* to the westward. It is not so distinct as to warrant specific designation as was done by Merriam (1897: 29) and Bailey (1905: 178).

The type specimen of *microdon* is the extreme in smallness of its dentition of any specimens examined of the subspecies. The dentition in the type specimen is smaller than in a young male from as nearby as Camargo, Tamaulipas, and considerably smaller than in a male from Bagdad, Tamaulipas. A "picked up" weathered skull of an animal probably about 7 months old from Rodriguez, Nuevo Leon, offers little satisfaction in identification. Geographically it should belong to *C. l. microdon;* the maxillary tooth row length is almost exactly that of the type specimen of *microdon,* although the upper carnassial is longer and heavier, and the first upper molar is somewhat broader. Two skulls of very young animals collected by Lieutenant Darius Nash Couch at Matamoros, Tamaulipas, are among the earlier specimens accessioned by the U. S. National Museum. Although the teeth in these Matamoros specimens are a little too large for typical *microdon,* the specimens are referred to this form. A series of nine specimens from Los Ratones, Zapata County, Texas, although showing in some skulls a slight approach toward *microdon* are referred to *Canis latrans texensis.*

Specimens examined.—Total number, 11, as follows:

Nuevo Leon: Rodriguez, 1.
Tamaulipas: Bagdad, 2; Camargo, 1; Matamoros, 2; Mier (type locality), 1.
Texas: Brownsville, Cameron County, 1; Lomita Ranch (6 miles north of Hidalgo), Hidalgo County, 1; Los Hojas, Starr County, 1; Roma, Starr County, 1.

Canis latrans impavidus Allen
Durango Coyote

Canis impavidus Allen, Bull. Amer. Mus. Nat. Hist. 19: 609, November 12, 1903.
Canis latrans impavidus Nelson, Proc. Biol. Soc. Washington 45: 224, November 26, 1932.

Type specimen.—No. 21,266, American Museum of Natural History; male young adult, skin and skull; collected February 13, 1903, by J. H. Batty.

Type locality.—Rio de las Bocas (altitude 7,000 feet), northwest Durango, Mexico.

Geographic range.—Pacific coast drainage of western Mexico between about 22° and 26° north latitude. Extreme southern Sonora, extreme southwestern Chihuahua, western Durango, western Zacatecas; Sinaloa.

Diagnostic characters.—Medium in size, reddish toned in color, skull small, dentition moderately weak. Similar to *Canis latrans cagottis* in color, about the same size or a trifle larger, carnassials and molar teeth somewhat smaller. Skull and dentition somewhat as *Canis l. mearnsi.*

Color.—General color tone a yellowish buff or near clay color, tending to be unusually yellowish buff on dorsal surface, particularly anteriorly on shoulders, head, and face. Color about that of *Canis latrans cagottis,* but somewhat paler.

Skull.—Essentially like that of *Canis latrans mearnsi.*

Measurements.—Adult female from Camoa, Rio Mayo, Sonora: Total length, 1,154; tail vertebrae, 362; hind foot, 194. *Skull:* Type specimen (young adult male) and young adult male from Escuinapa, Sinaloa, respectively: Condylobasal length, 184.6, 178.6; palatal length, 90.7, 91.0; squamosal constriction, 58.9, 56.9; zygomatic breadth, 92.9, 93.2; interorbital breadth, 30.0, 31.6; maxillary tooth row, 79.2, 82.8; upper carnassial length, 18.4, 17.7; first upper molar length, 12.5, 12.0; first upper molar breadth, 16.7, 16.0; lower carnassial length, 21.3, 20.1. Two young adult females from Camoa, Sonora, and Fresnillo, Zacatecas, respectively: Condylobasal length, 173.8, 170.5; palatal length, 89.3, 87.1; squamosal constriction, 57.4, 54.4; zygomatic breadth, 94.1, 90.0; interorbital breadth, 31.1, 31.5; maxillary tooth row, 80.7, 80.3; upper carnassial length, 18.3, 17.9; first upper molar length, 13.0, 11.6; first upper molar breadth, 16.0, 15.0; lower carnassial length, 21.8, 19.5.

Remarks.—The subspecies *impavidus* may be considered an intermediate form between *Canis latrans cagottis* and *C. l. mearnsi*, as which it has acquired the general color tone of the former and the skull characters of the latter. There is variation in color but all specimens of *impavidus* examined show the strong ochraceous color characteristic of south Mexican coyotes.

The series of five skins from Camoa (Rio Mayo), southern Sonora, is exceedingly variable in the amount of black and intensity of reddish in the coloration. Two of the specimens have so much black as to approach in appearance the type specimen of *Canis l. mearnsi*. Two other specimens, however have a dominant and intense reddish in their coloration. The skulls of these five specimens display dentition similar to *impavidus*, and none has the weak dentition and small teeth of *C. l. vigilis*. The skin from Escuinapa, Sinaloa, is very orange red or fulvous, though pale, much paler than the skins from Camoa, southern Sonora.

Specimens examined.—Total number, 27, as follows:

Chihuahua: Sierra Madre (near Guadelupe y Calvo), 1.
Durango: Rancha Baillon (Rio de las Bocas), 9[1]; Rio Sestin, 3[1]; Villo Ocampo, 3[1].
Sinaloa: Escuinapa, 9[2].
Sonora: Camoa (Rio Mayo), 5.
Zacatecas: Fresnillo, 5.

Canis latrans cagottis Hamilton Smith

Mexican Coyote

Lyciscus cagottis Hamilton Smith, Jardine's Naturalist's Library, vol. 18, Mammals, vol. 4, Dogs, vol. 1, p. 164, 1839.
Canis cagottis Merriam, Proc. Biol. Soc. Washington 11: 27, March 15, 1897.
Canis latrans cagottis Nelson, Proc. Biol. Soc. Washington 45: 224, November 26, 1932.

Type specimen.—Not designated.

Type locality.—Rio Frio, west slope of Mount Iztaccihuatl, Valley of Mexico, Mexico.

Geographic range.—Represented by specimens from States of Mexico, Oaxaca, San Luis Potosi, Pueblo, and Veracruz, Mexico. Range may possibly extend into southern Nuevo Leon and southern Tamaulipas.

Diagnostic characters.—A medium-sized dark reddish coyote

---

[1] Amer. Mus. Nat. Hist.
[2] Eight in Amer. Mus. Nat. Hist.

with full pelage having a liberal amount of black on upper parts, legs deep ochraceous usually with distinct black patches down front of forelegs, ears moderately large; skull medium in size, relatively short and broad, with base of rostrum broad; dentition moderately heavy.

Color.—(Based mainly on skin from North Slope of Volcano Toluca, State of Mexico, Mexico, September 10, 1893): Muzzle, near bister, or between snuff brown and bister; cheeks pinkish buff and forehead more tinged with vinaceous, both much grizzled; crown and nape near cinnamon; back of ears mikado brown; general tone of upper parts pinkish buff heavily mixed with black; tail slightly less mixed with black than back, paler below; legs near ochraceous tawny, the fore one moderately marked with an elongate black blotch down the front; under parts pinkish buff to light buff, the throat heavily mixed with grayish.

Skull.—Medium in size, relatively short and broad; audital bullae moderate; base of rostrum broad and deep; palate short; dentition rather heavy. Compared with the skull of *Canis latrans goldmani* that of *C. l. cagottis* is relatively slightly broader and shorter, has distinctly smaller audital bullae, somewhat shorter rostrum, and probably on the average weaker dentition.

Measurements.—Young adult male from Cerro San Felipe, Oaxaca, and adult male from Rio Blanco, west of Piedras Negras, Veracruz, respectively: Total length, 1,132, 1,189; tail vertebrae, 304, 360; hind foot, 195, 188. *Skull:* Young adult male from Cerro San Felipe, Oaxaca, and adult male from Rio Blanco, west of Piedras Negras, Veracruz, respectively: Condylobasal length, 173.2, 179.2; palatal length, 88.3, 91.2; squamosal constriction, 57.8, 61.4; zygomatic breadth, 99.4, 100.0; interorbital breadth, 30.7, 31.5; maxillary tooth row, 79.8, 84.6; upper carnassial length, 20.6, 19.3; first upper molar length, 13.1, 12.3; first upper molar breadth, 16.0, 15.7; lower carnassial length, 23.1, 22.7.

Remarks.—There is nothing distinctive or definitely descriptive about the subspecies *cagottis* in the original description; and until specimens are procured from near the type locality we must assume on zoogeographical grounds that the specimen from Cerro San Felipe, Oaxaca, nearest to the type locality of any available, represents the form. Hamilton Smith's original account of *cagottis* reads as follows: "The Caygotte of the Mexican Spaniards and most probably the Coyotl of the native Indians, is a second species, but slightly noticed by travellers. Mr. William Bullock observed it near Rio Frio, in the Mexican Territory, and was informed by muleteers, then with him, that it was the Caygotte, a very fierce kind of wolf; the individuals he saw were in size equal to a hound, of a brownish rusty grey, with buff coloured limbs, and rather a scanty brush" (Hamilton Smith, 1839: 164).

The only specimens of adult animals examined and here referred to *C. l. cagottis* other than the one from Cerro San Felipe, Oaxaca, are the two important specimens collected by W. W. Dalquest on Rio Blanco, west of Piedras Negras, Veracruz. Both of these specimens in cranial characters seem to be about as near to *C. l. goldmani* as to *cagottis*, and may in these characters be called intermediate. One of the skins (No. 19278, Kansas Univ. Mus.) in its rather worn pelage matches fairly closely the Cerro San Felipe, Oaxaca, specimen considered as representing typical *cagottis* except that it is more grayish on the cheeks and crown, the brown of the muzzle is a shade darker, and there is more admixture of blackish hairs dorsally. It thus appears darker than the type specimen of *C. l. goldmani*. The other skin from Piedras Negras (No. 19279, Kansas Univ. Mus.) in bright fresh pelage differs scarcely in color from a young (near 5 or 6 months old) male from the North Slope of Volcan de Toluca, Mexico, except that it is a shade brighter in color. The specimen from Atlixco, Puebla, a juvenile of about 6 months offers little as a study specimen. The male from Hacienda La Parada, San Luis Potosi, is also a young animal, but seems to fit well with *cagottis*.

Specimens examined.—Total number, 6, as follows:

Mexico: Volcano Toluca (north slope), 1.
Oaxaca: Cerro San Felipe, 1.
Puebla: Atlixco, 1.
San Luis Potosi: Hacienda La Parada, 1.
Veracruz: Piedras Negras (400 feet altitude, on Rio Blanco, 20 kilometers west), 1[1]; Piedras Negras (300 feet altitude, on Rio Blanco, 15 kilometers west), 1[1].

Canis latrans vigilis Merriam

Colima Coyote

Canis vigilis Merriam, Proc. Biol. Soc. Washington 11: 33, March 15, 1897.
Canis latrans vigilis Nelson, Proc. Biol. Soc. Washington 45: 224, November 26, 1932.

Type specimen.—No. $\frac{32627}{44550}$, U. S. National Museum, Biological Surveys collection; female young adult, skin and skull; collected February 6, 1892, by E. W. Nelson. Original number 1840.

Type locality.—Manzanillo, Colima, Mexico.

---

[1] Kansas Univ. Mus.

Geographic range.—Pacific coast, slope, and drainage of western Mexico between 16° and 22° north latitude.

Diagnostic characters.—A medium-sized, dark colored coyote, the ochraceous colors, particularly of the under fur being dark and bright, and the black hair tips of the back abundant and pronounced; skull rather flat, dentition weak, upper carnassial and molars being smaller than in *Canis l. mearnsi*, and exceeding only those of *Canis l. microdon* in size.

Color.—Not greatly different from that of *Canis latrans cagottis* except that the muzzle is somewhat paler; the black over the upper parts is less pronounced; the ochraceous of the back of the ears and the underfur is some darker and brighter; the black extends less down on the sides and the sides are more ochraceous; and the under parts are darker and more cinnamon colored.

Skull.—Medium size, averaging somewhat larger than that of either *Canis latrans mearnsi* or *Canis l. impavidus*; dentition weaker than in either *mearnsi* or *impavidus;* first upper molar usually deeply notched posteriorly; carnassials and molars smaller than in any subspecies except *microdon*.

Measurements.—Type specimen (young adult female): Total length, 1,155; tail vertebrae, 335; hind foot, 190. *Skull:* Type specimen (young adult female) and adult female from Las Canoas, Jalisco, Mexico, respectively: Condylobasal length, 174.0, 183.5; palatal length, 87.9, 93.2; squamosal constriction, 57.4, 61.5; zygomatic breadth, 87.3, 97.8; interorbital breadth, 30.5, 31.6; maxillary tooth row, 79.6, 83.3; upper carnassial length, 17.3, 16.7; first upper molar length, 11.3, 11.4; first upper molar breadth, 14.0, 15.7; lower carnassial length, 19.3, 19.5.

Remarks.—The Colima coyote is in some ways an intermediate form between *Canis l. cagottis* and *C. l. impavidus,* having the color and size similar to *cagottis,* but a skull more nearly like that of *impavidus.* It differs from both, however, in its weak dentition. Few specimens have been studied and we know too little of its status and geographic range.

Specimens examined.—Total number, 5, as follows:

Colima: Manzanillo (type locality), 1.
Jalisco: La Barca, 2; Las Canoas, 2.[1]

―――――
[1] Amer. Mus. Nat. Hist.

Canis latrans goldmani Merriam

Chiapas Coyote

Canis goldmani Merriam, Proc. Biol. Soc. Washington 17: 157, October 6, 1904.

Canis latrans goldmani Nelson, Proc. Biol. Soc. Washington 45: 224, November 26, 1932.

Type specimen.—No. 133,204, U. S. National Museum, Biological Surveys collection; female adult, skin and skull; collected April 25, 1904, by E. A. Goldman. Original number, 16,725.

Type locality.—San Vicente, Chiapas, Mexico, near the boundary of Guatemala.

Geographic range.—Known only from type locality, but may presumably be the coyote of western Guatemala.

Diagnostic characters.—Size large, probably the largest of the Mexican species; general color tone ochraceous, paler than *Canis latrans cagottis* or *Canis l. vigilis.* Skull rather heavy and broad, the audital bullae especially large; dentition heavy. Compared with that of *C. l. cagottis* the skull of *goldmani* is relatively not quite so broad and short, has distinctly larger bullae, somewhat longer rostrum, and on the average heavier dentition.

Color.—(Type specimen; worn April pelage): Ochraceous tones much as in *Canis l. cagottis,* the muzzle and back of ears slightly paler, the black on upper parts much reduced (more grayish) as compared to *cagottis,* and the under parts more deeply tinged with cinnamon.

Skull.—Large, rather heavy and broad; frontal region moderately depressed; audital bullae large, and flattened on outer side; dentition heavy.

Measurements.—Type specimen (adult female): Total length, 1,220; tail vertebrae, 355; hind foot, 216. *Skull:* Type specimen (adult female): Condylobasal length, 177.4; palatal length, 90.5; squamosal constriction, 61.5; zygomatic breadth, 100.0; interorbital breadth, 32.1; maxillary tooth row, 86.9; upper carnassial length, 18.9; first upper molar length, 12.1; first upper molar breadth, 16.1; lower carnassial length, 21.1.

Remarks.—The subspecies *goldmani* seems to be a well-marked race represented by material entirely too inadequate for study. The type specimen was a nursing female, and its large size, comparable to that of males of *Canis l. cagottis,* would indicate that it is probably the largest of the Mexican coyotes.

Specimens examined.—One, the type.

Canis latrans dickeyi Nelson
Salvador Coyote

Canis latrans dickeyi Nelson, Proc. Biol. Soc. Washington 45: 224, November 26, 1932.

Type specimen.—No. 12,260, collection of Donald R. Dickey; male young adult, skin and skull; collected December 29, 1926, by G. D. Stirton.

Type locality.—Cerro Magote Mountain, 2 miles west of Rio Goascoran, District of La Union (13° 30' north latitude), Salvador.

Geographic range.—Known by specimens only from type locality. Assumed to be the subspecies known to occur in parts of Costa Rica and other parts of Salvador, and possibly western Nicaragua.

Diagnostic characters.—Size medium to rather large, almost equaling that of *Canis latrans ochropus* of California, and slightly larger than its geographically near relatives *Canis l. hondurensis* of Honduras, *C. l. cagottis* of the Mexican tableland, or *C. l. vigilis* of the west coast of Mexico; hind foot large; skull and dentition about the size of that of *C. l. ochropus*, but rostrum relatively shorter, and premolars more closely spaced. Color rather dark, dull rusty rufous, tail heavily overlaid with black, under parts including those of tail with distinct rufous tinge.

Color.—*Winter pelage* (fresh; December): Muzzle and crown dull grayish with a distinct rusty tinge, shading into rusty rufous on sides of nose and into paler grayish buff on cheeks and nape; back of ears rusty rufous; upper parts and sides dark rusty rufous, washed with black, heavily on shoulders and rump; lower parts of flanks rusty buff, a paler shade of same (pinkish buff) extending over under parts; fore and hind legs dark rusty rufous, almost ochraceous tawny, the forelegs with black stripe on front.

Skull.—Larger than that of any of the three of the geographically nearest subspecies of *Canis latrans*, namely, *hondurensis*, *cagottis*, and *vigilis*; molariform teeth larger and heavier than in *goldmani*, *hondurensis*, or *vigilis*, but relatively smaller and weaker than in *cagottis*; inner cusp of upper carnassial strongly developed; supra-occipital plane relatively high from upper border of foramen magnum to junction with sagittal lambdoid crests.

Measurements.—Type specimen (young adult male): Total length, 1,280; tail vertebrae, 380; hind foot, 250. *Skull:* Type specimen (young adult male): Condylobasal length, 188.5; palatal length, 98.9; squamosal constriction, 62.6; zygomatic breadth, 101.2; interorbital breadth, 31.8; maxillary tooth row, 87.7; upper carnassial length, 19.3; first upper molar length, 12.7; first upper molar breadth, 16.9; lower carnassial length, 21.6. Topotype (young adult female): Condylobasal length, 181.4; palatal length, 95.1; squamosal constriction, 60.5; zygomatic breadth, 96.0; interorbital breadth, 29.4; maxillary tooth row, 83.8; upper carnassial length, 18.7; first upper molar length, 13.2; first upper molar breadth, 16.4; lower carnassial length, 22.3.

Remarks.—Only two specimens, the type and a topotype, have been examined of *Canis latrans dickeyi*. It is a well-defined subspecies, and may be the same subspecies of coyote that is known to occur in Costa Rica (Goodwin, 1946: 438-439).

Specimens examined.—Total number, 2, as follows:

Salvador: Cerro Magote Mountain, near Pasaguina, Rio Goascoran, 13° 30' north latitude, District of La Union, 2[1].

Canis latrans hondurensis Goldman
Honduras Coyote

Canis hondurensis Goldman, Journ. Washington Acad. Sci. 26 (1): 33, January 15, 1936.

Type specimen.—No. 251,447, U. S. National Museum, Biological Surveys collection; male adult, skin and skull; collected August 18, 1934, by C. F. Underwood. Original number 1247; Biological Surveys miscellaneous number 27,352X.

Type locality.—Cerro Quinote, northeast of Archaga, on the Talanga road north of Tegucigalpa, Honduras.

Geographic range.—Known only from the region of the type locality in southwest central Honduras.

Diagnostic characters.—A rather small, rufescent species, with coarse, thin pelage and a short, broad skull. Similar in color to *Canis latrans dickeyi*, of the Pacific coast region of Salvador, but smaller, and skull characters, especially the shorter tooth rows and more widely spreading zygomata, distinctive. Resembling *C. l. goldmani* of eastern Chiapas, Mexico, but back apparently more heavily overlaid with black and differing in various cranial features.

Color.—Type specimen (summer pelage, worn): Top of head and back coarsely grizzled buffy grayish mixed with black, the

---

[1] Collection Donald R. Dickey.

black tending to predominate on the back; muzzle, outer surfaces of ears, flanks, fore and hind limbs rusty rufous; a short, narrow line of black hairs along middle of anterior surface of forearm; under parts sparsely clothed, the hairs light buff across abdomen, becoming whitish on throat and inguinal region; a few inconspicuously dark-tipped hairs across under side of neck; tail above overlaid with black like back, below light buffy, giving way to black all around at tip.

Skull.—Similar in general to that of *C. l. dickeyi* but smaller, especially shorter, with more widely spreading zygomata; nasals much shorter, and broader between maxillae; palate relatively broader; audital bullae smaller; dentition similar, but maxillary and mandibular tooth rows shorter, the premolars more closely crowded. Compared with that of *C. l. goldmani* the skull is somewhat smaller, but with similarly wide spreading zygomata; frontal region broader, but rather highly arched as in *goldmani;* nasals broader between maxillae; lambdoid crest normal, not strongly projecting and broadly rounded in outline as in *goldmani;* interpterygoid fossa broader posteriorly; bullae smaller, more flattened, less distended along inner sides below; maxillary and mandibular tooth rows shorter; premolars more closely crowded; lower carnassial rather large, high and trenchant.

Measurements.—Type specimen (adult male): Total length, 1,240; tail vertebrae, 350; hind foot, 190. Adult female from type locality: Total length, 1,130; tail vertebrae, 290; hind foot, 190. *Skull:* Type specimen (adult male) and adult male from La Cueva, Honduras: Condylobasal length, 176.2, 189.6; palatal length, 91.6, 97.4; squamosal constriction, 58.4, 65.1; zygomatic breadth, 100.4, 110.2; interorbital breadth, 35.6, 36.2; maxillary tooth row, 78.3, 84.2; upper carnassial length, 20.0, 19.7; first upper molar length, 13.1, 12.9; first upper molar breadth, 17.0, 16.8; lower carnassial length, 23.0, 22.7.

Remarks.—When Goldman published the original description of this form he said: "It is probable that *Canis hondurensis* will eventually require reduction to subspecific status under the wide ranging *Canis latrans,* but in the absence of evidence of intergradation, and in view of the possibility of complete geographic isolation it seems best, meantime, to treat the animal as a full species" (Goldman, 1936: 33-34). The actual evidence of geographic intergradation is little more positive now than at the time Goldman described the species. In the opinon of the present reviser, however, *hondurensis* should be given only subspecific rank because of the overlapping individual variation that often smothers geographic variation. Goldman himself was of this opinion later.

C. F. Underwood, collector of the only known specimens describes the habitat of these coyotes as "open, sterile, and rocky country" and further states "They seem to prefer to make their dens amongst the rocks often within a league or so from cattle farms or haciendas where calves and chickens can be got. The natives resort to poison when they become too numerous. In several other parts of the country where conditions are analogous to the place where these were taken they are more or less abundant. They are very wary and difficult to shoot, but at times fall at night light hunting" (Underwood, 1935, ms. letter).

Specimens examined.—Total number, 4, as follows:

Honduras: Cerro Quinote (type locality; northeast of Archaga, north of Tegucigalpa), 3; La Cueva (Archaga, Department of Tegucigalpa), 1[1].

―――――

[1] Amer. Mus. Nat. Hist.

PHOTOGRAPHS
OF SKULLS

[All skulls are in U. S. National Museum
unless otherwise indicated; one-half
natural size unless otherwise indicated.]

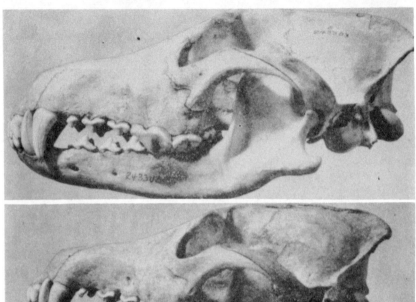

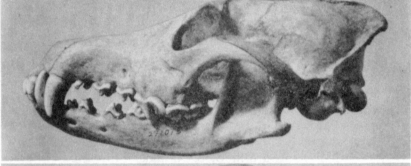

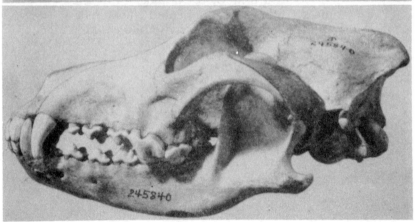

Plate 58. Upper: Mississippi Valley Wolf, *Canis niger gregoryi* Goldman; male, young adult; Simpson, Pope County, Arkansas. (No. 243,303, U. S. Nat. Mus., Biological Surveys collection.)

Middle: Southeastern Coyote, *Canis latrans frustror* Woodhouse; male, young adult; Deerfield, Vernon County, Missouri. (No. 271,075, U. S. Nat. Mus., Biological Surveys collection.)

Lower: Feral Domestic Dog, German Shepherd type, *Canis familiaris* Linnaeus; male, young adult; 15 miles southeast of Reserve, Catron County, New Mexico. (No. 245,840, U. S. Nat. Mus., Biological Surveys collection.)

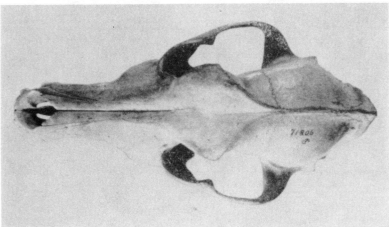

Plate 59. Upper: Plains Coyote, *Canis latrans latrans* Say; female, young adult; Beemer, Cuming County, Nebraska. (No. 149,723, U. S. Nat. Mus., Biological Surveys collection.)

Lower: Plains Coyote, *Canis latrans latrans* Say; male, young adult; Johnstown, Brown County, Nebraska. (No. 71,806, U. S. Nat. Mus., Biological Surveys collection.)

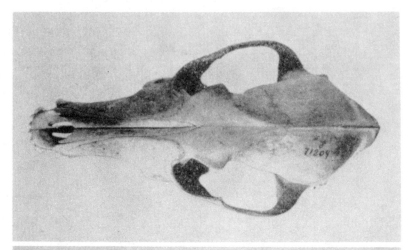

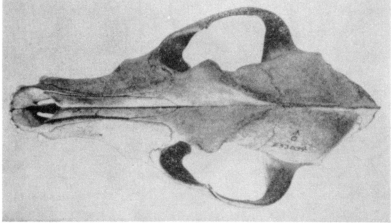

Plate 60. Upper: Northern Coyote, *Canis latrans incolatus* Hall; male, young adult; Stuart Lake (Fort St. James), British Columbia. (No. 71,209, U. S. Nat. Mus., Biological Surveys collection.)

Lower: Northeastern Coyote, *Canis latrans thamnos* Jackson; type specimen; male, young adult; Basswood Island, Ashland County, Wisconsin. (No. 233,034, U. S. Nat. Mus., Biological Surveys collection.)

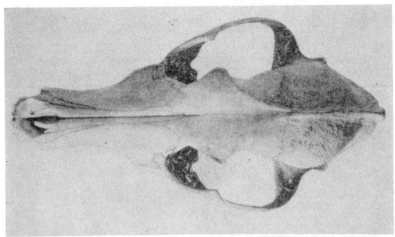

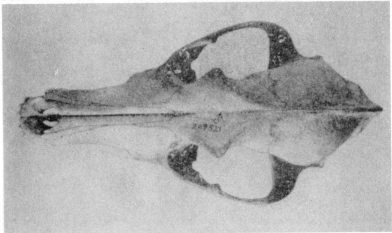

Plate 61. Upper: Southeastern Coyote, *Canis latrans frustror* Woodhouse; male, adult; Calumet, Canadian County, Oklahoma. (No. 235,602, U. S. Nat. Mus., Biological Surveys collection.)

Lower: Texas Plains Coyote, *Canis latrans texensis* Bailey; male, adult; Rankin, Upton County, Texas. (No. 209,521, U. S. Nat. Mus., Biological Surveys collection.)

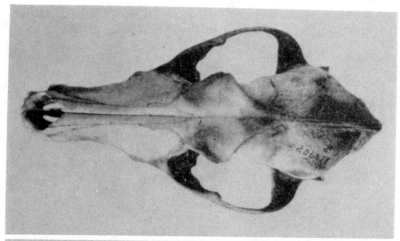

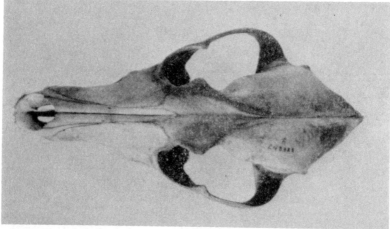

Plate 62. Upper: Mountain Coyote, *Canis latrans lestes* Merriam; male, adult; Gerlach, Washoe County, Nevada. (No. 206,679, U. S. Nat. Mus., Biological Surveys collection.)

Lower: Northwest Coast Coyote, *Canis latrans umpquensis* Jackson; male, young adult; Sequim, Clallam County, Washington. (No. 248,323, U. S. Nat. Mus., Biological Surveys collection.)

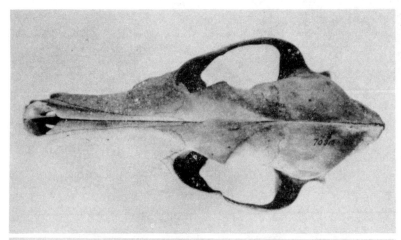

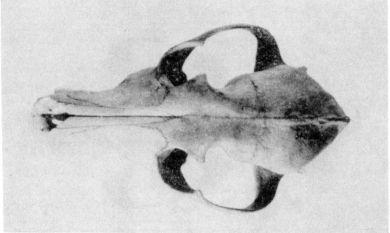

Plate 63. Upper: California Valley Coyote, *Canis latrans ochropus* Esch-scholtz; male, young adult; Tracy, San Joaquin County, California. (No. 70,315, U. S. Nat. Mus., Biological Surveys collection.)

Lower: San Pedro Martir Coyote, Canis latrans clepticus Elliot; male, young adult; La Grulla, Baja California, Mexico. (No. 140,365, U. S. Nat. Mus., Biological Surveys collection.)

324

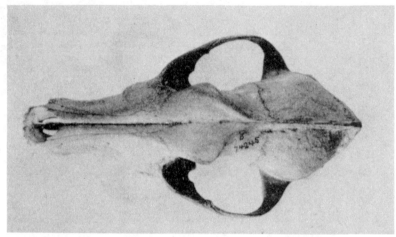

Plate 64. Upper: Peninsula Coyote, *Canis latrans peninsulae* Merriam; type specimen; male adult; Santa Anita, Baja California, Mexico. (No. 74,245, U. S. Nat. Mus., Biological Surveys collection.)

Lower: Mearns Coyote, *Canis latrans mearnsi* Merriam; male, adult; Gila Mountains, Yuma County, Arizona. (No. 203,158, U. S. Nat. Mus., Biological Surveys collection.)

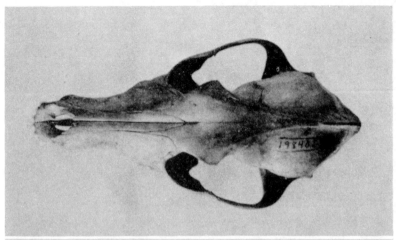

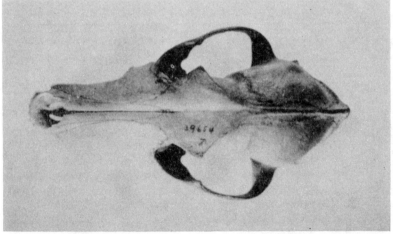

Plate 65. Upper: Tiburon Island Coyote, *Canis latrans jamesi* Townsend; type specimen; male, young adult; Tiburon Island, Baja California, Mexico. (No. 198,402, U. S. Nat. Mus.)

Lower: Lower Rio Grande Coyote, *Canis latrans microdon* Merriam; type specimen; male, adult; Mier, Tamaulipas, Mexico. (No. 39,654, U. S. Nat. Mus., Biological Surveys collection.)

326

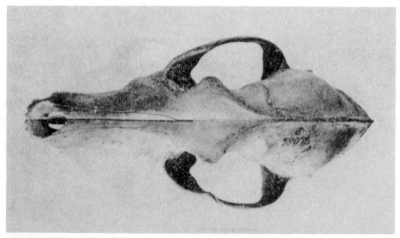

Plate 66. Upper: Durango Coyote, *Canis latrans impavidus* Allen; male, young adult; Esquinapa, Sinaloa, Mexico. (No. 98,076, U. S. Nat. Mus., Biological Surveys collection.)

Lower: Mexican Coyote, *Canis latrans cagottis* (Hamilton Smith); male, young adult; Cerro San Felipe, Oaxaca, Mexico. (No. 68,170, U. S. Nat. Mus., Biological Surveys collection.)

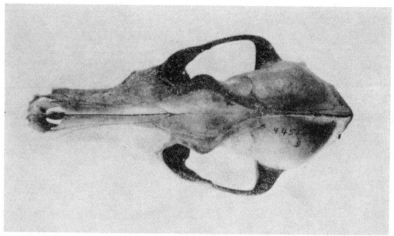

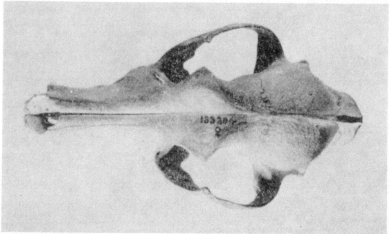

Plate 67. Upper: Colima Coyote, *Canis latrans vigilis* Merriam; type specimen; female. young adult; Manzanillo, Colima, Mexico. (No. 44,550, U. S. Nat. Mus., Biological Surveys collection.)

Lower: Chiapas Coyote, *Canis latrans goldmani* Merriam; type specimen; female, adult; San Vicente, Chiapas, Mexico. (No. 133,204, U. S. Nat. Mus., Biological Surveys collection.)

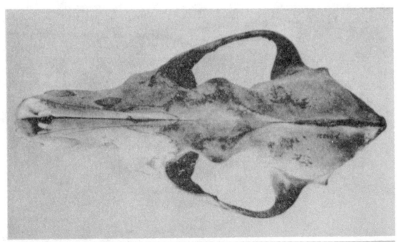

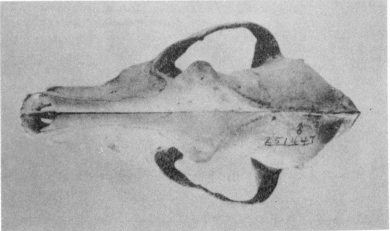

Plate 68. Upper: Salvador Coyote, *Canis latrans dickeyi* Nelson; type specimen; male, young adult; Rio Goascoran, Salvador. (No. 12,260, Donald R. Dickey collection.)

Lower: Honduras Coyote, *Canis latrans hondurensis* Goldman; type specimen; male, adult; Cerro Guinote, Honduras. (No. 251,447, U. S. Nat. Mus., Biological Surveys collection.)

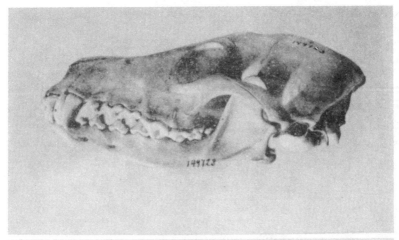

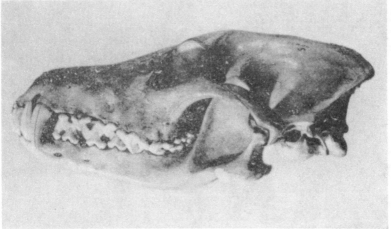

Plate 69. Upper: Plains Coyote, *Canis latrans latrans* Say; female, young adult; Beemer, Cuming County, Nebraska. (No. 149,723, U. S. Nat. Mus., Biological Surveys collection.)

Lower: Plains Coyote, *Canis latrans latrans* Say; male, young adult; Johnstown, Brown County, Nebraska. (No. 71,806, U. S. Nat. Mus., Biological Surveys collection.)

330

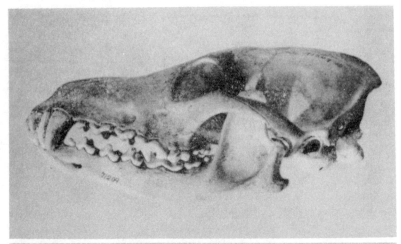

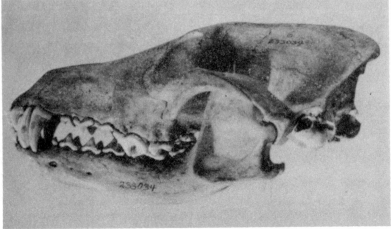

Plate 70. Upper: Northern Coyote, *Canis latrans incolatus* Hall; male, young adult; Stuart Lake (Fort Saint James), British Columbia. (No. 71,209, U. S. Nat. Mus., Biological Surveys collection.)

Lower: Northeastern Coyote, *Canis latrans thamnos* Jackson; type specimen; male, young adult; Basswood Island, Ashland County, Wisconsin. (No. 233,034, U. S. Nat. Mus., Biological Surveys collection.)

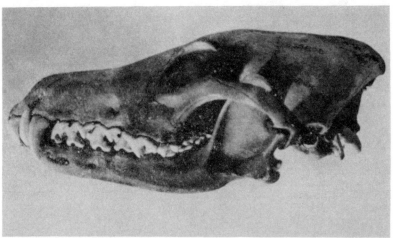

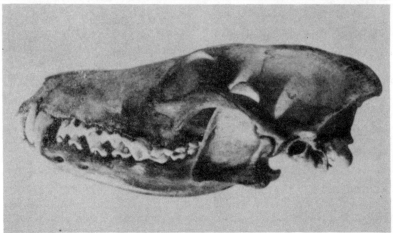

Plate 71. Upper: Southeastern Coyote, *Canis latrans frustror* Woodhouse; male, adult; Calumet, Canadian County, Oklahoma. (No. 235,602, U. S. Nat. Mus., Biological Surveys collection.)

Lower: Texas Plains Coyote. *Canis latrans texensis* Bailey; male, adult; Rankin, Upton County, Texas. (No. 209,521, U. S. Nat. Mus., Biological Surveys collection.)

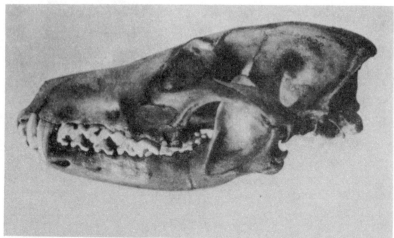

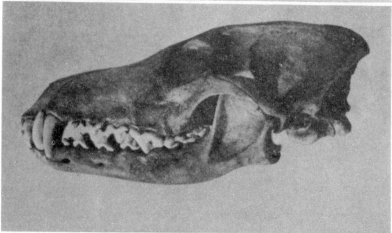

Plate 72. Upper: Mountain Coyote, *Canis latrans lestes* Merriam; male, adult; Gerlach, Washoe County, Nevada. (No. 206,679, U. S. Nat. Mus., Biological Surveys collection.)

Lower: Northwest Coast Coyote, *Canis latrans umpquensis* Jackson; male, young adult; Sequim, Clallam County, Washington. (No. 248,323, U. S. Nat. Mus., Biological Surveys collection.)

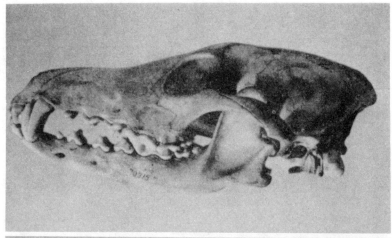

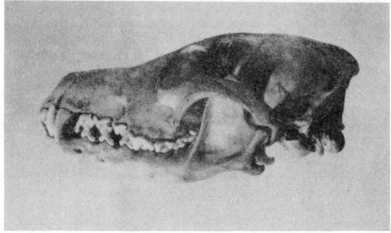

Plate 73. Upper: California Valley Coyote, *Canis latrans ochropus* Eschscholtz; male, young adult; Tracy, San Joaquin County, California. (No. 70,315, U. S. Nat. Mus., Biological Surveys collection.)

Lower: San Pedro Martir Coyote, *Canis latrans clepticus* Elliot; male, young adult; La Grulla, Baja California, Mexico. (No. 140,365, U. S. Nat. Mus., Biological Surveys collection.)

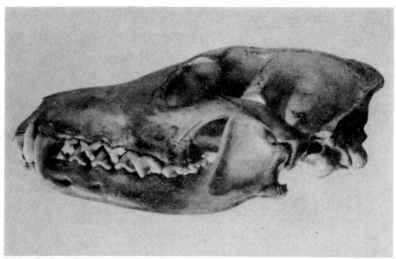

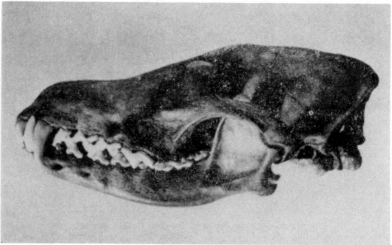

Plate 74. Upper: Peninsula Coyote, *Canis latrans peninsulae* Merriam; type specimen; male, adult; Santa Anita, Baja California, Mexico. (No. 74,245, U. S. Nat. Mus., Biological Surveys collection.)

Lower: Mearns Coyote, *Canis latrans mearnsi* Merriam; male, adult; Gila Mountains, Yuma County, Arizona. (No. 203,158, U. S. Nat. Mus., Biological Surveys collection.)

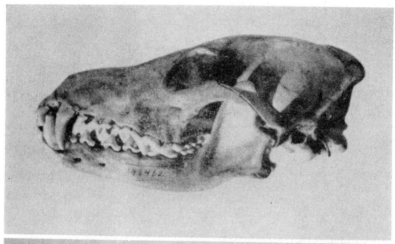

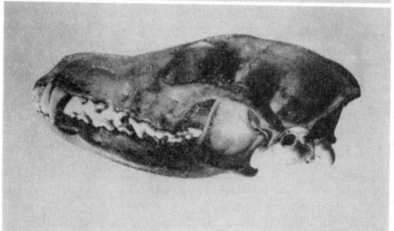

Plate 75. Upper: Tiburon Island Coyote, *Canis latrans jamesi* Townsend; type specimen; male, young adult; Tiburon Island, Baja California, Mexico. (No. 198,402, U. S. Nat. Mus.)

Lower: Lower Rio Grande Coyote, *Canis latrans microdon* Merriam; type specimen; male, adult; Mier, Tamaulipas, Mexico. (No. 39,654, U. S. Nat. Mus., Biological Surveys collection.)

336

Plate 76. Upper: Durango Coyote, *Canis latrans impavidus* Allen; male, young adult; Esquinapa, Sinaloa, Mexico. (No. 98,076, U. S. Nat. Mus., Biological Surveys collection.)

Lower: Mexican Coyote, *Canis latrans cagottis* (Hamilton Smith); male, young adult; Cerro San Felipe, Oaxaca, Mexico. (No. 68,170, U. S. Nat. Mus., Biological Surveys collection.)

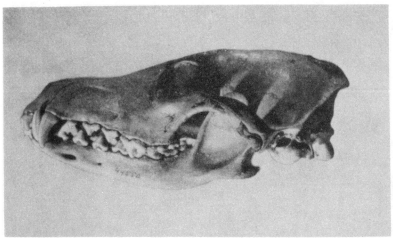

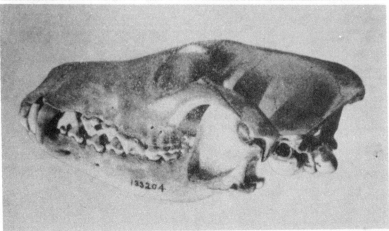

Plate 77. Upper: Colima Coyote, *Canis latrans vigilis* Merriam; type specimen; female, young adult; Manzanillo, Colima, Mexico. (No. 44,550, U. S. Nat. Mus., Biological Surveys collection.)

Lower: Chiapas Coyote, *Canis latrans goldmani* Merriam; type specimen; female, adult; San Vicente, Chiapas, Mexico. (No. 133,204, U. S. Nat. Mus., Biological Surveys collection.)

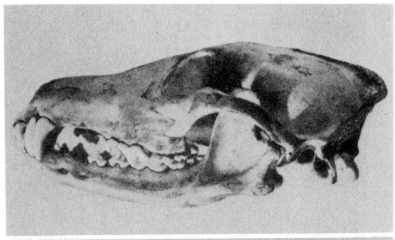

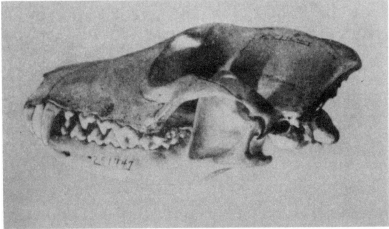

Plate 78. Upper: Salvador Coyote, *Canis latrans dickeyi* Nelson; type specimen; male, young adult; Rio Goascoran, Salvador. (No. 12,260, Donald R. Dickey collection.)

Lower: Honduras Coyote, *Canis latrans hondurensis* Goldman; type specimen; male, adult; Cerro Guinote, Honduras. (No. 251,447, U. S. Nat. Mus., Biological Surveys collection.)

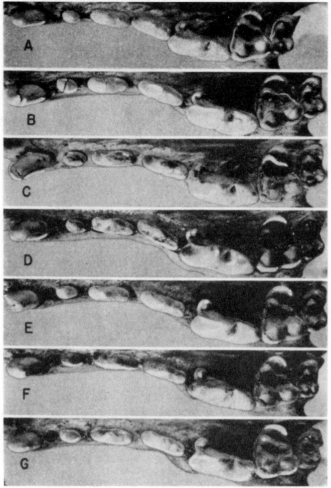

Plate 79. (Natural size.) (a) *Canis latrans latrans* Say; female, young adult; Beemer, Nebraska. (No. 149,723, U. S. Nat. Mus., Biological Surveys collection.)

(b) *Canis latrans latrans* Say; male, young adult; Johnstown, Nebraska. (No. 71,806, U. S. Nat. Mus., Biological Surveys collection.)

(c) *Canis latrans incolatus* Hall; male, young adult; Stuart Lake (Fort Saint James), British Columbia. (No. 71,209, U. S. Nat. Mus., Biological Surveys collection.)

(d) *Canis latrans thamnos* Jackson; type specimen; male, young adult; Basswood Island, Ashland County, Wisconsin. (No. 233,034, U. S. Nat. Mus., Biological Surveys collection.)

(e) *Canis latrans frustror* Woodhouse; male. adult; Calumet, Oklahoma. (No. 235,602, U. S. Nat. Mus., Biological Surveys collection.)

(f) *Canis latrans texensis* Bailey; male, adult; Rankin, Texas. (No. 209,521, U. S. Nat. Mus., Biological Surveys collection.)

(g) *Canis latrans lestes* Merriam; male, adult; Gerlach, Nevada. (No. 206,679, U. S. Nat. Mus., Biological Surveys collection.)

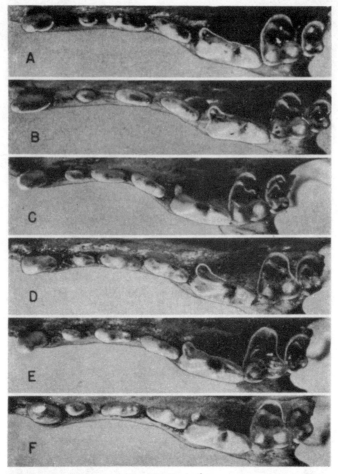

Plate 80. (Natural size.) (a) *Canis latrans umpquensis* Jackson; male, young adult; Sequim, Washington. (No. 248,323, U. S. Nat. Mus., Biological Surveys collection.)

(b) *Canis latrans ochropus* Eschscholtz; male, young adult; Tracy, California. (No. 70,315, U. S. Nat. Mus., Biological Surveys collection.)

(c) *Canis latrans clepticus* Elliot; male, young adult; La Grulla, Baja California, Mexico. (No. 140,365, U. S. Nat. Mus., Biological Surveys collection.)

(d) *Canis latrans peninsulae* Merriam; type specimen; male, adult; Santa Anita, Baja California, Mexico. (No. 74,245, U. S. Nat. Mus., Biological Surveys collection.)

(e) *Canis latrans mearnsi* Merriam; male, adult; Gila Mountains, Arizona. (No. 203,158, U. S. Nat. Mus., Biological Surveys collection.)

(f) *Canis latrans jamesi* Townsend; type specimen; male, young adult; Tiburon Island, Baja California, Mexico. (No. 198,402, U. S. Nat. Mus.)

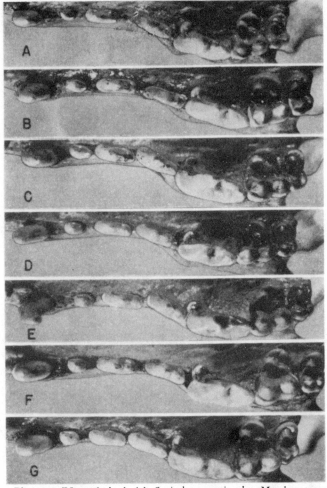

Plate 81. (Natural size.) (a) *Canis latrans microdon* Merriam; type specimen; male, adult; Mier, Tamaulipas, Mexico. (No. 39,654, U. S. Nat. Mus., Biological Surveys collection.)

(b) *Canis latrans impavidus* Allen; male, young adult; Esquinapa, Sinaloa, Mexico. (No. 98,076, U. S. Nat. Mus., Biological Surveys collection.)

(c) *Canis latrans cagottis* (Hamilton Smith); male, young adult; Cerro San Felipe, Oaxaca, Mexico. (No. 68,170, U. S. Nat. Mus., Biological Surveys collection.)

(d) *Canis latrans vigilis* Merriam; type specimen; female, young adult; Manzanillo, Colima, Mexico. (No. 44,550, U. S. Nat. Mus., Biological Surveys collection.)

(e) *Canis latrans goldmani* Merriam; type specimen; female, adult; San Vicente, Chiapas, Mexico. (No. 133,204, U. S. Nat. Mus., Biological Surveys collection.)

(f) *Canis latrans dickeyi* Nelson; type specimen; male, young adult; Rio Goascoran, Salvador. (No. 12,260, Donald R. Dickey collection.)

(g) *Canis latrans hondurensis* Goldman; type specimen; male adult; Cerro Quinote, Honduras. (No. 251,447, U. S. Nat. Mus., Biological Surveys collection.)

Chapter Fifteen

References and Selected Bibliography

Abernathy, John R.
    1936.   Catch 'em alive Jack. Reissue with extensive variations in text of the author's In Camp with Theodore Roosevelt. 224 pp. New York Assoc. Press. 1933.
           (Running coyotes and catching them with aid of dogs.)

Abert, J. W.
    1848.   Report of Lt. J. W. Abert of his examination of New Mexico in the years 1846-1847. U. S. House Executive Documents No. 41, 30th Cong., 1st Sess., 1847-1848, pp. 417-548, with maps; also a Senate Doc. No. 23, 30th Cong., 1st Sess., pp. 1-132.

Adams, Charles C.
    1906.   An ecology survey in northern Michigan. A Rept. from Univ. Mich. Mus. Zool. Pub. by State Bd. Geol. Survey as part of Rept. for 1905, pp. 133; p. 131.
    1924.   A review of Hewitt's "The Conservation of the Wildlife of Canada." Science n.s. 59: 279-281; 280.
    1926.   The economic and social importance of animals in forestry with special reference to wildlife. Roosevelt Wild Life Bull. 3 (4): 509-676, illus.; 584-587. October.
    1927.   The predatory mammal problem. Roosevelt Wild Life Bull. 4 (2); 283-284. June.

Aiton, John F.
    1936.   Whitetail deer in Glacier National Park. Trans. 2nd N. Amer. Wildlife Conf., Amer. Wildlife Inst., Washington, D. C., pp. 302-304.

Alcorn, J. R.
    1946.   On the decoying of coyotes. Jour. Mammal. 27 (2): 122-126, illus. May.

Aldous, C. M.
    1939.   Coyotes in Maine. Journ. Mammal. 20 (1): 104-106. February.

Alfaro, Anastasio
    1897.   Mamiferos de Costa Rica. La primera exposicion Centroamericana, San Jose, Costa Rica. Museo Nacional, pp. v + 51; 18-19.

Allen, J. A.
    1874a.   Notes on the mammals of portions of Kansas, Colorado, Wyoming, and Utah. Bull. Essex Inst. 6: 54.

1874b. Notes on the natural history of portions of Montana and Dakota. Proc. Boston Soc. Nat. Hist. 17: 1-69. June.
(At this time east of the Yellowstone coyotes reported as scarce —attributed to use of strychnine by "wolfers" of plains.)

1876a. Geographical variation among North American mammals, especially in respect to size. U. S. Geol. Survey Terr. Bull. 2 (4): 309-344; 311, 316. July 1.
(At this time it was averred that the coyote was not found much to the northward of the great "campestrian" region of the interior.)

Allen, J. A.

1876b. The extirpation of the larger indigenous mammals in the United States. Penn Monthly 7 (82): 794-806; 804. October.
(On the extensive poisoning of coyotes by professional wolfers on the Great Plains.)

1877. History of the American bison. U. S. Dept. Int., Geol. Survey, 9th Ann. Rept. for year 1875, pp. 443-587. June.

1878. The geographical distribution of the mammalia considered in relation to the principal ontological regions of the earth, and the laws that govern the distribution of animal life. U. S. Dept. Int.; Geol. & Geog. Survey Bull. 4 (2): 313-377. May 3.

1881. List of mammals collected by Dr. Edward Palmer in northeastern Mexico, with field notes by the collector. Mus. Comp. Zool. Bull. 8 (9): 183-189; 183. March.
(Mentions C. latrans scarce at this time because of "poisoning and shooting.")

1903. List of mammals collected by Mr. J. H. Batty in New Mexico and Durango, with descriptions of new species and subspecies. Amer. Mus. Nat. Hist. Bull. 19: 587-612. November 12.
(Describes Canis impavidus.)

1908. Northern extension of range of coyote. Amer. Mus. Nat. Hist. Bull. 24: 584-586.
(Re coyote killed February 1907 on Alsek River, Alaska, near Whitehorse; this was considered most northerly distribution of any form of coyote.)

Allen, Paul

1814. History of the expedition under command of Captains Lewis & Clark to the sources of the Missouri; thence across the Rocky Mountains and down the river Columbia to the Pacific Ocean. Performed during the years 1804-5-6. 2 vols., illus. Bradford & Inskeep, Philadelphia; and A. B. and M. H. Inskeep, New York.

Almirall, Leon V.

1926. Coyote coursing. 64 pp., illus. December 12. Denver, Colo.

1940. Open spaces and speedsters. Amer. Forests 46 (3): 121-122, 143, illus. March.

1941. Canines and coyotes. 150 pp., illus. Caxton Printers, Caldwell, Idaho.

Alston, Edward R.

1879-1882. Biologia Central-Americana Mammalia, with an introduction by P. L. Sclater. Pp. 66-67.
(An occurrence of coyote in Mexico, Guatemala, Costa Rica, at this early date were increasing in Costa Rica in the provinces of Guanacaste and Nicoya (northwestern provinces) destructive to sheep and young calves.)

Anderson, R. M.
 1928. The fluctuation in the population of wild mammals, and the relationship of this fluctuation to conservation. Canadian Field-Nat. 42: 189-191. November.
 1934. The distribution, abundance, and economic importance of the game and fur-bearing mammals of western North America, represented from the Proc. of the 5th Pacific Science Congress, Victoria and Vancouver, B. C., Canada. 1933. Univ. of Toronto Press, pp. 4055-4075 (p. 4060--table shows coyote pelts (Canadian) averaged $11.94 season 1930-31 for this Canadian area.)
 1937a. Faunas of Canada. Canada Yearbook 1937, Dominion Bureau of Statistics. Pp. 29-52, illus. Ottawa.
 1937b. Mammals and birds of the western Arctic Districts, Northwest Territories, Canada. Reprinted from Canada's Western Northland, pp. 97-122. Ottawa.
 1947. Catalogue of Canadian Recent Mammals. Bull. Natl. Mus. Canada, No. 102, (Biol. Ser. No. 31), pp. vi + 238. January 24.
   (*Canis latrans latrans* (p. 51); *Canis latrans incolatus* (p. 52); *Canis latrans lestes* (p. 52); *Canis latrans nebracensis* (p. 52).)
Annabel, Russell
 1941. Northern predator No. 1. The ravages of the coyote in Alaska. Field & Stream 46 (1): 30-31, 115.
Anonymous
 1830. Prairie wolf, Canis latrans. Cat. Nat. Hist. 1: 73-75, pl. 7.
 1868. The hounds of the jungle (Adventures with coyotes in Central America). Temple Bar 23: 66-75.
   (Occurrence of coyote in Costa Rica and description of animals cooperative method of hunting prey.)
 1870-71. A wolf hunt. La Porte City Progress, La Porte, Iowa. December 21, 28, January 4.
   (Announcement of "circular" wolf-coyote hunt, La Porte City, Iowa.)
 1879. The history of Warren County, Iowa. Union Historical Co., Des Moines. Pp. 320, 321.
 1881. A coyote chase on the Kansas Prairies. Amer. Field 15: 125.
 1884. History of Kossuth and Humboldt Counties, Iowa. Union Publishing Co., Springfield, Ill. P. 706.
   (Attractiveness of fresh pork to coyotes.)
 1885. Wolf hunting on the Little Missouri. Amer. Field 23: 413.
 1887a. Coyote hunting. Amer. Field 28: 53.
 1887b. Coyotes' strategy. Amer. Field 27: 7.
 1897. Noxious animals and animal pests. British Columbia Dept. Agr. Ann. Rept. 1895-96: 1167-1177.
 1903. Chased by coyotes. Current Literature 34: 69. January.
 1906. Some notes on wolves. Forest & Stream 66 (4): 135-136, 180-181, illus. January 27.
 1908. Thousands of mad wolves [coyotes]. Numbers increasing in Texas and rabies has spread among them. The Cincinnati Weekly Enquirer, January 2. Cincinnati, Ohio.
 1909. Life and sport in Labrador. Forest & Stream 73 (2): 55-56. July 10.
   (Notes on Comeau's book.)

1916. Many coyotes and bobcats killed in Wasco County. Oreg. Sportsman 4 (1): 58. January.

1921. Widely famous Custer wolf hits the long long trail. Weekly News Letter, U. S. Dept. Agr. 8 (26): 1, 16. Washington, D. C.

(In which 2 coyotes were observed feeding from wolf-kills, and traveled on wolf's flanks as kind of sentinels.)

1925. Sixty hounds in a coyote hunt in Texas. Literary Digest 84: 70-72. March 28.

1927. Giving the coyote a good name. Literary Digest 92: 61. March 26.

1928a. Fur-bearing animals of the United States. The coyote. Fur Jour. 2 (9): 18, 50-60, illus.

1928b. Tagged coyotes liberated. Heppner Gazette-Times, Heppner, Oreg. June 21.

(First experiment in study of coyote migration by ear tagging and release of the animal.)

1929. Killing predatory animals. Nat. Mag. 14 (4): 245. October.

(Mentions $30,000 appropriation for Alaska as an emergency measure for suppression of wolves and coyotes.)

1930. What is the fastest animal? Amer. Forests & Forest Life 36 (3): 178. March.

1931. More waterfowl by assisting nature. Pub. by More Game Birds in America, 500 5th Ave., New York. 106 pp.; 39-42. August.

(Coyotes as waterfowl predators.)

1932a. His hand was quicker than a wolf's jaw. Literary Digest 114: 23-24. September 3.

1932b. Go east, young coyote, go east! Literary Digest 112: 41-42. January 16.

1936a. Lone wolf. Literary Digest 112: 14-15. December 19.

1936b. Coyote moves east by modern methods. Scientific American 152: 328. June.

1937. Improved coyote trap. Natl. Wool Grower 27: 36. October.

1938. Dog runs with coyotes. Natl. Nat. News 2 (22): 6.

1940a. Documentary material on native protection and wildlife preservation in Latin America. Prepared for use of Comm. of Experts in nature protection, May 13-16; Vol. 1 (pt. 1): 103-125 (Mexico). Pan American Union, Washington, D. C.

(Status of the coyote, among other animals.)

1940b. Eagles attack coyotes. Maryland Conservationist 17 (2): 19.

1942a. Return of rabbits and coyotes. Editorial, Portland Oregonian, Portland, Oreg. January 25.

1942b. Wildlife Research News, Ill. Nat. Hist. Survey, Urbana, p. 16. March.

1943a. Photo of coyote killed in Clinton County. Outdoor Indiana 13 (4): 16. May.

1943b. Hunter trapped in cave eats coyote pups raw. Washington Evening Star, May 28. Washington, D. C.

1943c. Coyotes are killed by flyers while taking antelope census. South Dakota Conservation Digest 10 (5): 11. May.

(Hunting of coyotes by airplane in southwestern South Dakota while in an antelope county.)

1943d. Wildlife tragedy. Arizona Wildlife & Sportsman 5 (9): 9. September.
(Coyote overtaking young antelope in Arizona.)

1943e. Wildlife conditions in national parks, 1941. U. S. Dept. Int., Nat. Park Service, 58 pp.; 13. May.
(Resume of coyote big game relationship.)

1944a. Coyote seen running with deer in pursuit. Science News Letter 45 (14): 210. April 1.

1944b. Skinning a coyote. South Dakota Conservation Digest 11 (12): 14. December. Pierre, S. Dak.

1944c. The coyote. South Dakota Conservation Digest 11 (12): 6. Pierre, S. Dak.

1945a. Predatory animal bounty claims, 1944. South Dakota Conservation Digest 12 (5): 15. May. Pierre, S. Dak.
(Gives total of 1,317 adult coyotes and 6,012 coyote pups claimed for bounty in South Dakota for 1944.)

1945b. Dog-coyote hybrid caught in Missouri. Outdoor Georgia 5 (27): 2. February 15. Atlanta, Ga.

1945c. War on coyotes. Oklahoma Game & Fish News 1 (1): 8, illus. January.

1945d. Halifax enjoys part in Oklahoma coyote chase. Times-Herald, Washington, D. C., March 21.

1945e. [Lord] Halifax chases coyotes, misses all kills, calls it "Jolly." Washington Post, Washington, D. C., March 21, p. 7.

1945f. Two-legged coyote. New Mexico Magazine 23 (5): 22. May. Albuquerque, N. Mex.

1945g. Two-legged coyote. New Mexico Magazine 23 (6): 27, illus. June.
(Illus. from photo by W. T. Sherman. Good illus. of a peg-legged coyote.)

1945h. Coyotes and the luxury tax. New Mexico Magazine. National Fur News 17 (6): 16. July.

1945i. Timber-r-r-r. Outdoor Indiana 12 (4): 15. May-June. Indianapolis.
(On capture of den of coyotes numbering 7 in litter taken near Argos, Marshall County.)

1945j. Fox rabies. Pennsylvania Game News 16 (5): 22. August.
(Re rabies in foxes and coyotes, reprint in part from Current Medical Literature, July 7, 1945.)

1946a. Coyotes tree a bobcat. Service Survey 6 (1): 26. March. U. S. Dept. of Interior, Fish and Wildlife Service.

1946b. Iowa trappers net two and one-half million dollars. Iowa Conservationist 5 (4): 25, 28-29; 29. April 15.
(Value of coyote pelt, Iowa, 1930-46.)

1946c. Michigan coyote-dog pups. Pennsylvania Game News 17 (3): 23. June. Harrisburg, Pa.

1946d. Bounties don't do the job. Outdoor Nebraska 23 (4): 23. Lincoln, Nebr.
(An article against coyote bounty.)

1946e. Aerial coyote hunting. Oregon State Game Commission Bulletin 1 (2): 2. May.

1946f. Regulations governing the hunting of predatory animals with aircraft. North Dakota Outdoors 9 (5): 9. November.
(Re North Dakota's regulations in hunting predators from airplane.)

1946g. Unbalancing nature. North Dakota Outdoors 8 (11): 1-2. May. Bismarck, N. Dak.
(A plea for control not extermination of predators, including coyote.)

1946h. Extension predator control program. Missouri Conservationist 7 (6): 7-9, illus. June.
(Cooperative state-county-federal extension work in the art of tracking coyote trapping technic.)

1946i. (Study of airplane hunting of predatory animals, etc.) Pittman-Robertson Quarterly 6 (4): 169. October. U. S. Dept. Int., Fish and Wildlife Service.
(Sixty-three permit holders killed 3,290 coyotes from airplane in North Dakota winter 1945-46.)

1947a. New England [North Dakota] sportsmen wage war on coyotes. North Dakota Outdoors 9 (9): 7, illus. March.

1947b. Coyote hunting from air. Colorado Conservation Comments 10 (1): 13. March.
(An emphatic No! that anyone can make a living hunting coyotes by airplane.)

1947c. The coyote. Missouri Conservationist 8 (6): 8-9, illus. June.

1947d. Game statistics. Wisconsin Conservation Bulletin 12 (8): 12. August.
(Coyotes along with wolves increased to the highest point in twenty years per 1945-46 bounty records.)

1947e. Nebraska's flying farmers parade. The Washington Post, Sunday, September 7, Washington, D. C., pp. 17-19, illus.; 17.
(Use of airplane for killing coyotes, among other farm flying routines.)

1947f. Offer bounty for coyotes. New Mexico Magazine 25 (11): 26. November. Albuquerque, N. Mex.

1947g. This and that. Oregon State Game Commission Bulletin 11 (16): 3. Portland, Oreg.
(Report of a peg-leg coyote and a badger traveling along together in Wallowa County, Oreg., below Buck Creek.)

1947h. Trapped coyote survives. New Mexico Magazine 25 (12): 28. December.

1947i. Wildlife post mortem. Some "Inside" dope on predators. Outdoor Nebraska 25 (4): 16-17, illus.

1947j. Nebraska Trapper's Guide. Outdoor Nebraska 25 (4): 11, illus.

1947k. State law governs use of cyanide guns. Oklahoma Game & Fish News 3 (12): 9. December.

1948a. Aerial coyote hunting. Oregon State Game Commission Bull. 3 (1): 8. January.

1948b. A coyote goes "Hollywood," Inside Interior 5 (11): 3. February 16. U. S. Dept. of Interior, Washington, D. C.
(Coyote "Ranger" 2 years old, captured as pup in den being used for motion pictures of coyote.)

1948c. Coyote round-uppers hold annual festivities. Oklahoma Game & Fish News 4 (3): 19, illus. March.

1948d. Coyote roundup. Life 24 (10): 39. March 8.

1948e. Attack system of bounty. Mississippi Game & Fish 11 (9): 5. March.

1948f. Coyote "up and downs" not affected by bounty. Mich. Conservation 17 (3): 14. March.

1948g. Coyote hunting de luxe. Missouri Conservationist 9 (3): 11. March.

1948h. Coyotes aid job of finding leaks. Inside Interior 5 (13): 1. April. U. S. Dept. Interior, Washington, D. C.

———————[Manly F. Miner?]

1948i. Coyotes starve themselves out of Point Pelee (Canada) National Park. News Release, 1 p. Jack Miner Migratory Bird Foundation, Kingville, Ontario. June.

Anthony, A. W.

1923. A defense of the coyote. Calif. Fish & Game 9 (3): 111-112. July.

Anthony, H. E.

1913. Mammals of northern Malheur County, Oregon. Amer. Mus. Nat. Hist. Bull. 32 (art. 1): 1-27; 24. March 7. New York.
(Reports coyote very abundant, and take a large toll of poultry and sheep from ranchers.)

1928. Field book of North American mammals. 625 pp., illus. G. P. Putnam's Sons, New York and London.

1931. The control of predatory animals. Science 74 (1916): 288-290. September.

Armas, Juan Ignacio de

1888. La zoologia de Colon y de los primeros exploradores de America. (The zoology of Columbus and the first explorers of America.) 185 pp.; 44. Habana, Establ. Tipogr.

Arnold, Bridgewater M.

1925. Dictionary of fur names. Fur Industry Yearbook, pp. 39-47; 47. New York.
(Coyote listed under name of prairie wolf in raw fur trade.)

Ashbrook, F. G., and H. J. McMullen

1928. Fur-bearing animals of the United States. Fur Jour. 2 (9): 18, 59-60, illus.

Asdell, S[ydney] A[rthur]

1946. Patterns of mamalian reproduction. xii + 437 pp., 12 pls. Comstock Publishing Co., Ithaca.
(*Canis latrans*, pp. 156-157.)

Astle, Lloyd J.

1940. Leaves from our diaries. Yellowstone Nat. Notes 17 (11-12): 72. November-December. National Park Service.
(Unusual antics of coyote following for 1½ miles a man mounted on horseback.)

Audubon, John James, and John Bachman

1851-54. The quadrupeds of North America. 3 vols. Vol. 2, p. 152.
(Occurrence of coyote in western Arkansas.)

Aughey, Samuel

1884. Curious companionship of the coyote and badger. Amer. Naturalist 18 (6): 644-645. June.

Austin, Mary

1906. The flock. Houghton-Mifflin Co., Cambridge, Mass.

Bachrach, Max.
  1930. Fur—a practical treatise. 677 pp., illus. Prentice-Hall, Inc., N. Y.

Baegert, Jacob
  1864. An account of the aboriginal inhabitants of the California
          Peninsula. Trans. and arranged by Charles Rau, of New York City.
          Ann. Rept. Smithsn. Inst. 1863: 352-369; 355.
          (List of main mammals including coyote, occurring 18th
          century.)
          Baegert was a Jesuit missionary, a German, banished at time
          Chas. III of Spain decreed in 1767, to that effect concerning
          all Jesuit priests in Spain and her possessions where missions
          had been established. His volume was published in German 1773
          under nom-de-plume of Mannheim.

Bailey, Bernard
  1929. Mammals of Sherburne County, Minnesota. Journ. Mammal.
          10 (2): 153-164. May.
          (Coyotes first appeared in 1875.)

Bailey, Harold E.
  1930. Correcting inaccurate ranges of certain Florida mammals and
          others of Virginia and the Carolinas. Bailey Mus. & Lib. Nat.
          Hist. Bull. 5: 1-4; 2. December 1.
          (Coyote in Florida, probably escapee from a tourist.)

Bailey, Vernon
  1888. Report on some of the results of a trip through parts of Minne-
          sota and Dakota. Annual Rept. U. S. Dept. Agr. for year 1887;
          report of the ornithologist, pp. 431-454; 432.
  1905. A biological survey of Texas. U. S. Dept. Agr., Bur. Biol. Survey,
          North Amer. Fauna 25: 1-222, illus., p. 174. October 24.
  1907a. Wolves in relation to stock, game, and the National Forest
          Reserves. U. S. Dept. Agr., Forest Serv. Bull. 72: 1-31; 30-31.
          (Discusses measures of coyote control all comparable to those
          used for wolves.)
  1907b. Directions for the destruction of wolves and coyotes. U. S. Dept.
          Agr., Bur. Biol. Survey Circ. 55: 1-6, illus.
  1908a. Destruction of wolves and coyotes. U. S. Dept. Agr., Bur. Biol.
          Survey Circ. 63: 1-11, illus.
  1908b. Harmful and beneficial mammals of the arid interior. U. S. Dept.
          Agr. Farmers' Bull. 335: 1-31, illus.; 27-28.
  1909. Key to animals on which wolf and coyote bounties are often
          paid. U. S. Dept. Agr., Bur. Biol. Survey Circ. 69: 1-3, illus. May.
  1916. Wild animals of Glacier National Park. U. S. Dept. Int., Natl.
          Park Service, 210 pp., Mammals, pp. 1-102; 83.
  1924. Breeding, feeding, and other life habits of meadow mice
          (Microtus). Jour. Agr. Research 26 (8): 523-535, illus.; 524.
          February 23.
  1927. A biological survey of North Dakota. I. Physiography and life
          zones. II. The mammals. North Amer. Fauna No. 49, pp. vi +
          226, 21 pls. January 8.
          (Canis latrans latrans and Canis latrans nebracensis, pp.
          156-160.)
  1930a. Mammals of the Lone-Star State. Nature Magazine 16 (6):
          363-365, 386, illus. December.

1930b. Animal life of Yellowstone National Park. Chas. C. Thomas, Springfield, Ill., and Baltimore, Md., 241 pp., illus.; 137.

1932a. Mammals of New Mexico. North Amer. Fauna No. 53, 412 pp., 22 pls., March 1. Bur. Biol. Survey, U. S. Dept. Agr., Washington, D. C.

(*Canis latrans texensis, Canis latrans lestes, Canis latrans nebracensis, Canis latrans estor, and Canis mearnsi*, pp. 312-321.)

1932b. Can we bring back the Sierra Bighorn? Sierra Club Bull. 17 (2): 135, April.

(States coyote reduction necessary if 2,000 sheep were maintained in Yellowstone National Park.)

1935. Mammals of the Grand Canyon region. Grand Canyon Nat. Hist. Assoc. Bull. 1: 1-42; 32-33.

(Gives *Canis latrans lestes, Canis l. estor*, and *C. l. mearnsi* as occurring.)

1936. The mammals and life zones of Oregon. North Amer. Fauna 55: 276. Bur. Biol. Surv., U. S. Dept. Agr., Washington, D. C., 416 pp. June.

1939. Coyote fur. Pennsylvania Game News 10 (3): 12, 32, illus.

1940. Our fur bearing animals. Amer. Humane Assoc., Albany, N. Y., pp. 1-8, illus.

(Use of Verbail trap on coyotes.)

Bailey, Vernon, William B. Bell, and Melvin A. Brannon
1914. Preliminary report on the mammals of North Dakota. N. Dak. Agr. Exper. Sta. Circ. 3: 1-20; 16. Agr. College, N. Dak.

Baillie, J. L.
1939. First coyote. Evening Telegram, Toronto, Ontario, Canada. June 3.

Baird, Spencer Fullerton
1859a. Mammals of North America. Descriptions of species based chiefly on the collections in the museum of Smithsn. Inst., Wash., D. C. J. B. Lippincott & Co., Phila., Pa., 764 pp., illus.; 115.

1859b. Special report upon the mammals of the Mexican boundary with notes by the naturalists of the survey. 2 (Part 2): 1-62: 15.

Barclay, Lillian E.
1938. The coyote: animal and folk character. Coyote Wisdom, pp. 36-103. Texas Folk-Lore Society, Austin, Tex.

Barger, N. R.
1950. Coyote (*Canis latrans latrans*). Wisconsin Conserv. Bull. 15 (4): 32-33, illus. April.

Barker, E. S., and S. O. Barker
1921. Predatory animals and the game supply in New Mexico. Amer. Game Protect. Assoc. Bull. 10 (1): 6-8, illus.

Barker, Elliott S.
1944. Don coyote, saboteur. New Mexico Magazine 22 (3): 23, 25. March. Albuquerque, N. Mex.

1945. Coyotes and the luxury tax. New Mexico Magazine 23 (5): 21-22. May. Albuquerque, N. Mex.

(Reprinted in National Fur News 17 (6): 16, July, 1945.)

1948. Let's eliminate damage from coyotes. New Mexico Magazine 26 (3): 25, 27. March.

Barker, Franklin D.
  1911.   The trematode genus Opisthorchis R. Blanchard, 1895. Arch. de
           Parasitol. Par. 14 (4): 513-561, pls. 17-20.
Barker, S. Omar
  1947.   Coyote catastrophe. Western Sportsman 7 (9): 1-12, illus.
           March-April. Austin, Tex.
Barnes, Claude T.
  1922.   Utah mammals. Univ. Utah Bull. 12 (15): 117. April.
Barnes, R. M.
  1936a.   Albino coyote. The Oologist 53 (10): 137. October.
  1936b.   [Photo of two alb;no coyotes]. The Oologist 53 (11): 156.
           November.
Barnes, Will C.
  1935.   Arizona place names. Univ. of Arizona Bull. 6 (1): 115-116.
           General Bull. No. 2, 503 pp. January 1.
           (Re areas carrying name coyote such as Coyote Mountains in
           Pima County, etc.)
Baughman, J. L.
  1947.   The lady and the wolves [coyotes]. Texas Game and Fish 5
           (16): 4-5, 28-29, illus. September.
Baynes, E. H.
  1905.   My young coyote, Romulus. Woman's Home Companion 32: 16.
           March.
Beal, Robert P.
  1934.   Wawona deer, mountain lions and coyotes. Yosemite Nature Notes
           13 (5): 40. May.
           (Coyotes robbing a puma cache of deer.)
Beatty, Robert O.
  1947.   Predator control facts and fancies. Outdoor America 12 (11):
           6-8, illus. December.
Bebb, William
  1934.   Source of small birds eaten by the coyote. Journ. Mammal. 15:
           320-321.
  1935.   The coyote and the automobile. Journ. Mammal. 16 (4): 323.
Bee, James W., and E. Raymond Hall
  1951.   An instance of coyote-dog hybridization. Trans. Kans. Acad. Sci.
           54 (1): 73-77.
Beechey, F. W.
  1831.   Narrative of a voyage to the Pacific and Bering's Strait, to
           co-operate with the Polar Expeditions, in years 1825-26-27-28.
           London, 2 parts, pp. 1-742. Pt. 2, p. 403.
Bell, J. Frederick
  1945.   The infection of ticks (Dermacentor variabilis) with Pasteurella
           tularensis. Jour. Infectious Diseases 76 (2): 83-95. March-April.
Bell, William A.
  1876.   New tracks in North America. P. 274. London, 2nd Ed.
Bell, W. B.
  1921.   Hunting down stock killers. Yearbook, U. S. Dept. Agr. 1920:
           289-300, illus.
  1926.   Wolf and coyote control. The Producer 7 (9): 2-4; (10):
           6-8, illus.
  1927.   Wolves, coyotes take big toll from stockmen. Yearbook, U. S.
           Dept. Agr. 1926: 774-776.

Belt, Thomas
1928.   The naturalist in Nicaragua. London & Toronto. P. 40. J. M.
        Dent & Sons, Ltd., E. P. Dutton & Co., 2nd printing, 306 pp.,
        illus.

Bent, Arthur C.
1923.   Life histories of North American wild fowl. Order Anseres (part).
        U. S. Natl. Mus. Bull. 126: 1-250, illus.; 79.
        (Coyote depredation on nesting ducks.)

Bennitt, Rudolf, and Werner O. Nagel
1937.   A survey of the resident game and fur bearers of Missouri.
        Univ. Missouri Studies, Quart. of Research 12 (2): 1-215; 168-
        176. April, 1.
        (A good resume of coyote in Missouri.)

Benson, Seth B.
1948.   Decoying coyotes and deer. Jour. Mammal. 29 (4): 406-409.
        November.
        (Actual date of publication Jan. 8.)

Berryman, Jack H.
1949.   Facts of interest about Utah mammals. *Canis latrans*—Coyote.
        Utah Fish and Game Bull. 7 (5): 6-7.
        (Condensed life history of coyote and Utah bounty laws.)

Biddle, N.
1937.   The speed of mammals. Pennsylvania Game News 8 (5): 19.

Bingham, Cy. J.
1915.   Methods of poisoning coyotes. Oregon Sportsman 3 (3): 61-63.
        March.

Birdseye, Clarence
1912.   Some common mammals of western Montana in relation to
        agriculture and spotted fever. U. S. Dept. Agr., Farmers' Bull.
        484: 1-46, illus.; 46. March 9.

Black, J. D.
1937.   Mammals of Kansas. 30th Ann. Rept. Kans. State Bd. Agr.
        1935-36: 116-217, illus.; 167-169.

Blair, W. Frank
1938.   Ecological relationship of the mammals of the Bird Creek Region,
        northeastern Oklahoma. Amer. Midland Nat. 20 (3): 473-526;
        497-498, November.
        ("Probably is of the subspecies *latrans*.")

1939.   Faunal relationships and geographic distribution of mammals in
        Oklahoma. Amer. Midland Nat. 22 (1): 85-133; 107. July.
        Canis latrans nebracensis.

1940.   A contribution to the ecology and faunal relationships of the mam-
        mals of the Davis Mountain region, southwestern Texas. Univ.
        Mich. Mus. Zool., Misc. Pub. 46: 1-39, illus.; 25.

1941.   Annotated list of mammals of the Tularosa Basin, New Mexico.
        Amer. Midland Nat. 26 (1): 218-229; 220. July.

Bohl, Walter E.
1946.   An artist bags a turkey. Arizona Highways 22 (11): 1, 38-39,
        illus.; 38. November. Arizona Highway Dept., Phoenix, Ariz.
        (Observation of coyote endeavoring to stalk a flock of Mer-
        riam's wild turkeys.)

Bole, B. Patterson, Jr., and Philip N. Moulthrop
   1942.   The Ohio recent mammal collection in the Cleveland Museum
           of Natural History. Cleveland Mus. Nat. Hist. Sci. Pub. 5 (6):
           127. Sept. 11.
Bond, R. M.
   1939.   Coyote food habits on the Lava Beds National Monument.
           Journ. Wildlife Mgt. 3 (3); 180-198, illus.
Borell, Adrey E., and Ralph Ellis
   1934.   Mammals of the Ruby Mountains region of northeastern Nevada.
           Journ. Mammal. 15 (1): 12-44, illus; 22-23. February.
           (Gives interesting observations of coyote foods (grasshoppers),
           and antics of female coyote with young romping similar to
           domestic dogs.)
Bowman, Ed.
   1943.   Letter published in Arizona News Letter (a mimeographed
           weekly issued by the Arizona Cattle Growers' Association,
           Phoenix, Apr. 27).
           (Re spread of coyotes from Apache Indian Reservation to
           outside ranges.)
Bracket, U. S.
   1900.   Predatory beasts in Yellowstone Park. Recreation 12: 449-450.
           June.
Bradt, G. W.
   1947.   Michigan wildlife sketches. 47 pp. (not paged), illus. Michigan
           Dept. Conservation, Lansing, Mich. November.
   1948.   Wolf and coyote—wild dogs of forest and plains. Michigan
           Conservation 17 (1): 4-5.
Branch, E. Douglas
   1929.   The hunting of the buffalo. 240 pp., illus.; 11. D. Appleton &
           Co., New York and London.
Brandegee, Katherine
   1890.   Caenuris of the hare. Zoe 1: 265-268.
           (Coyote host to this tapeworm.)
Breckenridge, Walter J.
   1938.   A review of predator control. The Minnesota Conservationist
           57: 10-11, 23-26, illus. May. St. Paul, Minn.
Brennan, James M.
   1945.   Field investigations pertinent to Bullis fever. Preliminary report
           on the species of ticks and vertebrates occurring at Camp Bullis,
           Texas. Texas Repts. on Biol. and Medicine 3 (1) 112-121.
           (Reports finding of the tick (Ixodes scapularis) on coyote;
           also the Gulf Coast tick (Dermacentor variabilis).)
Brewer, William H.
   1930.   Up and down California in 1860-1864; the Journal of William
           H. Brewer, Ed. by Francis P. Farquhar. p. 277. Yale Univ. Press,
           New Haven.
Bristol, L. C.
   1946.   Our bounty law. South Dakota Conservation Digest 13 (2): 8.
           February. Pierre, S. Dak.
           (A plea for control of the coyote, not its extermination pur-
           suant to a high bounty in South Dakota.)
Bronson, Wilfrid S.
   1946.   Coyotes. 60 pp., illus. Harcourt, Brace & Co., Inc., New York.

Brooks, Allan
    1902.   Mammals of the Chilliwack District, B. C. Ottawa Naturalist 15:
            239-244; 242.
    1908.   Northerly range of the coyote. Forest and Stream 71 (21):
            812-813. November 21.
    1926.   Past and present big game conditions in British Columbia and
            the predatory mammal question. Journ. Mammal. 7 (1): 37-40.
    1930.   Early big-game conditions in the Mount Baker District of Wash-
            ington. The Murrelet 11 (3): 65-67; 66. September.
            (Says before 1892 coyotes were unknown in Mt. Baker,
            Wash., region, which year commenced to invade the region
            from the dry interior, now common.)
Brown, C. Emerson
    1936.   Rearing wild animals in captivity and gestation periods. Journ.
            Mammal. 17 (1): 10-13. February.
            (Gives gestation period of coyote, C. latrans, as 64 days
            Phila. Zool. Garden.)
Brown, James
    1926.   Coyotes and wolves in Alaska. Outdoor Life 58 (2): 162.
            August.
Brown, T. D.
    1918.   Report on Cypress Hill Game Preserve. Rept. Chief Game
            Guardian, Saskatchewan, p. 28.
            (Coyote abundant.)
Brown, W. S.
    1916.   Rabid coyotes in Modoc County. Calif. Fish & Game 2 (2):
            111-112.
Brunner, Josef
    1909.   Tracks and tracking. Outing Publishing Co., New York. Pp.
            1-219; 118-120.
Bryant, H. C.
    1920.   The coyote not afraid of water. Jour. Mammal. 1 (1): 87-88.
Buchanan, Angus
    1920.   Wildlife in Canada. John Murray, pp. 1-264, illus.; 217.
Bulger, B.
    1933.   Catching the coyote. Saturday Evening Post 206: 84-85. Sep-
            tember 23.
Burnett, Peter H.
    1880.   Recollections on opinions of an old pioneer. P. 394. New York.
Burr, J. G.
    1946.   Stalking the destroyer. Texas Game & Fish 4 (7): 4-5, 26-28,
            illus. June. Austin, Texas.
            ("In the preservation of the balance of nature, the rancher
            cannot be counted on, for his flocks come first.")
    1948a. Fanged fury. Texas Game & Fish 6 (6): 4, 18. May.
            (Two coyotes bark at treed bobcat in daylight.)
    1948b. A kind word for the coyote. Texas Game & Fish 6 (7): 9, 14,
            16. June.
Burt, William Henry
    1938.   Faunal relationships and geographic distribution of mammals
            in Sonora, Mexico. Misc. Pub., Mus. Zool., Univ. Mich., No. 39,
            pp. 1-77; 32-33. February 14.
            (On occurrence of coyote, C. l. vigilis.)

1946. The mammals of Michigan. Illustrated by Richard Philip Grossenheider. Univ. Mich. Press, Ann Arbor, Mich. Pp. xv-288; 159-192.

Cahalane, Victor H.
1939a. Mammals of the Chiricahua Mountains, Cochise County, Arizona. Jour. Mammal. 20 (4): 418-440; 425. November.
(On occurrence of *C. l. mearnsi* in San Simon Valley.)
1939b. The evolution of predator control policy in the national parks. Jour. Wildlife Management 3 (3): 229-237. July.
1946. Shall we save the larger carnivores? The Living Wilderness 11 (17): 17-21, illus.; 18. June.
(Coyotes still rare in Mt. McKinley National Park, 20 years after first recording. In 22 months of study only 4 coyotes were observed between 1939 and 1945.)
1947a. A deer coyote episode. Jour. Mammal. 28 (1): 36-39. February.
1947b. Mammals of North America. Pp. x+682; 35, 62, 66, 245-255, illus. Macmillan Co., New York.
1948. The status of mammals in the U. S. National Park system, 1947. Jour. Mammal. 29 (3): 247-259; 250. September 2.

Cahn, Alvin R.
1921. The mammals of Itasca County, Minnesota. Jour. Mammal. 2 (2): 68-74.
(Says "coyote" never called such in north woods, but called "Brush Wolf.")

Callison, I. P.
1948. Wolf predation in the North Country. I. P. Callison, Lloyd Bldg., Seattle 1, Washington. 89 pp., illus.
(Discusses wolves in North Country, their predations, bounties, and to a limited extent coyotes.)

Cameron, Jenks
1929. The Bureau of Biological Survey: Its history, activities, and organization. Service Monograph 54. Brookings Institution, Washington, D. C. Pp. i-x; 1-339.

Carey, J. L.
1946. Bounties and predator control. Rally Sheet, League of Maryland Sportsmen, Inc. 4 (7): 6. August. Baltimore.
(Bounties are an outmoded method of predator control.)

Carhart, Arthur H., and Stanley P. Young
1926. Senior Yip Yap. Sunset Mag. 6: 28-30, illus. December. San Francisco, Calif.

Carman, Ezra Ayers, and others
1892. Special report on the history and present condition of the sheep industry of the United States. Bur. Anim. Ind., U. S. Dept. Agr. 1,000 pp.; 828-829, 961. Washington, D. C.

Carney, Emerson
1899. Wyoming vermin bounties. Forest and Stream 52 (8): 145. February 25.
1902. Wolves in Wyoming and Colorado. Forest and Stream 58: 169. March 1.

Cary, Merritt
1911. A biological survey of Colorado. North Amer. Fauna 33: 1-256, illus.; 172-173. U. S. Dept. Agr., Bur. Biol. Survey.

Castro, William, and Clifford C. Presnall
    1944.   Comparison of coyote trapping methods. Jour. Wildlife Management 8 (1): 65-70. January.

Cates, E. C.
    1941.   Coyote runs amuck. Journ. Mammal. 22 (2): 203.

Chambers, A. P.
    1923.   Capturing a couple of killers in the Wind Cave Game Preserve. Amer. Game Protect. Assoc. Bull. 12 (3): 4-6, illus.

Chambliss, Peter C.
    1932.   Hunting notes. Baltimore Sun, Baltimore, Md.
        (Quoting E. Lee LeCompte.)

Chapman, A.
    1904.   Pariah of the skyline. Outing 44: 131-138. May.

Chapman, James W.
    1946.   Dramas of the wild. Fauna 8 (2): 37-39; 38. June. Pub. Zool. Soc. Phila., Pa.
        (Peculiar antics of a trapped and untrapped coyote.)

Chapman, Jim
    1946.   Tricky don coyote. Outdoorsman 88 (6): 34-36, illus.; 23. Whole No. 523.
        (Used on coyote-antelope relationship.)

Chittenden, Hiram Martin
    1935.   The American fur trade of the far west. The Press of the Pioneers, Inc., New York, 2: 819-820.

Clarke, C. H. D.
    1940.   A biological investigation of the Thelon Game Sanctuary with remarks on the natural history of the interior barren lands. Natl. Mus. Canada Bull. 96: 35, Biol. Ser. No. 25.
        (Occurrence of coyote at Timber Bay, Artillery Lake by an Indian. In 1937 one was taken at timber edge inland from Eskimo Point. R.C.M.P. recorded it in 1928 on Anderson River.)

Clarke, Frank C.
    1940.   Facts about, and experiences with coyotes. National Wool Grower 30 (5): 19. May.

Clarke, Tom E.
    1947.   When he lays his ears back, look out! Alaska Sportsman 13 (6): 14-17, 25-32, illus.; 15-16.
        (Coyote's taste for flesh of young moose on Kenai Peninsula, and the illegal use of such meat as coyote bait in trapping.)

Clemens, Samuel L. (Mark Twain)
    1872.   Roughing it. American Publishing Co., Hartford. Pp. 48-49, 51-52.
        (Mark Twain calls the coyote the "breathing allegory of want," and mentions its cooperation with food hunting (carrion) Indians and the desert buzzards.)

Cobb, M. S.
    1911.   Coyote hunt. Overland 57: 380-383. April.

Coke, Henry J.
    1852.   A ride over the Rocky Mountains to Oregon and California. Pp. 99-294. London.
        (Covers mammals from deer to prairie dogs, including coyotes.)

Colahan, Ellwood
1946. Coyotes from the air. Field & Stream 50 (9): 42-43, illus. January.

Collier, Eric
1947. Let us face the facts about predators. Cariboo and Northern British Columbia Digest 3 (3): 20-21, 86-89. Cariboo Digest Ltd., Quesnel, British Columbia.

Comeau, Napoleon A.
1909. Life and sport on the north shore of the Loser St. Lawrence and Gulf. 440 pp. Quebec.

Comstock, Theo. B.
1874. The Yellowstone National Park. Amer. Nat. 8: 65-79, 155-166; 75.
(One of the earliest pleas for protection of predatory animals in a national park, including the coyote.)

Condon, David de L.
1950. An uncanny record in the snow. Yellowstone Nature Notes 24 (1): 1-2. February. Mimeographed.

Conference, National Conservation Policy
1944. Sponsored by Amer. Wildlife Institute, Izaak Walton League of America. National Audubon Society, National Wildlife Federation, Washington, D. C., January 18, 19, 20. Pp. 1-107; 27.

Cook, Dave
1946. Concerning predators. Audubon Magazine 48 (3): 130-136, illus., by Walter J. Schoonmaker. May-June.
(Place of the predator, such as the coyote in nature's biological balance.)

Cooper, J. G., G. Suckley, and G. Gibbs
1860. The natural history of Washington Territory, with much relating to Minnesota, Nebraska, Kansas, Oregon, and California . . . 1853-1857, 3 pts. in 1 vol. Pac. R. R. Repts., Vol. 12, Book 2, 399 pp.

Cope, E. D.
1889. The Silver Lake of Oregon. American Nat. 23 (275): 970-982; 980.
(On occurrence of *C. latrans* in *Equus* beds of Silver Lake.)

Cosgrove, H. S., and C. B.
1932. The Swarts Ruin, a typical Mimbres site in southwestern New Mexico. Papers of the Peabody Museum, Harvard Univ., Vol. 20, No. 1, Pl. 218c.

Cottam, Clarence
1942. Coyote without external ears. Journ. Mammal. 23 (4): 450. November.
1945a. Research problems on the United States National Wildlife Refuges. Trans. 10th North Amer. Wildlife Conference, pp. 347-353; 350.
(Drift of coyotes to other areas, and become an economic liability problem is to determine this for facts.)
1945b. Speed and endurance of the coyote. Journ. Mammal. 26 (1): 94. February.
(In a 2-mile chase, last 0.6 mile coyote ran 35 mi. per hr.)

Couch, Leo K.
1928. Relationship of predatory animals and birds of prey to rodent life. Journ. Mammal. 9 (1): 73.

1932. River swimming coyotes. The Murrelet 13 (1): 24-25. January.

Coues, Elliott

1873. The prairie wolf or coyote, *Canis latrans.* Amer. Nat. 7 (7): 384-389. Salem, Mass.

1893. History of the Expedition under command of Lewis and Clark. 4 vols. Vol. 1, p. 297; Vol. 3, p. 846.
(20 or 25 miles west from Chelsea in Montana on the Missouri River reported on May 5, 1805 very plentiful. Vol. 3 discusses general range, description, habits.)

Coues, Elliott, and H. C. Yarrow

1873. Report upon the collection of mammals made in portions of Nevada, Utah, California, Colorado, New Mexico, and Arizona, during the years 1871, 1872, 1873, and 1874. Geogr. and Geol. Explor. and Surveys west of 100th Mer., pp. 44-45.
(Coyotes reported common from Fort Riley, Kansas to the Pacific.)

Cowan, Ian McTaggart

1939. The vertebrate fauna of the Peace River District of British Columbia. Occas. Pap. British Columbia Prov. Mus. No. 1, pp. 1-102, Illus.; 76.
(Found coyotes rare, apparently from overtrapping.)

1947. The timber wolf in the Rocky Mountain National Parks of Canada. Canad. Jour. Research (Sec. D) 25: 139-174, illus.; 157. October.
(Enmity between wolves and coyotes and coyotes as carrion eaters from wolf kills.)

1948. The occurrence of the granular tapeworm *Echinococcus granulosus* in wild game in North America. Jour. Wildlife Manag. 12 (1): 105-106; 105. January.

Cox, Ross

1831. Adventures on the Columbia River 1811-17. 2 vols., p. 228. London.
(Observations on coyotes from The Dalles, Oreg., to Spokane, Wash., 1811-1817.)

Coyner, David H.

1847. The lost trappers; a collection of interesting scenes and events in the Rocky Mountains, etc. Pp. xv + 255; 38. Hurst & Co., N. Y.
(States Indian dogs seem to be wolves of the smaller kind [coyotes].)

Crabb, E. D.

1925. The weight of an adult coyote. Okla. Acad. Sci. Proc. 4: 43.

Cram, E. B.

1926. Wild carnivores as hosts of the trematode previously found in dogs as the result of salmon poisoning. North Amer. Vet. 7 (7): 42-43.

Criddle, Norman

1925. The habits and economic importance of wolves in Canada. Canada Dept. Agr. Bull. 13 (n. s.): 13-16, illus.

Criddle, Norman E., and Stuart Criddle

1923. The coyote in Manitoba. Canadian Field-Naturalist 37 (3): 40-45.

Crider, Homer H.
  1948.   A coyote and wildcat episode. Yosemite Nature Notes 27 (3):
           59. March. Yosemite Nat. Hist. Assoc.
                (". . . two wildcats and two coyotes stalked one another for
           about forty minutes. The outcome was a draw.")
Cross, E. C.
  1937.   Wolf! Wolf. (Has Ontario just wasted money in paying wolf
           bounty? Yes, says this biologist. Here is food for thought for
           every conservationist—and for action!) Rod & Gun in Canada
           38 (8): 18-19, 32-33, illus. January.
                (This discusses wolves and coyotes, and the spread of the latter
           in this province.)
Cunningham, Albert Benjamin
  1925.   The prowler. DeMolay Councilor 3 (12): 11-12, 21, 23, 26-27,
           illus. January.
Cunningham, T. H.
  1948.   Mutiny on the bounty system. Hunting & Fishing 25 (1): 8,
           32. January.
Dall, W. H.
  1870.   Alaska and its resources. 628 pp. Boston.
Dalquest, Walter W.
  1948.   Mammals of Washington. Univ. Kans. Publ., Mus. Nat. Hist. 2:
           1-444, illus.; 226-231. April 9.
                (Canis latrans lestes,—"entire state except for northeastern
           Washington," Canis latrans incolatus, northeastern Wash.)
Darden, J. J.
  1950.   Coyote hunting from the air. Oklahoma Game and Fish News
           6 (3): 8. March.
Darling, Jay N.
  1934.   Report of Chief of Biological Survey, U. S. Dept. Agri. Pp. 1-32;
           30-31.
                (Increase of antelope in Nevada, Oregon and California by re-
           duction of coyotes.)
Davidson, R. P.
  1938.   Coyote menace. Natl. Wool Grower 28: 42-43. December.
  1939.   Coyotes or wildlife. Natl. Wool Grower 29: 28. September.
Davis, John J.
  1919.   Contributions to a knowledge of the natural enemies of Phyl-
           lophaga. Illinois State Nat. Hist. Survey Bull. 13: 53-136; 127-
           133, pls. 3-15. February.
                (Coyote among other mammals listed as enemy of the white
           grub.)
Davis, Ruth P.
  1945.   Dermacentor variabilis, the infection of ticks with Pasteurella
           tularensis. Journ. Infectious Diseases 76: 83. Univ. Chicago
           Press, Chicago. Ill.
Davis, William B.
  1939.   The recent mammals of Idaho. Pp. 1-400; 145. April 5. Caxton
           Printers, Caldwell, Idaho.
Day, A. M.
  1932.   Handbook for hunters of predatory animals. U. S. Dept. Agr.,
           Bur. Biol. Survey, 52 pp., illus.

1934.　Predator trap device safeguards species that are harmless. U. S. Dept. Agr. Yearbook for year 1934: 299-300 illus.

1935.　The case against the coyote. Outdoor Life 75 (5): 26-27, 90, illus.

Day, Albert M., and J. E. Shillinger

1935.　Predators and rodents are factors in the spread of disease. U. S. Dept. Agr. Yearbook 1935: 284-286.

Dearborn, Ned

1919.　Trapping on the farm. U. S. Dept. Agr. Yearbook 1919: 451-484, illus.

1920.　Maintenance of the fur supply. U. S. Dept. Agr. Circ. 135: 1-12, illus.; 5, 8.

1932.　Foods of some predatory fur-bearing animals of Michigan. School of Forestry and Conservation, Bull. No. 1, pp. 1-52. Univ. Michigan.

　　　　(Cover, food on opossum, raccoon, red fox, coyote, wild cat, mink, New York weasel, skunk, badger.)

DeHuff, Elizabeth Willis

1938a.　Coyote the sly trickster. Coyote Wisdom. Pp. 127-131. Texas Folk-Lore Society, Austin, Tex.

1938b.　The coyote's moon-child. Coyote Wisdom. Pp. 120-121. Texas Folk-Lore Society, Austin, Tex.

Denyse, T.

1919.　The bobcat and coyote as game destroyers. Outdoor Life 44: 375.

Dice, Lee R.

1919.　The mammals of southeastern Washington. Journ. Mammal. 1 (1): 10-21; 11-12. November.

1925.　The scientific value of predatory mammals. Journ. Mammal. 6 (1): 25-27.

1938.　Poison and ecology. Bird-Lore 40: 12-17.

　　　　(Control of mammals based on more ecological understanding of part mammals play in whole biological set-up.)

1942.　A family of dog-coyote hybrids. Journ. Mammal. 23 (2): 186-192, illus. May.

Dice, Lee R., and Philip M. Blossom

1937.　Studies of mammalian ecology in southwestern North America with special attention to the colors of desert animals. Carnegie Institution of Washington, Pub. No. 485: iv + 125, illus.; 19-20.

　　　　(Partial coyote distribution records.)

Dice, Lee R., and H. B. Sherman

1922.　Notes on the mammals of Gogebic and Ontonagon Counties, Michigan 1920. Occas. Papers Mus. Zool. No. 109: 1-40, illus.; 27. Univ. Mich., Ann Arbor.

　　　　(Coyote reported as numerous in region at north end of Lake Gogebic within past few years.)

Dixon, Joseph

1916.　The timber wolf in California. Calif. Fish & Game 2 (3): 125-128. July.

1920.　Control of the coyote in California. Calif. Agr. Exper. Sta. Bull. 320: 379-397.

1925.　Food predilections of predatory and fur-bearing mammals. Journ. Mammal. 6 (1): 34-46, illus.

1928a.　Doe pursues coyote. Yosemite Nat. Notes 7 (10): 86.

1928b. A coyote from Mount McKinley, Alaska. Journ. Mammal. 9 (1): 64. February.

1934. A study of the life history and food habits of mule deer in California. Reprint. Calif. Fish & Game 20 (3-4): 1-146, illus.; 7, 37, 49, 50, 52, 62, 97. July and October. San Francisco, Calif.

1938. Fauna of the National Parks of the United States. U. S. Dept. Int., Natl. Park Service Fauna Ser. No. 3: 163, illus.
(On the invasion of Mount McKinley Park, Alaska by the coyote, an exotic species here.)

Dobie, J. Frank
1945. Strange animal friendships. S. Dak. Conserv. Digest 12 (2): 2-3, 15.
(Affection shown by a nursing dog for coyote pup.)

1947. Fabulous little plains dweller. Western Sportsman 7 (11): 8. July-August.
(Coyote technique in catching prairie dogs.)

1948a. Coyote curiosity. Western Sportsman 8 (4): 16, 21. May-June.

1948b. Wild cunning. Western Sportsman 9 (1): 15, 18. November-December.
(Some fine notes on natural history of the coyote.)

Dobie, J. Frank
1949. The voice of the coyote. Pp. xx + 386, illus. April. Little, Brown & Co., Boston.
(Coyote life history, economics, and folk-lore.)

Dodge, Richard Irving
1877. The plains of the great west and their inhabitants. Pp. iv + 448, illus.; 209. G. P. Putnam's Sons, N. Y.

Donahue, Ralph J.
1936. Coyote. Literary Digest 122: 27. December 19.

Donham, C. R., and B. T. Simms
1927. Coyote susceptible to salmon poisoning. Jour. Amer. Vet. Med. Assn. 71: 215-217.

Donne, Joseph
1945. Coursing Kansas coyotes. Field & Stream 49 (12): 121-124, illus. April.

Dorf, R. H.
1947. The King Ranch solves the game problem. Texas Game & Fish 6 (1): 8, 23-24. December.
(Coyote main offender as predator on King Ranch.)

Douglas, Donald W., and A. M. Stebler
1946. Bounties don't work out as they are supposed to. Mich. Conservation 15 (2): 6-7, 10. February. Lansing, Mich.

Douglas, Walter B.
1911. Manuel Lisa. Missouri Hist. Soc. Coll. 3 (3): 233-268, 3 pls.; (4): 367-406, 6 pls.

Dragatt, F. M.
1926. Loss of deer by coyote. Outdoor Life 57: 143. February.

Dufresne, Frank
1940. First annual report of Alaska Game Commission to Secretary of Interior, July 1, 1939 to June 30, 1940, p. 11.

1942. Mammals and birds of Alaska. U. S. Dept. Int., Fish and Wildlife Service Circ. 3: 1-36, illus.; 26-27.

1946. Alaska's animals and fishes. Illustrated by Bob Hines. Pp. i-xvii, 1-297, illus.; 84-86. New York.

Duges, Alfredo
    1870.   Catalogo de animales vertebrados observados en la Republica
             Mexicana. La Naturaleza, Mexico 1: 137.
Dunn, Harry H.
    1907.   Hunting coyotes in Death Valley. Forest & Stream 69 (5): 172.
             August 3.
Dupuy, Frederick J.
    1924.   Coyote hunting in Alberta. Canad. Forest & Outdoors 20 (3):
             195-196.
             (Coursing coyotes with hounds.)
E. ———
    1896.   Coyotes catch cats. Forest & Stream 47 (16): 303. October 17.
             (Observation on coyotes consistently killing domestic house
             cats on a ranch near Shirley Basin, Wyo.)
Eads, Richard B.
    1948.   Ectoparasites from a series of Texas coyotes. Jour. Mammal.
             29 (3): 268-271. September 2.
Eakins, Wallace T.
    1924.   Shall we control rabies in New Jersey? Pub. Health News 9
             (6): 163-174. May. Dept. of Health, State of New Jersey.
Egbert, G. L.
    1939.   The coyote and his bad name. Michigan Conservation 8 (7): 5.
Einarsen, Arthur S.
    1948.   The pronghorn antelope and its management. Wildlife Man-
             agement Inst., Washington, D. C., 238 pp.; 75-79, 80.
             (Coyotes, uncontrolled, may be a series factor in limiting
             antelope kid crops.)
Elley, W. B.
    1945a.   What makes a bad coyote bad. South Dakota Conservation
             Digest 12 (3): 16. March. Pierre, S. Dak.
    1945b.   Coyote pup hunting. South Dakota Conservation Digest 12 (5):
             13, 16. May. Pierre, S. Dak.
Elliot, D. G.
    1903.   A list of mammals collected by Edmund Heller, in the San
             Pedro Martir and Hanson Laguna Mountains and the ac-
             companying Coast Regions of Lower California. Field Columbian
             Mus. Pub. No. 79, Zool. Ser. 3, pp. 199-232. June.
             (Canis clepticus described, p. 225.)
    1904.   The land and sea mammals of Middle America and the West
             Indies. Field Columbian Mus. Zool. Ser. Pub. 95 (vol. 4,
             pts. 1-2): 464-470, illus. August 2. Chicago.
    1905.   A check list of mammals of the North American continent, the
             West Indies, and the neighboring seas. Field Columbian Mus.
             Pub. 105, Zool. Ser. 6, 761 pp.
Elwell, Niska
    1946.   Curious coyote casualties. Fur-Fish-Game 83 (5): 14-15, illus.
             May.
Errington, Paul L.
    1946.   Predation and vertebrate populations. Quart. Rev. Biol. 21 (2):
             144-177; 158. June.
    1947.   A question of values. Jour. Wildlife Manag. 11 (3): 267-272;
             271. July.

Eschscholtz, Friedrich
  1829. Zoologischer Atlas, enhaltend Abbildungen und Beschreibungen neuer Thierarten, wahrend des Flottcaptains v. Kotzebue zweiter Reise um die Welt Drittes Heft, Tafel xi, pp. 1-2.
Evans, Herbert McLean, and Harold H. Cole
  1931. An introduction to the study of the oestrous cycle in the dog. Memoirs Univ. Calif. 9 (2): 65-103, pls. 12-18. December 19. Berkeley, Calif.
Evarts, Hal. G.
  1923. The spread of the coyote. Saturday Evening Post 196 (24): 44. December 15.
Evermann, B. W., and H. W. Clark
  1911. Notes on the mammals of the Lake Maxinkuckee region. Proc. Wash. Acad. Sci. 13 (1): 1-34.
Faile, Edward G.
  1920. Wolf, fox, or dog. Field & Stream 25 (4): 401. August.
Farley, Frank L.
  1925. Changes in the status of certain animals and birds during the past fifty years in central Alberta. Canad. Field Nat. 39 (9): 201-202. December.
Fauley, C. C.
  1937. Alert mother. Glacial Drift 10 (4): 36. October. National Park Service.
        (Observation on a female coyote in defense of her young until they were safely away from harm.)
Fenton, D. W.
  1899. Coyote hunt. Outing 33: 572-575. March.
Ferrero, Lee
  1944. Anchored poison guns kill coyotes. South Dakota Conservation Digest 11 (10): 6, 13, illus. October.
Fichter, Edson
  1950. Watching coyotes. Journ. Mamm. 31 (1): 66-73. February 25.
        (Coyote feeding habits in relation to pheasant populations.)
Finley, I.
  1927. Wild dog of the desert. Mentor 12: 28-29. August.
Finley, W. L., and I. Finley
  1925. Coyote, the prairie wolf. Nat. Mag. 5 (4): 223-227, illus.
  1930. Skeezix, a white coyote. Nat. Mag. 15: 227-229. April.
Fisher, A. K.
  1909. The economic value of predaceous birds and mammals. U. S. Dept. Agr. Yearbook 1908: 187-194, 3 pls.
  1919. Predatory animals and injurious rodents. The Producer 1 (3): 7-11, illus. Denver, Colo.
Fisher, Edna M.
  1934. Early fauna of the Monterey region, California. Jour. Mammal. 15 (3): 253. August.
        Coyote remains, C. ochropus ochropus, among shell mound deposits.)
Fisher, J. C.
  1851. [Observations on paper by S. W. Woodhouse on "The North American jackal—Canis frustror]. Proc. Acad. Nat. Sci. Philadelphia, 1850-1851 5: 147-148. June 30.

Fitch, Henry S.
  1947.   Ecology of a cottontail rabbit (*Sylvilagus auduboni*) population
          in central California. Calif. Fish & Game 33 (3): 159-184,
          illus.; 174. July.
          (An analysis of coyote food based on 1,173 scats shows cotton-
          tail rabbit leads by 45.4 per cent.)
  1948.   A study of coyote relationships on cattle range. Jour. Wildlife
          Manag. 12 (1): 73-78. January.
Fitch, Henry S., and Ben Glading
  1947.   A field study of a rattlesnake population. Calif. Fish & Game
          33 (2): 102-123, illus.; 120.
          (Rattlesnake as food of the coyote.)
Fitzgerald, O. A.
  1944.   Every hand against him. Country Gentleman 114 (2): 17, 58-59.
          February.
Flick, Chuck
  1913.   The weight of wild animals. Outdoor Life 31 (5): 425-427. May.
Flower, Stanley S.
  1931.   Contributions to our knowledge of the duration of life in
          vertebrate animals. Proc. Zool. Soc. London, pt. 1, pp. 172-173.
          March 3.
          (On longevity of coyote in captivity in zoos, London, and
          Washington, D. C.)
Fox, Herbert
  1923.   Diseases in captive wild animals and birds. 665 pp. J. B. Lippin-
          cott Co., Philadelphia.
Frantzius, A. V.
  1892.   Los mamiferos de Costa Rica. Contribucion al conocimiento de
          la extension geografica de los mamiferos de America [pp. 60-
          142], pp. 96-97. [In Barrantes, Francisco Montero. Geografia
          de Costa Rica, Comision de Babierno de la Republica para los
          Exposiciones Historica-Americana de Madrid y Universal de
          Chicago, Barcelona, pp. vii + 350, illus., 1 map.]
Frye, O. Earl, and Daniel W. Lay
  1943.   Fur resources and fur animals of Texas. Game, Fish & Oyster
          Comm. Bull. No. 25, pp. 1-42, illus.; 31-32. Austin, Texas.
Gabrielson, Ira N.
  1921.   Notes on the mammals observed in Marshall County, Iowa.
          Proc. Iowa Acad. Sci. 28: 147-149.
          (*Canis latrans latrans*, p. 148, occasional.)
  1935a. The antelope situation. American Game 24 (4): 54, 59, illus.
          July-August.
  1935b. Must the antelope go? American Forests 41 (10): 575-576,
          illus. October.
  1937.   Recent methods in coyote control. National Wool Grower 27:
          19-20. March.
  1941a. Wildlife conservation. 250 pp., illus. Macmillan Co., New York.
  1941b. In annual report, Sec'y of the Interior, Section on U. S. Fish
          and Wildlife Service. P. 386.
Gander, Frank F.
  1928.   Period of gestation in some American mammals. Journ. Mammal.
          9 (1): 75. February.
          (Records gestation period of *C. ochropus* as 65 days from
          last date of mating Jan. 26 to 29 inclusive.)

Garlough, F. E., and Justus C. Ward
  1932.   Possibilities of secondary poisoning of birds and mammals.
          Science 75 (1943): 335-337. March 25.
          (Discusses in part the effect of such poisoning on coyote.
          Poisons, effects of, etc.)
Garrison, L.
  1937.   Coyote appetites. Yosemite Nature Notes 16 (3): 19.
Gass, Patrick
  1808.   Journal of the travels of a corps of discovery under Captain
          Lewis and Captain Clark to the Pacific Ocean, in the years
          1804, 1805, and 1806. P. 56. London.
Gerstell, Richard
  1937.   The Pennsylvania bounty system. Pa. Game Comm. Research
          Bull. 1: 3. Harrisburg, Pa.
Gianini, C. A.
  1935.   Cougar and coyote. Journ. Mammal. 16 (3): 229.
Gidley, James William
  1914.   Preliminary report on a recently discovered Pleistocene Cave
          deposit near Cumberland, Maryland. Proc. U. S. Nat. Mus.
          46 (2014): 93-102, illus.
Gidley, James William, and C. Lewis Gazin
  1938.   The Pleistocene vertebrate fauna from Cumberland Cave,
          Maryland. U. S. Natl. Mus. Bull. 171: 1-99, illus.; 15-23.
Gilbert, Paul T.
  1945.   The coyote. Outdoor Nebraska 22 (4). Lincoln, Nebr.
          (A poem to the coyote on back of cover following p. 23.)
Gilfillan, Archer B.
  1929.   Sheep. Pp. 181-196. Little, Brown & Co., Boston.
Gilham, Chas. E.
  1945.   Memories of the Arizona game country as I knew it. Arizona
          Wildlife and Sportsman 6 (10): 5, 20. August. Tucson.
          (Comments on abundance of coyotes in 1924.)
Gilmore, Raymond M.
  1946.   Mammals in archeological collections from southwestern Penn-
          sylvania. Journ. Mammal. 27 (3): 227-234; 233. August 14.
  1947.   Report on a collection of mammal bones from archeologic cave-
          sites in Coahuila, Mexico. Journ. Mammal. 28 (2): 147-165;
          156. May.
Glading, Ben
  1938.   Studies on the nesting cycle of the California valley quail in
          1937. Calif. Fish & Game 24 (4): 318-340; 338.
          (Destruction of quail nests San Joaquin Exp. Range, 25 miles
          east of Madera, Madera County, Calif. Nests roughly destroyed
          and small bits of well-chewed eggs scattered about.)
Glading, Ben, David M. Selleck and Fred T. Ross
  1945.   Valley quail under private management at the Dune Lakes Club.
          Calif. Fish & Game 31 (4): 167-183, illus.; 178-179. October.
          San Francisco, Calif.
          (The coyote as a depredator on valley quail.)
Glazier, Willard
  1900.   Ocean to ocean on horseback. Pp. 433, 434. Edgewood Pub.
          Co., Philadelphia.

Gleeson, J. M.
  1904. Coyotes at home and in captivity. St. Nicholas 31: **606-607**. May.
Godfrey, W. C.
  1929. The coyote. Yosemite Nature Notes 8 (3): 33-34.
Goldman, E. A.
  1925. The predatory mammal problem and the balance of nature. Journ. Mammal. 6 (1): 28-33. February.
  1930. The coyote—archpredator. Journ. Mammal. 11 (3): 325-335. August.
  1932a. Management of our deer herds. Trans. 19th American Game Conference, November 28, 29, 30, New York City, N. Y. Pp. 49-61.
      (Contains comments re coyote depredations on Kaibab Arizona deer herd during 1920's.)
  1932b. The control of injurious mammals. Science (n.s.) 75 (1942): 309-311.
  1936. A new coyote from Honduras. Journ. Wash. Acad. Sci. 26 (1): 32-34. January 15.
Goodwin, E. D.
  1936. A glimpse of a mountain coyote. Yosemite Nature Notes 15 (2): 11-12.
Goodwin, George G.
  1942. Mammals of Honduras. Amer. Mus. Nat. Hist. Bull. 79 (Art. 2): 107-195; 183. May 29. New York.
      (Honduras coyote (*C. hondurensis*) known to frequent open savannas or semi-forested areas, subject to long dry season, along the Pacific coast as far south as Costa Rica. Records specimen from La Cueva Archago.)
  1946. Mammals of Costa Rica. Amer. Mus. Nat. Hist. Bull. 87 (Art. 5): 271-474, illus.; 438-439. New York.
Gorsuch, David
  1934. Life history of the Gambel quail in Arizona. Ariz. Univ. Bull. 5 (4) (Biol. Sci. Bull. 2): 1-89, illus.; 65, 66.
      (Findings show no appreciable effect of coyote on these game (birds out of 12 stomachs examined.)
Gourley, Lew L.
  1945. Hunting wolves [coyotes] with an airplane. Fur-Fish-Game, Harding's Mag. 79 (11): 12-13, illus. November.
  1946. Coyotes from the air. Field and Stream 50 (9): 42-43, illus. January.
      (Pictorial showing hunting of coyotes from airplane in Nevada.)
Graham, Edward H.
  1944. Natural principles of land use. Pp. xiii+274, illus.; 27, 53, 58, 131, 148, 149, 152, 213. Oxford University Press, London, New York, Toronto.
Grater, Russell K.
  1943. Coyote foods near Boulder Dam. Journ. Wildlife Management 7 (4): 422-423. October.
Graves, Henry S., and E. W. Nelson
  1919. Our national elk herds. U. S. Dept. Agr. Circ. 51: 1-34, illus.; 17.
Green, Dorr D.
  1947. Albino coyotes are rare. Journ. Mammal. 28 (1): 63. February.

Greene, Edward Lee
 1880. Botanizing on the Colorado Desert. American Naturalist 14: 787-793; 792.
  (On how Coyote Wells received its name.)
Greenwood, Charles
 1897. Coyotes also dope. Recreation 7 (3): 233. September.
Gregory, Tappan
 1936. Mammals of the Chicago region. Chicago Acad. Sci. Program Activities 7 (2-3): 46. July.
 1939. Eyes in the night. 243 pp. illus. New York. (Foxes and coyotes.)
Griffith, R. A.
 1917. The invasion of the north by coyotes. Outdoor Life 39 (5): 545. May.
Grimm, Rudolph L.
 1931. A coyote commuter. Yellowstone Nature Notes 8 (4): 30. April.
  (An interesting observation on a three-legged coyote stalking ducks, and his travels on a run approximating 60 miles.)
 1940. Trout and crayfish eaten by coyotes. Journ. Mammal. 21 (4): 458-459.
G[rinnell], G. B.
 1896. About wolves and coyotes. Forest and Stream 47 (26): 511-512. December 26.
Grinnell, George Bird
 1897. A coyote partnership. Forest and Stream 48 (6): 104. February 6.
 1904. American big game in its haunts. A book of the Boone & Crockett Club, pp. 1-497; 287. New York.
 1914. The wolf hunters. 303 pp. New York.
 1929. Eagles' prey. Journ. Mammal. 10 (1): 83. February.
  (Account of an eagle attacking a coyote in Montana mouth of Hausman Creek, St. Mary's River. Coyote was killed.)
Grinnell, Joseph
 1914. An account of the mammals and birds of the lower Colorado Valley with especial reference to the distributional problems presented. Univ. Calif. Publ. Zool. 12 (4): 51-294; 254. March 20.
  (An occurrence of C. l. estor along Colorado Valley. Gives weight of 3 adult males at 16, 18, and 21 pounds, and 2 females at 18 and 20 pounds.)
 1923. A systematic list of the mammals of California. Univ. Calif. Pub. Zool. 21 (10): 313-324; 315. January 27.
 1925. A conservationist's creed as to wildlife administration. Science, n.s. 62: 437-438.
 1937. Desert coyote. Calif. Acad. Sci. Proc. (ser. 4) 23 (9): 132. Aug. 7.
  (Re occurrence of coyote C. l. estor in Death Valley quite common.)
Grinnell, Joseph, and Joseph Dixon
 1918. California ground squirrels. Calif. State Comm. Hort. Bull. 7: 597-708. November-December.
  (Coyote-rodent relationship.)

Grinnell, Joseph, Joseph S. Dixon, and Jean M. Linsdale
1937.   Fur-bearing mammals of California, their natural history, systematic status, and relations to man. 2 vols. Vol. 2, pp. 472-525, illus. Univ. Calif. Press, Berkeley.
(Discusses mountain (*C. l. lestes*), valley (*C. l. ochropus*), and desert coyote (*C. l. estor*) recognized as occurring in California. A comprehensive account of these three races.)

Griswold, Gordon
1943.   Subsidizing coyote fur production. National Wool Grower 33 (11): 17-18. November.

Guberlet, John E.
1930.   Notes on relationships of parasitic flatworms to birds and mammals. The Murrelet 11 (1): 15-17. January.
(The cause of salmon poisoning in dogs.)

Gubser, H. H.
1931.   Report to the Governor of Alaska on cooperative predatory animal investigations and control in the territory for the period March 1, 1929, to February 28, 1931. Pp. 1-20, illus. March 1. Juneau, Alaska.
1936.   Suggestions on trapping coyotes and wolves in Alaska. U. S. Dept. Agri., Bur. Biol. Survey BS-62, 6 pp. (mimeographed).

Gunn, C. K.
1932a.   Color and primeness in variable mammals. Amer. Nat. 66: 546-559.
1932b.   Phenomena of primeness. Canad. Journ. Res. 6 (4): 387-397.

Gustafson, A. F., H. Ries, C. H. Guise, and W. J. Hamilton, Jr.
1944.   Conservation in the United States. Pp. 1-445, illus. 2nd Ed. revised. Comstock Pub. Co., Inc., Ithaca, N. Y.

Hagan, William A., et al.
1947.   The relation of diseases in the lower animals to human welfare. New York Acad. Sci. 226 pp., illus. New York.

Hahn, Walter L.
1907.   Mammals of Kankakee Valley. Proc. U. S. Nat. Mus. 32: 462. June 15.
(On extension of coyote's range in northern Indiana.)
1909.   The mammals of Indiana. 33rd Annual Rept. Ind. Dept. Geol. & Nat. Res., Indianapolis. Pp. 417-663, illus.; 561-565.

Hale, James B.
1950.   Is it coyote or dog? Wisconsin Conserv. Bull. 15 (7): 16-17. July.

Hall, E. Raymond
1927.   The deer of California. Calif. Fish and Game 13: 233-259, illus.; 248.
1931.   The coyote and his control. Calif. Fish and Game 17: 283-289, illus.
1934a.   The coyote and his control. Outdoor Life 73 (4): 30-32, illus.
1934b.   Mammals collected by T. T. and E. B. McCabe in the Bowron Lake Region of British Columbia. Univ. Calif. Pub. Zool. 40 (9): 363-386; 369-370.
(Description of new subspecies of coyote, *Canis latrans incolatus*, from Isaac Lake 3,000 ft. alt.)
1940.   A curious mutation in a coyote from Kern County, California. Calif. Fish and Game 26 (4): 394, illus. October.

1942. Fur bearers and the war. Trans. 7th North Amer. Wildlife Conference, Amer. Wildlife Institute, Washington, D. C., pp. 472-480.

1943. Cranial characters of a dog-coyote hybrid. Amer. Midland Nat. 29 (2): 371-374, illus. March.

1946. Mammals of Nevada. Contrib. Museum of Vertebrate Zool., Univ. Calif., Berkeley. Pp. xi + 710, illus.; 242-266. July 1. Univ. Calif. Press, Los Angeles and Berkeley.

Hall, F. S.
1930. The story of "Skeezix" an albino coyote. The Murrelet 11 (2): 16. May.

Hall, James
1838. Notes on the Western States. Pp. 113-114, 115, 119. Philadelphia.
1848. The West; its soil, surface, and production. Pp. 114, 119. Cincinnati.

Hall, Maurice C.
1911. The coyote as a host of *Multiceps multiceps*. Science, n.s. 33 (860): 975. June 23.

1912. A second case of *Multiceps multiceps* in the coyote. Science n.s. 35 (901): 556. April 5.

1914. A new nematode, *Rictularia splendida,* from the coyote, with notes on other coyote parasites. U. S. Nat. Mus. Proc. 46 (2012): 73-84, 6 figs. Octavo. Washington.

1920. The adult taenoid cestodes of dogs and cats, and of related carnivores in North America. U. S. Nat. Mus. Proc. 55 (2258): 1-94, illus.; 79.

1931. Parasite control in wild animals. Outdoor America 9 (12): 16-17, 46. July.
    (The coyote as a carrier of tapeworm that causes cysticerosis in deer.)

Halliday, Hugh
1948. Doe protects fallen deer by fighting three coyotes. Toronto Daily Star, Toronto, Ontario. P. 3. April 14.

Halloran, Arthur F.
1946. The carnivores of the San Andres Mountains, New Mexico. Jour. Mammal. 27 (2): 154-161; 158-159. May.
    (An occurrence of coyote and depredations and disturbances on Rocky Mountain sheep.)

Hamilton, W. J., Jr.
1939. American mammals; their lives, habits, and economic relations. 434 pp., illus. McGraw-Hill Book Co., Inc., New York and London.

1943. The mammals of eastern United States. An account of recent land mammals east of the Mississippi. Pp. 1-432, illus.; 178-182. Comstock Pub. Co., Inc.; Ithaca, N. Y.
    (On distribution and habits of coyote east of Mississippi River.)

1946. The bounty system doesn't work. Animal Kingdom (N. Y. Zool. Soc.) 49 (4): 130-138. August.
    (Gives reasons why bounties are not effective.)

1947. The bounty system. New York State Conservationist 2 (1): 4-5, illus. August-September.

Hamlett, G. W. D.
1938. The reproductive cycle of the coyote. U. S. Dept. Agr. Tech. Bull. 616: 1-11, illus.

Handlan, John W.
1946. Hunter slays Monroe "Wolf." West Virginia Conservation 10 (8): 13, 23, illus. December. (On probable occurrence of the coyote in Monroe County, West Virginia, on Peters Mountain.)

Handley, Charles O., Jr.
1950. Game mammals of Guatemala. U. S. Dept. Interior, Fish and Wildlife Service, Sp. Sci. Rept.: Wildlife No. 5, pp. 141-162. June.

Handley, Charles O., Jr. and Clyde P. Patton
1947. Wild mammals of Virginia. Pp vi + 220, illus.; 94, 126, 140. Richmond, Va.

Hankin, Dan
1945. Arizona united predator control. Arizona Wildlife and Sportsman 6 (6): 14. April. Tucson.

Harding, A. R.
1909. Wolf and coyote trapping. Pp. 1-252, illus. A. R. Harding Pub. Co., Columbus, Ohio.
1923. Wolves—timber and prairie. Outdoor Life 51 (1): 52. January.

Hardy, Ross
1947. Animals are a resource too. Utah Educational Review. March issue.

Harlan, James R.
1950. Wolf or coyote? Iowa Conservationist 9 (2): 11. February 15.

Harper, Francis
1932. Mammals of the Athabaska and Great Slave Lakes Region. Journ. Mammal. 13 (1): 19-36, illus.; 25-26. February. (Reported in 1914 as very common in vicinity of Chipewyan— C. latrans.)

Harrington, J. P., and Helen H. Roberts
1925-1926. Picuris children's tales with texts and songs. Ann. Rept., Bur. Amer Ethn., Smithsn. Inst. 43: 289-447.

Harris, Leo D.
1945. Captures rare specimen of coyote. North Dakota Outdoors 8 (6): 5-6, illus. December. Grand Forks, N. Dak. (Re capture of pure albino coyote in Killdeer Mountains, N. Dak.)

Harris, Wm. P., Jr.
1929. The book of Huron Mountain. P. 202. Pub. by Huron Mountain Club. (Re coyote as a newcomer in Northern Peninsula of Michigan.)

Hart, John D.
1948. Colorado fur trade, old and new. The Brand Book, official organ of The Westerners State Museum 4 (2): 1-17. February. Denver, Colo.

Hart, Rubin O.
1950. Unexplainable coyote activities. Yellowstone Nature notes 24 (1): 7. February. Mimeographed.

Harte, Bret
1869. Coyote. Overland 3: 93.

Hartman, J. S., and W. L. Thurston
  1940.   Combatting coyotes in the San Juan basin, Colo. Natl. Wool
          Grower 30: 27-28. June.
Hatt, Robert T.
  1938.   Notes concerning mammals collected in Yucatan. Journ. Mammal.
          19 (3): 333-337; 335. August.
          (Possibility of coyote occurring in Yucatan.)
Hawbecker, A. C.
  1939.   Coyotes prey on goats. Journ. Mammal. 20 (3): 371-372.
Hawkins, A. H.
  1907.   Coyote and badger. Ottawa Naturalist 21 (2): 37. May.
Hayden, Ferdinand Vandivar
  1862.   On the ethnography and philology of the Indian tribes of the
          Missouri Valley. Trans. Amer. Philos. Soc., n.s. 12 (pt. 2, art.
          3): 231-461. Philadelphia, Pa.
          (Says wolves on plains would offer a great hindrance to raising
          of sheep.)
  1863.   On the geology and natural history of the Upper Missouri.
          Trans. Amer. Philos. Soc., n.s. 12: 1-218; 141.
Hegner, Robert
  1935.   Parade of the animal kingdom. Pp. vi + 675, illus.; 603-604.
          Macmillan Co., New York.
          (General description of coyote.)
Heintzleman, B. F.
  1936.   Alaska from the Western Range—a great but neglected resource.
          U. S. Dept. Agr., Forest Service, Senate Doc. 199, Sept. 17,
          p. 592.
Heller, Edmund
  1914.   New subspecies of mammals from Equatorial Africa. Smithsn.
          Misc. Coll. 63 (7): 1-12, Pub. 2272. June 24.
          (Includes coyote in genus Thos.)
Heller, Edmund (with C. C. Adams, V. Bailey, J. Dixon, and E. A. Goldman)
  1928a. Report of the Committee on Wild Life Sanctuaries, including pro-
          vision for predatory animals. Jour. Mammal. 9 (4): 354-357.
  1928b. Supplementary report of the Committee on Wild Life Sanctu-
          aries, including provision for predatory mammals. Jour. Mammal.
          9 (4): 357-358.
Henderson, Walter C.
  1930.   The control of the coyote. Jour. Mammal. 11 (3): 336-353,
          illus. August.
Henry, Alexander, and David Thompson
  1897.   New light on the early history of the greater Northwest.
          Manuscript journals of Alexander Henry and of David Thomp-
          son, 1799-1814. 3 vols. Edited by Elliott Coues, New York.
Henshaw, Henry W.
  1908.   The policemen of the air. Nat. Geog. Mag. 19 (2): 79-118,
          illus.; 91-92, 98. February.
          (Re depredations of coyotes, and illustrating denning habitat.)
  1915.   Report of Chief of Bureau of Biological Survey, U. S. Dept.
          Agr., p. 3. August 31.
          (First demonstration on cooperative control of rabid coyotes
          by Federal Government in eastern Oregon and Nevada.)

1916. Report of Chief of Bureau of Biological Survey, U. S. Dept. Agr., pp. 1-2. August 31.
(First establishment of 8 cooperative predatory animal control districts on part of Federal Government. 1. Ariz.-New Mex.; 2. Calif. and Nev.; 3. Oreg. and Wash.; 4. Colo.; 5. Idaho; 6. Montana; 7. Utah; and 8. Wyoming.)

Henshaw, Henry W., and Clarence Birdseye
1911. The mammals of Bitterroot Valley, Montana, in their relation to spotted fever. U. S. Dept. Agr., Bur. Biol. Survey, Circ. No. 82, pp. 1 24, illus.; 5 6. August 3.

Herman, Carlton M.
1949. A new host for the eye worm, *Thelazia californiensis*. Calif. Fish & Game 35 (2): 139.

Herrera, Alfonso L.
1891. Notas acerca de los vertebrados del Valley de Mexico. La Naturaleza, (ser. 2) 1: 299-314, 1888-1890.

Herrick, C. L.
1892. Mammals of Minnesota. Geol. and Nat. Hist. Survey Minnesota, Bull. No. 7, 301 pp., 7 pls., 1 col. pl., 23 figs. Coyote, pp. 79-80.

Hesse, R., W. C. Allee, and K. P. Schmidt
1937. Ecological animal geography. pp. i-xiv; 1-597, illus.; 453, 554-555. John Wiley & Sons, New York; Chapman and Hall, Ltd., London.

Hewitt, C. Gordon
1921. The conservation of wild life of Canada. Pp. i-xx, 1-344, illus.; 193, 214. Chas. Scribner's Sons, New York.

Hibbard, Claude W.
1944. A checklist of Kansas mammals. Trans. Kansas Acad. Sci. 1943 47: 61-88.

Hichens, William
1930. Unwanted animals—a world problem. "Discovery," Monthly Jour. Know 11 (124): 133-136, illus. April. London.

Hicks, Ellis A., and George O. Hendrickson
1940. Fur-bearers and game mammals of Iowa. Agr. Exper. Sta., Iowa State College, Ames. Bull. P 3 (new series): 1-145, illus.; 117-118. Feb.

Hilderbrand, Milton
1948. Wildlife: conserve, manage, or lament? Sierra Club. Bull. 33 (3): 11-18.
(A well-stated paper on predator control objectives.)

Hill, John Eric
1945. Speedy animals. Natural History 54 (8): 359. October.
(States coyotes rarely exceed 30 miles per hour.)

Hinkle, T. C.
1925. Split-ear, a battling coyote. Pp. 1-269, illus. Rand McNally & Co., N. Y.

Hjelle, Brandt V.
1946. Airplane hunting of predatory animals in North Dakota—winter of 1945-46. North Dakota Outdoors 8 (12): 6. June.

Hoffman, W. J.
1878. List of mammals found in the vicinity of Grand River, D. T. Proc. Boston Soc. Nat. Hist. 19: 95-102. March.

1885.   Hugo Ried's account of the Indians of Los Angeles County, California [particularly the sub-tribe that was located in the vicinity of San Gabriel]. Bull. Essex Institute 17 (1): 1-33, illus.; 9.

Hoffmaster, P. J.
1942.   They need not vanish. A discussion of natural resources of Michigan. Ed. by Helen M. Martin. Michigan State Dept. of Conservation, pp. 1-294, illus.; 233-234.
          (Re original distribution of coyote in Michigan, and depredations on sheep, also bounties on it for 1935, 3,128: 1936, 2,920; 1937, 2,573; 1938, 2,593; and 1939, 2,066. Animal holding its own, but extending its range.)

Hoffmeister, Donald F.
1949.   The wolves and coyotes of Illinois. Illinois Wildlife 4 (2): 4-5. March.

Holder, C. F.
1875.   Coyote hunting, a sketch. All the year Round 34: 462.
1896.   Don Coyote. Land of Sunshine 4: 179-180. March.
1900.   Don Coyote. Current Literature 27: 261-262. March.
1909.   Don Coyote. Outing 54: 692-696. September.

Holmes, A.
1939.   Nature notelets. Yosemite Nature Notes 18 (1): 3. January.
          (Recording of 8 deer "ganging up" on a single coyote apparently bent on surrounding it so as to kill it.)

Holland, R. P.
1920a.   The spread of the coyote. Outers' Recreation 62: 453.
1920b.   Wolf, fox or dog? Field and Stream 25 (4): 401. August.

Hollister, N.
1920.   Report on the National Zoological Park. Ann. Rept. Smithsn. Institution for 1920, pp. 75-89; 80.

Hooper, Emmet T.
1941.   Mammals of the lava fields and adjoining areas in Valencia County, New Mexico. Miscl. Publ. Mus. Zool. Univ. Mich. 51: 1-47, illus.; 22. June 14.

Horn, E. E.
1941.   Some coyote-wildlife relationships. Trans. 6th North Amer. Wildlife Conference, American Wildlife Institute, Washington, D. C. Pp. 283-287.

Hornaday, Wm. T.
1904.   The American natural history . . . C. Scribner's Sons, New York, 449 pp.; 24.

Howard, W. E.
1949.   A means to distinguish skulls of coyotes and domestic dogs. Journ. Mamm. 30 (2): 169-171. May 26.

Howard, William Johnston
1937.   Notes on winter foods of Michigan deer. Journ. Mammal. 18 (1): 77-80; 77. February.
          (Says chief deer predator are coyotes (*C. latrans*) and bobcats (*L. rufus*).)

Howell, A. Brazier
1928.   A coyote surviving under difficulties. Journ. Mammal. 9 (1): 63-64. February.

1944. Speed in animals; their specialization for running and leaping. Pp. i-xii; 1-270, illus.; 49. Univ. Chicago Press, Chicago, Ill.

Howell, Arthur H.
1938. Revision of the North American ground squirrels, with a classification of the North American Sciuridae. U. S. Dept. Agr. North American Fauna 56: 1-256, illus.

Hoyt, Vance
1945. The doctor goes wild. Nature Magazine 38 (9): 482-498, illus. November.

Hubbard, Clarence A.
1947. Fleas of western North America, their relation to the public health. 533 pp., illus.

Hubbs, L. G.
1945. That darned old coyote problem. Arizona Wildlife and Sportsman 6 (10): 4.
(Advocates liberation of 3 ear-tagged coyotes in each county of Arizona to be redeemed by State Game Department at $100 per animal as further incentive for coyote control.)

Huey, L. M.
1937. El valle de la Trinidad, the coyote prisoner's proving ground. Journ. Mammal. 18 (1): 74-76.

Hull, Merlin
1917. Bounty laws. Information for the town chairman and descriptions of wolves and foxes. 8 pp. Secretary of State, Madison, Wisconsin.

Hulse, J. W.
1899. A woodland tragedy. Recreation 10 (3): 220. March.

Humphrey, Imogene
1933. "Kiyi," a coyote. Nature Magazine 22: 83-84. December.

Hunter, John
1787. Observations tending to show that the wolf, jackal, and dog, are all of the same species. Philos. Trans. Royal Soc. London 67 (pt. 2): 253-266. April 26.
(An interesting discourse on cross breeding of wolves, and jackals with domestic dogs in England such as mastiff bull-dog, and other dogs the breed of which is not stated.)

Hunter, J. S.
1946. Twenty-five years of the California Fish and Game Commission. Calif. Fish & Game 32 (2): 39-47; 44. April.
(Institution of coyote and bobcat control in 1928, 27,437 coyotes killed by December 31, 1945.)

Hurd, C. A.
1945. Coyote control methods. Colorado Conservation Comments 8 (3): 9-10. September 15. Denver, Colo.
(Prefers destruction of coyote dens as means of control rather than poisons or traps.)

Huxley, T. H.
1880. Cranial and dental characters of Canidae. Proc. Zool. Soc. London, 1880, pp. 238-288.

Illman, William I., and D. H. Hamly
1948. A report on the Ridgway Color Standards. Science 107 (2789): 626-628. June 11.

Ingersoll, Ernest
  1887.   Coyote, the hound of the plains. Popular Science Monthly
          30: 306.
  1937.   An adventure in etymology, origin and meaning of some animal
          names. Sci. Monthly 44: 157-165; 160. February.
          (Says coyote brought from Mexico its Anahuac (Indian) name
          coyotl.)
Ingles, Lloyd Glenn
  1947.   Mammals of California, Pp. xix + 258, illus.; 79-80. Stanford
          University Press, Calif.
Iowa, State of
  1858.   Laws of Iowa. Chapter 62.
          (Gives early day procedure for bounty claimant to follow in
          collecting wolf and coyote bounty.)
Jackson, Bud
  1946.   Coyotes—from the air. Fur-Fish-Game, Harding's Mag. 86 (8):
          12, 31-32, illus. August.
  1948.   Predator control. Sports Afield 119 (3): 59. March.
Jackson, Hartley H. T.
  1904.   Legislation for the destruction of noxious animals. Based after
          a consideration of evolutional and zoological factors. Unpub-
          lished thesis (Milton College); 19 pp. May. Milton, Wis.
  1908.   A preliminary list of Wisconsin mammals. Bull. Wisconsin Nat.
          Hist. Soc. 6 (1-2): 13-24; pl. 3. April. Milwaukee, Wis.
          (Coyote, p. 27.)
  1920.   An apparent effect of winter inactivity upon distribution of
          mammals. Journ. Mammal. 1 (2): 58-64. March 2.
          (Canis latrans latrans, p. 62.)
  1922.   A coyote in Maryland. Journ. Mammal. 3 (3): 186-187.
  1924a. Against destruction of predatory animals. Parks and Recrea-
          tion 7 (6): 658. July-August. Minot, North Dakota.
  1924b. Resolution on destruction of vermin and predatory animals.
          Science 59: 548. June 20.
  1930.   (Coyote in Wisconsin before 1875). Jour. Mammal. 11 (3):
          335. August 9.
  1949.   Two new coyotes from the United States. Proc. Biol. Soc. Wash-
          ington 62: 31-32, March 17.
Jackson, Hartley H. T., and H. E. Warfel
  1934.   Notes on the occurrence of mammals in the regions adjacent
          to the Salt Plains of northwestern Oklahoma. Pub. Univ. Okla.
          Biol. Survey 5 (1-4): 65-72; 68. Dec. 30, 1933. Actual date
          of publication February 28.
          (On the occurrence of the coyote on Salt Plains. Canis latrans
          nebracensis.)
Jackson, V. W.
  1926.   Fur and game resources of Manitoba. 56 pp., 10 pls.; p. 17.
          Industrial Development Board of Manitoba, Winnipeg.
          (Gives impression coyotes still holding their own in the
          Province.)
Jacobsen, W. C.
  1945.   The bounty system and predator control. California Fish & Game
          31 (2): 53-63. April. San Francisco, Calif.
          (An excellent expose of the frauds and inefficiency of the
          bounty methods as a real means of predator control such as the
          coyote.)

Jakeman, H. W.
  1918. Rabies, history, natural symptoms of the disease. What to do
        with animals suspected of having the disease. Shipping speci-
        mens for laboratory diagnosis. Dealing with animals that are
        exposed to infection. Agricultural Extension State Service Bull.
        19: 1-9. Univ. Nevada, Reno.
James, Edwin, and Stephen H.
  1823. Account of an expedition from Pittsburgh to the Rocky Moun-
        tains, performed in the years 1819 and 1820. 2 vols. Vol. 1,
        p. 168. Philadelphia.
        (Original description of coyote (*C. latrans*).)
Jardine, James T.
  1908. Preliminary report on grazing experiments in a coyote-proof
        pasture, with an introduction by Frederick V. Coville. U. S.
        Dept. Agr., Forest Service Circ. 156: 1-32, illus. Washington,
        D. C.
  1909. Coyote-proof pasture experiment, 1908. U. S. Dept. Agr., Forest
        Service Circ. 160: 1-40, illus.
  1911. Coyote-proof inclosures in connection with range lambing
        grounds. U. S. Dept. Agr., Forest Service Bull. 97: 1-32, illus.
Jardine, W. M.
  1929. Control of predatory animals. Ten-year program for U. S. House
        Document 496. U. S. Govt. Printing Office, Washington, D. C.
        Pp. 1-17.
Jewett, Stanley G.
  1931. Predatory animals in Oregon. Oregon Motorist 12 (2): 10-12,
        illus.
  1939. Hart Mountain Antelope Refuge. U. S. Dept. Agr., Bur. Biol.
        Survey Miscl. Publ. 355: 1-25, illus.; 11, 19.
Joffe, Joseph
  1931. How fast is a coyote? Yellowstone Nature Notes 8 (1): 2.
        (Chased by an auto for 1.6 miles coyote recorded speed was
        never less than 25 miles per hour, and maximum of 35 miles
        along a road.)
Johnson, Charles E.
  1930. Recollections of the mammals of northwestern Minnesota. Journ.
        Mammal. 11 (4): 435-452; 442-443. November.
        (An interesting account of *C. latrans*, i.e. eating of bodies of
        their own kind, and following man.)
  1934. Recollections of the prairie chicken and the sharp-tailed grouse
        in northwestern Minnesota. Wilson Bulletin 46: 3-17; 13-14.
        (No finding of coyote a serious enemy in snow-beds of these
        game birds.)
Johnson, Jerry
  1936. Coyote and bull snake. Journ. Mammal. 17: 169-170.
Johnson, Maynard S.
  1930. Common injurious mammals of Minnesota. Univ. Minn. Agr.
        Exper. Sta. Bull. 259: 1-66, illus.; 61-63. January. St. Paul,
        Minn.
Jones, Paul V., Jr.
  1949. Antelope management. Texas Game and Fish 7 (12): 4-5, 18-20,
        24-25, 28-29, illus. November.
        (Coyote predation on antelope fawns is main factor in limiting
        increase of pronghorns in upper and lower plains areas of Texas.)

Jotter, E. V.
1919.   The coyote as a deer killer. California Fish & Game 5 (1): 26-29, illus.
Kalmbach, E. R.
1943.   The armadillo: its relation to agriculture and game. Publ. by Texas Game, Fish, and Oyster Commission in cooperation with Fish and Wildlife Service, U. S. Dept. Int., 61 pp., illus.; 21. Austin, Texas.
         (While coyote presumed to be enemy, 569 coyote stomachs collected in Texas failed to reveal remains of an armadillo.)
Kartchner, K. C.
1941.   Desirability for control of predators in wildlife management as experienced in Arizona. Trans. 6th N. Amer. Wildlife Conference, American Wildlife Institute, Washington, D. C. Pp. 273-277.
Keane, Charles
1927.   The outbreak of foot and mouth disease among deer in the Stanislaus National Forest (California). Calif. State Dept. Agr. Monthly Bull. 16 (4): 213-226, illus; 216. April.
Kebbe, Chester E.
1946.   Oregon's fur resources. Oregon Game Commission Bull. 1 (8): 1, 6-7; 7. November. Portland, Oreg.
         (On spread of coyote to coastal mountains where they are becoming quite numerous by opening up of forests by fire and logging.)
Keller, L. Floyd
1935.   Porcupines killed and eaten by a coyote. Journ. Mammal. 16 (3): 232.
Kellogg, Charles E.
1938.   Review of Hamlett's "Reproductive cycle of the coyote." N. Amer. Wildlife Conf. Trans. 3: 524.
Kellogg, Remington
1939.   Annotated list of Tennessee mammals. Proc. U. S. Nat. Mus. 86 (3051): 1-303; 267.
Kennicott, Robert
1855.   Catalogue of animals observed in Cook County, Illinois. Trans. Illinois State Agr. Soc. 1: 578.
Kimball, Jim
1946.   Wildlife in South Dakota predator control. South Dakota Conservation Digest 13 (8): 12. August.
         (Bounties on predators has to date never effectively controlled predators; in 13 months State paid out $262,683.50 with payments still increasing.)
Kimball, J. W.
1946.   A Nebraska "wolf" hunt. Outdoor Nebraska 23 (4): 15-17, illus.
         (Describes circular ring-hunt for coyotes.)
Kincaid, Edgar B.
1931.   "The Mexican Pastor." Southwestern Lore 9: 63-64. Texas Folklore Society.
Kipe, L.
1872.   Coyote Canyon. Overland 9: 27.
Kircher, W. H.
1941.   Ranchers organize for coyote control. The Farmer 59 (17): 5, 12. August 23. St. Paul, Minn.

Klatt, B.
1928. Vergleichende Untersuchangen an Caniden und Procyniden. Zool. Jahrb. Abt. allg. Zool., Vol. 45.

Knowles, L.
1928. Antelope repel coyote attack. U. S. Dept. Agr., Forest Service Bull. pp. 4-5. (Mimeographed.)

Knowles, R. K.
1939. Happy hunting grounds for coyote in a Yosemite meadow. Yosemite Nat. Notes 18 (7): 84-85.

Kotzebue, Otto von
1830. A new voyage round the World, in the years 1823, 24, 25, and 26. Vol. 2, 362 pp. Colburn and Bentley, London.

Kroeker, H. W.
1909. Navajo's fairy tale. Overland 54: 456-458. November.

Kunkel, G. M.
1930. Report of case of tularemia contracted from a coyote (*Canis lestes*) in New Mexico. U. S. Public Health Repts. 45 (9): 439-440. February 28.

Kurz, Rudolph Friederick
1937. Journal of Rudolph Kurz. Smithsn. Inst. Bull., Amer. Ethnology 115: 212, 299.

L., E. R.
1945. Coyote hunt at Gettysburg. South Dakota Conservation Digest 12 (1): 11, 15, illus. January.

Laing, H. M.
1915. Wanted a coyote. Outing 66: 316-326. June.

Laing, H. M., and R. M. Anderson
1929. Mammals of Upper Chitna River, Alaska. Ann. Rept. for 1927, Nat. Mus. Canada Bull. 56: 98.

Lambert, P. L.
1917. Coyotes and their habits. Outlook 115: 568. March 28.

Landis, C. S.
1947. A rifle for coyotes. Rod & Gun in Canada 49 (1): 33. June.

Landon, C. R.
1920. Predatory animal situation in Texas. Sheep and Goat Raisers' Mag. 1 (2): 8-10.

1931. Predatory animal control. Sheep and Goat Raisers' Mag. 11 (8): 210-211. March. San Angelo, Tex.

Lantz, David E.
1905a. The relation of coyotes to stock raising in the West. U. S. Dept. Agr. Farmers' Bull. 226: 1-24, illus.

1905b. Coyotes in their economic relations. U. S. Dept. Agr., Bur. Biol. Survey Bull. 20: 1-28.

1905c. Kansas mammals in their relation to agriculture. Exper. Sta. Kans. State Agr. College Bull. 129: 331-404; 381-383. December 1904 (issued April 1905). Manhattan, Kans.

1908a. Bounty laws in force in the United States July 1, 1907. U. S. Dept. Agr. Yearbook 1907: 560-565.

1908b. Use of poisons for destroying noxious mammals. U. S. Dept. Agr. Yearbook: 421-432; 427.

1910. The muskrat. U. S. Dept. Agr., Bur. Biol. Survey, Farmers' Bull. 396: 1-38, illus.; 35.
(Coyote as enemy of muskrat.)

1916. Destroying rodent pests on the farm. U. S. Dept. Agr., Yearbook Sep. 708: 17. Washington, D. C.
(Relation of carnivores as rodent pest destroyers including the coyote.)

Lapham, I. A.
1853. A systematic catalogue of the animals of Wisconsin. Trans. Wisconsin State Agr. Soc. (1852) 2: 337-340.

Latham, Roger M.
1948. Does predator control pay. Field & Stream 52 (9): 40, 94-95. January.

Lawrence, Barbara
1934. Wild coyote with an undershot jaw. Jour. Mammal. 15 (4): 319-320.

Lawrence, W. B.
1922. Predatory animal control on Spring Valley Water Company property. Calif. Fish and Game 8 (4): 230-31. October.

Leavitt, Scot
1930. Control of predatory animals. Hearing before the Committee on Agriculture, House of Rep., 71st Congress, 2nd Sess. on H. R. 9599. April 29, 30, and May 1, 1930. Serial O, pp. 1-100.

Lehman, V. W., and W. G. Fuller
1943. Don coyote, arch enemy of nesting bobwhites. Texas Game and Fish 1 (9): 9, 15, 3 illus. August.

Lehman, Valgene W.
1946. Bobwhite quail reproduction in southwestern Texas. Journ. Wildlife Management 10 (2): 111-123. April.
(Of 194 quail nests, coyotes destroyed 83%, next to rainfall in importance as important factor.)

Leopold, Aldo
1936. Game management. Chas. Scribner's Sons, New York and London, pp. i-xxi, 1-481, illus.

1945. Deer, wolves, foxes and pheasants. Wis. Conservation Bull. 10 (4): 3-5. April. Wisconsin Conservation Department, Madison, Wis.

Leopold, Aldo, Lyle K. Sowls, and David L. Spencer
1947. A survey of over-populated deer ranges in the United States. Jour. Wildlife Manag. 11 (2): 162-177; 176. April.
(Rules out the coyote as effective deer predator.)

Leopold, A. Starker
1949. Adios Gavilan. Pacific Discovery 2 (1): 4-13; 9. January-February. Calif. Acad. Sci., San Francisco, Calif.
(Wolves keep coyotes out of the back country.)

Lichtenstein, H. von
1830. Erlauterungen der Nachrichten des Franc. Hernandez von den vierfussigen Thieren Neuspaniens. Abhandl. Konig. Akad. der Wis., Berlin, 1827, pp. 89-123; 105.

Ligon, J. Stokley
1927. Wild life of New Mexico. New Mexico State Game Commission, Sante Fe, N. Mex. Pp. 1-212, illus.

1930. The coyote peril to mountain and forest dwelling game. Address at annual meeting of New Mexico Game Protective Association, Albuquerque, N. Mex., September 2. (In files Fish and Wildlife Service.)

Lindsey, N. M.
   1940.   Trapping coyotes. Fur-Fish-Game 71 (4): 14-15.
Lippincott, Wm.
   1926.   Siskiyou County pays a bounty on coyotes. Calif. Fish & Game
           12 (2): 108.
Long, Albert, et al.
   1941.   Leaves from our diaries. Yellowstone Nat. Notes 18 (3-4): 23-
           24. March-April.
Long, Stephen H., and Edwin James
   1823.   Account of an expedition from Pittsburgh to the Rocky Moun-
           tains performed in the years 1819 and 1820. 2 vols. Vol. 1, p.
           168. Philadelphia.
Longanecker, D. S.
   1945.   A field study of latent tularemia in rodents with a list of all
           known naturally infected vertebrates. Journ. Infectious Diseases
           76: 115. Univ. Chicago Press, Chicago, Ill.
Lopez, Carlos M., and Carlos Lopez
   1911.   Caza Mexicana, xix + 629 pp., illus.; pp. 334-341.
Lucas, Frederick A.
   1889.   Animals recently extinct or threatened with extermination, as
           represented in the collections of the U. S. National Museum.
           Rept. of U. S. National Museum for year ending June 30, 1889,
           pp. 609-649; 612.
           (Decrease of coyotes due to bounties with corresponding in-
           crease in jack rabbits in western Kansas.)
Lummis, C. F.
   1895.   The coyote. Land of sunshine 3: 215-217. October.
Lyon, Marcus Ward, Jr., and Wilfred H. Osgood
   1909.   Catalogue of type-specimens of mammals in the United States
           National Museum, including the Biological Survey collection.
           U. S. Natl. Mus. Bull. 62: x + 325; 215-217.
Lystrup, Herbert F.
   1941.   The cunning coyote. Yellowstone Nat. Notes 18 (9-10): 49-50.
           September-October.
           (An unusual eye-witness account of how a coyote outwitted
           a grizzly bear in Yellowstone National Park in obtaining a
           piece of meat.)
MacFarlane, Roderick Ross
   1905.   Notes on mammals collected and observed in the northern
           Mackenzie River district, Northwest Territories of Canada. Proc.
           U. S. Natl. Mus. 28 (1405): 694.
Maerz, A., and M. Rea Paul
   1930.   A dictionary of color. 207 pp. New York.
Mahaffey, Juanita
   1946.   Coyote roundup. Oklahoma Game and Fish News 1 (2): 4-6,
           17, illus. January.
Maine, State of
           Rabies (Hydrophobia). State Dept. of Health Circ. 124: 1-8.
Mann, Walter G., and S. B. Locke
   1931.   The Kaibab deer—a brief history and recent developments.
           Mimeographed report with colored map. 67 pp.; 62. Prepared
           by Forest Service, U. S. Dept. Agr.
           (Recommends keeping coyotes to a minimum.)

Mann, William M.
    1943.   Wild animals in and out of the Zoo. Smithsn. Sci. Ser. 6: 1-374,
             illus., 107.
             (P. 300 gives longevity records of coyotes in captivity.)

Mara, W. A., and E. M. Canfield
    1932.   New ways of keeping the wolf from the door. American Maga-
             zine 114: 66. October.

Markley, Merle H.
    1945.   Seasonal fur primeness of the coyote in the western United
             States. Journ. Wildlife Mgt. 9 (3): 227-231. July.

Marsh, E. G., Jr.
    1943.   Predators. Texas Game and Fish 1 (4): 4, 15, illus. March.

Martin, Fred
    1946.   Sport in Arizona. Fur-Fish-Game 85 (12): 51-52, illus. Decem-
             ber.
             (Coyote trapping in Arizona.)

Martin, Joe
    1943.   Timber wolves. Fur Trade Journal of Canada, pp. 30-31, illus.
             May. Toronto, Ontario, Canada.
             (Brief description differences between wolves and coyotes.)

Mast, J. F.
    1932.   Coyote and wildcat trapping. 78 pp., illus. Ontario, Calif.

Mather, Stephen T.
    1923.   Report of the Director, National Park Service, U. S. Dept. Int.,
             pp. 1-198; 23, 64, 156, 170, 177.
             (Park Service policy at this time was extermination of preda-
             tors presumably pumas and coyotes, and also rodents within
             national parks.)

Matheson, Colin
    1944.   The gray wolf. Journ. of the Society for the Preservation of
             Fauna of the Empire n.s. (pt. 1): 31-42. December. Zool. Soc.
             London, Regents Park, London.
             (This article is a reprint from Antiquity 17 (1943): 11-18.
             The gray wolf.)

Matthew, W. D.
    1930.   The phylogeny of dogs. Journ. Mammal. 11 (2): 117-138, illus.
             May.

Matthews, W.
    1886.   Deities and demons of the Navajos. American Naturalist 20
             (10): 841-850. October.
             (Discusses part the coyote plays in Navajo myths—a prominent
             animal in this respect.)

Maximilian, Prince of Wied
    1841.   Reise Innere Nord-America 2: 278, 307.
             (Occurrence of coyote (C. latrans) near Fort Clark on the
             Missouri River, February 26, 1834.)

McAtee, W. L.
    1933.   Game management is not just vermin control. Outdoor Life
             72 (5): 24-25.

McClure, S. W.
    1938.   Coyotes destroyed. National Wool Grower 28: 22. September.

McCowan, Dan
  1936.   Animals of the Canadian Rockies. 302 pp.; 139 New York.
  1947.   Fastest on four feet. The Beaver, Outfit 277: 36-39, illus.; 38.
          Hudson's Bay Co., Winnipeg, Manitoba.
          (Coyote as one of the principal enemies of antelope.)
McCoy, J. G.
  1940.   Historic sketches of the cattle trade. The Southwest Historical
          Series 8: 1-397. Ed. by Ralph P. Bieber. The Arthur H. Clark
          Co., Glendale, Calif.
McIlvaine, C.
  1906.   How coyote got his marks. Delineator 67: 207. February.
McKean, William T.
  1948.   Winter foods of North Dakota predatory animals. North Dakota
          Outdoors 10 (8): 8-9.
McKenna, James A.
  1936.   Black Range tales. P. 59. Wilson-Ericson, Inc.
McLean, Donald D.
  1934.   Predatory animal studies. Calif. Fish & Game 20: 30-36.
McMurry, F. B.
  1942.   Cryporchidism in a coyote. Jour. Mammal. 23 (2): 220.
Meachem, A.
  1903.   The coyote as a strategist. Forest & Stream 60 (8): 48. Janu-
          ary 17.
Mearns, Edgar Alexander
  1907.   Mammals of the Mexican boundary of the United States. U. S.
          Natl. Mus. Bull. 56: 1-530.
Mengarini, Father
  1872.   Flathead Indians. Amer. Nat. 6: 180-183.
          (Coyote in religion of Flathead Indians.)
Merriam, C. Hart
  1890.   Results of a biological survey of the San Francisco Mountains
          region and desert of the Little Colorado, Arizona. U. S. Dept.
          Agr., North Amer. Fauna 3: 38.
          (Coyotes reported as very common in San Francisco Mountain
          and Desert Region of Arizona.)
  1897.   Revision of the coyotes or prairie wolves, with description of
          new forms. Proc. Biol. Soc. Washington 11: 19-33. March 15.
          (Describes as new *Canis pallidus*, *C. lestes*, *C. peninsulae*, *C.
          microdon*, *C. mearnsi*, *C. estor*, and *C. vigilis*.)
  1898.   New names for Spermophilus brevicaudus, *Canis pallidus*, and
          Sorex caudatus Merriam. Science, n.s. 8 (205): 782 Decem-
          ber 2.
  1899.   Results of a biological survey of Mount Shasta, northern Cali-
          fornia. U. S. Dept. Agr., North Amer. Fauna 16: 103.
  1904.   A new coyote from southern Mexico. Proc. Biol. Soc. Wash.
          17: 157.
Merriam, John C.
  1911-12.   The fauna of Rancho La Brea. Mem. Univ. Calif. (Pts. 1-2)
          1 (2): 199-262, illus.
Millard, F. B.
  1891.   Coyote that bites. Overland 18: 471.

Miller, Gerrit S., Jr.
  1912. List of North American land mammals in the United States
        National Museum, 1911. U. S. Natl. Mus. Bull. 79: xiv + 455.
        December 31.
  1920. (Review of) Einar Lonnberg. Remarks on some South American
        Canidae. Arkiv for Zoologi, Stockholm 12 (13): 1-18, 4 figs.
        September 3, 1919. Jour. Mamm. 1 (3): 149-150. May.
        (Re domestic dogs ancestry linked up with wild Canidae "orig-
        inal domestication somewhere within northern area inhabited by
        true *Canis*.")
Miller, Gerrit S., Jr., and James A. G. Rehn
  1901. Systematic results of the study of North American land mammals
        to the close of the year 1900. Proc. Boston Soc. Nat. Hist. 30
        (1): 1-352. December 27.
Miller, Loye Holmes
  1907. Deafness in wild animals. Science, n.s. 25 (628): 67. Janu-
        ary 11.
Miller, Ryland A.
  1947. Cooperation and coyotes. Missouri Conservationist 8 (11): 83,
        illus. November.
Mills, Enos A.
  1932. Watched by wild animals. 243 pp., illus.; 89, 96. Houghton-
        Mifflin Co., Boston and New York.
Mills, Harlow Burgess
  1937. A preliminary study of the bighorn of Yellowstone National
        Park. Jour. Mammal. 18: 205-212; 210.
        (No evidence coyote factor on bighorn sheep.)
Mills, Joe
  1926. The comeback. Illus. by Howard L. Hastings. Pub. by J. H.
        Sears & Co., New York. 221 pp.
Missouri, State of
  1825. Revised statutes. p. 797.
Mivart, St. George
  1890. A monograph of the Canidae. 2 vols. London.
Moe, Alfred K.
  1904. Honduras. 58th Cong., 3rd Sess., House of Rep. Doc. 145
        (part 4): 242 pp., illus.; 19. Washington, D. C.
Moffitt, James
  1933. Food habits of coyotes [a review]. Calif. Fish and Game 19:
        284-286.
Mohler, John R.
  1923. Rabies or hydrophobia. U. S. Dept. Agr. Farmers' Bull. 449:
        1-14.
Moore, Robert D.
  1929. *Canis latrans lestes*, Merriam feeding on tadpoles and frogs.
        Jour. Mammal. 10 (2): 255.
Morton, Samuel George
  1852a. Observations on the antiquity of some races of dogs. Proc.
         Acad. Nat. Sci. Phila. 5: 84-89. 1850.
         (Coyote in its relation to American Indian dog.)
  1852b. Communications on the races of dogs. Proc. Acad. Nat. Sci.
         Phila. 5: 139-140. 1851.
         (Comments on the vast extent the coyote is crossed up with
         ranch dogs near Fort Duncan, Texas.)

Mossman, F.
1929. Wild animal pests of the United States. Wide World Mag. 64 (381): 197-203.

Muleahy, J. V.
1924. The laboratory examination of rabid animals. Public Health News 9 (6): 174-179, illus. May. Dist. of Health, State of New Jersey.

Mullin, R. H.
1915. Rabies. Univ. Nevada Bull. 9 (9): 1-13. December 23.

Munro, J. A.
1940. Animal predation. Canadian Field-Nat. 54 (6): 82-83.
1945. Preliminary report on the birds and mammals of Glacier National Park, British Columbia. Canadian Field-Nat. 59 (6): 175-190; 186. November-December.
   (States coyotes come in with the deer in the spring, and leave with them in fall.)
1947. Observations of birds and mammals in central British Columbia. Occas. Papers, British Columbia Provincial Museum 6: 120-123. January. Victoria.
   (Coyote population cyclic as depicted by bounty payments.)

Murie, Adolph
1940. Ecology of the coyote in the Yellowstone. U. S. Dept. Int., Natl. Park Service Fauna Ser. 4: xxi + 206 pp., 56 figs.
1944. The wolves of Mount McKinley. U. S. Dept. Int., Natl. Park Service Fauna Ser. 5: xix + 238 pp.; 15, 17, 55, 96-97, 125, 161, 216-217, 231. Washington, D. C.

Murie, Olaus J.
1935a. Alaska-Yukon caribou. U. S. Dept. Agr., Bur. Biol. Survey, North Amer. Fauna 54: 1-93, illus.; 8. June.
   (At time this material comprising the fauna was compiled, the depredation of coyotes on caribou had not been determined.)
1935b. Food habits of the coyote in Jackson Hole, Wyoming. U. S. Dept. Agr. Circ. 362: 1-24.
1936. Dog skulls from St. Lawrence Island, Alaska. Appendix IV in Geist and Rainey Archaeological excavations at Kukulik, St. Lawrence Island. Vol. 2 of Miscl. Publ., Univ. of Alaska, pp. 349-357, illus. U. S. Govt. Printing Office.
   (Pages 355-356 discuss mating of Colorado coyote raised in Wyoming with a 40-lb. dog coming from St. Lawrence Island, Alaska. Breeding took place in early March; 65 days later mother coyote died just before giving birth to litter. Three pups were in the litter weighing 2 lbs. 14 oz., a male and female weighed 1 lb. each, and the third a male weighed 14 oz. Dog and coyote characters were well mixed in the foetuses.)
1945. Notes on coyote food habits in Montana and British Columbia. Jour. Mammal. 26 (1): 33-40. February.
1946. Evaluation duplications in analysis of coyote scats. Jour. Wildlife Management 10 (3): 275-276. July.
1948. Wonder dog. Audubon Magazine 50 (5): 269-276, illus. September-October.
   (A defense of the coyote.)

Murray, Charles Augustus
1839. Travels in North America. 2 vols. Vol. 1, pp. 51-321; vol. 2, pp. 20-133. New York.
(Covers mammalian life throughout buffalo-land, including the large wolves and coyotes.)

Musgrave, Mark E.
1919. Destruction to livestock by predatory animals and their practical means of destruction. Arizona Cattle Growers Assoc. Proc. 12: 111-113.

Nagel, W. O.
1947. The real meaning of predation. Wyoming Wildlife 11 (1-2): 4-7, 37, illus. January-February. Cheyenne, Wyoming.
(A reprint from the Missouri Conservationist.)

Negus, N. C.
1948. A coyote, Canis latrans, from Preble County, Ohio. Jour. Mammal. 29 (3): 295. September 2.

Nelson, E. W.
1916. The larger North American mammals. Nat. Geog. Mag. 30 (5): 385-472, illus.; 423-424. November.
(Re plains and Arizona or Mearns coyote.)
1917. Doing the work of the U. S. Government. The Bureau of Biological Survey. Export American Industries, pp. 77-82, illus. December.
1918. Smaller mammals of North America. Nat. Geog. Mag. 33 (5): 371-493, illus.
(List coyote as enemy of armadillo.)
1920. Report of Chief of Bureau of Biological Survey, U. S. Dept. Agr., p. 4. September 4.
(Coyote nightly depredations on 3 to 6 lambs from one ranch in New Mexico.)
1921. Lower California and its natural resources. Mem. Nat. Acad. Sci. 16 (1): 1-194, illus.; 25, 90, 110, 127, 132. Washington, D. C.
1922. Report of the Chief of the Bureau of Biological Survey, U. S. Dept. Agr., p. 5.
1923. Biological Survey, U. S. Dept. Agr., Report of the Chief, 1923, 44 pp.
1925. Status of the prong-horned antelope, 1922-1924. U. S. Dept. Agr. Bull. 1346: 64 pp., illus. August.
(Mentions vulnerability of antelopes to predatory animals, mainly coyotes.)
1932. Remarks on coyotes with description of a new subspecies from Salvador. Proc. Biol. Soc. Washington 45: 223-226. November 26.
(Most southerly of coyotes (C. l. dickeyi) with exception of one taken at Guanacaste, western Costa Rica. Describes as new Canis latrans dickeyi (p. 224), and places all forms of coyotes as subspecies of latrans.)

Nelson, L. A.
1916. Hunting down mad coyotes. Illustrated World 25: 508-509. June.

Neubrech, Walter
1946. History of predator control in the State of Washington. Washington Outdoors 1 (5-6): 5, 15. August-September. Tacoma.

1948. History of predator control in the State of Washington. Northwest Sportsman 3 (6): 10-12. Vancouver, British Columbia, Canada.
(Points out difficulties of controlling coyote and other predators by bounty system.)

Nevada, State of
1916a. Report of the Bureau of Biological Survey on the rabies eradication campaign in the State of Nevada to the Nevada Rabies Commission, April-May, 1916.

1916b. Rabies eradication in Nevada. Report by Bureau of Biological Survey, U. S. Dept. Agr., to Nevada Rabies Commission, June, July, August, 1916, pp. 1-7, illus.

1917. Biennial report of the State Board of Stock Commissioners, 1915-1916. Pp. 1-23. Carson City, Nevada.

1919. Biennial report of the State Rabies Commission, 1917-1918, pp. 1-10.

1921. Biennial report of the State Rabies Commission, 1919-1920, pp. 1-8.

1923. Biennial report of the State Rabies Commission, 1921-1922, pp. 1-11.

1931. Biennial report of the State Rabies Commission, 1929-1930, pp. 1-9.

1934. Biennial report of the State Rabies Commission for period July 1, 1932 to June 30, 1934, inclusive, pp. 1-8.

New Mexico, State of
1936. Practical predator control featuring coyote trapping. Dept. of Game and Fish, Santa Fe, N. Mex., pp. 1-16, illus.

Noland, William
1948. Coyotes are sport to them. Missouri Conservationist 9 (5): 12. May.
(Spotting coyotes from air, then later coursing with dogs.)

Nordyke, Lewis
1944. Coyote cunning. Nature Mag. 37 (3): 120-124, illus. March. Washington, D. C.

O'Connor, J.
1936. Furry gangsters of the desert. Readers Digest 28: 47-49. June.
(Condensed from Field and Stream, April 1936.)

Oliver, H.
1930. Trapping the coyote. Natl. Wool Grower 20 (5): 30-31, illus.

Olson, Sigurd F.
1938. A study in predatory relationship with particular reference to the wolf. Scientific Monthly 46: 323-336. April.

Oregon, State of
1893. General and special laws and memorials passed and adopted by the 17th Regular Session Jan. 9, February 18, p. 38 [H.B. 8].
(Empowers county courts to pay bounties on predators; to pay not less than $1.00 or more than $20.00 for each coyote.)

Ormond, Clyde
1945. Try coyotes. Field and Stream 49 (10): 24-25, 94-95, illus. February.

Osborn, Henry Fairfield
1906. The causes of extinction of mammalia. Amer. Nat. 40 (479, 480): 769-795, 829-859. November-December.
(Interesting comments when considering the spread of the coyote in the past 100 years.)
1914. "Preservation of the wild animals of North America." In: American big game in its haunts (The Book of the Boone & Crockett Club), pp. 349-373; 354. New York.

Osborn, Henry Fairfield, and Harold E. Anthony
1922. Can we save the mammals? Natural History 22 (5): 388-405; 393. Amer. Mus. Nat. Hist., New York City, N. Y.
(Wolf used in fur-trade 1919-21 figure given undoubtedly includes coyote pelts.)

Osgood, Wilfred H.
1934. The genera and subgenera of South American Canids. Journ. Mammal. 15 (1): 45-50. February.

Packard, A. S.
1885. Origin of the American varieties of the dog. American Naturalist 19 (9): 896-901. September.
(Shows that several varieties of North American domestic dogs originated from gray or prairie wolf (coyote).)

Packard, Fred Mallery
1940. Beaver killed by coyotes. Journ. Mammal. 21 (3): 359-360. August.
(Colorado State trappers believe that coyotes rank first among species that prey on beaver in that State.)
1946. An ecological study of the bighorn sheep in Rocky Mountain National Park, Colorado. Jour. Mammal. 27 (1): 3-28, illus.; 10-11. February.
(Coyote predation of bighorn sheep.)

Palmer, T. S.
1896. Extermination of noxious animals by bounties. U. S. Dept. Agr. Yearbook 1896: 55-68.
1897. The jack rabbits of the United States. U. S. Dept. Agr., Bur. Biol. Survey Bull. 8: 1-88, illus.; 44-45, revised edition.
1899. Report of Acting Chief, Division of Biological Survey. In Rept. Secy. Agr. 1899: 59-70; 65.
(Re so-called "west-wide" plan of predatory animal bounty. Amer. Nat. Livestock Assn., annual convention, Denver, Colo. 1899.)

Parkman, Francis
1872. The Oregon trail. 381 pp.; 57. Little, Brown and Co., Boston.

Paschall, A. L.
1917. How to combat rabbits, gophers, prairie dogs, coyotes, ants, and grasshoppers. Ariz. Agr. Expt. Sta. Bull. 81: 322-338, illus.

Pauley, Sylvan J.
1941. The stockman's viewpoint on conservation. Trans. 6th North Amer. Wildlife Conf., Amer. Wildlife Institute, Washington, D. C. pp. 19-23.

Pellett, Frank C.
1911. The prairie wolf in Iowa. Forest & Stream 76 (12): 452. March 25.

Petersen, William J.
    1940. Wolves in Iowa. Iowa Journ. Hist. & Politics 38 (1): 50-93.
           January. State Hist. Soc., Iowa City, Iowa.

Peterson, Randolph L.
    1946. Recent and Pleistocene Mammalian Fauna of Brazos County,
           Texas. Jour. Mammal. 27 (2): 162-168, illus.; 166. May.
           (Occurrence of a fragment of coyote in Pleistocene deposits.)

Petrie, G.
    1937. Airplanes for coyotes. Natl. Wool Grower 27: 29-30. June.

Petrie, H.
    1927. Habits of the coyote. Outdoor Life 59 (4): 83-84.

Phillips, J. C.
    1930. American game mammals and birds—a catalogue of books,
           Houghton Mifflin & Co., New York.
           1582-1925, on sport, natural history, and conservation. 638 pp.

Pine, George W.
    1870. Beyond the West. Pp. xii + 444, illus.; 307. Utica, N. Y.

Piper, S. E.
    1909. The Nevada mouse plague of 1907-8. U. S. Dept. Agr. Farmers'
           Bull. 352: 1-23, illus.
    1923. Sage grouse or coyotes? Colo. Game & Fish Prot. Assn. Bull.
           3 (1): 2-3, illus. January. Denver, Colo.
    1928. The mouse infestation of Buena Vista Lake Basin, Kern County,
           California, September 1926 to February 1927. Calif. Dept. Agr.
           Monthly Bull. 17 (10): 538-560, illus.; 551.
           (Coyotes eating house mice.)

Pocock, R. I.
    1914. On the feet and other external features of the Canidae and
           Ursidae. Proc. Zool. Soc. London, pp. 913-941.

Poole, Arthur J., and Viola S. Schantz
    1942. Catalog of the type specimens of mammals in the United States
           National Museum, including the Biological Surveys collection.
           U. S. Natl. Mus. Bull. 178: xiii + 705. April 9.
           (Coyote types listed, pp. 41-45.)

Poole, C. G.
    1928. Coyote not strictly carnivorous. Calif. Fish & Game 14 (2): 151.
    1931. Ten years of predatory animal control. Monthly Bull. Dept.
           Agr. State of Calif. 20: 467-469.
    1933. Some facts about predatory animal control. Calif. Fish & Game
           19 (1): 1-9, illus. January.

Poole, C. G., and W. C. Jacobsen
    1929. Predatory animal control. Calif. Dept. Agr. Monthly Bull. 18:
           794-795.

Porsild, A. E.
    1945. The mammals of the Mackenzie Delta. Canad. Field-Nat. 59
           (1): 4-22; 12. January-February.

Potter, Waylan
    1949. Poison afield. Dog and wildlife slaughter mounts in organized
           poisoning campaign. Hunting and Fishing [Philadelphia] 26
           (3): 18-21, illus. August.
           (Rabid plan against poisoning and the Fish and Wildlife
           Service.)

Power, Stephen
1872.   Afoot and alone. 299 pp. Columbian Book Co., Hartford, Conn.
Pratt, Henry Sherring
1940.   A manual of the land and fresh water vertebrate animals of
the United States (exclusive of birds). Pp. xvii + 416, illus.;
266-267. P. Blakiston's Sons & Co., Inc., Philadelphia, Pa.
(Gives key to species *Canis*.)
Pratz, Du Le Page
1758.   Voyage de Louisiana. Vol 2, p. 54. London.
Preble, E. A.
1908.   A biological investigation of the Athabaska-Mackenzie region.
North Amer. Fauna 27: 1-574, illus.; 214. Bur. Biol. Survey,
U. S. Dept. Agr., Washington, D. C. October 26.
Presnall, Clifford C.
1948.   Applied ecology of predation on livestock ranges. Journ.
Mammal. 29 (2): 155-161. May.
(The role of the coyote with other predators upon domestic
prey species.)
Presnall, C. C., and Harold J. Rush
1941.   Coyote-cattle relationships on the San Carlos Indian Reserva-
tion. Unpublished report in files of Fish and Wildlife Service,
Washington, D. C.
(Estimate of coyote population of 49 per township on cattle
ranges of this Indian Reservation, Arizona.)
Quarles, E. A.
1919.   The day of the coyote. Field and Stream 23 (12): 928. April.
Quinn, Davis
1930.   The antelope's S. O. S. 16 pp. Emergency Conservation Committee, N. Y.
Raine, William MacLeod, and Will C. Barnes
1930.   Cattle. 340 pp. New York.
Rakes, L. W.
1927.   Shaggy fellow. Catholic World 125: 217-221. May.
Ramirez, Roman
1909.   Coyotes O Lobos del Campo. Government Bulletin. Mexico.
Rand, A. L.
1944.   The southern half of the Alaska highway and its mammals.
Nat. Mus. Canada Bull. 98 (Biol. Ser. 27): 1-50, illus., 39. Dept.
Mines and Nat. Res., Ottawa.
1945a.   Mammals of the Ottawa District. Canad. Field-Nat. 59 (4):
111-132; 122. July-August.
1945b.   Mammal investigations on the Canol Road, Yukon and Northwest Territories, 1944. Nat. Mus. Canada Bull. 99 (Biol. Ser.
28): 1-52, illus.; 33.
1945c.   Mammals of Yukon, Canada. Nat. Mus. Canada Bull. 100
(Biol. Ser. 29): 1-93, illus.; 35-36.
(Says coyote is a recent addition to the fauna appearing in
Pelley Valley about 1912.)
1948.   Mammals of the Eastern Rockies and Western Plains of Canada.
Nat. Mus. Canada Bull. 108 (Biol. Ser. 35): 1-237, illus.; 109-
112. September.

Randle, Allan C.
1943. Relationship of predatory control and big-game problem areas. Trans. 8th North Amer. Wildlife Conf., pp. 329-333. Amer. Wildlife Institute, Washington, D. C.

Rasmussen, D. Irwin, and William T. McKean
1945. The pheasant in the Intermountain Irrigated Region. [The ring-necked pheasant and its management in North America.] Amer. Wildlife Institute, Washington, D. C., 330 pp., illus.; 234-253.
(Coyote not definitely established as an outstanding predator on pheasant, although remains of the bird has on occasion been taken from its stomach.)

Records, Edward
1919-1934. Biennial report of the State Rabies Commission [Nevada] for 1917-1918, pp. 1-10, 1919; for 1919-1920, pp. 1-8; for 1921-1922, pp. 1-11, 1923; for 1923-1924, pp. 1-10, 1925; for 1925-1926, pp. 1-9, 1927; for 1927-1928, pp. 1-10, 1929; for 1929-1930, pp. 1-9, 1931; for January 1, 1931 to June 30, 1932, pp. 1-8, 1932; for July 1, 1932 to June 30, 1934, pp. 1-8. State Printing Office, Carson City, Nevada, included in appendices of Senate and Assembly of Legislature of State of Nevada.
(Summary of coyote specimens examined for rabies found negative or positive.)

Redington, P. G.
1928. Reduce losses by rodents and predatory animals. Amer. Hereford Jour. 19 (12): 132-134.

1930a. The federal program of wildlife control. Natl. Wool Grower 20 (12): 41-42, illus.

1930b. Report of Chief, Bureau Biological Survey, U. S. Dept. Agr., p. 26.

1931a. Report of the Chief of the Bureau of Biological Survey, U. S. Dept. Agr., p. 28.

1931b. Federal program of wild-life control. Producer 12 (8): 6-8.

1931c. Report of the Chief of the Bureau of Biological Survey for fiscal year ended June 30, 1931. August 31. P. 27.
(On the appearance of the coyote as far north in Alaska as Point Barrow.)

Redburn, Ralph
1933. A coyote tale. Grand Canyon Nat. Notes 7 (12): 128. March. National Park Service.

Reed, John S.
1889. The coyote song. Outing 14: 1.

Rhoads, Samuel N.
1898. "Noxious" or "Beneficial"? False Premises in economic zoology. Amer. Naturalist 32: 571-581.

Richard, F. J.
1915. The life story of a coyote. Outdoor Life 36 (6): 516-522, illus, December.

Richardson, John
1829.   Fauna Boreali Americana. Part 1, pp. xlvi + 300, illus. P. 73.
(Re the abundance of coyotes on plains of Saskatchewan,
Canada, and that boundary (north of coyote range) at this time
was north boundary of Alberta and Saskatchewan or about the
55th parallel.)
1836.   Zoological remarks, appendix, of narrative of the Arctic Land
expedition. P. 493.

Ricksecker, L. E.
1890.   A few notes on the yellow-haired porcupine (Erethizon epixan-
thus Brandt). Zoe 1 (8): 235-237; 237. October.
(Coyote teamwork in killing of the porcupine.)

Ridgway, Robert
1912.   Color standards and color nomenclature. iv + 44 pp., 53 col.
pls. Baltimore.

Riggs, Thos., Jr.
1919.   Report of the Governor of Alaska on the Alaska game laws,
1919. U. S. Dept. Agr., Dept. Circ. 88: 1-18; 11.

Riter, William E.
1941.   Predator control and wildlife management. Trans. 6th N. Amer.
Wildlife Conf., pp. 294-299. Amer. Wildlife Institute, Washington, D. C.

Roberts, Thos. S.
1917.   Methods of controlling "vermin." Fins, Feathers and Fur, No.
10, pp. 1-3; 1. June.
(Quoting I. B. Nayler, then Asst. Sec. State of Wisconsin.)

Robinson, Weldon B.
1943a. Coyote-getter, for coyote control. Jour. Wildlife Manag. 7 (2):
179. April.
1943b. The "Humane Coyote-Getter" vs. the steel trap. Natl. Wool
Grower 33 (11): 20-21, illus. November.

Robinson, Weldon B., and M. W. Cummings
1947.   Notes on behavior of coyotes. Journ. Mammal. 28 (1): 63-65.
February.

Roosevelt, Theodore
1905.   Wolf hunt in Oklahoma. Scribner's 38: 513-532. November.

Roosevelt, Theodore, T. S. Van Dyke, D. G. Elliot, and A. J. Stone
1902.   The deer family. Macmillan Co., N. Y. Pp. i-ix, 1-334, illus.;
44, 111.
(Observation of 2 coyotes running down a young mule deer in
Colorado.)
(Antelope an overmatch for a single coyote, and a doe will
fight gallantly for her kid.)

Rottier, John M.
1948.   Coyote Commando. Western Sportsman 8 (2): 11, 24, illus.
January-February. Austin, Texas.

Rush, William Marshall
1932.   Northern Yellowstone elk study. Montana Fish and Game Commission. 131 pp., illus.; 88.
(Description of deer killing by two or more coyotes.)
1946.   When animals get sick. American Forests 52 (1): 24. January.

Russell, Andy
    1947.   Little gray wolf. Field and Stream 52 (5): 26-27, 129-131, illus. September.
        (Coyote observations in Alberta.)

Russell, Frank
    1904-1905.   The Pima Indians. Annual Rept., Bur. Amer. Ethnology, Smithsn. Institution 26: 3-389.

Sabin, E. L.
    1908.   Story of coyote. Overland 21: 274-279. May.

Sampson, Frank W.
    1945.   The coyote problem in Missouri. Missouri Conservationist 6 (7): 4-5, 14-15, illus. July. Jefferson City, Mo.
        (Depredations, economic status, life-habits, and control practices of the coyote in Missouri.)

Sampson, Frank W., and Rudolf Bennitt
    1947.   Ways and means in wolf-coyote-bobcat control. Missouri Conservationist 8 (12): 4-6, illus. December.
    1948.   Ways and means in wolf-coyote-bobcat control. Missouri Conservationist 9 (1): 4-5, illus.; 5. January.

Sanborn, William B.
    1950.   An unusual encounter with a coyote. Yellowstone Nature Notes 24 (1): 7-8. February. Mimeographed.

Sarett, Lew
    1941.   The collected poems of Lew Sarett with a foreword by Carl Sandburg. Pp. xxviii + 383; 33, 166. Henry Holt & Co., New York.

Say, Thomas
    1823.   In Stephen H. Long and Edwin James "Account of an expedition from Pittsburgh to the Rocky Mountains performed in the years 1819 and '20."

Schmidt, Rex Gary
    1947.   The coyote. Missouri Conservationist 8 (6): 8-9, illus. June. Jefferson City.

Scholl, E. E., and J. W. Neil
    1918.   The control of destructive animals. Texas Dept. Agr. Bull. 60: 1-19.

Schoolcraft, H. R.
    1821.   Travels to the sources of the Mississippi River, Albany, N. Y. P. 285.

Scott, T. G.
    1937.   Mammals of Iowa. Iowa State College Journ. Sci. 12: 43-97.

Scott, William Berryman
    1913.   A history of land mammals in the western hemisphere. 693 pp., illus. Also 1937 ed., 786 pp. New York.

Sedgwick, C. B.
    1891.   Hunting the coyote for scalps. Overland 19: 192.

Seton, E. T.
    1900.   "Tito," the coyote that learned how. Scribner's 28: 131-145. August.
    1909.   Handbook of Manitoba. P. 188.
        (Coyote in all S. W. half of province probably as numerous as in the day before settlement.)

1911. The Arctic Prairies. Pp. xvi + 415, illus.; 350, 352. Chas. Scribner's Sons, N. Y.
       (On extension of coyote's range northward. Wolf foe of coyote, records killing of coyote by wolf after chase of 1 mile.)

1920. English names of mammals. Journ. Mammal. 1 (2): 104-105. February.
       (Mention of pronunciation of *Canis latrans*, "Small Prairie Wolf"; coy-o'-te; coy'-ote; ky'-ute.)

1923. The mane on the tail of the gray fox. Journ. Mammal. 4 (3): 180-182, illus.
       (Discuss musk gland of coyotes on upper side of the tail near base.)

1929. Lives of game animals. 4 vols. Vol. 1, Part 2, pp. 355-422, illus. Doubleday, Doran & Co., Inc., Garden City, N. Y.

Sheldon, H. H.
1933. The deer of California. Mus. Nat. Hist., Occas. Papers No. 3, pp. 1-71; 57, 19 pls. November 1. Santa Barbara.
       (Venison on coyote bill of fare.)

Shelford, V. E.
1940. The smaller animals of the great plains. Science 91 (2355): 167-168.

1942. Biological control of rodents and predators. Scientific Monthly 55: 331-341, illus. October.

1944. Deciduous forest man and the grassland fauna. Science 100 (2590, 2591): 135-140, 160-162. August 18 and 25.

Sheppard, Morris
1933. Tribute to Dr. A. K. Fisher. Congressional Record 76 (67): 5154. February 25.

Sherman, H. B.
1937. A list of the recent land mammals of Florida. Proc. Fla. Acad. Sci. for 1936 1: 102-128; 112.

Shiras, George, 3rd
1921. The wild life of Lake Superior, past and present. Natl. Geog. Mag. 40 (2): 113-204.

Shoemaker, T.
1912. Kiote. Outlook 101: 679. July 27.

Simpson, George Gaylord
1945. The principles of classification and a classification of mammals. Bull. Amer. Mus. Nat. Hist. 85: xvi + 350; 109.

Skinner, M. P.
1922. The prong-horn. Jour. Mammal. 3 (2): 82-105; 102.
       (States coyotes when in packs are most dangerous of the antelope's enemies.)

1924. The American antelope in Yellowstone National Park; an account of the life history and habits of America's most unique animal. Roosevelt Wildlife Forest Exp. Sta., 32 pp., illus.; 21. Syracuse, New York.
       (Revised and extended from "The prong-horn," Jour. Mammal. 3: 82-105, illus., 1922.)

1927. The predatory and fur-bearing animals of the Yellowstone National Park. Roosevelt Wild Life Forest Exp. Sta. Bull. 4 (2): 163-281, illus. June. Syracuse University.

Smith, Allen J., and Herbert Fox
  1908.   Note on occurrence of a ciliate (*Opalinopsis nucleobata*, n.s.)
          in the liver of a mammal (*Canis latrans*). Proc. Path. Soc.
          Phila., n.s. 11: 282-287.
Smith, Chas. Hamilton
  1846.   Mammalia, Dogs. Vol. 1. The Naturalist's Library, 2nd issue,
          vol. 18, edited by Sir William Jardine. Pp. 1-267; 162-166.
          Edinburgh. First issue 1839.
          (Original description of *Lyciscus cagottis*.)
Smith, G. Stanton
  1909.   When the wildwood was in flower. J. S. Ogilvie Pub. Co., N. Y.
          Pp. 24-25,
              (The friendliness of certain farm dogs with coyotes on the early
          frontier.)
Smokey, George
  1943.   Coyotes. South Dakota Conservation Digest 10 (12): 11, 13.
          December. S. Dak. Game and Fish Dept., Pierre, S. Dak.
Snyder, L. L.
  1942.   Mammals of the Sault Ste. Marie Region. Contrib. of the Royal
          Ontario Museum of Zoology No. 21: A faunal investigation of
          the Sault Ste. Marie region, Ontario 24 (Pt. 1): 105-120; 116.
Solinsky, Frank
  1931.   Protection for the coyotes. Crater Lake Nature Notes 4 (1).
          July. Nat. Park Service.
Sooter, Clarence A.
  1943.   Speed of predator and prey. Journ. Mammal. 24 (1): 102-103.
  1946.   Habits of coyotes in destroying nests and eggs of waterfowl.
          Journ. Wildlife Management 10 (1): 33-38, illus. January.
Soper, J. Dewey
  1942.   Mammals of Wood Buffalo Park, northern Alberta, and Dis-
          trict of Mackenzie. Journ. Mammal. 23 (2): 1-131, illus. May.
              (Coyote ranges throughout whole of park. The species has in-
          creased considerably past 40 years.)
  1944.   Report [typewritten] on wildlife investigations in the Grande
          Prairie—Peace River region of northwestern Alberta, Canada.
          Nat. Parks Bureau Lands, Parks, and Forest Branch, Dept.
          Mines & Resources, Winnipeg, Manitoba, 1-189, illus.; 171.
              (States coyote ranges throughout whole of territory, and on the
          increase past several years.)
  1945.   Report on wildlife investigations in Wood Buffalo Park and
          vicinity, Alberta and Northwest Territories, Canada. In files of
          Nat. Mus. Canada, pp. 1-71, illus. (Typewritten). Ottawa.
  1946.   Mammals of the northern Great Plains along the international
          boundary in Canada. Jour. Mammal. 27 (2): 127-153, illus.;
          138-139. May.
              (Occurrence of coyote in eastern Manitoba and Alberta, also
          Saskatchewan.)
  1947.   Obervations on mammals and birds in the Rocky Mountains of
          Alberta. Canad. Field-Nat. 61 (5): 143-173; 149. October.
Soulen, G. H.
  1938.   Food habits of the coyote. Minnesota Conservationist 58:
          20, 27-30, 32, illus.

Sperry, Charles C.
1933.   Autumn food habits of coyotes, a report of progress, 1932. Jour. Mammal. 14: 216-220, illus.
1934.   Winter food habits of coyotes: A report of progress, 1933. Jour. Mammal. 15: 286-290, illus.
1939.   Food habits of peg-leg coyotes. Journ. Mammal. 20: 190-194, illus.
1941.   Food habits of the coyote. U. S. Dept. Int., Fish & Wildlife Service, Wildlife Research Bull. 4: 1-70, illus.

Sproat, H.
1925.   The government's share in coyote control. Natl. Wool Grower 15 (11): 33-34.
1943.   Coyote control. National Wool Grower 33 (7): 27-28. July.

Squier, E. L.
1923.   Coyote who talked with God. Good Housekeeping 77: 30-31. December.

Squire, L.
1931.   Coyote of the plains. Nature Magazine 17: 162-167. March.
1933.   The hunt of the coyote. Nat. Mag. 22 (4): 151-154, illus.

Squires, Paul R.
1946.   The red fox in Indiana. Outdoor Indiana 13 (2): 8-9, 15; 9. March-April. Indianapolis, Ind.
         (Re bounty: says no bounty shows results other than large expenditure of funds, cites Michigan's coyote bounty.)

Stanwell-Fletcher, John F., and Theodora C.
1940.   Naturalists in the wilds of British Columbia. III. The summer and preparations for our second winter. Sci. Monthly 50 (3): 215, March.
         (On the feeding of a coyote whelp with milk and cooked fish, a female,—a food which she relished during 4 days in captivity, Driftwood River between Tacla Lake and Bear Lake, B. C., Canada.)

Stanwell-Fletcher, Theodora C.
1946.   Driftwood Valley. Pp. ix + 384. Illus. by John F. Stanwell-Fletcher. Little, Brown & Co., Boston.

Stearns, M. M.
1928.   Black coyote. Colliers 81: 23-24. February 25.

Stebler, A. M.
1939.   The tracking technique in the study of the larger predatory animals. Trans. 4th North Amer. Wildlife Conf., Amer. Wildlife Inst., Washington, D. C., pp. 203-208.
1944.   Fox and coyote trapping simplified. Mich. Dept. Conservation, 15 pp. Lansing.

Steele, J. W.
1907.   The figurehead of the frontier. Outing 50: 407-410. July.

Steffa, D.
1910.   The war against the coyote. Outdoor Life 25: 371-378.

Stephens, Frank
1906.   California mammals. 351 pp., illus.; 213-216. San Diego, Calif.

Stephl, Otto E.
   1927.   The prairie dog in Montana. Montana Extension Service in
          Agriculture and Home Economics, Montana State College, Boze-
          man. Bull. No. 83, pp. 1-13, illus.; 7. March.
          (The coyote as a national enemy of the prairie dog.)

Stevens, DeLyle R.
   1948.   Coyotes along the Yellowstone River. Yellowstone Nat. Notes
          22 (3): 19, March-April [May]. (Mimeographed.)

Stevenson, E.
   1936.   The case of Reddy—a coyote. Nature Magazine 27: 140-142.
          March.

Stevenson, William
   1944.   Teamwork by coyotes. Yosemite Nature Notes 23 (4): 42-43.
          April. Yosemite.

Stiles, C. W., and Clara Edith Baker
   1935.   Key-catalogue of parasites reported for Carnivora (cats, dogs,
          bears, etc.) with their possible public health importance. U. S.
          Public Health Service, Treasury Dept. Bull. 163: 913-1223.

Stiles, Chas. Wardell, and Albert Hassall
   1894.   A preliminary catalogue of parasites contained in the collections
          of the U. S. Bur. Animal Industry, U. S. Army Medical Mus.,
          Biol. Dept., Univ. of Pennsylvania (Coll. Leidy) and in Coll.
          Stiles and Coll. Hassall Vet. Mag., Phila. 1 (4): 245-253,
          April; (5): 331-354, May.

Stimson, A. M.
   1910.   Facts and problems of rabies. U. S. Public Health & Marine
          Service. Hygienic Lab. Bull. 65: 1-90, illus. June. Washington,
          D. C.

Stock, Chester
   1929.   A census of the Pleistocene mammals of Rancho La Brea, based
          on the collections of the Los Angeles Museum. Journ. Mamm.
          10 (4): 281-289, illus.

Stoner, Emerson A.
   1931.   Marsh hawks vs. coyotes. Auk 48: 599.

Storm, Dan
   1938.   The little animals of Mexico. Coyote Wisdom 14: 8-34. Folk-
          Lore Society, Austin, Tex.

Storer, Tracy I.
   1923.   Rabies in a mountain lion. Calif. Fish and Game 9 (2): 45-48;
          48. April.
          (Mention of "extensive epidemic of this disease [rabies] among
          coyotes N.E. California.")

Strecker, John K.
   1924.   The mammals of McLennan County, Texas. The Baylor Bull.
          (pt. 1), 27 (3): 1-20; 12. Baylor University, Waco, Tex.
   1926.   The mammals of McLennan County, Texas. 2nd paper supple-
          mentary notes. Contrib. from Baylor University Museum, No. 9,
          pp. 1-15; 5. Oct. 15. Waco, Tex.

Stroman, G. N.
   1925.   An albino coyote. Journ. Hered. 16: 342-343.

Struwing, Nels. J.
1946. Report on the North Dakota fur harvest. North Dakota Outdoors 8 (1): 11. July.
(Average price of coyote 1941-1942—$9.00; to 1945-46 incl.— $5.85, $5.05, $4.85.)
1947. North Dakota's fur harvest for '46-'47 season. North Dakota Outdoors 10 (2): 6-7, illus. August.
(Coyote kill shows a drop of 56 percent.)

Stuart, R. Y.
1931. Report of the Forester. Ann. Rept. U. S. Dept. Agr. 1931, pp. 1-82.

Sturgis, Robert S.
1939. The Wichita Mountains Wild Life Refuge. Chicago Nat. 2 (1): 12. March. Chicago Acad. Sci., Chicago.

Suckley, George, and George Gibbs
1860. Report of exploration and surveys to ascertain most practical and economical route for a railroad from the Mississippi to the Pacific Ocean, 1853-55. 36th Cong., 1st sess., Sen. Ex. Doc. No. 56, Vol. 12, (bk. 2, ch. 3, Zoology), p. 111.

Surber, Thaddeus
1932. The mammals of Minnesota. 84 pp., illus. Bull. Minn. Dept. Conserv., Div. Game & Fish, St. Paul. P. 55.

Svihla, Arthur, and Ruth D. Svihla
1933. Mammals of Clallam County, Washington. The Murrelet 14 (2): 37-41; 39. May.
(The mountain coyote invading eastern part of Olympic Peninsula as lumbering and clearing proceeds.)

Svihla, Ruth D.
1931. Mammals of the Uinta Mountain region. Journ. Mammal. 12 (3): 256-266, illus. August.

Swanson, Gustav, Thaddeus Surber, and Thomas S. Roberts
1945. The mammals of Minnesota. Minn. Dept. Conserv. Tech. Bull. 2: 1-108, illus.; 32, 48, 72.

Swanton, J. R.
1904-1905. The Ningit Indians. Ann. Rept., Bur. Amer. Ethn., Smithsn. Inst. 26: 391-485.

Swarth, Harry S.
1936. Mammals of the Atlin Region, northwestern British Columbia. Jour. Mammal. 17 (4): 388-405; 401. November.
(Occurrence of C. latrans incolatus.)

Swenk, Myron H.
1908. A preliminary review of the mammals of Nebraska. Studies from Zool. Lab. Univ. Nebraska, No. 89, 88 pp. September. Lincoln, Nebraska.
(Canis latrans Say and Canis nebracensis Merriam, p. 64.)

T. N. A.
1888. Bullsnake and white wolf. Forest & Stream 39 (15): 288. May 3.

Tanner, Clara Lee
1946. Antelope trappers. Arizona Highways 22 (1): 12-19, illus.; 19. January.
(A good account on antelope trapping for redistribution, and competition with other creatures including the coyote.)

Taylor, Walter P.
  1931.   Predatory mammal policies of the Biological Survey for Arizona, New Mexico, Texas. 138 pp. (In files of Fish and Wildlife Service, Washington, D. C.)
  1935.   Ecology and life history of the porcupine (*Erethizon epizanthum*) as related to the forests of Arizona and the southwestern United States. Univ. Ariz., Biol. Science Bull. 3: 1-177, illus.; 123-124, July 1.
          (Coyote as enemy of porcupine.)
Taylor, Walter P., and William T. Shaw
  1927.   Mammals and birds of Mount Rainier National Park, 249 pp.; 41. U. S. Dept. Interior, Nat. Park Service, Washington, D. C.
Texas, State of
  1930.   Report of Texas Game, Fish, and Oyster Commission for the year ending August 31, 1930. P. 32.
Thompson, David
  1916.   David Thompson's narrative of his explorations in western America, 1784-1812, pp. 1-512; 186, edited by J. B. Tyrrell, Toronto.
          (Early day wolf infestation mitigates against sheep raising.)
Thompson, Ernest E.
  1886.   A list of the mammals of Manitoba. Trans. Manitoba Sci. & Hist. Soc. No. 23: 1-26; 25. May. Toronto.
          (Coyote common in prairie regions.)
Thompson, Raymond
  1945.   Crafty coyotes. The Outdoorsman 87 (1) (Whole No. 512): 18-19, 24-25, illus. January-February.
Thoms, C. S.
  1907.   The coyote's conflict with civilization. Outdoor Life 19: 333-338.
Tindall, Cordell
  1942.   Killers on the farm front. Missouri Ruralist: 6, 14, illus. December 12.
Toner, G. C.
  1946.   Notes on the mammals of the lower Chilcotin River region, Cariboo District, B. C. Canad. Field-Nat. 60 (4): 86-89; 87. July-August.
Towne, Charles Wayland, and Edward Norris Wentworth
  1945.   Shepherd's Empire. Pp. xii + 364, illus.; 213-238. Univ. Oklahoma Press, Norman, Okla.
Townsend, Charles Haskins
  1912.   Mammals collected by the "Albatross" Expedition in Lower California in 1911, with description of a new species. Bull. Amer. Mus. Nat. Hist. 31: 117-130, illus.; 130. June.
          (Describes *Canis jamesi* sp. nov.)
Townsend, John K.
  1839.   Narrative of a journey across the Rocky Mountains to the Columbia River. 352 pp.; 311. Philadelphia, Pa.
Tozzer, Alfred M., and Glover M. Allen
  1910.   Animal figures in Maya Codices. Papers, Peabody Mus., Amer. Arch. & Ethn. 4 (3): 280-372, illus.; 358-359, pl. 35. February. Harvard University, Cambridge, Mass.
          (Figs. 1 and 2 of Pl. 35 presumed to be figures of coyotes as taken from Nuttall Codex, but no drawings of the coyote have been noted in the Maya codices.)

Trembley, Helen Louise and F. C. Bishop
1940.   Distribution and hosts of some fleas of economic importance. Journ. Economic Entomology 33 (4): 701-703. September 28.

True, Frederick W.
1884.   A provisional list of the mammals of North and Central America, and the West Indian Islands. Proc. U. S. Nat. Mus. 7: 1-610.
         (At this time range of coyote was given as extending from Saskatchewan to Costa Rica.)

True, John Preston
1888.   Wolves and the Tonkaways. Forest and Stream 30 (9): 165. March 22.

Tyrrell, J. B.
1888.   The Mammalia of Canada. Read before Can. Inst. April 7, and publ. in advance. 28 pp.; 9. Toronto.
1896.   Report on the country between Athabaska Lake and Churchill River with notes on two routes travelled between Churchill and Saskatchewan Rivers. Annual Report Can. Geol. Surv. (n.s.) 8 (pt. D): 5 D-120 D; 13 D.

Twain, Mark
1871.   Roughing it. Harpers. New York.

United States Government
1921.   Agricultural Appropriation Bill, 1922. Extracts from hearing before sub-committee of House Committee on Appropriations; Agricultural appropriation bill for 1922; 66th Congress, 3d session.
1928.   An act making appropriation for the Department of Agriculture for fiscal year ending June 30, 1929, and for other purposes. P. 23. [Public. No. 392, 70th Congress.] [H.R. 11577]
1929.   Control of predatory animals. House Doc. No. 496, 70th Congress, 2nd sess.
1930.   Control of predatory animals. Hearing before Comm. on Agr., House of Rep., 71st Cong. 2nd sess. April 29, 30, May 1, on H.R. 9599.
1931a.   Control of predatory animals. Hearings before the Comm. on Agr. and Forestry, U. S. Senate, 71st Cong., 2nd and 3rd sess., on S. 3483, May 8, 1930, and January 28 and 29, 1931, 192 pp.
1931b.   [Public No. 776–71st Congress] (H.R. 9599) March 2.
1936.   The western range. 74th Cong., 2d Sess. Sen. Doc. No. 199, 620 pp.; 352, 359, 592.

United States House of Representatives
1934.   Hearings before special committee on conservation of wildlife. House of Representatives, 73rd Cong., 2nd Sess. Pursuant to H. Res. 237, pp. vii + 320; 10-11.
         (Statement of Chief, Biological Survey (J. N. Darling) re predator control.)

United States Public Health Service
1947.   Control of rabies. Public Health Reports 62 (34): 1215-1237. August 22.

United States Senate
1907.   Report on work of the Biological Survey. 60th Congress, 1st Sess. Doc. No. 132, 29 pp. December 21.
1930.   Control of predatory animals (Confidential Report). Hearing before Comm. on Agr. & Forestry, U. S. Senate, 71st Cong., 2nd Sess. Senate Rept., 3483, 28 pp. May 8.

1940. The status of wildlife in the United States. Rept. of the Special Committee on the conservation of wildlife resources pursuant to S. Res. 24 (71st Congress), Senate Rept. No. 1203, 76th Cong., 3rd Session, pp. 1-457, illus.; 111-116, 361-362.

Van Cleve, Harry
1945. Pelting equipment and how to skin, flesh, stretch and dry pelts. Trans. 10th North Amer. Wildlife Conf., pp. 86-90. American Wildlife Institute, Washington, D. C.

Victor, F. F. (Mrs.)
1872. All over Oregon and Washington. Pp. 300-307. San Francisco.

Von Blon, J. L.
1920. Commercializing on coyotes. Scientific American 122: 246. March 6.

Vorhies, Charles T.
1931. Report to the Special Committee on problems of predatory mammal control of the American Society of Mammalogists on predatory mammal policies of the Biological Survey—Arizona, New Mexico, Texas. 140 pp. January 29. (In files of Fish and Wildlife Service, Washington, D. C.)

Vorhies, Charles T., and Walter P. Taylor
1933. The life histories and ecology of jack rabbits in relation to grazing in Arizona. Univ. of Ariz., Tucson, Tech. Bull. 49: 471-587, illus.; 543-546. May 31.
(The pros and cons as to the effectiveness of the coyote in the control of the jack rabbit.)
1940. Life history and ecology of the white-throated woodrat, Neotoma albigula albigula Hartley in relation to grazing in Arizona. Univ. Ariz., Tucson, Tech. Bull. 86: 455-529; 507-508. June 1.
(Coyote as enemy of woodrat.)

Wafer, Lionel
1934. A new description of the Isthmus of America by Lionel Wafer, surgeon on buccaneering expeditions in Darien, the West Indies, and the Pacific from 1680 to 1688; with Wafer's secret report (1698) and Davis expedition to the gold mines (1704) edited, with introduction, notes, and appendices by L. E. Elliott Joyce. Oxford, England, printed for the Hakluyt Society, pp. lxvi + 221; 113, illus.
(Coyote in Honduras or Nicaragua observed in year 1685.)

Walcott, Charles D.
1917. National Parks as a scientific asset. Proc. Nat. Parks Conference, 1917, pp. 113-117. Government Printing Office, Washington, D. C.

Walker, Lewis Wayne
1950. A defense of the western prairie dog. Nat. Humane Rev. 38 (6): 22, 29, illus. June.

Ward, Henry Baldwin
1895. The parasitic worms of man and the domestic animals. Ann. Rept. Nebraska Bd. Agr., Lincoln (1894), pp. 225-348, figs. 1-82, 2 pls., figs. 1-16.
(A Trematoda from the gall ducts of Canis latrans.)

Warfel, H. E.
1937. A coyote in Hampshire County, Massachusetts. Journ. Mammal. 18 (2): 241.

Warren, Edward R.
    1926a. A study of the beaver in the Yancy region of Yellowstone National Park. Roosevelt Wildlife Annals 1 (1-2): 5-191, illus.; 165. Roosevelt Wildlife Forest Expt. Sta. of N. Y. State College of Forestry, Syracuse University.
    1926b. Notes on the beaver colonies in the Long's Peak region of Estes Park, Colo. Roosevelt Wildlife Annals (1-2): 193-234, illus.; 233. Roosevelt Wildlife Forest Expt. Sta. of N. Y. State College of Forestry, Syracuse University.
    1927. The beaver: Its work and its ways. Amer. Soc. Mammal. Monograph 2, pp. xx + 177, illus.; 146-149.
        (Lists and cites example of coyote depredation on beaver.)
    1942. The mammals of Colorado. 2nd revised edition, 330 pp., illus.; 95-99.
        (Lists 4 coyotes: *C. l. nebracensis, lestes, mearnsi,* and *estor* as probably occurring in Colorado, with comment on natural history of the coyote.)

Wasco, County of Oregon
    1947. Agricultural Planning Conference containing committee reports approved by conference held in The Dalles, Oregon, Jan. 22. Livestock committee report, pp. 3-8; 5.
        (Coyotes prevent needed sheep increase.)

Webster, E. B.
    1920. The King of the Olympics. 227 pp., illus.; 213.

Weiss, Harry B., and Grace M. Ziegler
    1931. Thomas Say, early American naturalist. 260 pp., illus. December. Springfield, Illinois.

Wentworth, Edward Norris
    1948. America's sheep trails, history personalities. Iowa State College Press, Ames, Iowa. Pp. 470-490.
        (The effect of coyotes and other predators on the sheep industry in the United States.)

Wetmore, Alexander
    1921. Wild ducks and duck foods of the Bear River marshes, Utah. U. S. Dept. Agr. Bull. 936: 1-20, illus.; 17-18.
        (Coyote depredations on young ducks and ducklings and mature ducks disabled by duck sickness.)

Wheeler, Olin D.
    1904. The trail of Lewis & Clark. 2 vols., illus. G. P. Putnam Sons, New York and London.

Whitacre, Donald
    1948. The mysterious coyote pack of Ohio. The Ohio Conservation Bull. 12 (3): 29. March.

White, Jim
    1906. Traps and poison. Hunter, Trader, Trapper 13 (1): 41-42; 42. October.
        (Describes the poisoning by use of strychnine of 81 coyotes and 14 gray wolves in one week's time 60 miles northwest of Sundance, Wyo., the winter of 1885.)

Whiteman, E. E.
    1940. Habits and pelage changes in captive coyotes. Journ. Mammal. 21 (4): 435-438.

Whitney, D. J.
1936. To organize war on the coyote. Calif. Cult. 83: 749-750. October.
1938. Trapping the wily coyote. Calif. Cult. 85: 12. January 1.
Whitney, J. Park
1906. Reminiscences of a sportsman. Forest and Stream Pub. Co. Pp.
273-274.
Wilbur, Charles G.
1946. Mammals of the Knik River Valley, Alaska. Journ. Mammal.
27 (3): 215.
(Occurrence of the coyote rather common in this area)
Willhoft, W.
1928. Coyotes via airplane and round-up. Forest and Stream 98 (6):
338-339, 370-372, illus.
Williams, H. P.
1930. "Killing the killers." Northern Sportsman 1 (5): 5-6.
Williams, M. Y.
1942. Notes on the fauna of Bruce Peninsula, Manitoulin and adjacent
islands. Canadian Field-Naturalist 56 (6): 92-93. September.
(On the occurrence of coyote Manitoulin Island, Ontario. None
known 1912-20, but in 1935 reported as common.)
1946. Notes on the vertebrates of the southern plains of Canada 1923-
1926. Canadian Field-Naturalist 60 (3): 47-60; 59. Sutton West,
Canada.
(On occurrence of coyote, seemingly abundant at the time.)
Wilmot, Lew
1897. Coyotes hunting in bands. Forest and Stream 48 (15): 284.
April 10.
Winters, S. R.
1921. The predatory animal pest. Outdoor Life 48: 181-182, illus.
Wood, Kerry
1947a. That canny coyote. Fauna 9 (1): 2-5, illus. March. Philadelphia.
1947b. Stoney Joe and the Coyote Hound. Rod and Gun in Canada
48 (12): 14, 48. May.
Wood, Norman A.
1914. Annotated check list of Michigan mammals. Univ. Mich. Mus.
Zool., Occas. Pap. 4: 1-13; 8. April 1. Ann Arbor.
1922. The mammals of Washtenaw County. Univ. Mich. Mus. Zool.,
Occas. Papers 123: 1-23; 8-9. Ann Arbor.
Wood, William
1911. Animal sanctuaries in Labrador. 2nd Ann. Meeting Canad. Comn.
of Conservation, pp. 1-37.
1912. Supplement to "Animal Sanctuaries in Labrador," pp. 1-38.
Canad. Commission of Conservation.
Woodhouse, S. W.
1852. The North American jackal—*Canis frustror*. Proc. Acad. Nat.
Sci. Philadelphia 1851 5: 147-148. June 30.
Woodring, George B.
1930. News items. Migrant (Quart. Jour. Tenn. Orn. Soc.) 1 (3-4): 19.
December.
Woodward, H. B.
1933. How should we pronounce c-o-y-o-t-e? Yellowstone Nat. Notes 10
(1-2): 7.

Wortman, J. L., and W. D. Matthew
1899. The ancestry of certain members of the Canidae, Viverridae, and Procyonidae. Bull. Amer. Mus. Nat. Hist. 12: 109-139, 10 figs.

Wright, G. M., and B. H. Thompson
1935. Fauna of the national parks of the United States. Wildlife Management in the National Parks, U. S. National Park Service. Fauna Series 2: 1-142, illus.

Yeager, Dorr G.
1931. Our wilderness neighbors. A. C. McClurg & Co., Chicago; 160 pp., illus.; 55, 85, 154.
(Coyote-deer and coyote-antelope relationship.)

Yore, Clem
1928. Coyote danger. Saturday Evening Post 201: 205-206. October 13.

Young, Stanley P.
1924. Coyote infestation in Colorado. Colo. Game & Fish Prot. Assoc. Bull. 4 (4): 6. December.
1926. The coyote and examples of its persistency. Outdoor Life 57 (1): 17. January. Denver, Colo.
1928. Senor Yip Yap. Sunset Mag. 6: 28-30, 5 illus. December. San Francisco, Calif. (In collaboration Arthur H. Carhart.)
1930. Hints on coyote and wolf trapping. Leaflet 59, illus. U. S. Dept. Agr. July.
1932. Predatory-animal and rodent control to be conducted under a ten year program. U. S. Dept. Agr. Yearbook 1932: 312-315.
1934. Our federal predator control work. Amer. Game Conf. Trans. 20: 172-174. January.
1935. Our Federal cooperative predator control work. Southern Agriculturist 65 (12): 34, illus. December.
1939. The coyote marches on. American Forests Mag. 45 (11): 538-540, 574-576. November.
1941a. Hints on wolf and coyote trapping. U. S. Dept. Int., Fish and Wildlife Service Circ. 2: 1-8, illus.
1941b. Wanderlust from the plains. Western Sportsman 7 (2): 9-12, illus.; 11. July.
1943. What was the early Indian dog? American Forests 49 (12): 571-573, 599, 603, illus. December. (Concluded in Vol. 50, No. 1, pp. 26-28, 32, 45, illus., January, 1944.)
1944. Other working dogs and the wild species. Nat. Geog. Mag. 86 (3): 363-384, 12 illus. from photos, 9 original paintings by Walter Weber. September.
1946a. Sketches of American wildlife. Pp. xiii + 142, illus. Monumental Press, Baltimore, Md.
1946b. The wolf in North American History. Pp. 1-149, illus. Caxton Printers, Caldwell, Idaho.
1947. The case against the bounty. Northwest Sportsmen 2 (4): 11. February. Vancouver, British Columbia.

Young, Stanley P., and Harold W. Dobyns
1937. Den hunting as a means of coyote control. U. S. Dept. Agr. Leaflet 132. October. Washington, D. C.
1945. Coyote control by means of den hunting. U. S. Dept. Int., Fish and Wildlife Service Circ. 7: 1-8, illus.

Young, Stanley P., and Edward A. Goldman
1944.   The wolves of North America. 660 pp., illus. American Wildlife Institute, Washington, D. C. May 29.
1946.   The puma—mysterious American cat. Pp. xiv + 358, illus.; 44, 132, 135, 136, 142. American Wildlife Institute, Washington, D. C.
Zimmerman, R. Scott
1943.   A coyote's speed and endurance. Journ. Mammal. 24 (3): 400. August.
Zinser, Juan
1936.   Wildlife in Mexico. Proc. North Amer. Wildlife Conference called by President Franklin D. Roosevelt, Washington, D. C., February 3-7. Printed for the use of the Special Comm. on Conservation and Wildlife Resources, 74th Cong., 2nd Sess., Washington, D. C., pp. 6-11; 9.
          (A closed season on coyote, for farmers in northern Mexico. States desired such because of coyotes living on rabbits and hares, a pest to agricultural crops.)

Index

[New names and principal page references to a species in boldface; synonyms in *italic*]

407